NICARAGUA
BETRAYED

NICARAGUA BETRAYED

by

ANASTASIO SOMOZA

as told to

JACK COX

WESTERN ISLANDS

PUBLISHERS

BOSTON   LOS ANGELES

First printing, August 1980   25,000 copies
Second printing, January 1981   25,000 copies

Published by
Western Islands
395 Concord Avenue
Belmont, Massachusetts 02178

Printed in the United States of America
ISBN: 0-88279-235-0

Dedication

I dedicate this book to all of the courageous and freedom-loving people of Nicaragua, who now live under the yoke of Communism. In particular, I dedicate this effort to the loyal and faithful men and women of the Guardia Nacional and the Partido Liberal Nacionalista. To those thousands who now languish in prison, I can only say that it is my hope and my daily prayer that one day you shall know freedom again.

A. Somoza

CONTENTS

Foreword

Anastasio Somoza Debayle was born in Leon, Nicaragua on December 5, 1925. His father was General Anastasio Somoza Garcia and his mother was Salvadora Debayle Sacasa.

Young Anastasio, or Tachito, as he was called by his father and friends, attended grammar school in Nicaragua. In 1936 he began his long and close relationship with the United States by attending St. Leo School in Florida and then La Salle Military Academy in Long Island, New York. He passed the examination for West Point, entered the U.S. Military Academy on July 3, 1943, and graduated from West Point on June 6, 1946.

On December 10, 1950 he married Hope Portocarrero Debayle. They have five children: Anastasio, Julio, Carolina, Carla, and Roberto.

His father, General Somoza, was elected President of Nicaragua in 1937 and served as President in three periods: 1937–1941; 1941–1947; 1950–1956. He was serving as President when he was felled by an assassin's bullet in 1956.

Anastasio Somoza Debayle was elected President of Nicaragua on May 1, 1967. He served that country for nine years. His last elective term began December 1, 1974 and would have expired in 1981. He remained in office until July 17, 1979, when a resolution from the Organization of American States (OAS) demanded his resignation and forced him to leave the country.

Nicaragua is a small Central American country with approximately 2.2 million people. Yet from this small country came a man known in most parts of the world. Anastasio Somoza Debayle most assuredly left his mark in the history books.

When a disastrous earthquake destroyed Managua, the capital city of Nicaragua, in 1972, General Somoza was Chief of the Armed Forces. He was named Military Governor by the three-member ruling junta. In this capacity he directed all relief and reconstruction operations. Even his critics praised his leadership ability in the crisis. According to his friends and foes alike, Somoza held Nicaragua together during this most troublesome time.

He was and is strongly pro-Western in democratic ideals. Until the Communist-supported rebel victory, Somoza was

considered to be the staunchest supporter of the United States
and Western ideology in all of Latin America. His country
never deviated from its support of the U.S. on any vote in the
United Nations.

When his hour of peril came and his loyal Guardia Nacional
was being pressed on all sides by superior Communist-trained
forces, the United States did not live up to her existing treaties
with Nicaragua. There is evidence that the U.S. actually
contributed to his downfall.

It is documented that the rebel Sandinistas, a name derived
from General Augusto Cesar Sandino who had fought the U.S.
Marines in his rebellious activities in Nicaragua many years
before, received men, arms, equipment, and supplies from
Soviet Russia, Cuba, Panama, Venezuela, the PLO, and the
Dominican Republic. All of which names, you will note, are of
countries or organizations of the pro-Communist camp.

In the end, General Somoza and his Guardia Nacional were
simply out-gunned. Observers of the war say that Somoza's
men were never out-fought. But with the United States government unilaterally and insistently calling the shots for a
surrender to the Communist-backed Sandinistas, Somoza
called it quits and flew to Miami. Later he went to Paraguay
where he now resides.

                                            Jack Cox

Preface

The comments of an "outsider" about the military and domestic affairs of a nation might offend some people in that nation. So far as the United States is concerned, I do not feel like an "outsider," and in so many ways I'm not.

When I was ten years old I came to the United States to go to school. That was in Florida, and until this day I remember thinking, "I'm in the States and I'm all by myself." Except for those first four years, all of my education was received in the U.S.A. I took my high school course at La Salle in New York. Later, I passed the examinations for the United States Military Academy at West Point, and graduated from that outstanding military institution in 1946.

At that time, I can truthfully say that I knew more about the United States than I did about my own country. My ties with the United States will be with me all of my life. So far as the United States is concerned, I am not an outsider. The United States shall always be a part of me; and in my heart I shall always be a part of the United States of America.

As a result of those early years in my life, and the governmental years which followed, I have friends in practically every state in the Union. With a fervor for the American way of life and a deep-rooted sense of loyalty to those principles which made the United States the great nation she is, I believe I have earned the privilege to address myself to the dangers which confront the United States today.

Additionally, when the United States assumes leadership, in a conspiratorial fashion, to annihilate anti-Communist nations, I believe it is my duty to speak out. When I have factual evidence that the United States of America has actually aided and abetted the evil forces of Communism, I believe the people of the United States should share in such facts and incontrovertible manifestations. When I, as President of a free and democratic nation closely allied with the United States, witness the betrayal and subsequent defeat of that nation, I firmly believe the citizens of the United States are entitled to know the details of that betrayal. When I have indisputable knowledge as to the perpetrator of such an insidious betrayal, I feel destined to reveal that identity, because I believe that the people of the United States should be privy to that knowledge.

It should be understood that I have the utmost respect for the office of the Presidency of the United States. To me, that office has always epitomized the ultimate public position in the world. This, in my opinion, does not mean that those men who have attained that ethereal public position automatically achieve greatness and command world respect. It follows that one can be critical of the President of the United States without denigrating that esteemed office.

When I criticize the present holder of that office, I do so because I am firmly convinced he is leading the free world into a cataclysmic political eclipse which will bring darkness to free peoples everywhere. Therefore, it is with a compelling sense of responsibility to the people of the United States, that I relate the facts and events which propelled my country into political darkness. This is my revelation of Nicaragua BETRAYED.

A. Somoza

NICARAGUA
BETRAYED

Chapter One

THE TRAGEDY OF '72 — EARTHQUAKE

Since the discovery of the Americas, Nicaragua has been a nation of importance in the power centers of the world. Primarily, this importance has been due to her transoceanic possibilities. Before the Panama Canal was built serious consideration was given to the construction in Nicaragua of a sea-level canal from the Atlantic to the Pacific. Long ago this project was considered feasible and it still is. With the uncertainty which surrounds the Panama Canal today, and the new non-atomic technology, the idea of a sea-level canal through Nicaragua will most likely receive renewed attention.

With the exception of the past forty years the history of Nicaragua relates to ups and downs. There were periods of turmoil and periods of limited progress. But one thing stood out above all else, the people of Nicaragua were willing to work and they were loyal to their country. Things changed during the last forty years or so. They changed for the better. During this period, Nicaragua had stability of government, stability of currency, and individual prosperity. These attributes set Nicaragua apart from most countries of Central and South America. She was recognized throughout the world, and Nicaragua conducted trade and government-to-government relations with most nations of the world.

Therefore, a country even without the benefit of natural resources, such as oil and gas, could attract foreign investors. They came from everywhere and they were willing to invest their capital in Nicaragua. To my way of thinking, this is hard-core evidence of total confidence.

When investments in Central America were considered, the word on Wall Street and other financial centers was "place your money in Nicaragua." This recommendation always gave me a sense of pride — in my government and pride in the people of Nicaragua.

So, under a stable government and with dedicated people, Nicaragua prospered. My dream was to make my country a shining example of free enterprise at work. My dream was to build the best highway system in Central America and this we did. My dream was to provide better schools for all our children and to create for the children of Nicaragua an atmosphere of freedom in which each child could attain the limit of his God-given ability. My dream was to provide a University equal to any in the world so that those young men and women with special qualifications could achieve educational equivalency with any student in any part of the world. As President of Nicaragua, a position I exercised during nine years, my dream was for a prosperous Nicaragua and a better way of life for all of our proud people.

These hopes and aspirations, many of which had been achieved, received a sudden and jolting shock on the night of December 23, 1972. In retrospect, how tragic it all seems.

Having spent many a Christmas in the United States, I know how the birth of Christ is celebrated. At one and the same time there is fun, frivolity, and solemnity. There are decorations, Christmas trees, cards, and constant reminders of this glorious day of celebration. I must say, however, that nowhere in the world is Christmas so religiously celebrated as it is in Latin America. It is difficult to describe the feeling and emotion which permeate all walks of life. There is a deep inward sense of religious devotion and an outward display of love for your fellow man. Oh, it is something to see and something to experience.

On the night of that fateful December 22nd–23rd, I remember looking out over our capital city of Managua and thinking that Christmas is really here. The tall business structures were decorated with lights of all kinds. The residences, almost without exception, displayed some sort of electrical reminder that the Christmas season was upon us.

And then came the jolt. Earthquake! I sensed immediately

that this was not a tremor. Managua was literally being torn apart. The devastating shock hit at 12:30 A.M. Then there was total darkness. One moment the entire city was lit up like a giant Christmas tree and, in the next moment, the entire city was black. Then came the sounds. These I shall never forget. The sounds of tumbling buildings, the sound of metal scraping against metal, and the eerie sound in my own home — these are with me still. Later I was to hear an even more nerve-shattering sound — the sound of human agony and despair.

In those few short minutes, some ten thousand people died in Managua. It was a city without electrical power, a city without water, a city without telephones and, for a brief period of time, a city totally out of touch with the rest of the world.

For me and the rest of the people of Managua, there was no sleep that night and many nights to come. Here was a city of 75,000 homes and of these 90 percent were declared totally destroyed. For those who survived, there would be no sleep for a long time. Sadly, almost every family in the capital city lost a member of the family or a loved one to that eternal sleep.

I recall very vividly the morning following the earthquake. The early morning sun revealed a city covered by an enormous black pall of smoke. The earthquake had started fires in every section of the city and there was no water with which to fight them. And if there had been, all the fire-fighting equipment was buried under a crumbled building.

I then called for a helicopter so as to evaluate the damage more accurately. What I found exceeded my worst fears. The presidential house was destroyed, the military headquarters was destroyed, the U.S. Embassy, which was 150 meters from the military headquarters, was also destroyed. The destruction was unbelievable.

The previous night we received reports that many U.S. Embassy secretaries were trapped in the Embassy housing. A team was dispatched to rescue them. All were saved except one, and she was dead when the rescue team reached her.

Upon returning to my residence from the helicopter inspection trip, I remember thinking that this was indeed the worst moment in the history of Nicaragua. As Chief of the Army, I felt a particular responsibility to our brave people who had suffered such devastation. At that moment we had 450,000 people without homes, without food, without water, without transportation, without lights, and without any means of acquiring those services. The situation was most appalling and I meditated as to what course of action should be followed.

I recall that on the very night of the earthquake, U.S. Ambassador Turner Shelton laboriously made his way to my home. He and I discussed the alternatives. We agreed that a message of distress should be sent out to the world. At that time, Nicaragua was governed by a three-man junta. The Ambassador and I agreed that the junta should send the message. However, it was impossible to locate the ruling junta. So, as Chief of the Army, I felt it incumbent upon me to assume the responsibility and send the urgent message of distress. I recall writing the message on the trunk of my car. The U.S. Embassy had strategic radio equipment which was operated by a courtesy license of the Guardia Nacional of Nicaragua. The message went to all Central American countries and the United States. I requested that the U.S. relay the message to other governments of the world.

The response was immediate. Nicaragua will always be grateful for the aid which came from so many countries, and particularly the United States of America. Without the medical supplies, food, and clothing, many additional people would have perished. I sent expressions of gratitude to all of those nations who had responded to our request for assistance. It is regrettable that these acts of kindness and generosity would later be clouded by false accusations concerning the distribution of much-needed aid which came to Nicaragua.

Some elements of the U.S. media, Viron Vaky, Assistant Secretary of State for Inter-American Affairs, and my political opponents in Nicaragua claimed that international relief was exploited for my own personal gain. Nothing could be further from the truth.

For verification of the just distribution of all economic assistance rendered Nicaragua, I refer the reader to a statement made before the U.S. House Subcommittee on International Development. This House of Representatives Subcommittee was convened for the purpose of investigating the alleged misuse of economic assistance in Nicaragua.

On March 9, 1978, Terence Todman, the U.S. Assistant

Secretary of State for Inter-American Affairs, testified before the investigating Subcommittee. He said:

"Since the 1972 earthquake, 28 major audits, two separate congressional staff surveys, and a General Accounting Office report on reconstruction activities have been completed. We are pleased to note that no diversion or misuse of official U.S. assistance has been revealed by these reports." Now, Viron Vaky also worked for the State Department. So who was telling the truth? When hit with this question, the State Department had to answer. The State Department's answer was as follows:

"Assistant Secretary Todman was speaking about the results of a specific GAO investigation and other audits held with regard to specific U.S. relief funds. None of these investigations or audits revealed diversion or misuse of U.S. funds." So there you have it in black and white. But until this day, there are those in high places who still falsely accuse me. I can't help but wonder how many other relief operations in other parts of the world have been investigated twenty-eight times? To be sure, the world now knew that Viron Vaky was lying.

The day following the earthquake, the ruling junta came to my home and declared martial law. Generally speaking, when disaster hits a particular area or country, martial law is declared. This simply means that the military commander in that designated area represents the highest authority. As Chief of the Army, I became the government authority for the city of Managua. In military terms, I was the Military Governor.

Unfortunately, my designation as Military Governor was belatedly opposed by Dr. Fernando Aguero, a member of the opposition political party and a member of the ruling junta. Mutual friends, and even members of the opposition political party, advised that it was simply petty jealousy. From that point forward, however, Dr. Aguero attempted to torpedo each and every move the government made in its effort to save Managua from this catastrophe. It seems strange to me that in the beginning he offered complete cooperation and suddenly opposed every move that was made. Perhaps there is an explanation.

At that time, Dr. Aguero was very close to a Mr. James Cheek of the U.S. Embassy. Well-founded sources advised me that Cheek was encouraging Dr. Aguero to harass me in every way possible. At a time when we needed full cooperation, disunity, spearheaded by one individual in the U.S. Embassy, was the last thing we wanted. It is well known, and it was written in many newspapers, that various leaders in the opposition came to me with the acknowledgement that in an hour of dire peril, I was holding the country together. I thought then and I think now that the challenge was monumental. I think now that I successfully met that challenge and brought order out of chaos, hope out of despair, and progress out of rubble.

On the night of the earthquake, when I realized this was a major catastrophe, I tried immediately to contact all police precincts, the Army and the airforce. To my dismay, however, no one was on duty. To the last man, they had left to check on their families. In actuality, Managua was completely without any semblance of law and order, or any structure of government.

My own security guard consisted of thirty men and I remember thinking that I should check on these men. There was a problem! All of them wanted to leave to check on their families. To my way of thinking, this was the only organized military unit left in a city of 600,000 people. I could not let them leave. I finally had to tell these men that I would severely punish any man who left his post of duty.

At that moment, many thoughts were running through my head. I felt certain that it would be almost impossible to impose law and order because we didn't have the men to do it. Looting and stealing were sure to occur, but how could we tell the good guys from the bad guys? Right then and there I decided that enforcement of the law would have to depend on the good people of Managua. This decision might be classified as benign neglect, because we had to depend upon the people.

At that time I began an effort to organize what was left of the armed forces in Managua, and this was no more than 110 men. I then prepared a message to be sent to all sixteen department commanders of Nicaragua. I requested that each one send me as many men as he could spare. General Heberto Sanchez Barquero, who was then the Minister of Defense for Nicaragua, took this message by car and personally delivered it to all department commanders. By morning we had about three hundred men come into Managua from the outlying areas.

Those first three days after the earthquake were crucial, and I am convinced that's where a lot of the animosity against me began. I realized the full extent of the tragedy but the individual organizations did not. Perhaps the magnitude of the catastrophe can best be illustrated by analogy. It was as though 30 percent of the population of the United States were suddenly hit by disaster. If that should happen to the U.S., someone would have to take charge and it would not likely be the Commander and Chief of all Armed Forces. This was the position I took, and I immediately ran into opposition from the International Red Cross, the Catholic Church, various business groups, and the service clubs. Each group wanted to do things its own way. I realized that all efforts had to be coordinated, even though this decision meant that I would be opposed by many powerful elements of our society, and world organizations.

For some forty-five days the Emergency Committee, consisting of three hundred people representing every social and economic level in Managua, met in my home. Incidentally, this home was designed by an architect from San Antonio, Texas, and was built according to the State of California Code 3 specifications. Therefore, it withstood the earthquake.

The Committee and I were gravely concerned about an epidemic. Dead bodies were everywhere, there were no means of disposing of human waste, and there was practically no purified water. So, we called in a team of epidemiologists. They recommended that we evacuate the city. That was a tremendous responsibility for me and the Committee. Nevertheless, we decided to take their advice and I remember a U.S. Army colonel, who was an advisor to me, saying that it would be impossible to evacuate 350,000 people in a small country like Nicaragua.

Further, he said that we didn't have the transportation network to move that many people. I told him we could do it, and we started to work on setting up an emergency transportation system.

For evacuation purposes, I decided to use the headquarters of my political party, the Liberal Party. I then called upon the good people of Managua to come forward with every truck and bus that would roll so as to evacuate 350,000 people. We had the authority to commandeer such vehicles, but this was not necessary. The true character of our people once again evidenced itself. We assembled some two thousand trucks and buses which were all privately owned. For evacuation purposes, we set up three exit routes out of Managua — one in the East, one in the West, and one in the South.

Now, the question was, where would we send all of these people? I knew that the residents of Managua came from all over the country and that each family had relatives in a particular place of origin. So, I sent them to their relatives. We completed the evacuation in two days. Now, these were the people who had no means of transportation. Thousands of others departed by their own transportation. I should point out that those who had no relatives were placed in primary and secondary schools upon reaching their destination, but all had food and shelter. Through the earthquake relief effort, we were feeding 650,000 people.

Meanwhile, the center of Managua was still burning and there was no way to put out the fires. A detachment of the U.S. Corps of Army Engineers from Panama decided there was only one alternative — dynamite the entire area. I agreed that such action was the only way to stop the fires. On that day when they were setting the charges, I went into the Presidential Archives to determine who was in command during the previous earthquake, the one in 1931. I knew that in that earthquake dynamite was used by the U.S. Marines; and, as a result, there was much ill feeling directed toward the Marines.

When I checked the Presidential Archives, I found that the man in charge of all earthquake relief was my father. He was president of the Nicaragua Red Cross at that time. Recalling the ill feeling toward the U.S. Marines, I determined that this should not happen to the U.S. Corps of Army Engineers. I told them to place the charges but a Nicaraguan would set off the explosives, and that's exactly what happened.

Before detonating the explosives, however, a building-to-building check was made to be certain that no one was in those buildings. This was not done by the Marines in 1931, and there was a persistent rumor that when the explosives were detonated, a few people were inside the buildings. Thus, there was another alleged cause for animosity toward the Marines. This time I made certain that there would be no rumors and no ill will directed at the Corps of Army Engineers. So, the fires were extinguished and Old Managua, as we called our downtown area, was no more.

In the meantime, the bickering and back-stabbing continued. Dr. Aguero continued to oppose every move I made, and by this time I was certain that he was being prompted by James Cheek of the U.S. Embassy. Now this is the same James Cheek who, at one time, urged me to overthrow the ruling junta in a coup d'état.

Also, I continued to have difficulty with the Catholic leadership. This opposition was led by Bishop Obando Bravo. Ironically, the Bishop was the man I wanted to join me and serve as vice chairman of the Emergency Committee. I had personally invited him to the first organizational meeting at my home, but he did not attend.

I continued to have difficulty with business groups and service organizations. And at a very critical moment in our relief program, the International Red Cross threatened to cease all of their efforts. It was the same old story. Each group, but particularly the Red Cross and the Catholic Church, wanted to do its own thing. This simply could not be. There had to be cooperation and there had to be a coordinated effort. Otherwise, there would have been total chaos.

By this time, the relief effort was in full swing. At Las Mercedes Airport over one thousand planes were landing each day. Most of these planes came from the United States, but they were coming from other countries as well. It's difficult to imagine the confusion attendant on the unloading, sorting of relief supplies, and classifying of these supplies for distribution.

It was decided that we should use the hangars at the airport for storage and distribution. It's difficult to comprehend the multitude that descended upon the airport and the unbelievable effort made by some people to receive special favors. It was obvious to me that I needed a special "storekeeper." In my son, Tachito, who was then attending Harvard University, I found the man I wanted. He was not in Managua when the earthquake occurred and, therefore, I felt he could be totally objective in his assigned responsibilities. This assumption proved to be correct. He did an excellent job but, due to the nature of his responsibility, he received much unwarranted criticism. It was impossible for him to satisfy the requests of all the people, and constant political pressure was exerted upon him. This was no easy job and it was to continue for some time.

Of interest is the fact that at the time of the earthquake there was solidarity and unity amongst the Central American countries. Immediately after the earthquake, the presidents of Guatemala, Honduras, El Salvador, and Costa Rica came to visit Nicaragua. For small, relatively poor nations, each of these countries gave generously to the people of Nicaragua.

In thinking of aid and assistance, I recall being surprised at some of the countries which came to our assistance. This is one of the reasons I find it difficult to understand why the United States turned against Nicaragua. We received aid from Russia, Communist China, North Korea, South Viet Nam, Cuba, Nationalist China, Eastern European countries, Libya, Iran, Israel, Japan, and so many other countries. We even received a donation from a gold mine. The gold mine was named Compañia Minera del Septentrion, and we received $150,000 from that generous establishment. On one day when there was no beef, I personally donated four hundred steers.

Not all donations were accepted. I remember clearly the day that the NABISCO representative in Managua came to see me. He said he had a tremendous supply of crackers in his warehouse, and he said that I should send Army personnel to pick up the crackers. I told the man that we wouldn't be able to pay for the crackers. I recall his words well. He said, "Forget it. I will declare that the warehouse was looted and let the insurance company pay." I refused to take the crackers, and I did not see the man again. To me, this man displayed a weakness in character and this fault I cannot tolerate.

I should recognize also that there was some looting on the part of a few Army officers. It is not my intention to portray all of my officers and men as saints. Some of them took advantage of a disastrous situation for personal gain. I recall one incident where information came to me that four fairly high-ranking officers were seen looting a building. Confronted with the evidence, each one admitted his guilt. Forthwith all were dismissed from the Army. Even though there were mitigating circumstances, I felt this action was necessary.

The four officers had removed goods from buildings that were on fire and abandoned by their owners. Their contention, and it was a valid contention, was that everything in the stores would have burned anyway, so they weren't really looting. Nevertheless, my order stood. Some merchandise was recovered and returned to the rightful owners.

It's only natural that peoples and countries removed geographically from such a disaster as we experienced would tend to forget that this was a continuing tragedy. Somebody has said that there is nothing so impersonal as death to a stranger one hundred miles away. Well, we were a stranger to most of the world and we were more than a hundred miles away. This is not to say that aid did not continue to come to us. It is to say that the emotional impact of the tragedy subsided.

For nine long months we continued to provide food for 650,000 people. For an outsider, it's difficult to understand the continuing problem of logistics, of transportation, and of distribution. Even though the immediate impact of the earthquake had passed, the United States continued her lifesaving aid. President Richard Nixon, his administration, and the American people did not forget us.

The U.S. Ambassador, Turner Shelton, had completely briefed President Nixon as to the extent of the catastrophe. So Nixon was aware of our grave situation. He dispatched hospitals — portable airforce hospitals, and a large two-hundred-bed field hospital from Fort Hood, Texas. France sent a portable twenty-five-bed hospital. In conjunction with these efforts, all kinds of medical supplies were also sent. Such medical assistance meant that countless numbers of our people were saved.

It didn't take long to establish our communications system. Very shortly we were able to communicate with any part of the world, and the network proved invaluable. A field telephone was set up in the garage at my home. With this system, I could talk to almost any given locale anywhere on earth. The importance of such communications had become clear when Ambassador Shelton advised me that President Nixon would call me on December 24th. I had great respect for Nixon and I took personal pride in the fact that he would call, even though I was

not the Chief of State. I considered myself his friend. I had
been his guest at the White House in 1971 when I attended the
25th year celebration of my West Point class.

Nixon did call and we had a most amiable telephone visit.
He was compassionate and pointed out to me that he and the
American people would assist Nicaragua in any way possible.
Naturally, I thanked him profusely for the unmatched generosity of the United States. I remember thinking that this man
truly understands the gravity of our situation; and then, when
the conversation was about to terminate, Nixon said: "Pat and I
wish you and your family a happy Christmas, if you can have a
happy Christmas under those circumstances." This conversation touched me deeply. The genuine concern of the President
of the United States gave me the feeling that the people of
Nicaragua and I were not alone. I fully realized then that our
traditional ally and long-standing friend, the United States,
was backing us all the way.

After the conversation with Nixon, my family and I began a
small celebration. This was not with the traditional turkey with
all the trimmings, but with a local dish called nacatamales.
Now, nacatamales are made principally out of corn and beef.
But I recall thinking that we were all fortunate to be together
and how fitting it was that our "feast" that evening was an
inexpensive native dish.

At midnight an unusual thing happened. I was gazing out my
window toward the eastern parts of the city when suddenly I
saw a tremendous display of fireworks. My first reaction was
anger. I thought, "These zealous Christians will set the city on
fire." After my moment of anger, I said to my family, "Damn
it, you have to hand it to these people, because they have spirit.
They may be down but they are not out — not by a long shot
they're not." It also occurred to me that there wasn't anything
to burn, so why worry about it.

I would be remiss if some mention were not made about the
assistance given to Nicaragua by the Mexican government.
Compared to the United States, their contribution was relatively small. What they did contribute, however, was people-and-
earthquake know-how. One person who deserves singular recognition is the Minister of Public Works for Mexico, Braca-
monte. His presence seemed to lift our spirits, and he and his

experts laid out a complete plan for the relocation of Managua.

One of my first priorities was the rebuilding of all schools. With funds obtained from AID and the World Bank, we were able to rebuild all the classrooms in one year. This meant that the children of Managua didn't lose a school year and this was of great importance to me.

With virtually every business destroyed, unemployment was a serious problem. Our people had to have work. So, I created the Civil Reconstruction Corps. At its peak, the Reconstruction Corps employed some 3,500 men. Essentially, their job was to clean up the rubble. Also, they separated usable lumber from unusable, and they placed in huge piles any and all metals which could be recycled. This group rendered good service, and, more importantly, they were working.

As usual, however, I was criticized. This time the criticism came from the international community. There were charges that these men would form the backbone of a private army for Somoza. Such charges received more than a little attention, and as a result of the accusations, Senator Mark Hatfield of Oregon and Senator Lawton Chiles of Florida came to Nicaragua to investigate. They checked the work program, they talked to the men, and completed a thorough investigation. When their investigative task was terminated, we had a personal visit. I remember Senator Hatfield saying to me that he had heard a lot about the Somozas, but, he said, "It's quite a different thing to hear about them and talk to them eye-ball to eye-ball." Further, he said, "I now know what you guys are doing here." Suffice it to say that the Civil Reconstruction Corps performed a most useful function for the country.

At that time, serious consideration was being given to the relocation of the capital city of Managua. The Emergency Committee wanted the best information possible, because this decision, like so many of the others, was a serious one. I entrusted this assignment to a West Point classmate of mine, A.R. McBirney, who is a volcanologist. He is considered to be one of the top men in this field, and I had confidence in him. The results of this study revealed two options. We could either rebuild on the Pacific side, or the Atlantic side. It was revealed, however, that either site had serious drawbacks. Faced with what I called a "draw," I decided we should not relocate Managua. Obviously, then, we would follow the recommendations of the Mexicans and the other prominent seismologists, such as the team headed by Dr. Toshi Matsumoto of the University of Texas. This simply meant that we would rebuild on the outskirts of Managua.

There is no doubt in my mind that the decision to rebuild on the outskirts represented the turning point in my support from the business and financial community. It's not too difficult to understand their sentiment. Prior to the earthquake, the downtown area of Managua had been extremely valuable property. Rebuilding on the perimeter of the city meant this once valuable property would be worthless. My concern, though, was the future. I did not want Managua to be destroyed again. It was a hard decision and it hurt many of my friends. For the good of Managua and the entire country, I'm certain I reached the correct decision. Later, however, I was to learn that many of the capitalists in Nicaragua never forgave me. And, as we shall see, vengeance would be theirs.

After conditions had somewhat stabilized, the U.S. sent a team to Nicaragua to evaluate our total reconstruction plan. The team was headed by Ambassador Williams, and subsequent to his trip, a complete report on his findings and recommendations was made to President Nixon. This was early in 1973.

For reconstruction purposes, the U.S. was willing to match funds with Nicaragua. But one must understand that at that time the government of Nicaragua did not have any extra funds. At that point, Williams, Shelton, and I had a conference to determine how Nicaragua could meet her part of the fundraising plan. We finally arrived at a solution but one which I did not like. However, it was the only way to get the money. This plan required that Nicaragua levy a 10 percent export tax, F.O.B., on all exports from Nicaragua. There were a few exemptions, such as bananas, but I think it is important to note that there were no exemptions on anything produced by the Somoza family. As a result of the export tax plan, the government of Nicaragua collected approximately thirty million dollars annually.

It should be recognized that the export tax plan was,

politically, not a popular project. I was strongly advised by members of my own political party that such action would turn the business people completely against me. Naturally, such a tax bill had to be passed by the Congress and it was not an easy thing to do. In my opinion, it took political courage to recommend such a measure and push for its passage. None of my decisions had been easy, and certainly the export tax plan was a difficult political decision. Many of the businessmen, who were later to oppose me, simply couldn't understand that Nicaragua had to have funds, and quickly!

With funds, we could immediately begin building homes for those working people who had a place of employment. In this instance, the good Lord was looking after me. We had an excellent site on which these homes could be built at once.

Prior to leaving the presidency in 1972 and *before the earthquake*, I had asked for an urban study of Nicaragua. The city was growing so rapidly that I knew serious consideration should be given to new urban development areas. My advisors suggested that we establish a Land Bank whereby urban development land could be acquired. This was done and 340 acres were purchased. No one knew we were going to have an earthquake but I knew we had to have land for future urban development. When the U.S. set aside eleven million dollars for eleven thousand small homes, we had the land on which to build those homes. In this regard, we were lucky because even expedited purchases of land, which had been declared for public use, would have taken three months.

An example of Nicaraguan dedication is the fact that we built eleven thousand wooden structure homes in ninety days. By the time the rainy season arrived, we had eighty thousand people living in those small pine houses. It should be pointed out that these houses were not allocated on the basis of any political interest or party affiliation. We conducted a census of all workers whose occupational source was still functioning in Managua. These workers were then brought back and these houses were assigned to them. We called the housing project *The Americas*.

In Central America, at least, this was an unequalled accomplishment. No one believed we could do it. And of course it was a great step toward stabilizing the working class. They saw an effort on the part of the U.S. and their own government to get them out of tents and into houses.

Even so, some of the workers were resentful of the fact that they had to move into plain wooden houses. They didn't realize there wasn't enough stone, sand, cement, and steel to build the amount of housing which was so desperately needed in such a short time. Shortly before I left Nicaragua, Radio Catolica, which is run by the Bishop, was still critical of "The Americas" and stated the project was unworthy of the United States.

The critics didn't understand then, and they don't understand now, that we had to provide shelter for these people — and in short order. Now, "The Americas" are efficiency apartments with running water, electricity, and collective transportation. In retrospect, it was a valiant effort, and I'm proud of the role I played in the creation of "The Americas."

It must be noted that after the earthquake, and for some time to come, a vital area which required utmost attention, supervision, and guidance was that of medical care. By medical care, I mean hospitalization, medical supplies, care for the ill and wounded, and food for the helpless. My wife, Mrs. Hope Somoza, headed up this entire effort, gratuitously. Whether day or night, she could be found in the middle of the gigantic effort. She gladly gave of her time and her energy. I know that part of her life can still be felt in Managua. She gave so much to so many.

The significance of our rebuilding effort can be attested to by the fact that U.S. Secretary of State William Rogers came to Managua to lay the cornerstone of the first hospital which was built by matching funds with AID.

It is noteworthy too, that while he was in Managua Secretary Rogers decorated U.S. Ambassador Turner Shelton for his gallant service to the people of Nicaragua. It was an honor well deserved. Few Americans realize the contribution this man made to our country. The Leftists in the U.S. State Department did an excellent job in covering up the outstanding performance of Turner Shelton. I considered him a personal friend and, beyond a doubt, he was a friend of the people of Nicaragua. Perhaps that's the real reason he was later criticized in the U.S. press.

As I have already mentioned, in the relief program we had a continual battle with Bishop Obando Bravo. He was the Bishop for Managua. The controversy began over distribution of relief supplies. The Bishop wanted to distribute supplies through the parochial divisions of the Catholic Church. The parochial divisions could not serve this function because the churches were destroyed. Instead, we decided to distribute through the polling precincts where the people knew each other, and this system worked quite well.

Knowing the importance of the church and being of the Catholic faith, I decided to invite Bishop Bravo to my office and show him the confidential map which revealed the relocation of the city. Furthermore, I told him I would give him a copy of the map so he could then get with his people and determine where they wanted to place their churches. I then told him to let me know the sites they desired and the land would be donated. The Bishop never came back. However, this same Bishop Bravo was most anxious to get over $400,000 from the government of Nicaragua for an empty lot near the Palacio Nacional, which he sold to the government.

The obstacles created by the Bishops reached the bizarre stage. President Nixon had diverted a supply ship from Viet Nam to the Port of Corinto. The ship unloaded in Corinto and I decided to ship these supplies to Managua by train. Somehow Bishop Salazar of the city of Leon heard about the shipment plans. The supply route carried the train through Leon. Well, the Bishop stopped the train and said, "These supplies are mine." Then he and his followers proceeded to unload every single item on the entire train. I remember that Ambassador Shelton was about to have a fit. He said, "What will I tell President Nixon?" I told him to tell the President the truth and simply say: "Mr. President, I regret to inform you that the supplies which you diverted to Managua from Viet Nam were highjacked by a Catholic Bishop." Now that's humorous but it is also tragic. It illustrates the total lack of cooperation between the Catholic Church of Nicaragua and the government of Nicaragua. The Church simply had to do its own thing.

In most tragedies some humor can be found. Admittedly it may be difficult to find, but if you search meticulously it will be there. One such instance relates to the total destruction of the main hospital of one thousand beds in Managua. It took some doing but we finally rescued all the patients and salvaged some equipment and medical supplies. After this was accomplished, we suddenly realized that a container of cobalt, which was used for cancer treatment, was still in that demolished building. This almost created a panic and there was thought of evacuating the area.

We sent for Geiger counters from Panama and a team came from the States in an effort to locate the cobalt bomb. Finally we pinpointed the location of the container and all of us left the demolished building. When we came out, someone said we would all be sterile as a result of cobalt exposure. One woman there said, "Thank God for the unexpected gifts which come from an earthquake."

Colonel Jose Ivan Allegrett, a brave and daring soldier, retrieved the monster and, luckily, the shield had not been broken. So even in the middle of a disaster it's possible to find some humor.

Dr. Aguero continued to harass me, the government, the relief effort, and the reconstruction program. He was, by this time, holding secret meetings in Massaya in an effort to stir up opposition. This man had some influence, because he was President of the Conservative Party and a member of the three-man ruling junta.

I then decided to call a meeting of the leaders of the Conservative Party and to have that meeting in my house office. What I told the leaders of the opposition political party was not new to them. They simply were not familiar with the details of Aguero's activities and the extent to which he had gone.

With such a preponderance of evidence against Dr. Aguero, the leaders of his own party decided to remove him from office. He was relieved of his duties as President of the Conservative Party, and he was replaced as a member of the ruling junta.

Here, again, an analogy might help to clarify the significance of this action. If a Democratic President of the U.S., for example, should call in the Chairman of the National Republican Party, and say to him that he didn't appreciate the activities of the Senate Minority Leader, a Republican, and wanted him removed from his leadership position, it would parallel my problem in requesting the removal of Dr. Aguero. In my situation, the Conservative Party did support me and Dr. Aguero was removed.

After the removal of Aguero, Edmundo Paguaga was installed as President of the Conservative Party and a member of the junta. Apparently he was the kind of leader they desired because he was the Conservative Party's candidate for the presidency of Nicaragua in 1974.

As it should have been, the U.S. Ambassador and I had regular meetings. In one of these meetings he brought along James Cheek of the U.S. Embassy staff. Now this is the same James Cheek who had been collaborating with Dr. Aguero. In that session I outlined the activities of Aguero and the damage he was doing to our rebuilding effort. I remember Cheek saying to me, "Well, General, why don't you pull a coup d'état, throw the junta out, and assume the presidency?" I turned to him and said, "Mr. Cheek, that's the last thing I want to do. First, the world would say I used the earthquake as an excuse to obtain the presidency; and, second, it would violate the democratic principles of Nicaragua." Cheek did not like my retort, and I thought, "What kind of a chameleon is this man?" It could have been a trap, or he might have been trying to impress Ambassador Shelton. At any rate, I didn't trust him and wanted nothing to do with his ilk.

The new Managua would bear no resemblance to the old. Shopping centers, service centers, office buildings, and all those facilities which are required in any major city would be built several kilometers from the epicenter of the earthquake. Also, this new construction would be spread out over a wide area.

Slowly but surely I saw coming together the various segments which represent the makeup of a vibrant city. But each day as I gazed out upon the old Managua, the hurt returned, and I felt nostalgia.

I saw still standing the ghostly skeletons of wrecked edifices, never to be rebuilt again. I saw the man-made protrusion into Lake Managua which came from the dumping of the rubble that was once upon a time our city. How strange it seemed that of all the mortar, bricks, and stones which man had laboriously placed together to form homes and buildings, the finale of that effort would be bits and pieces deposited in Lake Managua.

All of this served as a reminder to me that in this world of ours, there are few lasting things. Perhaps change is the one true constant. I had not been present at the sunrise of old Managua, but I was there for the dusk. Out of the beginning and the end of Old Managua would evolve something new, and this represented change. With eyes and heart set on the future of my country, I could not help but reflect on the past. With God's help and with more determination than I have ever known, I vowed to make my country a better place in which to live. As my eyes covered an area of windswept desolation, I knew that Managua would change, and I fervently hoped that change would be for the better.

Chapter Two

HOW IT ALL BEGAN

As far back as 1963, there was guerrilla activity in Nicaragua. These were sporadic attempts by the Leftist movement to influence and control people in some of the remote areas. At that time, the Sandinistas represented no serious threat to the government of Nicaragua.

While the government was in the throes of recovering from the earthquake, the guerrillas stepped up their activities in the mountainous northeast section of Nicaragua. This was done after a group of Cubans had crossed over the border on foot and conferred with the rebels. They were told by the Cubans that if they could recruit eight hundred fighting men, they would get all the arms and ammunition they wanted.

The rebel Sandinistas then began sporadic raids in the smaller communities of the northeast. In these raids they murdered eighty justices of the peace. In the eyes of the rebels, these were the local representatives of the government, so they were killed. The rebels even overran the small town of Rio Blanco and, for a short time, held it. So, I dispatched "Bravo" Salazar to this area and he and his men brought an end to that guerrilla activity. However, it was like a malignant cancer. You could stamp out the disease in one part of the body politic and it would suddenly appear in another part.

Had I been a dictator, as was claimed by my political opponents and the international press, I could have eliminated the cancer entirely. This would have meant drastic action on my part and curtailment of the freedom I wanted the people of Nicaragua to have. It would have meant banishment of those

Jesuit priests who preached Communism. These priests sought out the youngsters from the upper class families and indoctrinated them to the Leftist cause. Their effort never ceased.

One must understand that within the Jesuit organization there are two religious concepts. One concept is based upon the theological thesis that a priest should be apolitical. This thesis adheres to the philosophy that the Catholic Church has no place in partisan politics. Now, the other thesis is that it is the responsibility of a priest to become directly involved in partisan politics. But there is a "catcher" to all this. These priests teach Communism. They believe that Jesus Christ was a Communist; and that we will have world peace when all the world is communistic. They teach that capitalism is evil and that all material things should be shunned. It is noteworthy that Pope John Paul II adheres to the thesis that all priests should be apolitical and should not engage in partisan politics.

This religious philosophy has a significant impact upon those young minds which are in the formative stages. This is why children from successful families in Nicaragua turned against their parents. To use a phrase which evolved from the Korean War, it's a form of "brainwashing."

An interesting report appeared in the July 11, 1979 issue of *Accuracy In Media, Inc.* This is a publication which comes out of Washington, D.C. In that issue, AIM quoted Mr. Robert Moss, who writes for the London *Daily Telegraph*, as follows:

> Moss reports that the Sandinista "roving Ambassador," Fr. Ernesto Cardenal, showed up in Teheran last April, where he had long talks with the Ayatollah Khomeini. He broadcast praise for Khomeini over the Teheran Radio on April 8. Moss says that Cardenal has described experiencing his "second conversion" during a three months stay in Cuba in 1970. He established a Catholic commune on an island in Lake Nicaragua, which became a Sandinista recruiting base . . . .

We knew where Cardenal stood and we knew he was not merely a "philosopher poet," as he was described by some members of the press. He was only *one* priest whose political philosophy was exposed to a limited number of people. Most of them, working under the cloak of priesthood, conducted their subversive activities without the exposure of public scrutiny.

I can't stress strongly enough the role that the Communist

priests played in the Sandinista movement. I say again that the influence they exercised on their young students was far greater than an outsider could comprehend. And the quote from Mr. Robert Moss is revealing in another way. It shows the relationship between the Sandinistas and the Ayatollah Khomeini.

In Nicaragua there were many priests who actively opposed our government and continually painted me as some sort of an ogre. A number of these priests came from the United States and Spain, and they seemed more dedicated to the Communist cause than the local priests. Naturally, I knew who these men were and I knew what they were teaching. Of course, we had intelligence sources and at any given moment I could have told you the names of those priests who wanted me dead and the government in the hands of the Communists.

Had I been a dictator, such as Fidel Castro, or the leaders in any of the Soviet-controlled countries, these priests would have been banished or they would have been liquidated. After all, they were truly subversives and they were advocating the overthrow of the government. But I have always believed in freedom of religion and, even though these misguided priests sought to destroy me, I chose not to impose sanctions against them. Rather, I tried to monitor their activities and curtail, as much as possible, their field of influence.

If I had taken hostile action against this segment of the Catholic Church, I can visualize the hasty retaliation by the international press. SOMOZA DENIES RELIGIOUS FREEDOM IN NICARAGUA, or, DICTATOR SOMOZA KICKS PRIESTS IN THE TEETH — so the headlines would have read. Automatically, world opinion would have been against the government of Nicaragua and I would have been the devil with horns. With only one side of the story, the Vatican would have had misgivings, the U.S. Congress would have denounced me, and condemnation would have come from every section of the world. It's ironical, but there are literally thousands of loyal Catholics in Nicaragua today who wish I had taken such a course.

I encountered substantial opposition from certain university staff members and students. They opposed me, my government, and the free enterprise system. The university was a hotbed of Communist activity and Leftist indoctrination was a way of life on the campus.

The same question is propounded again. Why did I permit such subversive activity at the National University? There is a parallel here to freedom of religion. I'm a great believer in excellence in higher education, and "libertad de catedra." In order to achieve excellence, I believe this sector of our society must not be fenced in. In other words, I feel it is wrong to impose educational limits. Such limitation can only deter mental expansion. The mind is a wonder to behold and intelligence capabilities will not be achieved if we autocratically install horizons beyond which a scholar cannot reach.

In all Communist countries, as in Nicaragua now, there are strict governmental controls on what can be taught and what can't be taught. This is particularly true in the fields of history, philosophy, sociology, and any subject relating to the humanities. In intellect, therefore, the students who graduate from those universities have peripheral limitations.

With my high school education at La Salle in the United States and my most excellent education at West Point, I learned the meaning of expanded intellectual horizons. Not only did I study science, mathematics, physics, and other such engineering background courses, I was privileged to learn about other peoples, other governments, other languages, and a broad range of philosophical adventures were open to me. This kind of system is what I wanted for Nicaragua. And perhaps this explains why I opposed educational control. It was my dream that one day the National University of Nicaragua would have equivalency with any university in the world.

A dictator would have stepped in and said, you can teach this course and you can teach that course but here are a list of subjects you cannot teach. Contrary to the image created by the international news media, I was duly elected President of Nicaragua by the people of Nicaragua, and it was not a dictatorial position from which I could rule the country by decree. The National University of Nicaragua had autonomy and my political party and I believed it should be autonomous.

Like all universities in the United States and countries of the free world, our university was run by a board of regents. The makeup of that board would astonish you. The government had only one member on the board; the rest of the board covered the entire political spectrum. However, most of them were Leftists, and some were known Communists. I did not choose to interfere with the board of regents. I represented the controlling Liberal Party and our party controlled the Congress on a 60 percent–40 percent division. Had we chosen to do so, we could have passed legislation which would have placed control of the regents in the hands of the government. This we did not do.

Of course we had the names of the Sandino Communist professors, and their leaders, and the students who continually berated me and the government. The dean of the university was Tunmerman Berhaim, an admitted Socialist, who now happens to be Minister of Education, and we knew his background. Under a dictator, all of these people would have been shot or they would have been imprisoned for long terms. The irony is that these people were promoting and espousing a cause which would destroy all individual freedom. They are learning now that once freedom is lost, it cannot be regained. Let one of those professors or one of those students speak out against the Sandino Communist government, or Fidel Castro, and see what happens. Unfortunately for them, the board of regents must now conform to governmental edicts. The students are still permitted the privilege of berating Somoza but they cannot condemn the government.

The one man who was directly connected to all the Leftist, Sandinista activity was Pedro Joaquin Chamorro. He overtly worked with the Jesuit priests, the university officials and students, and the FSLN. His activities were well known to all of us in government. Yet, he was not banished or imprisoned.

It's interesting to note that he was also co-owner and publisher of the opposition newspaper, *La Prensa*. Chamorro used this newspaper to blast me and my administration every day. Unless I made the headlines in his newspaper, there was something wrong. If I didn't make his headlines, my friends would say to me that Chamorro must be ill today.

My close friends and associates in the Liberal Party often suggested that the government should close the doors of *La Prensa*, because the publication promoted the Communist cause and, in essence, advocated overthrow of the government. I

never considered this course of action, and *La Prensa* continued to be published until we were actually in serious battle with
the Sandinistas.

Why did I permit such flagrant action on the part of
Chamorro? Here again, the principle of freedom was involved.
In the Constitution of the United States of America, the First
Amendment guarantees freedom of speech and freedom of the
press. Well, I happen to believe strongly in those tenets.
Chamorro hated my guts, and he publicly called me an SOB
practically every day. I didn't like it, but it was his newspaper
and he had the right to place in print those things he desired to
express. So, he could run his newspaper, even though he was the
biggest Sandinista in Nicaragua.

I had another reason to dislike Chamorro, and this was
personal. My father, General Anastasio Somoza Garcia, was
assassinated in 1956 by a group of Sandinistas — I should say
Communists. Pedro Joaquin Chamorro was privy to the entire
plot to attack and kill my father. Knowing of his involvement
in the plan to assassinate my father, I still respected his right to
freedom of the press.

When dignitaries from various parts of the world came to
see me, they were always amazed at the contents of *La Prensa*.
To all of them, I could point to it and say, "Perhaps now you
can believe that we do have freedom of the press in Nicaragua."

It should be mentioned here that at a very crucial moment in
Nicaragua's battle with the Sandinistas, Pedro Joaquin Chamorro was killed. It was only natural that the Communists, the
Sandinistas, and the international press blamed the government of Nicaragua. The world seemed to know of his hatred
for me and the government.

What the world didn't know was that Chamorro was the last
man I wanted to be killed. To those who called me "dictator"
and worse, I could always point to Chamorro and *La Prensa* as
obvious evidence of our free press policy. Also I knew that
Chamorro was a symbol of the anti-Somocistas. His death could
only mean martyrdom and Chamorro was the last man in Nicaragua that I wanted to be a martyr. Later I will give detailed
attention to Pedro Joaquin Chamorro.

The news media depicted a Nicaragua controlled, a Nicaragua suppressed, and a Nicaragua without freedom. How strange that this image should be portrayed. If any one thing precipitated the colossal predicament in which the government of Nicaragua would later find itself, it was an excess of freedom. For this excess, I take full responsibility.

It seemed incredible, but in the midst of all the rebuilding activity it became necessary to devote some thought to politics. With day-and-night devotion to earthquake needs, politics had been placed on the back burner. Now, however, leaders in the Liberal Party were pressing me to discuss the upcoming presidential election.

For background purposes, perhaps it would be well to discuss briefly the election laws of Nicaragua as they existed at that time. I say "at that time" because it appears that free elections in Nicaragua are now a thing of the past.

Contrary to information disseminated by the U.S. press, our election laws were patterned after the laws of the United States. The statutes were researched and drawn by Professor Dobbs of Princeton University. So far as I can determine, our elective procedure was exactly the same as the U.S. We did have some constitutional provisions which did not exist in the United States. For example, we had a provision which stipulated that no President could succeed himself in office. Since the three-man junta, with one person from the Conservative Party and two people from the Liberal Party, had been ruling Nicaragua, I was qualified, under the Constitution, to run for the presidency again. In other words, I would not be succeeding myself.

Much like the United States, Nicaragua was principally a two-party country. However, if any political group petitioned with as much as 5 percent of the last registered vote, that group had the right to be recognized as a political party. This procedure meant that third parties could not be excluded. Each party selected delegates to a national convention, and these delegates then nominated its candidate. Generally speaking, maneuvering for delegates began about six months prior to election time. Due to the earthquake emergency in Nicaragua, the year 1973 was somewhat different. The normal process would be delayed. However, one thing was certain, elections were mandatory and each political party had to face up to that responsibility.

I discussed my own personal situation with my party associates. I told them that my day-and-night effort after the earthquake had left me exhausted and that perhaps consideration should be given to another candidate. They pointed out that there was no one in the party who possessed the needed national prominence and the required leadership ability but myself. Oh, they gave me a hundred reasons why I should be the candidate. They stressed the role I had played in, as they put it, "saving Nicaragua from disaster." They reminded me that I had an obligation to the international community and, furthermore, that in all of Nicaragua only I had a person-to-person relationship with the leaders around the world. There was something to their argument. I did have a responsibility to Nicaragua, but I also had a personal responsibility to my family and to myself. So, I told them that I wanted to discuss the matter with my family.

Well, we had some kind of a family debate. All the pros and cons were thoroughly kicked around. It was apparent that my wife, Hope, was not too happy about another campaign and another term in office. Finally we agreed that this was the last campaign for me and that I would not seek the presidency again. With the family in accord, I decided to run for the position one more time.

The Liberal Party leaders were advised of my decision and the campaign was under way. At the appropriate time, our party held its convention. Out of some 220 delegates, there were 5 who expressed opposition to me. In the end, however, the vote was unanimous. I had my party's nomination.

In the meantime, the Conservative Party had its political machinery in motion. They were choosing delegates and, amongst themselves, trying to decide on a viable candidate. Their choice was Dr. Edmundo Paguaga, a well-known politician in Managua. He had the credentials to lead their party. He was President of the Conservative Party and a member of the ruling junta. His hat was in the ring.

Again, the procedure of both parties was similar to the nominating process in the U.S. For example, I made my acceptance speech and outlined the platform on which I would seek the presidency. Dr. Paguaga did the same thing.

Perhaps it was because I knew this would be my last campaign, or perhaps it was because Nicaragua was on the move and that we were winning the "earthquake battle" — whatever the reason, I entered the campaign in a state of euphoria. It was a vigorous contest, and in my opinion, I conducted this campaign with vim and élan.

It was my goal to speak in every city and municipality of Nicaragua. This goal I achieved. I wanted to see the people, and I wanted them to see me. Further, I wanted them to hear my message about the future of Nicaragua. It was a good message and it related to sound economic progress for all the people. Basically it was the same message I outlined in my acceptance speech.

As anyone familiar with politics knows, an acceptance speech touches on a variety of subjects and it should inspire the delegates as well as the people at home. Somehow, I don't think that particular acceptance speech followed the norm. I did touch on a number of things but I stressed in particular two areas of economic importance to all the people of Nicaragua.

This was in 1973, a long time before the Shah of Iran was unceremoniously thrown out and a long time before the Persian Gulf oil crisis. It was clear to me, though, that a petroleum crisis was coming. At 1973 crude oil prices, our balance of payments suffered because we imported all of our oil. Therefore, energy had to be an important issue in my campaign. We had to find a way to escape the coming financial crunch of high oil prices which might reach as much as $15 to $20 per barrel. Little did I dream that spot prices would reach $30 to $35 per barrel.

In this context, I tried to alert the presidents of other Central American countries concerning the coming energy crisis. There is very little oil production in all of Central America and most of the countries are totally dependent upon oil imports. The same can be said for most so-called Third World powers. I can say unequivocally that unless those Third World powers find alternate sources of energy, they will all go broke, and that includes Nicaragua. They simply cannot keep their countries on a sound economic basis and pay the current price for oil. This fact I recognized in 1973.

In my acceptance speech, I emphasized this problem for

Nicaragua. I told the delegates, and I was later to take this message to the people, that alternate sources of energy had to be developed and that we had one such source in Nicaragua — geothermal power.

Back in 1969, I conceived the idea of such a power source and asked that a study be performed. The study verified my contention. The volcano Momotombo was, scientifically speaking, the ideal source and it was feasible. The price of imported oil and gas was putting constant pressure on our balance of payments, and this was the reason for my concern. Since the cornerstone of my socioeconomic policy, and that of the Liberal Party, was stability of the cordoba and the suppression of inflation, I wanted to have either hydroelectric power or geothermal electricity. With either source of energy, we could offset inflation.

I announced that we would continue with the geothermal project and indicated that by 1981, Nicaragua should have inexpensive electricity on steam, thanks to "Momo," as we called Momotombo. In this project we were working closely with the Japanese. Their engineers, in concert with ours, recommended that initially three generating plants be erected with a capacity of 35,000 K.W. I had completed arrangements for financing of this project with the overseas Economic Cooperation Fund of the Japanese government.

For the future of Nicaragua, this project assumed great importance. When I explained geothermal power to the delegates, and even to the uneducated worker, they knew what I was talking about. Also, expressions of gratitude came from everywhere. The people were delighted that someone was looking ahead and thinking about their future.

Agriculture was another area to which I gave special economic attention. I predicted a food crisis but, in reality, it didn't take much foresight to predict a greater demand for food. The world's population was expanding exponentially, and they would need food to survive.

Nicaragua was in a fortunate position. We had thousands upon thousands of undeveloped acres which were suitable for farming. This land was free to the farmers. All they had to do was clear the land and they were in business. In our country, everyone works — men, women, and children. Therefore, a family, with hard work and dedication, could clear a considerable amount of land and make it productive. This would help the farmer and it would help our economy. In my mind, this was free enterprise at work. If there was one particular theme to my campaign it was "Invest in Agriculture."

I tried to be the kind of leader for my country who could foresee problems before they arose. In my first administration, we established a network of drying centers and grain silos. The only grain infrastructure of national level in Latin America. I foresaw that Nicaragua would be the principal exporter of grain for Central America. This proved to be a wise decision. In this campaign, I could foresee the coming demand for agricultural products, and I continually discussed the agricultural issue.

It will probably surprise the U.S. press but I regularly discussed the injustice of giving tax advantages and incentives to industry and none to agriculture. Throughout Central America, tax exemptions and other advantages are given to industry. If an industrial organization or a factory has good management, it's a cinch to succeed because they don't have to pay taxes. To my way of thinking, everyone should pay his fair share of the tax burden. In this sense, I could be called a reformer.

The agricultural sector of Nicaragua knew that my interest in the small farmers was not a campaign gimmick. I was deeply concerned about their welfare and sought to use all the resources at my command to improve their way of life and their standard of living.

In my previous administration, I had instituted certain educational reforms in the primary schools. One of these reforms called for the teaching of basic agriculture as the initial science for the students of Nicaragua. I felt that such a program would stimulate agricultural interest in the student at a very early age. If a student were so inclined, he or she could pursue that interest to the highest educational level. Even if that were not the case, the student would have benefited from the program.

In that same administration, we had a far-reaching program to improve seeds, fertilizers, and insecticides. This endeavor drew the attention of the appropriate people with the United States AID program. As a result, our farmers improved their technology and their productivity increased.

In my visits throughout the country, I determined that the small farmer was probably the poorest person in Nicaragua. Prior to leaving office in 1972, a committee, of which I became chairman, was formed to study the agricultural sector at the level of the poorest people in the country. The committee made a detailed study and the results reflected badly on our society. The study gave me the feeling that those of us who enjoyed a decent standard of living had been guilty of iniquitous conduct, so far as the poor farmer was concerned.

Actually, this was a diagnosis of the condition of the poorest people in Nicaragua. The prognosis indicated survival for these poor people, provided certain reforms were carried out so as to make available to them new agricultural technology, better seeds, better fertilizer, and sufficient arable land on which a living could be made. So far as I know, this was the first detailed agricultural study made in all Latin America.

In my last term of office, the first national activity to receive my attention was agriculture. We created a department called INVIERNO (Instituto De Bienestar Campesino). This department guaranteed to the small farmer that he could acquire sufficient land to provide a decent living for himself and his family. If open government land was available and it was suitable to him, he could have it. If it meant that he needed a small amount of acreage from a larger landowner next door, the government would assist him in obtaining that land. In essence, this changed the land tenure law in Nicaragua. As a part of INVIERNO's program, we proposed to increase taxes on idle ground. That is, land that was not being utilized for farming or ranching.

I take pride in the fact that the formation of INVIERNO, the studies of INVIERNO, the progress and results of INVIERNO, were taken to Hong Kong by Robert Culberson, Chief of AID, as an example of what a government could do to assist a small "dirt poor" farmer.

I had great compassion for the poor farmers of Nicaragua. The government made every effort to provide agricultural opportunity for this segment of our society. Most importantly,

we were succeeding. When I left Nicaragua, we had INVIER-
NO operating in Matagalpa, Esteli, Jinotega, and Carazo.
Since this was an AID — sponsored function, the General Accounting Office (GAO) of the United States conducted two
investigations and audits. Each time, INVIERNO was in perfect
condition and given a "clean bill of health."

I kept the campaign trail hot. As I mentioned, I covered the
country from one end to the other. Our campaign was well
financed and, therefore, I could reach most of the people with
my message. The same cannot be said for Dr. Paguaga.

Due to the success of the earthquake relief and reconstruction program, and the prosperity of the entire country, the
leadership of the Conservative Party was lachrymose. In essence, they were crying in their beer. They could see our
campaign moving and theirs was not. They could see the
turnout of people for our rallies, while their rallies attracted
very few people. Thus they failed to contribute the finances
which my opponent needed in order to run a first-class
campaign. The campaign of Dr. Paguaga simply never got off
the ground.

As in the United States, our voters were required to register.
In Nicaragua you wouldn't find the voter apathy which exists
in the U.S. Out of a population of 2,250,000 people, over one
million people registered and these people voted.

In our Liberal constitutional reform of 1893, all males over
eighteen years of age were eligible to vote. Then with women's
suffrage, all females over eighteen were eligible to vote. That's
the reason we had such a high percentage of our people register
and vote.

The day of the election arrived and there was an unprecedented turnout. Over one million people registered and some
850,000 voted. To say that I was happy with the results, is an
understatement. I received over 750,000 votes and my opponent
received in excess of 100,000 votes.

There was a unique agreement between the Liberal Party
and the Conservative Party. Whichever party won the presidency would have sixty percent of the representation in the Senate
and sixty percent of the representation in the House. Although
the Conservative Party received far less than forty percent of
the popular vote, they had forty percent of the entire Congress.

An interesting thing happened toward the end of the campaign. Pedro Joaquin Chamorro and other Sandinista leaders
publicly announced that the people should not vote because
there was really no choice. Such notices were run in Chamorro's
newspaper, *La Prensa*. In other words, the Sandinistas were
advising the people to boycott the election. Such action on the
part of the Sandinistas was against the election laws of
Nicaragua. Therefore, each of those men who advocated
violating the law was brought into court, found guilty, and his
civil rights were suspended for a period of time. However,
Chamorro continued to publish *La Prensa*. The court could
have halted publication for a period of time but they chose to
be lenient with Chamorro.

After the election, the junta continued to rule Nicaragua
until I was sworn into office on December 1, 1974. The
inauguration was something I shall always remember. It was the
first time in the history of Central America that the presidents
of Guatemala, El Salvador, Honduras, and Costa Rica had
attended an inauguration. A member of Chile's ruling junta
also came. This inauguration represented a change in power,
and they all came. It had not happened before and it has not
happened since. This was truly an historical event.

The international press had criticized my election. The
presence of the presidents from Costa Rica, Guatemala, El
Salvador, and Honduras was positive proof of the legitimacy of
my election. In this regard, prior to the presidential election, the
Organization of American States (OAS) was invited to send
observers and poll watchers on this election. I wanted no
charges of rigged election and voter coercion. The OAS did
send a team to Nicaragua and they travelled from polling place
to polling place. They reported no irregularities. Conclusion —
Nicaragua had an honest election and I was elected. I might also
point out that an invitation was extended to the press to be
present at the polling places on election day. Very few of them
showed up.

At about that time, President Carlos Andres Perez of Venezuela was feeling smug and prosperous. As a result of the
increased price of petroleum, millions of dollars were pouring
into his country each day. With a feeling of power, he launched

a drive to exert geopolitical influence in the entire Caribbean area. As a kickoff in this power move, he invited the five presidents of Central America and Omar Torrijos of Panama to Venezuela.

This, in reality, was to be a staged show for Perez and a display of his generosity to all of the poor Central American countries. Prior to the meeting in Venezuela, all of us who were invited were advised as to the purpose of the session. We were all purchasing petroleum from Venezuela and President Perez knew the new prices were hitting us in our most vulnerable economic point. So he proposed to extend a loan to each country to make up for some of the price differential. This was to cover a period of five years, and Perez would decide upon an interest rate to be charged for the loan.

For me, the invitation from the president of Venezuela was somewhat of an embarrassment. Had Carlos Andres Perez and I met on the street twenty-five years ago, we would have met with pistols and one of us would have been dead. Twenty-five years ago he was the private secretary of President Romulo Betancourt and I was the right-hand man of my father, General Somoza. General Somoza and Betancourt were enemies because Betancourt followed communistic policies and was a self-declared Communist. It was no secret that my father hated the Communists. When the invitation from Perez arrived, I felt uncomfortable.

However, when you are elected as president of your country, your personal likes and dislikes must give way to your mandated position — representative of all the people. Even though it was going to be a traumatic experience, in the interest of my people and my country, I accepted the invitation.

Nicaragua has always been an austere country. Therefore, the government didn't have an Air Force One, or an Air Force Two. Now we might have had an Air Force Ten, but that plane would not have made it to Venezuela. So, how was I to travel to this highfalutin affair? After my first term, I had ordered a Rockwell Turbo-prop, inasmuch as I needed good transportation to travel through Central America. The order was placed and I expected delivery in time to make the meeting in Venezuela. I don't know whether I was fortunate or unfortunate, but the plane didn't arrive in time for the trip to

Venezuela. In its place though, Rockwell sent a Sabre-60. For this particular trip, I would receive a free ride and I would be going in style.

Having good pilots and an excellent airplane, my flight time to Puerto Ordaz, Venezuela could be calculated with accuracy. I took off so as to arrive at exactly the time which had been designated on my invitation. We were twenty minutes out of Puerto Ordaz, when we received a call from the tower advising us to proceed to Ciudad Bolivar. No reason was given for the change in our flight plan but we followed the tower directive. As it turned out, President Perez had been to a celebration in Peru and was late on his return trip to Venezuela. Naturally, he didn't want his guests to arrive before he did. As every Chief of State knows, there is a certain amount of pomp and ceremony attendant to arrivals and departures. Personally, I could do without most of the fanfare, but custom and tradition seem to demand it.

After an hour on the ground in Ciudad Bolivar, we were notified that we could now take off for our original destination. We landed and taxied to the spot which had been marked for us and I left the airplane. There stood Carlos Andres Perez, dressed in a tan suit with matching colors, and wearing a rather stern look on his face. I walked up to him, put out my hand, and said, "I'm General Somoza, President of Nicaragua." He sponded, "I'm Carlos Andres Perez." He then surprised me by saying, "You were the last man with whom I wanted to shake hands, but I'm glad you are the first." I thought to myself, "Somoza, it's a good beginning and everything is turning out as you expected."

I found myself in an interesting situation. I was standing beside President Perez and as the other Central American presidents arrived, I greeted them along with Perez. We were then ushered into the airport terminal and departed for the hotel.

That night Perez invited all the presidents to dinner. Prior to dinner, the other presidents and I had an opportunity to discuss strategy. If I can help it, I will never go into a meeting, such as the one with Perez, unprepared. In our own private session, we had an opportunity to express ourselves. Incidentally, Omar Torrijos of Panama had not yet arrived. He was delayed in

Colombia, and had sent word that he would arrive that night.

For me, this planning session proved to be rather frustrating. Daniel Oduber of Costa Rica spoke first and pointed out that he had been host for Perez while he was in exile from Venezuela. Therefore, he didn't want to do or say anything that would tarnish his friendship with Perez. Arturo Armando Molina of El Salvador said, "Look, I don't know the guy, and, besides, I don't know anything about this loan business." Langeraud Garcia of Guatemala said he didn't know anything about this kind of business. Since I had more experience in financial matters than they had, I was asked to be their spokesman. In such a situation, what could I say? I told the group of presidents that I would do my best.

So we went to dinner. On the way to dinner, I decided that I was going to ask certain questions of Carlos Andres Perez and make him feel good. The dinner lasted two and one-half hours. We reached the point when questions were appropriate. As previously discussed by the group of presidents, I acted as spokesman and proceeded to ask questions of Perez. My questions were of a friendly nature and gave Perez an opportunity to expound on his philosophy. This was the stage he wanted, and I gave it to him. He criticized the new government in Peru and, to draw an analogy, he said he had been to a bullfight where the bull did not come up to the expectations of the crowd. In this instance the new government had not come up to the expectations of the people. It was obvious that Perez was in a happy mood. It was my feeling that my relationship with him was now less tense. It seemed the ice had been broken.

The next morning we had a grand show. President Perez sat at a dais and was flanked by his ministers and advisors. Each of the six presidents sat at an assigned table with his own delegation. From his commanding position, Perez laid out his proposal.

For me, the atmosphere was uncomfortable. Lined up at the other five tables were five presidents with advisors and none of them wanted to say anything. I had already suggested to the other presidents that we tie the interest rate on the loan to the rate which was given us by the Inter-American Development Bank. It was regrettable to me that the details of such a financial arrangement had to be discussed in an open forum.

The plenary session adjourned for lunch, and it was decided that during this period, the technical people and the Central Bank representatives would discuss the loan and the interest rate. This was because I had strenuously opposed the high interest rate which Perez wanted to charge us.

On the way out of the plenary session, Omar Torrijos came up to me and said, "Tachito, why are you being so hardheaded about accepting the money which Perez has offered us? Look," he said, "the most expensive money is the money you never receive." I found his remarks to be hilarious. Torrijos was out of touch with financial reality and didn't have the vaguest notion as to the strategy I was trying to follow. What Torrijos was really telling me was that he was broke and, regardless of terms, he needed the money. But this was the way he handled the finances of Panama. He was always in financial trouble. You can be sure that Torrijos will have Panama in financial straits again. Only this time he won't have the Canal to trade on or anything else.

As part of the visit, Perez had planned a trip to the largest dam in Venezuela. Of the entire group to visit the dam, I was the only person with an engineering background and I was the only one, including Perez, who understood anything about dam construction. I had built dams, so this type of project was not new to me. When the dam authorities came over to visit with this group of presidents, I discussed the moment, the cubic feet per second, the kilowatts, the watershed, and other important engineering functions relating to such a project. At that point, Carlos Andres Perez came over to me and said, "How come you know so much about dams?" I told him that I was a practical man, an engineer, and that it was important to me and my country to know about such things. While we were at the dam, another interesting conversation ensued.

We began to discuss U.S. relations with Latin America. I wanted to find out firsthand how Perez felt about the United States. In such a setting, I thought he would let his hair down and tell me how he really felt. He did, and so far as the U.S. was concerned it was not good. Actually, he had nothing good to say about the government of the U.S., and he was particularly critical of the private business sector. I determined for certain that President Perez of Venezuela was not a friend of the United States.

After the dam visit, we went to lunch. Seated at that luncheon table was quite an array of presidents. There sat Perez of Venezuela, Langeraud Garcia of Guatemala, Oduber of Costa Rica, Molina of El Salvador, Torrijos of Panama, and myself. Then began a general discussion. At one of those quiet moments which comes in any group conversation, Perez turned to me and, in a voice so that all could hear, said, "You were the last man with whom I wanted to shake hands, but now that I have met you, I'm glad that I did."

Well, this comment almost caused me to fall out of my chair. Much of his attention had been directed toward me and this made me uneasy, because I knew how the other presidents must feel. In retort to his personal comment about me, I said: "Mr. President, those are the circumstances of life." I pointed out to him that in the past he had been secretary to an important person and I was the chief aide to another important person. "At that time," I said, "each of us had orders. Now we meet and make policy decisions."

The loan agreement and financial arrangements were completed and the necessary papers signed. It was now time to leave Puerto Ordaz for Caracas. Before leaving, however, I asked for an audience with President Perez. I merely wanted to say goodbye and thank him for his hospitality. I must admit, though, that there was an ulterior motive.

I went to his suite and we had an amiable visit. But there was international intrigue here. I wanted to find out, if possible, why Venezuela was now pushing to establish normal relations with Cuba, when this same country had fought for the isolation of Cuba. Prior to my visit to Venezuela I had received a call from Julio C. Turbay of Colombia in which the vote for Cuba had been solicited. This bothered me. Why had Venezuela changed her position?

It was known to me that Castro sabotaged Betancourt's election. Betancourt, formerly a self-proclaimed Communist, had come to the realization that Communism was evil and so he was having trouble with Castro. Now here was Perez, former secretary to Betancourt and former Minister of the Interior, seeking support for Castro. As Minister of the Interior, Perez had been ruthless, and in his support of Betancourt was responsible for the death of thousands of people. This was indeed a puzzle and I wasn't able to put all the pieces together.

This goodbye visit rapidly turned into more intrigue. Before I could obtain answers on Venezuela's support of Cuba, the conversation turned in a different direction. Perez wanted to know about Pedro Joaquin Chamorro. I knew that Chamorro and Perez had been in Costa Rica at the same time and that they had become friends. I told him not to worry about Chamorro because he was my best ally. I told him that Chamorro hated my guts, but he was an ally because he helped keep my government clean with his opposing newspaper. I told Perez not to worry about Chamorro because nothing would happen to him. I pointed out that on four different occasions I had the opportunity to eliminate him when he was in the bush with the revolutionaries. The concern of Perez for Chamorro was obvious.

How much did I know about the relationship between the two men? I knew more than Perez realized. For example, when Chamorro left Costa Rica to come back to Nicaragua, he gave his refrigerator to Perez. Refrigerators were hard to come by and this was a meaningful gesture of friendship. At that time, Perez was very poor and the refrigerator meant much. I could tell that Perez was pleased with my report on Chamorro.

Then, I came back to my strategic question so as not to let Perez off the hook. I said, "Why, Mr. President, having been the Minister of the Interior, having fought Castro and knowing full well what he is capable of doing, why have you asked to lift the sanctions against Cuba?" He replied, "In the first place, I want to be honest about the whole thing. I don't want to be like the Caldera government that did business with Cuba under cover, violating the OAS resolution." He said, "If I do business with Cuba, I want to do it openly." He went on to point out that during the Caldera Administration in Venezuela, countless ships loaded with supplies of all kinds sailed for Cuba. That didn't surprise me very much.

Again, I pressed the point. I said, "Mr. President, what is the real reason you want to lift the sanctions against Communist Cuba?" The answer was surprising. The President of Venezuela replied, "I don't want Castro to hurt my government." How could this be? Here you had a man, elected in a democratic process and representing a powerful government in South

America, genuflecting before Castro. He was actually afraid of what Castro might do to him. He even said, "I don't want to face up to Castro."

The frightening thing is that this is the man, this same President Carlos Andres Perez, that President Jimmy Carter picked as his strongman in Latin America. This shows you how solid Mr. Carter's base was. I find it to be absolutely incredible. Mr. Carter's assessment and judgement compare to those of a high-school dropout. Perez was Carter's choice of a leader in Latin and, in Perez, he had nothing.

Thereupon, I again thanked Perez for his hospitality and took my leave. I left with an empty feeling in my stomach. I no longer had any respect for the man. I recall thinking that if all the major governments of Latin America were headed by weak men like Carlos Andres Perez, we were in a hell of a spot.

Then we went to Caracas and there we were still guests of President Perez. At dinner that night, in the presence of all the presidents of Central America, President Perez pointed me out and said, "Somoza, when are you going to make any kind of declaration against the United States?" This was an embarrassing question but one to which I thought I should respond. I said, "Mr. President, I will make such a declaration when I'm sure I can back up what I say. I do not believe in frustrating the people of Nicaragua with idle declarations which cannot be enforced. To me, the peace of mind of my people is far more important than making useless declarations which can never be accomplished." Now, this retort was aimed directly at Perez. He was always making declarations against the United States, but these declarations were just so much hot air. Perez asked for it and I let him have it — right on the head.

With the mission to Venezuela accomplished, my advisor and I headed back to Managua. I felt happy about the economic results and looked forward to a joyous Christmas.

At that time I worked closely with the U.S. State Department. The events which transpired in Venezuela were reported in full to the proper people in the U.S. government. After all, they were my friends.

Chapter Three

TERRORISM IN MANAGUA

Christmas was approaching and we had much for which to be thankful. Following the earthquake, we were making great strides in our reconstruction effort. I had just concluded a financial arrangement with Venezuela which promised to aid our economy. The people of Nicaragua were working and our exports for the year were greater than we anticipated. Indeed, this should be an outstanding Christmas for everyone.

I previously mentioned the importance of Christmas to the people of Nicaragua. I failed to mention that this is truly party time in Managua. It seems that everyone who can wants to give a party for friends and loved ones. For over two weeks there is a social function to attend every night.

I remember well the day of December 18, 1974. On that day I had lunch with two very dear friends of mine, Jose Maria "Chema" Castillo and Ambassador Guillermo Lang, who was formerly Nicaragua's Ambassador to the United Nations. We had drinks, good food, and warm fellowship. Each of us expressed love for the other and pledged undying friendship. For some reason, at Christmas it's easier to express our sentiments.

Before leaving, Chema Castillo advised me that he was giving a farewell party that night for U.S. Ambassador Turner B. Shelton and he wanted me to come. My friend, Turner Shelton, was being assigned to another diplomatic post. I told him there were so many things going on that I didn't think I could make it. Little did I dream that this was the last time I would see Chema alive.

Chema always gave a good party and that night was no

exception. It proved to be his last party. As guests mixed and mingled in an atmosphere of gaiety and friendship, the calm of night was shattered by a burst of gunfire outside Chema's home. All of those at the party knew immediately that the sounds they heard were not Christmas firecrackers. Before they had time to react, Sandinista terrorists were shooting their way into Chema's home. The gunfire heard outside had ended the lives of two chauffeurs who had driven guests to the party. As terrorists entered the home, Chema made a wrong move and he was killed with an automatic weapon. Quickly and efficiently, these killers had taken over the entire home and garden and some forty-five distinguished guests were being held at gunpoint. They were now hostages and would be for some time. Another nightmare for Managua had begun.

I received the news from my brother, Jose, who had been notified by the police. Not realizing that the terrorists were trained killers, we sent the police to move in to retake the home. The policemen surveyed the situation and decided their best approach was quietly to vault the brick wall which surrounded the garden. These were good policemen and they had been trained to operate in risky situations. It was no clumsy, half-hearted effort that took them over the wall and into the garden. Unbeknown to the police, they were expected, and as soon as their feet touched the ground, they were greeted with machine-gun fire. Once again, death struck the ill-fated Christmas party. As was revealed later, those were no amateurs. Their fire spread was small, indeed, and would have done justice to an automatic weapon expert with the FBI. We were to learn later that this group had received the best training Castro could offer.

At that time, I decided we should not force the situation. It was now readily apparent that this well-trained group of killers would, without the slightest hesitation, shoot all of the hostages and anyone who tried to enter the house. My chief concern was the safety and well-being of those poor souls being held. Also, inside that house were some of the most outstanding people in all of Nicaragua, as well as foreign dignitaries.

For example, in that home in a life-and-death situation were my brother-in-law, Guillermo Sevilla Sacasa, dean of the diplomatic corps in Washington; the Foreign Minister of Nicaragua; and, the former Ambassador to the United Nations from ,Nicaragua, with whom I had had lunch that very day. Also, there were Noel Pallais Debayle, my first cousin; Danilo Lacayo, representative for Esso in Nicaragua; Franco Chamorro, a prominent Nicaraguan; the ambassador from Chile; and the mayor of the city, Luis Valle Olivares. I cannot reveal all of those who were present, but it is evident that this was no ordinary gathering. Most of the men present were accompanied by their wives and some children were there. As best we could determine, there were forty-five people being held in that house and the host, Chema Castillo, was already dead. Fortunately, the guest of honor, Ambassador Turner Shelton, had attended the party and decided to leave early. Otherwise he would have been taken along with all the others.

I decided to keep all telephone lines open so that we could be assured of receiving any calls coming from the hostages or the terrorists. The terrorists had all given themselves a numerical designation. These numerical designations started with zero and went to twelve. The first call was from Zero to General Jose Somoza, demanding that the police and military personnel be removed from fifty to one hundred yards from the house. In that same conversation, they demanded that we get Monsignor Obando Bravo to come to the house and visit with them. This is the same Bravo with whom I had had so much difficulty in the aftermath of the earthquake.

We looked for Bravo but we couldn't find him until early the next morning. After he was located, I asked him to come to my office. He came to my office and it was a visit I shall never forget. I remember that visit not because of the dialogue, but due to the appearance of the man. Normally, Bravo had very dark skin, but not on that day. His face was ashen and except for obvious life, it was like looking at the face of a dead man. I noticed also that his mouth was dry. He kept trying to lick his lips, but there was no moisture there. His whole demeanor was surprising to me.

In my many years of dealing with people, I have learned something about psychology. Bravo's appearance and his demeanor told me that something traumatic was happening within that man. My hasty analysis, which later was proven to be correct, was that this leader in the Catholic Church had known the hostage action was going to be taken in Managua. He didn't know where it was going to happen but he knew the criminal activity was to occur that night.

We later learned that three days previously, this same terrorist group had been in Managua to learn the details of various Christmas parties. They had given serious consideration to hitting the 25th Wedding Anniversary party of my first cousin, Noel Pallais Debayle. However, I attended that party and my military guard was present. The presence of the military guard dissuaded the group. So, they did not hit Noel's party. Had I gone to Chema Castillo's party, he probably would not have been the victim. You can be sure, however, that someone else would have been hit.

We were then advised that unless we began serious negotiations at once, they would systematically kill one hostage at regular intervals of time. I could see that this was going to be an ordeal. When I recall all the events which transpired, I become angry. In evaluating my own actions and reactions, I think perhaps I was too nice. But, then, you cannot go against your moral principles.

The night the terrorists took over the house of Chema Castillo, a couple of people were wounded. In one of their telephone conversations, a doctor's assistance was requested. We told the kidnappers that we didn't know of one single doctor who would willingly walk into that situation. These people were prepared because they then gave us the name of a doctor to call. It was Dr. Briceño, chief of the Pavlov Clinic in Managua, who had been trained in Moscow. We couldn't find Dr. Briceño, so we asked them to name another one. This time they nominated Dr. Gutierrez Sacasa. Dr. Sacasa is Vice Minister of Health for the Communist government now ruling Nicaragua, so his connection with the rebels becomes very clear.

Before going to the house, Dr. Gutierrez Sacasa came to see me. I told him that he had been picked by the terrorists to come to the house and see to the needs of the wounded. At that point, he didn't know that I associated him with the rebels. I told the doctor that his mission of mercy would not be held against him and that he had my solemn pledge that there would be no recriminations.

The doctor went to the house and the terrorists showed him

only one man who was wounded, Mr. Danilo Lacayo, the Esso representative. He was not shown the body of Castillo. The wounded man received medical attention and Dr. Gutierrez Sacasa returned. I questioned him about the condition of the hostages and asked him if he had seen other wounded people. He said he had not seen anything, that he had attended the wounded man and departed.

Dealing with these killers was a delicate matter, because a misdirected order or a mistake of any kind could cost the lives of some of the hostages. Obviously, many officials in government were in and out of the presidential complex. There were Cabinet members, the Army Chief of Staff and his group, and others who held important positions. With so much traffic on the part of these respected officials, it was possible that misinformation could be disseminated and, as a result, the hostages could suffer. So as to avoid this possibility, I closed the presidential complex and all telephone lines, save one. Then we had confined in the presidential complex the entire Cabinet, the defense attaché of the U.S.A., various ministers, and members of the General Staff of the Army. By so doing, I could be certain that there would be no foul-up in orders and, at the same time, I would have immediate access to all of these people.

Until this day, I get bitter when I think of the attitude of Bishop Bravo. With government essentially paralyzed and, under executive order, all top officials sequestered in the presidential complex, this man was playing games with a bunch of murderers. He went back to visit with these people and on this visit he was presented with their demands. Then he came back to see me. My patience with Obando Bravo was wearing thin because it was apparent that he was working on the side of the terrorists.

I asked him if he had tried to reason with the group, and he said that he had not because you couldn't reason with them. In exasperation, I told the Bishop: "Look, these people identify with you, they have empathy with you, so surely you can talk to them." He responded with a one-liner — "No, you can't talk to them." He then laid out their demands. They wanted an airplane so they could fly to Cuba. The hostages, all of them, would have to go with them, and they wanted something in the order of ten million dollars. These demands, according to Bravo, had to be met the following day. These demands could not be met and we had to play for time.

It occurred to me that there was one area in which even Bravo would have a modicum of compassion, and that area related to the women and children. I sent the Bishop back to negotiate their release. The possibility of death hung heavy over the heads of all the hostages and I wanted to get as many people out as was possible, particularly the women and children. The Bishop did convince the terrorists to release the women and children. They had been held captive for two days.

After another discussion with Bishop Bravo, I was firmly convinced that he was working more for the criminals than he was for the release of the hostages. In a confrontation such as this, a negotiator must be able to talk with both sides in the confrontation. Here we had a negotiator who could see only one side. It appeared to me that he was not willing to do anything to solve the problem. With this type of negotiator, it was evident that we would accomplish nothing.

Since one of the hostages was a Chilean diplomat, I decided to set up a conference with the entire diplomatic corps in Nicaragua. At that meeting I explained our predicament and revealed to them the attitude and activities of Bravo. With the entire picture placed squarely before them, the diplomatic corps was worried. Out of this conference came a good recommendation. The recommendation was that we select the Nuncio Monsignor Gabriel Montalvo as the principal negotiator. This was an excellent idea. Being the representative of the Pope, he was automatically dean of the diplomatic corps in Nicaragua. In other capitals, the dean of the diplomatic corps is selected on the basis of longevity. In Nicaragua, however, that position goes to the representative of the Pope.

We tried to contact the Monsignor but found he was in Tegucigalpa, Honduras. Due to the extreme emergency, I sent a special plane to get him. Upon his arrival, he and I had a meeting. He was thoroughly briefed and during the briefing I learned that he was aware of Obando Bravo's attitude and activities. It was pleasing to me to know that we would have an intelligent, fair-minded man to act as negotiator. It was not until Monsignor Montalvo began talking to the kidnappers that we received any semblance of dialogue.

Meanwhile, the terrorists continued with their threats of killing one hostage at regular time intervals. By putting bits and pieces of information together, I had come to the conclusion that someone in the house was already dead. When the terrorists refused to show all the kidnapped people to the Nuncio, it confirmed my theory that someone was dead.

It was a terrible thing. They had killed Castillo and placed him in an air-conditioned room so as to keep the body in fairly good condition. They were simply keeping this dead man in "cold storage," so to speak, so that when evidence of an execution was needed, they could display his body.

I called their bluff and told them I knew they had a dead man in the house and that I was sending Bishop Bravo and another Leftist priest to fetch the body. After so much time had passed, the body had begun to throw off an offensive odor. There are photographs of the body being brought out of the house, and the stench was so bad that Bishop Bravo held a handkerchief over his face.

We continued to negotiate with these people. The idea was to get them to spend as much time as possible in order to lower their resistance. We cut off the water and we cut off the food. We then learned that they had water bags and supplies on which they could subsist for a week to ten days.

During this time, they were continually putting various hostages on the telephone to talk to their relatives. This tactic, of course, was used as a device to break down our resistance. In a manner of speaking, it was a war of nerves. I can remember talking to my brother-in-law, Ambassador Sacasa, ten times. He showed signs of intimidation and that was understandable. In each conversation he asked me please to accelerate negotiations. I learned later that each time he talked to me, one of the terrorists held a cocked 38-caliber pistol at his head. Even the bravest would feel pressure at such a moment.

With Bishop Bravo, we accomplished nothing. With Monsignor Nuncio Montalvo, we were making progress. We now asked that their demands be reduced to writing and submitted to us. This was done, and there had been no substantial change in those demands.

I knew one thing for certain, we would not permit the terrorists to take the hostages to Cuba. Consider the fact that a

Chilean diplomat was a hostage. Under international law, each government is responsible for the safety of those foreign diplomats stationed in that country. This is as it should be. If anything were to happen to the diplomat from Chile, it was my opinion that the government of Nicaragua would have been liable for any demands made by the Chilean government. Therefore, the hostages would not be taken to Cuba. On this point I was adamant.

In my opinion, this point was resolved in our favor. The hostages would not go to Cuba but, to assure safe passage, the terrorists submitted a list of those who *would* be required to accompany them on their flight. Among those named were the ambassador from Spain, Bishop Obando Bravo, and Monsignor Montalvo. Although there was danger involved, all agreed to make the flight to Havana.

The terrorists also demanded and received the release of approximately twenty prisoners. All of these people had been tried in an open court of law and had been convicted of felonies up to and including murder. Among those convicted felons were Daniel Ortega — now a member of the ruling Marxist junta — and Lenin Cerna, a Marxist who is today in charge of State Security.

While all of this was going on, we were working on another serious matter. Money! The terrorists had demanded a tremendous amount of cash, $10,000,000. I checked the Central Bank to ascertain the amount of dollars the bank had in the vault. We had only $150,000 and I knew this would not suffice. We then called the Federal Reserve Bank in New York and made arrangements for the delivery of $5,000,000 in cash.

As I stated earlier, the government of Nicaragua had no jet aircraft. Again, I was happy that with my own money I had purchased the Rockwell turboprop aircraft. Carlos Dubon, my personal aide and secretary, and Leo Broadhead, my personal pilot, flew to New York to pick up the money.

In New York, they met with the Federal Reserve authorities and counted the money. It takes a lot of counting to catch up to five million dollars. With the cash tucked away in appropriate containers, Dubon, Broadhead, and a caravan of police escorts headed for the airport at Newark, New Jersey. It had been previously decided that this was the airport which would be used. They were escorted directly to their aircraft and the money was put aboard. Then the two men were alone and a long flight lay ahead of them. They made it to Managua and we had the money.

I had asked the Federal Reserve Board for five million dollars because I was not certain what the final negotiated figure would be. As it turned out, we agreed on one million dollars, so we had money to spare. The thought of paying that amount of money to Communist-trained terrorists, who had kidnapped and killed, caused me to suffer mental agony. But what was I to do? There was no way I could place a dollar value on the lives of the people involved. It had to be done.

The moral fiber of Bishop Bravo was now detected by all. He was one of "them." On the other hand, it's difficult to describe the excellent performance of Monsignor Nuncio Montalvo. He worked incessantly to bring about an agreement. Finally we had a plan, a plan which laid out all the details in a precise manner. We knew how the hostages were to be handled and where they would be released. We knew when and where the money was to change hands. We knew exactly who was to accompany the terrorists on their flight and when they were to join the group. We knew what aircraft would be used and where it would be going. It had to work.

There was only one point of the agreement on which the terrorists failed to keep their word. It had been agreed that a bus would be used to transport hostages, terrorists, and the accompanying group to the airport. It was agreed that the bus would stop one kilometer before the air terminal was reached and there the hostages would be freed. Well, the bus didn't stop at the designated point. The driver was ordered to go directly to the airport. This brought some uneasy moments. Had the entire plan been scuttled? Would the hostages be forced to go to Havana? If one little seam started to unravel, there could be a shoot-out and all aboard the bus knew it.

As it developed, the terrorists had the bus driven to one of the taxi strips on the airport and there the hostages were set free. Then the bus went directly to the airplane. It was a LANICA (Lineas Aereas de Nicaragua, S.A.) Convair 880 and it would be piloted by two of LANICA's regular pilots.

When the Convair 880 was reached, there stood Carlos

Dubon with the money in his hand. Dubon is a man of intelligence, dedication, and courage. His role in that entire unfortunate episode was significant and courageous. He handed the money to one masked terrorist and they began to climb aboard the airplane. All of the terrorists wore stocking masks, as they had done throughout the ordeal. Then they were aboard. One by one the four jet engines began to purr and there was relief because there had been no malfunction. The bulky "880" taxied to its takeoff position and started its run. In a matter of seconds the plane was airborne. As the plane and its weird assortment of passengers disappeared from view, one government official at the airport aptly described the feeling of all who had been involved. He said, "It was a dream. It was a goddamned dream and it really didn't happen."

The plane departed Las Mercedes airport in Managua at approximately 10:00 A.M. It was on the ground in Havana for approximately four hours and was back in Managua at 6:00 P.M. If I do say so, it was one hell of a day. From the beginning to the end of the crisis, the elapsed time amounted to three days. When word was flashed to me at the presidential complex that the hostages were free and with their loved ones, I wept. In the presence of generals and government staff members I wept, without shame.

Later, after I had time to talk personally to the hostages, and review all the facts which had been assimilated, I was able to reach some solid conclusions. Number one, the Sandinista terrorists had a hard core group of Leftist priests with whom they could work and from whom they could obtain intelligence information. Number two, the rebel movement was without men and money, and they felt the necessity of performing some spectacular criminal act in order to attract international attention. Number three, the women among the terrorists who held the hostages were far more vicious than the men. This characteristic would be reaffirmed in events that were to follow.

After the terrorist activity, a different atmosphere prevailed in Managua. Every diplomatic function was guarded with military forces. People were reluctant to give parties and if they did, some kind of security was provided. Previously, our people had felt safe in their homes. Now there was doubt. Now there was fear.

The attitude of the United States still amazes me. For some time prior to the terrorist kidnapping event, I had been advising the appropriate people in Washington that my real enemy was Fidel Castro and Cuba. I gave them hard evidence to substantiate my claims. I concluded that they didn't care. While the terrorists were holding the hostages, I called the State Department in Washington and was put in touch with their so-called expert on these matters.

After all, this was my first experience in such matters and I needed some expert advice. I explained who they were, what they were, and what they were doing. His advice to me was, "Wear them out." That's it! Just wear them out. For heaven's sake, how do you wear out a bunch of wild killers who have already demonstrated what they are capable of doing? How do you wear out wild-eyed radicals who are willing to die if they don't get their way? Besides, the wives and families of the hostages were calling me every day, pressuring me to act with the utmost caution, so as not to expose their loved ones to any more danger than already existed. There was no way I could wear them out.

After the terrorists demonstrated to the world that their connection was Cuba, I thought, now the United States will believe me and now the United States will act. How wrong I was!

So what was expected to be a happy and glorious Christmas turned out to be a rather sad one. Of course, all of us were happy that the hostages had been saved. Many prayers of thankfulness were given and I was one of those who gave praise to the Almighty. Even so, the spirit of Managua had been dampened. The earthquake, the pain of rebuilding, and now this. Since December 22, 1972, our people had been forced to tread a convoluted path, and it would not get better.

The spectacular showing of the terrorists in Managua led me to believe that we could expect more rebel activity in the northeast. This expectation came to fruition. Theirs was a "hit and run" operation. Sporadic raids in small communities and outlying areas of the northeast continued. There was one element of consistency with those Cuban-trained guerrillas — they always left death behind them. On one occasion they completely overran the small town of Rio Blanco, and, for a few hours, controlled the town. Here again certain people were selected to be shot. The U.S. Ambassador in Nicaragua was kept abreast of these activities as well as the authorities in Washington.

After the relationship between the Sandinistas and Cuba had been well established, logic dictated to me that the U.S. government would recognize that Nicaragua and the U.S. had a common enemy — Cuba. It was unilateral logic because Washington refused to recognize the common enemy.

To my perturbation and utter disbelief, I found anti-Nicaragua sentiment being expressed in Washington. I wanted to find the source of such malignity and I did. The Leftist priests in Nicaragua, seeing they couldn't destroy me and my government in Nicaragua, decided that they should take their battle to Washington, the seat of power in the Western Hemisphere. And this they did. Father Miguel d'Escoto and Father Fernando Cardinal and a few other Jesuit priests started a campaign with known Left-leaning members of the U.S. Congress.

An organization known as WOLA (Washington Office for Latin America) assisted in this entire operation. This campaign was designed to terminate military assistance to Nicaragua and cause a breach between the United States and her staunchest and most loyal ally in all of Latin America. These Jesuit priests had brains and they knew something about politics. As a starter in their campaign, they used the issue of Human Rights. In their corner, they lined up Clarence Long of Maryland, Edward Koch of New York, and David Obey of Wisconsin. Now Obey is not only a Liberal, he is a Leftist.

The Leftist Jesuit priests from Nicaragua did their job. They supplied friends in the U.S. Congress with all kinds of information. More aptly put, it was misinformation. With Liberal and Leftist members of the U.S. Congress, the State Department, the executive branch of government, and with WOLA serving as a central distribution point for anti-Nicaragua information, opposition in Washington to me and my government was gathering momentum. All of these elements of government knew that the terrorists in Managua were Cuban-trained and supported by Castro. This knowledge, however, made no difference at all to these people.

For the moment, then, despite earthquakes, terrorist kidnappings and murders, Leftist activity in the Church, and opposition in the U.S. government, Nicaragua was still alive and doing well.

At this point in time, the Guardia Nacional practically eliminated the guerrillas. So at Christmas time, 1974, the Sandinistas were hard pressed. They had no men and it looked as though they were defeated. That's why they had to do something spectacular that would draw international attention. That's why they were so desperate and would stop at nothing to achieve some showings of successful audacity.

Chapter Four

THE UNEXPECTED

As 1975 began to fade, I could sense a change in the U.S. State Department, and this worried me. I had the feeling that an anti-Nixon list had been prepared and that I was on that list. I do not pretend to know, nor do I understand, the political machinations behind Watergate. I do know that for the first time in history a President of the United States was forced to resign. I have asked many Republicans and Democrats alike, Why was Richard Nixon forced to resign? I get one answer — "He lied about having knowledge of the Watergate coverup."

Apparently this allegation was true. Mr. Nixon did have knowledge of the Watergate affair and as a result of this knowledge and his subsequent denial, he was forced to resign as President of the United States. The effect of that resignation was felt throughout the United States. In reality, the Nixon-Watergate incident touched every fiber of the U.S. political structure. The Nixon lie, however, affected only the domestic body politic of the United States. In other words, it was a U.S. political problem and did not relate to other governments in other parts of the world.

Nixon's fabrication, basically, was a domestic political problem with domestic repercussions. But what about President Carter? Has he lied? The answer is most assuredly yes, but to lay bare the details of his lies would take an international board of inquiry. There is a difference in the Nixon lie and the lies of Mr. Carter. Mr. Nixon's untruth was confined to U.S. politics; whereas, Mr. Carter's falsehoods reached nations around the world on matters in which the United States was

involved. As a starter, Mr. Carter lied about Nicaragua; he lied
about Iran; he lied about Israel; he lied about the Republic of
China; and so on ad infinitum. For a long time to come, the
United States and the free world will pay for the fabrications
of Mr. Carter.

The effect of Nixon's departure came home to me very
quickly. Turner Shelton was replaced as U.S. Ambassador to
Nicaragua by James Theberge. In our first visit, Mr. Theberge
told me that he had been advised by the State Department to
keep his distance from me. This came as a shock and it was
hard to take. Next to Nicaragua, I loved the U.S. more than any
place in the world. But I had been told by the new Ambassador
that he should keep distance between us. I thought, whom in
the State Department have I offended? What would precipitate such a drastic comment from a member of the diplomatic
corps?

There were more surprises. Ambassador Theberge began to
associate with Pedro Joaquin Chamorro, a known Sandinista.
He was entertained by these people in Granada and other
places. It seemed to me that Theberge was bent on establishing
close relations with the wrong side — an opposition coalition. It
seemed to me that I must be on the Nixon list and if that were
true, my country and I were in for trouble. A good indication
that trouble was on its way was provided by James Cheek.
Remember him? He was the staff member with the U.S.
Embassy in Nicaragua who collaborated with Dr. Aguero. Well,
he was taken back to Washington and decorated with the
Rifkin Foreign Service Award. Cheek was so honored because
of his dissenting political reports out of Nicaragua. He had disagreed with Ambassador Shelton, so he was given a medal. Dr.
Henry Kissinger was present for the award ceremony.

That should have been more than an indication to me of our
forthcoming problems with the State Department. I'm reminded of the time a friend of mine was attending the horse
races in Mexico City. A fellow in the adjoining box had bet
heavily on a particular horse, which happened to be the
favorite in the race, and it appeared the horse would win easily.
Before the finish line was reached, the horse seemed to pull up
and a long shot won the race. The fellow in the next box
jumped to his feet, shook his fist, and shouted: "The race was

fixed!" My friend asked him how he knew it was fixed. He replied, "Well, my first clue was when the jockey stood up and pulled back on the reins." My first clue should have been just as obvious as the racetrack clue, because the State Department suddenly stood up in the stirrups which straddled Nicaragua and pulled back on the reins.

We followed with great interest the presidential campaign between Gerald R. Ford and James Earl Carter. The consensus in Latin America was that Ford would win but that the race would be close. Well, the race was close but Carter won. This democratic victory caused us no great alarm because we had worked harmoniously with previous Republican and Democratic administrations. We were confident that Carter would see the strategic value of Nicaragua and that he would take into consideration our long-standing friendship and unswerving loyalty to the U.S. It didn't take long for this confidence to dissipate.

In the first month of his administration, Carter and the new Secretary of State, Cyrus Vance, selected those governments to which they would no longer provide military aid. They singled out Nicaragua.

With the knowledge that Nicaragua was to be stricken from the list of those countries receiving military assistance, I had to determine the course I would follow. Nicaragua is a proud country and my training as a youth and my training at West Point instilled in me the importance of personal pride. Although the action of the Carter Administration was crippling, it was not a death-dealing blow. Some countries to which military assistance was denied requested that the U.S. military mission be removed from their soil, and some went so far as to cancel the mutual military defense pact. This is what Brazil did.

It was naïve thinking but I reasoned that due to the common interests of Nicaragua and the United States, I could, through negotiations, change her mind. After all, we both had capitalistic states, we both had constitutional republics in which the President and the Congress were chosen through the democratic process, and both countries stood for individual liberty. All this, I thought, would count for something. I consulted with my friends in the U.S. Congress and they agreed with my approach. They felt that I showed more rationale than leaders in some of the other countries and that no useful purpose would be served by assuming a retaliatory posture. Hoping to change minds in Washington, dialogue was commenced.

We were now getting another U.S. Ambassador. Mr. Theberge was leaving and he was being replaced by Ambassador Mauricio Solaun. Apparently his instructions were similar to those received by Theberge — don't get too close to Somoza. However, he came asking a favor. He wanted me to invite the Human Rights Commission of the Organization of American States to Nicaragua. Automatically, this was a red flag. Our continuing battle with the Sandinistas was well known and, through the efforts of the Leftist priests in Nicaragua, certain congressmen in the U.S. had already accused me and my government of all kinds of rights violations. Then when I looked at the composition of the Commission, I knew the deck was stacked against me.

Heading the Commission was Aguilar of Venezuela. So far as the people of Nicaragua were concerned, there was no doubt in anyone's mind where Venezuela stood. This, then, was the tipoff as to the complexion of the Commission. We did have some support on the Commission but they were in the minority. Knowing the political makeup of the Human Rights Commission, I was convinced their conclusions were preconceived and, therefore, a visit to Nicaragua would only further aggravate our position.

I think people in the United States and elsewhere now understand that the Human Rights Commission is political. It shouldn't be but it is. For example, the Commission went to Panama for an investigation. This visit to Panama was, without a doubt, politically motivated. Mr. Carter needed a favorable human rights report so as to influence the U.S. Senate on the Canal Treaty vote. If you can imagine, Panama received a clean bill of health. I know Torrijos. I know that he is a dictator and I know that the people of Panama have few rights. They do not have free elections and basic individual rights are probably more flagrantly violated in Panama than in any country in Latin America. This is not a new thought on my part and it takes no great intellectual depth to comprehend the lack of human rights in Panama.

So when the Human Rights Commission came out with its glowing report on Panama, I was absolutely convinced the organization was strictly political and I wanted no part of it. The very name is a misnomer. It should be called the "Carter Hatchet Commission" because that's what it is.

Conceptually, the idea of a Human Rights Commission is good. I'm convinced that the Western Hemisphere is blessed with people of good intentions, such as the belief in basic rights of all people. But if those good intentions are going to be manipulated for political purposes like the Human Rights Commission is manipulated, you will have a lot of countries in upheaval. How can five people go into a foreign country, spend a few days, talk to a few selected people, and come out with an honest report on the sociopolitical conditions in that country?

Let's turn the thing around for a moment. Let me pick five, six, or seven people to serve on a Human Rights Commission and let me send them to the United States to do a study. Now under the rules and guidelines, this Commission could pick and choose those people they want to interview. When all is said and done, I could present you a report that would make the United States look worse than Nazi Germany. That's because the Commission would be politically motivated and could be manipulated. Naturally, such a report would not accurately represent conditions in the United States. It would, however, reflect the preconceived ideas of the Commission which had been selected with political bias. With the foregoing in mind, I want to develop further the theme of human rights.

With the advent of the Carter Administration, a new phrase appeared on the international scene. That phrase was "Human Rights." In speech after speech, Mr. Carter emphasized that the United States would, henceforth, concern itself with the rights of people all over the world. In itself, that's not a new concept, so far as human values are concerned. It was the first time, however, that the leader of a major power brought to the foreground the rights of people, no matter where they might live. My first reaction, when I read of this bold new plan, was an affirmative response. After all, there are many parts of the world in which people are virtual slaves and have no rights at all. What harm could be done, then, if the spotlight of public opinion were focused on those areas?

This positive attitude toward Mr. Carter's bold stance did not last too long. His program of Human Rights, I found, only applied to certain countries, and the values changed from one geopolitical area to another. Then I found that the experts on this program had preconceived ideas about a country, before they ever saw that country. Generally speaking, this preconception was determined by a political evaluation. Simply put, this meant did the field investigators for Human Rights like the leader of a particular country, or didn't they? If they had negative vibrations about a given leader, that leader was determined to be guilty of violating this humane concept before the team of experts ever set foot in his country.

As this scenario began to unfold, I thought it was time for me to take an introspective view of my own appraisal of human rights. How did I perceive human rights? What about human rights in my own country of Nicaragua? Had my government and I been guilty of violating the guidelines laid down by Mr. Carter? This meant that I had to examine my own philosophy in regard to my people.

When I began to examine my deep-rooted personal beliefs on human rights, I remembered an event of importance to me. In 1949, I represented my country and took part in the signing of the U.S. Declaration of Human Rights in Paris. I also recalled something of significance which I had learned at La Salle Military Academy in New York. It began like this: "We hold these truths to be self-evident, that all men are created equal, that they are endowed by their Creator with certain inalienable Rights, and that among these are Life, Liberty and the pursuit of Happiness . . . ." These words had meaning. These words had depth and no wonder — they could be found in the Declaration of Independence of those thirteen colonies struggling for freedom. If Thomas Jefferson wrote them, he knew the true meaning of human rights. I could identify with those words and that's what I wanted for the people of Nicaragua. Now, in applying that yardstick of moral measurement, did my country possess those ingredients found in the Declaration of Independence?

Since any discussion of human rights would relate to liberty, that, I felt, should be considered first. In the category of liberty, how did Nicaragua fare? Well, our people were free to work where they chose; they were free to travel about without interference from the military or local constabulary; they were free to select their own doctor; education was free and, we might have strayed here, it was compulsory. They had the right of collective bargaining and could go on strike, if they chose to do so. Though predominantly Catholic, our people could belong to the church of their choice; they could choose their own home and live where they desired. They could travel to other countries, and see how other people lived; and, very important, we had freedom of the press. In essence, they were free to do whatever they chose to do, so long as they didn't trespass upon the rights of others. So far as liberty is concerned, I'm convinced we passed the test with flying colors.

". . . Life, Liberty and the pursuit of Happiness." It is my belief that all of these are interrelated. If you have liberty, then you have the possibility of happiness and a good life. Happiness, of course, depends upon the mental attitude of each individual. With freedom, though, an individual is free to do those things which make for a better life, and attain the ultimate of his own God-given abilities.

It turned out that Mr. Carter didn't see things the way we did in Nicaragua. He and his State Department wanted to send us political "experts" rather than people who understood what human rights are all about. The preconceived consensus — Nicaragua was in gross violation of human rights.

As I viewed other countries in Latin America, Russia, Communist China, and even the United States, I thought, "My God, these people don't know what they are talking about." Then I began observing the pattern followed by Mr. Carter and the revelation came to me.

Mr. Carter was concerning himself with human rights in only the small and militarily weak countries. I made another observation. Generally speaking, these were anti-Communist countries such as Nicaragua, Chile, Argentina, and Paraguay. He didn't concern himself with human rights in Russia or Red China. Doesn't that seem a little strange?

In the Soviet Union, the citizen has no basic freedom. He is told where to work, where to go to school, what to think, where he can travel, and what he can watch on television. There is no freedom of the press. Very frankly, in Russia the individual

has no rights at all. Everything and everyone is subservient to
the State. But Mr. Carter and his human rights people didn't
concern themselves with the rights of the Russian people. The
hallowed team of experts couldn't get into Russia, even if they
had wanted to do so.

If we are kind, we could call Mr. Carter's attitude toward
the utter lack of human rights in the socialist countries benign
neglect. A logical question would follow. Is Mr. Carter's attitude of benign neglect toward these socialist powers an indication that he loathes the capitalistic system which prevails in
the Western camp?

What has been said about the Soviet Union could be said
about Red China. Since the United States sold Chiang Kai-shek
down the river and turned China over to the Communists,
literally millions of human beings have been slaughtered. The
slaughter continues, and yet Mr. Carter doesn't complain about
the violation of human rights in China. In that huge nation,
there is no freedom at all and the individual is as nothing.

If the value of a human being is important in Nicaragua, it
should be just as important, if not more so, in the larger and
more powerful countries.

To evaluate human rights properly, Mr. Carter doesn't have
to go to Nicaragua, Chile, or Argentina. What about human
rights violations in the United States? To observe gross human
rights violations, all one has to do is visit any Indian reservation
in the United States. There you can see how these once proud
people are treated as children by the federal government. The
widespread exploitation of the Mexican "wetback" labor force
is certainly an area in which human rights are grossly violated
in the United States.

When I think of the attention focused on my small country,
I get angry. I get angry because I know that the people of
Nicaragua were free — free to live, free to dream, and free to
pursue happiness in their own way. Yet, Mr. Carter used the
phony issue of Human Rights to turn much of U.S. public
opinion against me and my government. As a result of his
policy, the people of Nicaragua are now devoid of human
rights.

Now that the Communists have Nicaragua under control,
the silence surrounding the Human Rights issue is deafening.

Since the fall of my government on July 17, 1979, some three thousand men, women, and children have been slaughtered in Nicaragua and buried in mass graves. This is now a matter of public record, so I cannot be accused of misrepresentation.

Jose Esteban Gonzalez, until recently President of the Nicaraguan Permanent Commission on Human Rights, revealed some of the gory details of these mass executions. It should be stated that this was a man who opposed me and was in the opposition party. Gonzalez stated publicly that in the city of Granada, the only large city where no fighting occurred, some four hundred people were executed. "These people were not killed in the fighting," said Gonzalez. They were killed after the Sandinista take-over. Gonzalez went on to report that shallow mass graves had been found in Leon, Masatepe, Nueve Guinea, Jinotepe, and Esteli. Gonzalez said: "Our experience is that this went on all over the country." Even Interior Minister Tomás Borge, the Communist strongman in Nicaragua, admitted that there had been torture and illegal executions. However, Borge played down the number of executions, saying that one hundred people had been illegally killed.

The Communists in Nicaragua didn't want Gonzalez to disclose this horrible slaughter of human beings. In information released to the press, Gonzalez said: "They have told us to close down the Commission, they have tried to oblige me to resign, they have threatened other officials in other parts of the country, and some of our people have resigned. Today, there is a tremendous fear in this country; and an equal fear of admitting this condition exists," Gonzalez added.

When I read of facts such as these, I become nauseated. There is no way I can mentally remove myself from the suffering of the people in Nicaragua. How, I ask myself, can Carter and his crowd condone the Communist slaughter in Nicaragua? I listen, I listen very intently, but I do not hear one single protest of human rights violations out of Washington. Knowing the logic previously followed by Carter, perhaps there is an explanation. That logic would indicate that since the people of Nicaragua now have no rights at all, how can there be a violation of human rights?

The Human Rights issue, as advocated by President Carter,

Patricia M. Derian, Mark Schneider, Bob Pastor, and the Leftist news media, turned public opinion in the U.S. against me and my government. If their aim was absolutely to destroy human rights, if their aim was to assist in establishing a Communist base of operations in Central America, they were successful.

We had a free country, we had progress, and we had patriotism. Our system of government, our election laws, our practice of free enterprise, and even our mode of wearing apparel were all patterned after the United States. Our loyalty to the United States was unquestioned. Somehow, Carter was able to destroy all of this, and quickly. The tool of destruction he used in the beginning was Human Rights. That was an unadulterated farce and President Carter and Secretary of State Cyrus Vance both knew it.

Under the guise of Human Rights, Mr. Carter brought into the federal government a retinue of radicals. These are not elected officials who must answer to the voters of the United States. These are handpicked subordinates who answer to Mr. Carter. With this group of appointees, Mr. Carter is changing the socioeconomic structure of the U.S. They may call it something else, but the new economic philosophy is Socialism. The actors are radical, their plan is radical, and the capitalistic, free enterprise system that made the United States the productive wonder of the world is undergoing radical surgery.

Again, the Declaration of Independence clearly outlines my concept of government and, more particularly, Human Rights — "We hold these truths to be self-evident, that all men are created equal, that they are endowed by their Creator with certain inalienable rights, and that among these are Life, Liberty and the pursuit of Happiness — [and that] governments are instituted among men, deriving their just powers from the consent of the governed." These words are worth repeating, just from memory, again and again and again.

The possibility of a halt in arms and ammunition shipments to Nicaragua from the U.S. still haunted me. I didn't realize that Carter and the State Department had already ordered the sale of all such weaponry for Nicaragua to be stopped, and this was done one week after Carter took office. Normally, the president of a country would be advised of such serious action by the ambassador of the other country involved. This was not the case. I learned that small arms exports from the U.S. to Nicaragua had been stopped from the man who handled the shipments. I confronted the man and admonished him for failure to deliver our small arms and ammunition. He said, "Mr. President, I don't have a license to deliver to you. It has been cancelled." This was before Ambassador Theberge had left Nicaragua and when he came to my office, he was nervous and most upset with the U.S. State Department because he had not received instructions to advise me of this action. I recall thinking that the State Department was now being sneaky.

The Carter Administration was determined in its effort to punish Nicaragua, and, in so doing, lend support to Communist-dominated Sandinistas. With the Nicaragua opposition nerve center, Washington Office for Latin America (WOLA), supplying an abundance of misinformation; with the support of the Leftist priests in Nicaragua; and with the congressional support of such Leftists as Edward Koch, David Obey, and Clarence Long, Mr. Carter thought it was time to make a congressional move against Nicaragua. So in the 1977 session of Congress, a bill was introduced to cut off all military assistance to Nicaragua. This meant that my friends in the Congress had to gear up for a fray. My brother-in-law, Ambassador Sacasa, was not quite up to such a political battle. This meant that my government had to obtain legal assistance in Washington to fight this bill.

Anyone familiar with the legislative process in the United States knows that the first hurdle for a bill is the subcommittee to which the bill is assigned. If the bill is passed in the subcommittee, it then goes to the full committee. If the full committee approves the legislation, it then goes before the full House of Representatives for debate. There the legislation will either be passed or it will be killed.

The bill to cut off military assistance to Nicaragua passed the subcommittee. In the full committee it passed but by only one vote. This meant that our only hope was that in a full debate in the House, the measure would fail.

In this same bill, Nicaragua found itself in the company of several other countries such as Argentina, Guatemala, El Salvador, Brazil, and Chile.

On June 23, 1977, Congressman Charles Wilson of Texas offered his amendment to the U.S. Military Assistance Bill and it was one of the shortest amendments in history. It simply said: "On page 20, line 21, of the bill, in section 505, delete 'Nicaragua'." The amendment was adopted by a margin of 225 votes for, to 180 votes against. Nicaragua stayed in the military assistance bill, even though Mr. Carter and Mr. Vance exerted pressure on the House of Representatives to condemn Nicaragua. Since this amendment was very important to Nicaragua, I believe it is fitting and appropriate that attention be given to Mr. Wilson's remarks on that day. The following is taken from the *Congressional Record* of June 23, 1977:

(Mr. Charles Wilson of Texas) Mr. Chairman, this amendment is very simple. It simply reinstates Nicaragua as a recipient of U.S. military assistance.

First of all, the most important point which needs to be made is that, in my judgement, Nicaragua is not a gross violator of human rights. Nicaragua's main sin seems to me to be that it is friendly to the United States. What is the situation in Managua? The largest newspaper in Nicaragua, *La Prensa*, is in vigorous opposition to the Somoza regime. In any country which we think of as being in gross violation of human rights we very seldom see a vigorous, large, major newspaper that is anti the President. But there is active opposition to the President of Nicaragua. The last election there was monitored by the Organization of American States. The very people who helped my good friend from New York orchestrate the case against human rights in Nicaragua are now back in Nicaragua continuing their opposition to the government.

How many countries can we think of that are accused of being in gross violation of human rights would allow their people to come to the United States, testify against their country, and then go home and remain free? Certainly that does not fit my description of a country that violates human rights, nor that of most Members.

We did have some Catholic priests making allegations, and we had a bishop's letter of some sort that alleged great violations of human rights there. I am suspicious of this, however.

In my district I have 500,000 white Protestants, mostly Baptists; I have 100,000 black Protestants, mostly Baptists. As a result of this and as a result of only being exposed to Protestant preachers and in many cases to evangelists, I became very suspicious of radical preachers as a very young boy. Since I came to Washington I have expanded that suspicion to include radical rabbis, radical priests, and radical Korean gurus. We should rely on our own State Department and not on religious opinion in these matters, especially when religious opinion has a stake in the results.

Before the government took power in Nicaragua, the church was much more powerful and the church owned much more land.

It has been said by my friend, the gentleman from Wisconsin (Mr. OBEY), that the gentleman from New York (Mr. KOCH) has indeed made a case against Nicaragua, in fact a compelling case against Nicaragua. I submit to the Members that any Members of this House can make a compelling case against any country on this Earth. No one is perfect, no one is pure.

I would like to show the Members some things I would use if I were making cases against people that I did not particularly like for one reason or another. I could show the police in Houston pictured as "brutal and unchecked." But my friend, the gentleman from New York (Mr. KOCH), could say, "What would you expect from barbarians such as those?"

And so in addition to that, I might say to my friend, the gentleman from New York: "Attica — a premeditated massacre. They came to Attica to kill and to torture — Attica where time ran out."

The recipient countries of about one-third of the funds in this bill have also been accused of violations of human rights. Israel is pictured as an "occupier, using excessive force, and enforcing strict security." This resulted in a five-month investigation, where reporters have shown that Israeli interrogators routinely mistreat and often torture Arab prisoners.

That is not true. I have been there many times, and I know it is not true. The Israeli occupation of the West Bank is probably the most humane occupation in the history of civilization. Just because some reporters who wanted to write a story said it violates human rights does not make it true.

In the same light, because some dissident bishop came up here and said these things about Nicaragua does not make them true.

On the international scene there are over one hundred countries that are said to be violators of human rights; and money for many of them is contained in this bill. We should not single out one country, and if we are going to single out one country, we should not single out one of our best friends in this hemisphere."

As everyone knows, the Washington political scene is rough and tumble. For this victory I could not claim credit. Credit should go to those members of the House of Representatives who understood what this political battle was all about and voted for Nicaragua. Credit should go to the Cuban community in the U.S. They understood what this battle was about. And credit should also go to the Friends of Nicaragua and the many Spanish-American organizations throughout the U.S. who stood solidly behind my country.

Prior to Carter's appointment of the new U.S. Ambassador to Nicaragua, I decided to use what influence I could command to get an ambassador who would at least be fair with Nicaragua. Knowing of Carter's efforts to appeal to minority groups in the U.S., I contacted my Cuban friends to see if they could make a sound recommendation to Carter.

Major Mauricio Ferre of Miami recommended this man Solaun. He was born in Cuba and was a naturalized American citizen. He was a former university professor and when I reviewed his curriculum vitae, I had the feeling that this man was probably over his head in this assignment. I felt that being a naturalized citizen of the U.S. would work to his disadvantage. He simply would not have the influence in the State Department that a person born in the U.S. would have.

I'll say this for Mr. Solaun, he did his best. However, he was not forceful enough and he didn't have the clout to impress his superiors in the State Department. Also, he was constantly being undercut by the political officer at the U.S. Embassy. I think Solaun wanted to do a good job. What Nicaragua needed was a U.S. Ambassador who understood the country, our people, and the nature of the rebel group with whom we had problems. Mr. Solaun never fully understood and if he had, he would not have been able to convince those in Washington.

The attitude of the Carter Administration toward the government of Nicaragua became more flagrant with each passing day. I was becoming worried, very worried. It was the first time I had doubt about my ability to serve out my constitutionally elected term of office. Somehow I had to find the strength and support to carry me until May 1, 1981. A man can take so much and can stand just so much harassment and, believe me, I was being harassed by the United States.

In July, 1977, Nicaragua was still making progress. We had started drilling our first geothermal field, and my expectations were great for this project. We had just completed a feasibility study on a dam that would provide a ten-year supply of energy for Nicaragua. We were building roads all over the country and opening up new areas for development. All the while, though, I was deeply concerned about our deteriorating relations with the U.S. but believed, with my many friends in the U.S. Congress, that this unhappy situation could be improved.

I did not anticipate that Carlos Andres Perez, President of Venezuela, would, at this point, extend his effort to many other countries in his attempt to topple me. His influence was more than I expected. But when you are rich and you possess a commodity which is badly needed, it should be foreseen that such a position would command influence. Venezuela had money and she had oil. So Perez could demand and receive an audience anywhere he desired. Thus, he enlisted the support of Colombia, Costa Rica, Panama, and other countries as well. With this bloc, he could apply added pressure on Washington and exacerbate the position of Nicaragua.

I felt that Nicaragua was standing on the wrong side of a weak dam which was holding back an ocean of water. I knew if that dam should break, Nicaragua and all of Central America would be flooded out. How could I shore up our position? Nicaragua was a small country, relatively poor, and we had no known deposits of oil and gas. The most tangible thing we had going for us was our long friendship with the United States. And it was apparent that forces were at work in the United States to annihilate that friendship. This was our reinforcement against the weakened dam. Oh, how I prayed that this reinforcement would stand firm and strong. But in July, 1977, our position was precarious.

At this point of confusion, doubt, stress, and constant pressure, I received a telling blow — right in the middle of my chest. I suffered a serious heart attack. That's something for which you are never prepared.

Chapter Five

HEART AND OTHER TROUBLE

The heart attack came on July 28, 1977. As in many heart cases, I had a warning but didn't realize it. Every morning for fifteen years I had done the Canadian Airforce exercise routine. On the day previous to the attack, I had completed my exercises and was driving to the office when a sudden pain hit me in the left elbow. In a few minutes it was gone and I thought no more of it. The next day the attack came on in full force. My brother, Luis, had died of a massive coronary at the age of 44, and that's the first thing that came to my mind. I thought, well, it's happening to me.

In retrospect, I'm convinced those fifteen years of exercise saved my life. It didn't take much medical knowledge to know that I was a prime candidate for a heart attack. My weight was 267 pounds, I was under constant stress and strain, and each day I demanded more of my body than I should have. Through the rigorous exercise program, I had developed collateral circulation. This circulation kept me alive.

On the morning of the attack, I was doing my exercises when I noticed that my throat seemed to be stopping up. I felt as though I had a large piece of steak in my throat. I stopped exercising and took a shower. After the shower, I felt better and decided to do some running in place. All of a sudden I felt deep burning heat run across my chest. I knew then it was a genuine heart attack.

My cardiologist, Dr. Blandon, was called and he could not be found. Then Dr. Bernheim was called and he came over and ran an EKG. Dr. Bernheim then called Dr. Aron Tucker, a heart specialist, and I remember he told me that between the two of them they could handle me. These doctors did an excellent job but, even so, I wanted Dr. William Phillips of Miami. He was head of the Heart Institute in Miami and I had tremendous faith in him. He was flown to Managua to attend me. He was accompanied by Dr. Trad who was an open heart surgeon. It was determined that I should be flown to Miami for medical treatment.

Since the decision was made to fly me to Miami, my son called the United States to obtain transportation in an Airforce plane. To my surprise, the U.S. balked. This I couldn't believe. It was as though your closest friend for fifty years turned a deaf ear when you asked him for help. During my hospital stay in Miami, this thought kept going over and over in my mind. The U.S. Airforce did finally agree to send a plane, after we agreed to pay for the transportation. The records will show that we paid thirty thousand dollars for the flight. The plane was a converted DC-9, and the flight to Miami took seven hours.

After arriving at the hospital in Miami, I had severe pains that night. Dr. Phillips told me that it looked as though an angiogram would be necessary. I asked him if there was any danger involved, and he bluntly replied, "You could die from it." This kind of news makes one realize that legal affairs should always be in order, because no one knows what the future holds. I realized that I did not have an up-to-date will and I asked Dr. Phillips if he could give me two days so as to prepare my last will and testament. He said that was agreeable so I sent for Dr. Oscar Sevilla Sacasa of Managua, an excellent attorney. Dr. Sacasa came to Miami and my will was prepared. Then we were ready for the angiogram and that was an experience to be remembered. Interestingly enough, the doctor who performed my angiogram was the same doctor who did the angiogram on my brother, Luis, when he had his fatal heart attack.

Those who have had an angiogram know the technique. To me it was amazing. After my arm was opened, and the proper tube was inserted, things began to happen. I could actually see my heart on the screen before me. I was flabbergasted when, with my untrained eye, I could see that one side of the heart was functioning normally and one side was barely going. Dr.

Phillips then explained what was happening. I had experienced a frontal coronary and as a result one side of my heart was receiving sufficient blood and one side was not. More than ever, I appreciated those fifteen years of Canadian Airforce exercises. The collateral circulation which resulted from those exercises saved my life.

A tight and guarded routine was established for me. I was placed on four hundred calories per day and that isn't much food. I was completely cut off from the outside world. I could receive no telephone calls and I could make none. I could not receive any mail and I could not write letters. I could see only immediate members of my family, my nurses, and the doctors. One of the few people permitted to see me was my old friend and classmate, Congressman Jack Murphy of New York. This situation prevailed for the month of August, but by the middle of August I was permitted to walk. On that first day of exercise, I could walk only ten yards and then I had to get back to bed. My total lack of strength and endurance surprised me.

In early September, while I was still in the hospital, I received a surprising telephone call. General Omar Torrijos called and invited me to attend the Canal treaty signing celebration in Washington. For some unknown reason, I wanted to go. So I asked Dr. Phillips if I could make the trip to Washington. His voice was stern and strong when he said, "Absolutely not!" So that was that and I had to send regrets.

I named Dr. Cornelio Hueck, who was President of the Congress of Nicaragua, to represent me at the signing ceremony in Washington. Later, Dr. Cornelio Hueck was to die a horrible death at the hands of the Communist guerrillas in Nicaragua.

While in the hospital, I had time to do much soul searching. My doctor and I had many serious discussions about my physical capability to continue as President of Nicaragua. Of one thing I was certain, I would most assuredly follow the professional advice of my doctor.

Dr. Phillips told me that if I lost weight and did the prescribed exercises, I could function as well as I did before the heart attack. I remember asking Dr. Phillips if he thought I should resign from the presidency. He said there was no reason I should resign and he pointed out President Dwight Eisenhower and President Lyndon Johnson as prime examples of presidents who functioned normally after a similar illness. For me, that determined my future. I would return to Nicaragua and, at the proper time, resume my full work schedule.

Before I left the hospital in Miami, the doctor outlined a complete rehabilitation program for me. For this rehabilitation period, it was decided that I should go to the family beach home at Montelimar. There I developed a routine which brought good results. My diet was limited, so I continued to lose weight. I took sunshine and performed the designated exercises.

At the beach home I was not cut off from the outside world. My Cabinet members and my secretaries came out regularly. It was while I was recuperating at the beach home that I felt the first overt hostility of the Venezuelan government.

That year, Nicaragua was to serve as the host nation for the Army Chiefs of Staff of the Americas. That meant that every nation in all of Latin America, as well as the United States, would participate. To illustrate the importance of this seminar, this meeting would bring together the top military authority from each of these many countries, and for four days this group would consider the most pressing problems of the time.

A United States general by the name of Bogart started this function in Panama many years ago. It became an annual function and was recognized as the military function of the year. Naturally, I was pleased and proud to have this important affair in Nicaragua.

I was dumbfounded when the Nicaraguan Minister of Defense, General Guillermo Noguera, came to the beach home and announced to me that Venezuela would not participate and would not send a representative of any kind. This was another effort on the part of my old nemesis, Carlos Andres Perez, to discredit me and my government. This shock should have brought on another heart attack, but it didn't. With the information I had received from General Guillermo Noguera, I knew that Perez would put pressure on other nations to boycott the meeting in Nicaragua. Confirmation of this assumption followed shortly.

I received word from inside the U.S. Embassy that Omar Torrijos had asked the United States to refrain from sending General Brown, the U.S. Army Chief of Staff. Let's face reality, Torrijos had and still has exceptional power in Washington. The United States accommodated Torrijos, because they sent the Deputy Chief of Staff. Next I learned that Perez had persuaded Peru to send her Deputy Chief of Staff.

Actually, the entire effort to sabotage the meeting in Nicaragua was prompted by Carlos Andres Perez. Torrijos was prompted by Perez and he delivered. Torrijos told the U.S. Ambassador that sending General Brown to Nicaragua would be like sending the Pope to bless me. This is the same Torrijos who had called me in the hospital and asked me to come to Washington for his big moment. The path that some government leaders follow is, indeed, a convoluted course.

So far as our meeting in Nicaragua was concerned, there was absolutely no reason for Perez to assume a dichotomous attitude. Since our meeting in Puerto Ordaz, Venezuela, I had endeavored to cooperate with Venezuela. When that country was hit by a disastrous flood and thousands of their cattle perished, I authorized the sale and shipment of 25,000 brahma heifers to Venezuela. Their herds were decimated and they needed to be replenished.

Perez was devious and Perez was deceitful. While he was pinning medals on my front, he was stabbing me in the back. Yes, he had the Venezuelan government decorate me. This, of course, was for "outstanding service." Perez sent the Chief of the Venezuelan National Guard and the Chief of the Airforce, a general I had known since we were young men, to give me a "well-earned" decoration. Now this show of respect and recognition was bestowed upon me in 1977, before my heart attack.

Naturally, I was completely aghast at the decision of Perez to disrupt the military function in Nicaragua. I reached the conclusion that Venezuela, Panama, and the United States were having close conversations about me and the government of Nicaragua. It was also clear to me that Torrijos and Perez had powerful influence in Washington.

My personal concern for a successful Army Chiefs of Staff meeting cannot be overemphasized. From its inception in Panama until 1967, I had attended every such conference. In

1967, I was President of Nicaragua so, naturally, the Army Chief of Staff attended.

All of those who attended these conferences derived much benefit. Ideas were exchanged, intelligence reports were given, and this was of particular importance because communistic activities were always explored. Additionally, the person-to-person contact with these generals proved invaluable. While attending those Chiefs of Staff conferences, I met and came to know the future presidents of Brazil, Argentina, Bolivia, El Salvador, and Guatemala. To illustrate further the importance of these meetings, I hark back to the Chiefs of Staff meeting in Caracas, Venezuela in 1973.

In that year I was Army Chief of Staff for Nicaragua, so I attended the meeting. At that time, the revolution in Peru was at its height. I recall that the Peruvians, in connivance with the Venezuelans, the Ecuadorians, the Panamanians, and the Colombians, were attempting to create a change in direction for the conference. This group wanted to include Communism within its scope. This, to me, was a contumacious attitude on the part of these Chiefs of Staff and represented a 180-degree turn from the posture taken in all previous conferences. I was determined that this philosophy would not be accepted. In conjunction with General Abrahams, Chief of Staff for the U.S. Army and the Chief of Staff from Brazil, we maneuvered the conference so as to exclude that Leftist proposal. We were able to achieve anti-Communist results without the cacophony that normally goes with such ideological differences.

By taking such a stand, I made enemies who, like the proverbial elephant, would not forget. These countries would later be part of a bloc whose aim would be to destroy Somoza and the government of Nicaragua.

I make this point to substantiate my claim that I was a tried and true ally of the United States of America. There should be no question as to my determined loyalty to the Western democracies. On foreign policy matters, I stood back to back with the U.S. and gave my friend and ally all the support I could muster. In this event, it was Brazil, Nicaragua, and the United States forming a front to oppose a Leftist move.

I challenge Carter and Cyrus Vance to examine the record and see if there is any president anywhere who supported the policies of the United States more devoutly than I did. The record will show that no such loyalty existed anywhere. This is not to say that I was trying to get something for nothing. I merely wanted Nicaragua to have progress and to have good interdependent relations with other countries.

It must be understood that Nicaragua identified with the United States. Nicaragua is a small country but the anti-Communist attitude of our people was well known. Philosophically, our country could relate to all of those precepts which had made the U.S. the great country she was and is. It was natural, too, that the side of the United States was our side. And that was the side we took in Caracas at the 1973 Army Chiefs of Staff meeting. At that time, I thought nothing would ever shake that solid relationship. These things went through my mind as I was undergoing rehabilitation while my country was host to the Chiefs of Staff in 1977.

At my beach home, I had a visit with General Kerwin, Assistant Army Chief of Staff for the U.S., and General Gordon Sumner, President of the Inter-American Defense Board, and I even had a talk with the son of Jules Dubois, that famous journalist who always opposed the Somozas. Out of these many conversations, one common thought emerged. All of these people were amazed at the freedom which existed in Nicaragua. They listened to the radio, they read the opposition newspaper, and they talked to the people. They were amazed at the tranquility and the attitude of the people. The international press had told them one thing, but what they found was something totally different. They found that propaganda had twisted reality into some ethereal dream of the Left.

In retrospect, though, I must have failed in my effort to show Nicaragua as she really was — a free country. So many of these guests were complimentary of our government and, to me, their statements were sincere. I have to believe that these people supported me and they supported our government, but it was not they who made the final international policy decisions.

Even though strenuous effort had been exerted to sabotage the meeting, it was a success. I was unable to attend the seminar, because I was still recuperating. However, I did have a party for the entire military group and their wives at my beach home. I was pleased with the entire affair. It was the first time this important seminar had been held in a small country, and Nicaragua showed herself beautifully.

While I was recuperating at the family beach home, all the presidents of Central America came to see me. To me, this was a high honor and it made me feel that these leaders had respect for me and that they were genuinely concerned about my health. It was important to me that they came to my inauguration, but it was more important that they came to see me while I was ill. All of them did not come at one time and that was good, because I could spend more time visiting with each individual.

Soon after I returned from the Miami hospital, President Daniel Oduber of Costa Rica came to see me. Our relationship was unusual. Politically and philosophically we disagreed in many areas. However, we understood each other and each of us respected the right of the other to follow the principles to which he adhered. He, as President of Costa Rica, and I, as President of Nicaragua, had many visits. These were always warm and pleasant visits. Our countries adjoined each other and our people enjoyed about the same standard of living. So we always had things to discuss. I then considered Daniel a friend and I still do. After all that has happened to me, I hope he still considers me his friend.

I recall vividly the day of his visit. He spent most of the day, we had lunch, and we discussed the problems of Central America and those things and events which affected both our countries.

The conversation which I am about to relate has never been told before. While Daniel was still President of Costa Rica I could not, out of fairness to him, publicly release the contents of our personal conversation. This revelation could have caused problems for Daniel with the Carter Administration. And, as I can affirm, our small countries didn't need additional problems with Mr. Carter.

Mrs. Carter, the President's wife, had just been to Costa Rica on what was billed as a "good will tour." During this tour she also visited other countries. Accompanying Mrs. Carter was Mr. Robert Pastor, a White House National Security Advisor. Daniel told me that he had several lengthy discussions with Mr. Pastor. The contents of those discussions shocked me to my very roots. For openers, Daniel quoted Mr. Robert Pastor as saying to him: "When are we going to get that son of a bitch up to the north out of the presidency?" He was, of course, referring to me. Daniel said he spent more than an hour trying to explain to Pastor the good things that were happening in Nicaragua. During this period, he said he strongly advised Pastor of the evolution Nicaragua had experienced economically, politically, and socially. Daniel then said to me: "I have come to tell you this because you are my friend and I wouldn't want your country to be harassed by the United States. So you had best get yourself prepared."

I surmised that Mr. Pastor, utilizing Mrs. Carter's trip as an excuse, talked to all the countries which were visited on that same theme, and that theme was to get Somoza. This was in September of 1977 and that was a long time before my government fell to Communist forces on July 17, 1979.

In this instance, and it's shocking to realize, Mr. Pastor was representing the White House. He was speaking for the executive branch of government in the United States of America. More specifically, he was speaking for James Earl Carter. If that information had been revealed at that time, it could easily have meant a congressional investigation. The President of the U.S. was directly interfering in the internal affairs of another republic. More importantly, this republic was a long-time friend, ally, and supporter of U.S. policy. The U.S. Congress and the American people are entitled to know why Mr. Carter was supporting Castro and the Communists in their bid to destroy an anti-Communist nation in the Western Hemisphere. As I have pointed out, Mr. Carter and the State Department had concrete evidence as to the Communist effort in Nicaragua.

The next to visit me was General Carlos Humberto Romero, President of El Salvador. He told me that his people had recently captured a Communist labor leader and that the man had some interesting things to say about Nicaragua. The Communist told his captors that no one could imagine what was going to happen in Nicaragua. The man was quoted as saying, "Very shortly, all hell is going to break loose there." Here again, President Romero came to me as a friend. He felt that I should be warned that the Communists were planning something "big" for Nicaragua.

With all this information coming to me in a time of

recuperation, I should have been back in the hospital. However, my heart stood the test.

The Constitution of Nicaragua sets forth the order of succession to the presidency. In the event the President dies or becomes incapacitated to the extent that the duties of office cannot be met, immediately next in line to that office is the Minister of the Interior. When I had the heart attack and departed for Miami, Minister of the Interior Antonio Mora Rostran became Acting President of Nicaragua. Until I returned to Nicaragua on September 10, 1977, he served in that capacity. The duties of the office were carried out in an orderly manner and the Constitution served us well.

Chapter Six

SANDINO AND SANDINISTAS

By late 1977, the international propaganda against me and the government had reached proportions beyond imagination. Never have I seen such concerted effort by the international news media to destroy one individual. This was particularly true in the United States. Writers and television news teams who, in reality, knew nothing about me or the government and the people of Nicaragua, became overnight experts on the ills and ails of Nicaragua. There was nothing good for them to see and nothing good for them to report. It was as though a button had been punched in Washington, D.C., and a big, red light had suddenly appeared in Nicaragua. This red light was the signal to swarm and attack.

As I look backward and think of all the distortions, misrepresentations, and out-and-out lies which abruptly fell upon me, a previous notion now becomes a strong conviction. There is a Leftist power structure that controls the news media. This power structure is not limited to the United States in its area of control. The tentacles of this mind-moulding machine reach out to every section of the globe.

If an event important to the ideological Left occurs in Red China, it's immediately front-page news in the *Washington Post*. If Castro makes a move or gesture which can be interpreted as favorable for the Leftist cause, it's forthwith front-page news in the *New York Times*. If Pinochet of Chile breathes an anti-Communist word or strikes an anti-Communist blow, all three major television networks in the U.S. hit the six o'clock news with some indirect praise of

Allende, the former Communist president of Chile. What a control system they must have! I'm an engineer but this international communications system, controlled by that mysterious power structure, is beyond my comprehension.

I will agree that in the field of electronics, there are accomplishments which approach wizardry. But this system developed by the brains of the Left exceeds wizardry. There is truly instantaneous transmission; and with this transmission there is something even more amazing. The technique of desired instantaneous response has been developed. That old psychological theorist and practitioner, Ivan Petrovich Pavlov, would shrink from the conditioned reflex which has been developed today. He wouldn't have to worry about ringing bells and flashing lights. Pavlov, if he were alive today, could touch a button in the Orient and immediately a light would respond to that slight touch in the West. And with the light would come a message and instructions on how most effectively to disseminate that message.

Perhaps the foregoing seems farfetched. But, hopefully, it will indicate the tremendous control which is exercised over the news media. Of this you can be certain. That control will *not* be exercised on behalf of anti-Left news. For verification of this contention, all you will have to do is read the newspaper and watch the news on television.

In late 1977, I was the object of this international news control monster. From experience, I can relate to you that once this monster descends upon you, there is no escape. It has the ability and the know-how to discredit any human being in the free world. That's frightening, don't you agree? The irony of this is that the Leftist power structure does not reach into Communist-controlled countries, because in these countries there is no freedom of the press. As one individual who has always believed in and advocated freedom of the press, almost unto death, I hope this power structure does not succeed in pushing the Western world into the Communist camp.

At the time the international press really took after me, favorable articles about the Sandinistas began appearing. These were glowing articles in which the Sandinistas were depicted as being young idealists who, with their bare hands,

were fighting a horrible dictator named Somoza. How wrong
they were. All of the leaders had been trained in Cuba,
Czechoslovakia, the PLO, Libya, and Panama; and they were
tough. They knew tactics and their knowledge of weaponry
was first rate.

As a result of the Jesuit priests' training and as a result
of the favorable international news coverage, many young
idealists did join the Sandinistas. Their movement now began
to gather some momentum.

Late in 1977 the Sandinistas made a daring move. They
made a simultaneous attack on the Massaya police station,
the San Carlos police station, on the battalion of Army
Engineers in Managua, and they also made an attack on the
Honduran frontier. In these attacks, many people were killed
on both sides. Some of the Sandinistas in Massaya and San
Carlos were captured, and many escaped over the border into
Costa Rica.

Even though I was still in rehabilitation, I could not
remain on the sidelines. I requested that an aero commander
be sent to pick me up so that I could observe the fighting
firsthand. My doctor, my nurse, and my aide accompanied
me on that flight. We scouted Massaya and San Carlos at an
altitude of seven thousand feet. This altitude was maintained so that small arms fire could not reach us. With field
glasses I had an accurate view of the destruction being
wrought upon these areas. During these periods, I was quite
nervous. I was not so much concerned about the small arms
fire as I was about suffering another heart attack. At that
altitude, oxygen is more difficult to come by and this could
be dangerous for a heart patient. However, I experienced no
angina, and this made me feel much better.

We spent approximately four hours on that flight and
returned to Las Mercedes Airport in Managua. We refueled,
had luncheon refreshments, and returned to the air. By that
time, it was obvious that the government forces had control
of the situation. There were still pockets of resistance, but
these would soon be eliminated.

The tactics used by the Communist-trained guerrillas
should be examined, because this initial plan would be used
over and over again. In combating these tactics, the govern-

ment forces received undeserved criticisms from the press. At any rate, the Communist-trained leaders would make plans to attack an area, such as Massaya. They would move into that area and recruit whatever help they could get. Often times their momentary military assistance came from teenagers who weren't even old enough to qualify for military service. Some of these boys would be fourteen or fifteen years of age. The Communist-trained leaders would remain in the fight until it became apparent that the government forces would win, and then they would escape while there was still an escape route. The local youths who had joined in the fight would remain and continue to fire their weapons.

If you happened to be a young captain in the Guardia Nacional, what would you do? To be sure, you would not walk out in the open, admonish the boys, and tell them to stop that nonsense. Some of my men tried that approach and they are dead. Sadly, you had to fight them. Through death-learning experiences, those who fought in Indo-China learned that an eleven-year-old boy, or an innocent-looking little old lady, can render you dead just the same as can a thirty-year-old combat veteran. In this manner, several young boys were killed. Of course, they killed some of our men. This always happened. But the news stories and the photographs which went out all over the world centered on the young boys who had lost their lives fighting Somoza.

I didn't appreciate the kind of warfare being conducted by the Communist-trained leaders, and neither did the government forces. We were forced to fight on their terms and we did. As General Douglas MacArthur once said: "In war, there is no substitute for victory." As trained and disciplined soldiers, my men were trying to win, and this was as it should be.

After the attacks which have been described, we began to realize the makeup of the forces which were opposing and fighting the constitutional government of Nicaragua. In Massaya, for example, we captured the wounded son of a wealthy Nicaraguan cattle rancher by the name of Belli. We also found that in San Carlos, the employees of the San Antonio sugar mill were in the forefront of those joining the

Sandinistas. This group attacked the police station and killed some of the enlisted men.

We knew the Sandinistas were Communists, but it surprised us to learn they had successfully convinced sons of solid Conservative families actually to join them in battle. We knew the Leftist Jesuits had done a good job of indoctrination, but we didn't fully realize just how effective that indoctrination had been.

The name Sandinista has been made familiar in news publications around the world. How did the Communists come by that name? That question should be answered because the name will continue to reverberate from one Communist guerrilla camp to another. The name Sandinista was derived from a revolutionary in Nicaragua, General Augusto Cesar Sandino. It is fitting that I introduce the reader to General Sandino.

This man was born in Niquinomo, Nicaragua. He and my father, at different times, attended the same school in Jinotepe, Nicaragua. He apparently had a normal growing up period, learned his numbers, and learned to read and write. His first job of importance was with a Mr. Potters, who owned a gold mine in Nicaragua. Due to the fact that he could read and write, Sandino became the warehouseman.

When President Juan Bautista Sacasa of the Liberal Party made a constitutional comeback, and a year later became President of the country, he was violently opposed by the Conservative Party which was then backed by the U.S. Marines. A revolution occurred, and the next we heard of Sandino, he had joined the revolution on the side of the Liberal Party. Under the leadership of General Jose Maria Moncada, and Sacasa, Sandino travelled with the revolutionary group all the way to Boaco. At that juncture, the group was met by Henry L. Stimson, who was later to become Secretary of War for the United States, and Moncada was told that if he advanced any further toward Managua, he would have to fight the U.S. Marines. Moncada said he never intended to fight the U.S.

At that point in time, both parties, in consultation with the U.S.A, agreed to a free, direct, one-man, one-vote popular election, with the provision that the elections would be controlled by the U.S. government. When Moncada returned from this conference in which an agreement had been struck, he gave a full report to the other generals under his command. All the generals, except one, agreed to the popular election process and that general was Sandino. He then made his famous statement that would be echoed in years to come. He said: "To hell with it. I'm going out into the bush and fight the damn U.S. Marines." At that instant, Sandino became the idol and hero of all those who opposed the American intervention and the presence of the tough U.S. Marines.

It should be noted that at one time, the Liberal revolution carried the banner against American intervention. When all the conditions were laid out to the leadership of the Liberal Party and it appeared they would have to fight the United States of America, they knew this could never be. These were responsible people and they did not seek to destroy themselves. Also, it was apparent that the United States was being fair to both the Conservative Party and Liberal Party.

The United States disarmed the revolutionary forces, no one was put in jail, everyone was given some money, and then they were sent home. Preparation then began for the big popular election which was to be controlled by the U.S. government.

While all this was going on, Sandino took off for San Rafael del Norte in Jinotepe. There he endeavored to copy Pancho Villa of Mexico and constantly enunciated the familiar anti-U.S. slogans. Many of these are still popular around the world today. He then became the flag bearer of anti-American imperialism. There is no doubt that Sandino, at that time, had the sympathy of the people of Nicaragua. The presence of U.S. troops was an irritant and Sandino capitalized upon that irritation.

However, the widespread popularity of Sandino didn't last too long. He soon began to follow a course of non-discrimination. This is to say that he did not discriminate between the U.S. Marines and the people of Nicaragua. He would rob, steal, murder, rape, and burn. He had a law all his own — Sandino's law. As can well be surmised, this made him unpopular. So long as he ranted about U.S. imperialism and fought the U.S. Marines, that posture was laudable. When he began to ravage his own people, that was an entirely different matter.

In the U.S.-supervised election of 1929, Moncada, of the Liberal Party, won the presidency. Apparently the people of Nicaragua were pleased with the performance of the Liberal Party because in 1933 the party won again and Sacasa became President. This election was also supervised by the U.S.

History tells us that Lieutenant Maxwell D. Taylor was stationed in Nicaragua at that time and was one of those officers counting the votes. Chester Puller, a U.S. Marine who was later to gain fame in the Marine invasion of Guadalcanal, was also stationed in Nicaragua.

In 1933, Franklin D. Roosevelt established the Good Neighbor Policy and the U.S. Marines were pulled out of Nicaragua. Thus ended a very important phase of Nicaraguan history. Many U.S. Marines liked Nicaragua and decided to remain. One, Russell Brown, was later to become a member of my staff.

Regarding this period of Nicaraguan history, the news media have conveyed and kept alive a gross inaccuracy. It has been printed over and over again that the U.S. Marines put my father in office. Nothing could be further from the truth. As previously stated, the U.S. government supervised two elections, with Moncada winning in 1929 and Sacasa winning in 1933. I shall relate exactly how my father came to prominence in Nicaragua, and this involves a touch of family background.

General Somoza was educated in the United States. He attended the Pierce Business School in Philadelphia to become a mercantile accountant. He married Salvadora Somoza who was the niece of Dr. Sacasa. General Somoza was also the second cousin of Moncada, the leader of the revolution in which some twenty thousand people lost their lives.

When it came time for the U.S. Marines to depart, it was necessary that a Commander of the Nicaragua Guardia Nacional be selected. There were three candidates being considered for that position, and one of them was my father. The other two candidates were Carlos Pasos and Carlos Catrowassmer. In all candor, I doubt that General Somoza would have been selected had he not been married to the niece of President Sacasa.

However, Somoza's background in the family was also one of well-cemented relations with the Conservative Party. His father had been a Senator of the Republic, and his whole family was tied to Conservative partisanship. General Somoza did have combat experience in the revolution and he had served in a high administrative position in the Department of Leon. So he did have qualifications. President Sacasa nominated General Somoza and this nomination met the approval of Moncada, who happened to be my father's cousin. This nomination was then submitted to General Matthews of the U.S. Marine Corps and U.S. Ambassador Hanna. The selection of General Somoza met with their approval and that's how General Somoza became Commander of the Nicaragua Guardia Nacional.

To insure fairness to both the Liberal Party and the Conservative Party, fifty percent of the officers in the Guardia Nacional were from one political party and fifty percent were from the other. So in the Army of Nicaragua, each party had an equal share of the officer contingent.

When the U.S. Marines left Nicaragua, Sandino continued fighting. Only now all of his misdeeds were directed against the people of Nicaragua. He then became identified as a bandit. No longer was he recognized as a nationalistic hero who was struggling against U.S. imperialism in Nicaragua.

He was still looked upon as a dichotomous factor in an otherwise peaceful Nicaragua. Efforts were made to appease Sandino but these efforts were in vain. His proposal to the constitutionally elected government was that Nicaragua be divided into two parts — east and west. He proposed that President Sacasa govern the western half of Nicaragua and he, Sandino, would take the eastern half. The eastern half of the country was where the gold mines and other valuable hard minerals existed. This, of course, President Sacasa refused to do.

It became obvious, then, that there was no way an accommodation could be reached with Sandino. He had absolutely refused to accept the results of the popular elections which had been supervised by the U.S. government. During the entire Moncada Administration and into the Sacasa Administration, he violated every law known to man. These vile criminal acts were perpetrated against his own people. He abhorred the United States and he had come to hate the people of Nicaragua. He found respect only in the band of guerrillas who followed him and, in the main, that respect came out of fear.

Sandino was captured by the Guardia Nacional and he was shot. Thus the violent life of August Cesar Sandino came to an end, and from this man, the Sandinistas derived their name.

After his death, the Sandino movement died. His followers were given amnesty and they disbanded. They were guaranteed a peaceful life and no charges were brought against them. This is quite contrary to what the present Marxist government has done to the loyal members of the Guardia Nacional and members of my government. They are all in prison waiting to be tried by "kangaroo courts."

For many years, nothing was heard of the name Sandino. Then along came a Communist by the name of Carlos Fonseca Amador. He was the illegitimate son of the administrator of our family's sugar plantations. This man began the modern movement known as Frente Sandinista de Liberacion Nacional. Carlos Fonseca stole the name Sandino, but the ideals of the new movement were communistic. He followed the pattern established by Castro in Cuba.

In 1971, Carlos Fonseca Amador sent a message to the Communist Party Congress in Moscow. He wanted to be certain that the Communist Party knew of his loyalty and devotion. In that message he described the Sandinistas as the "successor to the Bolshevik Revolution" and said further that "the ideals of Lenin are a guiding star in the struggle which the revolutionaries in Nicaragua are waging." With a few malcontents, he began robbing small stores, business establishments, and graduated to robbing banks. Due to the fact that Carlos Fonseca's father worked for us, I saved his life on four different occasions. I couldn't save his life the fifth time. He had decided to abandon the urban areas and went to the bush with other guerrillas. In an encounter with the Guardia Nacional in the bush, Carlos Fonseca Amador was shot and killed. Then the FSLN, or the Sandinistas, had no leader.

At that time, the Leftist priests moved in to fill a void. They continued the work of Carlos Fonseca but at a much higher economic level. In the Jesuit schools, the seeds of discontent and, basically, the seeds of Communism, were sown. Their doctrine was spread to the children from affluent families, and with many the doctrine was accepted. You had young men like the Carrion Cruz boys, and the Langs Sacasa for example. They became avowed Communists and they had received their training from the Jesuit priests.

Perhaps the foregoing again illustrates the liberty which existed in Nicaragua. Not a single school in which the Jesuits were teaching their communistic philosophy was ever closed. It is my belief that Nicaragua was pinpointed in Latin America as the key government to destroy, and that the Jesuit priests figured prominently in the planning.

One might ask why, of all the countries in Central America, was Nicaragua pinpointed as the country to be taken? The answer is that we had a successful government. Our country was financially sound. Nicaragua had progress and the future looked bright for all of our people. Also, we had a successful political system based upon a constitutional form of government. More importantly, the people of Nicaragua were, and still are, anti-Communist. They believed in individual liberty and they were proud of their country. Moreover, Nicaragua had earned the respect of her neighbors. Their belief, and it was a sound concept, was that if Nicaragua could be taken by the Left, then the remaining countries in Central America could not stand the pressure. And one by one, they would also succumb to the Leftist onslaught.

With the death of Carlos Fonseca Amador, there was no one single leader of the Sandinistas. This situation would not last long. Shortly, the Sandinistas would have three distinct factions. These were the Communists, the Christian Sandinistas and the Terciary group. Carlos Fonseca was gone and it was believed the movement could be easily stolen. They didn't realize that at that very moment, Castro had three hundred men trained to be leaders in the movement, and these were the men who took control of it. Additionally, we knew of many who had gone to the Soviet Union and to the Palestine Liberation Organization (PLO) to be trained. Some of the Sandinistas had been active with the PLO in Israel ten years previously.

All in all, it can be stated with finality that the Sandinistas represent *the* movement of the people in Latin America which is against the United States. I have talked to Sandinistas who are not Nicaraguans and who are not Communists, but they support the movement because it is strongly against the United States.

One who is not familiar with the modus operandi of the Leftist priests might think that Somoza has to pick on someone, so why not the priests? On this important issue, there is complete verification and my word doesn't have to be taken. To make verification as current as possible, I refer anyone to the *New York Times* issue of February 8, 1980. The article by the *Times* writer, Alan Riding, is quite revealing. His article is headlined as follows: NEW NICARAGUA REGIME RECOGNIZES CHURCH'S POTENT ROLE. From my viewpoint, this is a fascinating article because it backs up my every contention in reference to the Jesuit priests. First, Riding recognizes there are two factions amongst the priests — the apolitical and political. In reference to the political segment, Mr. Riding had this to say:

In Nicaragua, this change was first apparent among priests, often Jesuits, teaching in private Catholic schools: by the mid-1970's, many of their former students, children of wealthy families, had joined the guerrillas. And as the fight against President Anastasio Somoza Debayle intensified, several priests joined the Sandinistas, while others helped organize slum neighborhoods in preparation for last year's successful insurrection.

But at the level of the priests, the church was participating fully in the revolution. The Rev. Miguel d'Escoto was named Foreign Minister, the Rev. Ernesto Cardinal became Minister of Culture, the Rev. Fernando Cardenal was placed in charge of the literacy crusade and the Rev. Xavier Gorostiaga was given a key role in the Ministry of Planning. Many parish priests, who had collaborated with the rebels, began organizing their community for the reconstruction effort.

How could it be stated more clearly, and how could I ask for a more clearly defined position of the Jesuit priests? It's all there. It should be made clear, however, that, at the priest level, the Communists have successfully infiltrated Catholic orders other than the Jesuits.

My sympathy goes out to the people of Guatemala, El Salvador, and Honduras. The Jesuit priests, in collaboration with the Cuban-trained guerrillas, are following the same course in those countries that they followed in Nicaragua. If they are able to pursue effectively their preconceived plan of action, then those countries, too, will fall.

The plague of the Sandinistas and the ghost of Augusto Cesar Sandino have already fallen upon those other Central American Republics. It's one down and four to go in Central America but, in reality, it's one down and nineteen to go in Latin America.

Chapter Seven

BRICK WALLS — U.S. STYLE

Those not directly involved in the Nicaraguan contest may have forgotten the amount of pressure which was being heaped upon me and my government. By late 1977, each day in Managua one could find television teams, foreign correspondents, syndicated writers, independent writers, and all manner and means of worldwide communications. In face of all this press commotion, it's difficult to function in a normal way. You know without asking that these people are against you, and you know they are searching for sensationalism. Even with this constant "circus atmosphere." the government maintained its poise. That was a credit to all of those who held responsible positions and to the people of Nicaragua.

At that time, the press decided to take a different course. Instead of attacking me head-on, as they had always done, they began a campaign against my Cabinet members. These men were attacked collectively and they were attacked individually. Nothing was sacred — not their personal lives, nor their governmental functions — and their very being was suspect. I had been subjected to this kind of treatment, but my Cabinet members had not.

Perhaps I yielded to the overwhelming pressure, or perhaps it was an effort on my part to appease but, whatever the motivation was, I decided the government would best be served if the Cabinet members resigned and a new Cabinet was appointed. Unlike the United States, the underdeveloped nations of the world are limited in the availability of qualified people for top assignments. This was true in Nicaragua, but I had good people. Nevertheless, I decided to proceed with a new Cabinet. I then called in each of these men and explained the situation to them. Their attitude couldn't have been better and their acceptance, without question, of my decision made me feel less pain.

The vitriolic attack by the press and certain areas of Communist influence had been successful. The Cabinet was replaced. Out of all of this, I learned a lesson. It's impossible to appease an insatiable appetite. I confess, I had tried to appease the forces against me and my government, and it didn't work. After the bones of my Cabinet members had been picked clean, those same forces came right back for more. Only now, they were more determined than ever to get *me*.

While this was transpiring, we were hit from another direction. The Comité de Solidaridad con el Pueblo de Nicaragua was formed to fight me and my government. Translated, this means the Committee of Solidarity for the People of Nicaragua. On the surface, that sounds like a committee which could have been formed after the earthquake to help the people of Nicaragua. But experience has taught me that the Left is most adept at forming noble-sounding committees to do its dirty work.

We found that the origin of this committee was Havana, and that it had been formed by the Communists in Honduras. This committee was given funds by Havana to travel to Mexico, Costa Rica, and Panama. Venezuela had also formed a committee under the same name with the same purpose. In this manner, the Communists had begun a campaign to pressure various Latin American governments to oppose me. I must say the committee had some effect. However, their influence in Honduras was not what they hoped for. Through our intelligence sources, we learned that the Chief of Intelligence in Panama had made an urgent trip to Honduras to get that country to make war against Nicaragua. He failed completely. Torrijos was doing everything in his power to destroy me and I wasn't sure who was exerting more influence on him, Carter or Perez.

There was no question in my mind about the political philosophy of Omar Torrijos. Since Mr. Carter, Mr. Vance, and the U.S. State Department have embraced this man, it might be well to examine his ideology. When I say embrace, I do so with the literal meaning. On nationwide television, Mr. Carter fondly embraced Omar Torrijos, and gave him the Panama Canal with four billion dollars of the U.S. taxpayers' money. This display of affection was photographically presented to the world.

For his present position of influence in all of Latin America, Torrijos should give thanks to the Carter Administration. So, the two men must share common interests, have mutual respect for each other, or it might be a combination of both.

At the time Mr. Carter handed over the Canal and a U.S. obligation for all that money, the President of the United States knew that, at least, Torrijos was a socialist dictator. He knew that Torrijos had handpicked Aristides Royo, an avowed Marxist, to be President of Panama. He knew that Torrijos was an admirer of Fidel Castro and that the two men had a close relationship. Further, Mr. Carter knew that Torrijos was in blatant violation of the OAS Charter in his overt effort to overthrow the constitutional government of Nicaragua. There should be a huge question in the minds of the American people as to why Carter and Torrijos became "political bedfellows."

Mr. Carter can't claim ignorance as to the Leftist philosophy of the Panama dictator. He had all kinds of intelligence reports on this man. One such report was written by a much-decorated lieutenant general of the U.S. Army. That would be General Gordon Sumner. He was no "swivel chair" general. Among his military decorations you will find the following: Distinguished Service Medal, Silver Star, Legion of Merit (with three Oak Leaf Clusters), Distinguished Flying Cross (with thirteen Oak Leaf Clusters), Bronze Star Medal "V" Device, Army Commendation Medal (with one Oak Leaf Cluster), and the Purple Heart.

Previously, I alluded to the fact that in 1977 General Sumner attended the Army Chiefs of Staff Conference in Managua. At that time he was Chairman of the Inter-American Defense Board in Washington — a position he held from August, 1975 until his retirement from the military on May 31, 1978. By way of explanation, the Inter-American Defense Board is a product of the Rio Treaty and each of the nineteen signatory nations to that treaty is represented on the IADB.

In Managua, General Sumner had casually mentioned that

at the termination of our seminar he was proceeding to Panama. Until his June 7, 1979 appearance before the U.S. House of Representatives Subcommittee on the Panama Canal, I did not know that the General had had an appointment to see Omar Torrijos; and, obviously, I had no knowledge of their conversation. General Sumner is a patriotic American and a man who is well informed on Latin American affairs. His testimony is revealing and clearly outlines the ideology of Omar Torrijos. Keep in mind that this testimony was given to members of Congress on June 7, 1979. With only my emphasis added, here is a part of what General Sumner said:

> *Unfortunately the facts of Panamanian involvement in supporting leftist/communist terrorist groups in Central America have been denied the American people.* I saw a great deal of this when I was Chairman of the Inter-American Defense Board. *There was a blackout of this particular subject, not only in the media, but also, I felt, in the U.S. Government.*
>
> But I think of even greater importance is the strategic significance of these efforts by Gen. Omar Torrijos in de-establishing the entire Central American Region. This is only one part, obviously important, of a strategic effort by the Soviets and their surrogates, the Cubans, to deny the United States access to the Caribe basin.
>
> *I have watched this over three years experience as the Chairman of the Inter-American Defense Board; and the frustration of being unable to get this, though, to the American people, but also to the officials of the Federal Government. That is one reason why I retired from active military duty.*
>
> . . . Almost all of the countries that have been under attack by the leftist terrorists have produced extensive white papers, documenting the Cuban/Soviet involvement, and it is a matter of daily discussion over at the Inter-American Defense Board.
>
> As a matter of fact, yesterday the Chief of the Nicaraguan Delegation asked for and there was a special session of the Inter-American Defense Board to discuss this very subject.
>
> Less obvious, and less discussed, however, has been the Panamanian involvement in this effort. From the standpoint of the Inter-American Defense Board, the matter has been, and I am sure it is today, one of acute embarrassment. As a member of the Inter-American Defense Board, Panama was officially committed to the security of the hemisphere, not its subversion. They are members of the Rio Treaty, and they have kept a delegation in Washington at the Inter-American Defense Board since its inception.
>
> As a matter of fact, in my position as the Chairman of the Defense Board, Gen. Omar Torrijos was one of my bosses, as was President

Somoza and President Carter. I was, under the terms of the treaty, under their control.

My personal knowledge of Panama's involvement came from a 2-hour conversation with Gen. Omar Torrijos in November, 1977. *He told me then of his intention to support the Sandinistas, to support the insurrection in not only Nicaragua but also El Salvador; and during this 2-hour conversation, he expressed the opinions that the Sandinistas were his good friends. The Sandinistas were just a bunch of good old boys.* This meeting followed our biannual meeting of the Conference of the American Armies in Managua, Nicaragua, I traveled to Panama where a meeting with Gen. Torrijos had been arranged by the Chief of the Delegation, at that time, Major Dubrai; at the meeting, with just Omar Torrijos and myself and my aide, Major Dubrai, who was born in Panama, and is a native speaker in the language.

While I was in the conference in Managua, which lasted a week, I had several private conversations with President Somoza, during which time he outlined, in great detail, the problems he was having with the Sandinistas. He told me at that time that he felt they were not only receiving support from Havana, but that some of the support was being funneled through Panama; and of course, he was very disturbed about this, and in turn I became disturbed, because *the fact that the Panamanians were involved in this was a potentially disruptive development for the Inter-American Defense Board.*

. . . The Panama Canal negotiations were getting cranked up, and I saw at this time that this was really a bad development.

When I met with General Torrijos, I brought this up, and I expected him to give me a denial. Well, much to my surprise, he not only did not deny it, but as I say, he said *he would continue the support, and defended the Sandinistas.* He told me at that time, he said you people on the Board get too worried about these Communists. This is not really a problem. He said you know there is a lot going on, *socialism is the way of the future,* and you people are behind the power curve on this. He had quite a bit to say about this.

. . . One point he made which I did not really pick up on at the time, after talking about the Sandinistas, he turned to El Salvador and he said, you know, my classmate, General Romero, wants to use tanks rather than talking. He said he is wrong, and I am going to do something about that situation, too.

. . . I was on my way down the continent. Upon my return to Washington, I reduced this conversation, the salient points of the conversation with General Torrijos, to a memorandum, which I forwarded to the late Gen. George Brown, Chairman of the Joint Chiefs of Staff. I also reported on the meeting that we had in Managua, where I felt things went very badly for the United States.

I also made a point, out of talking to the other responsible officials in both State and Defense.

. . . My decision to testify against the Panama Canal treaties before the Senate Armed Services Committee was, in part, influenced by my experience both in Managua and Panama. *It was quite clear that General Torrijos was expanding his horizons to include support for revolution in Central America, and I believed then, and I believe today, that he is under the influence of Communist/Marxists within Panama and Cuba,* and particularly Colonel, or I believe it is General, Noriega.

General Torrijos expressed to me great admiration for Fidel Castro at this meeting. The whole tone of the meeting was one, as far as I could determine, and I had not detected this degree earlier, that Omar Torrijos was moving very quickly to the left as he expressed it that he was getting out in front of the movement to lead it. *I believe the unseemly haste of the group of people advising President Carter at that time to consummate these treaties was just one more piece in a plan which was designed to polarize this hemisphere into left and right;* and I think that from a strategic standpoint, that is a tragedy for this country.

We divided up all of Latin America into good guys and bad guys. They are being designated as *"human righteous." This is all being done by a very small group in the White House and State. The fact that these "Good Guys," the guys with the white hats, are supplying arms, which you see here, they are supplying the training, money, support, a lot of this is coming out of the U.S. taxpayers' pockets, perhaps indirectly, to murder and maim as General Noriega did in Nicaragua, without discrimination. As far as I'm concerned, that makes a mockery out of the President's human rights policy.*

. . . I think the fact that the Mexican oil reserves are limiting at this time makes this area a strategic objective as far as the Soviets are concerned. I do not think the United States can afford to watch this area be stabilized by Fidel Castro, by Gen. Omar Torrijos, or the Soviets or anyone.

We have a vital interest in this area and it is about time we realized it. I think Gen. Omar Torrijos is actively aiding and abetting leftist subversion in this area. It is apparent to me that *he has nothing but scorn and contempt for this country, and our apparent weakness*: the fact that he would stir this one up at this time to set a critical juncture in the whole Panama Canal negotiations and the implications of these treaties is another indicator of this attitude.

I repeat, this testimony was given before the U.S. House of Representatives Subcommittee on the Panama Canal on June 7, 1979. That was over a month before the Marxist take-over in Nicaragua. More importantly, this same information was presented to General George Brown, Chairman of the Joint Chiefs of Staff, General McAuliffe, U.S. Commander of the Southern Command, the Defense Department, and the State Department in November, 1977.

Yes, Mr. Carter and his entire coterie of radicals were warned, briefed, and presented conclusive proof as to the political philosophy of Omar Torrijos. Furthermore, they had the message direct from the mouth of Torrijos that he was after Nicaragua and then he would turn his attention to El Salvador. Apparently, this knowledge pushed the Carter Administration into high gear. Somehow they had to get the Canal treaties signed before the American people became enlightened as to who and what Torrijos was.

The same can be said about Nicaragua. The Carter Administration never admitted that they had any proof that Torrijos was working with Castro in support of the Sandinistas in Nicaragua. They had the proof, but they chose to ignore it. If any person is interested in all the evidence presented and the testimony given to the aforementioned subcommittee, that information can be obtained from the U.S. Government Printing Office. Simply ask for a booklet entitled *Panama Gunrunning: Hearings before the Subcommittee On The Panama Canal, U.S. House of Representatives, June 6, 7, and July 10, 1979, Serial No. 96-22.*

So, with that intimate background on Omar Torrijos, let's proceed to other activities of late 1977 and early 1978. To be sure, I was concerned about the Havana-backed Committee of Solidarity for the People of Nicaragua, but I was more concerned about the stepped-up activities of Torrijos.

Toward the end of 1977, we had once again to turn some of our attention toward Nicaraguan politics. According to the Constitution, on the first Sunday in February, 1978 we were required to hold municipal elections throughout the country. With the exception of Managua, mayors would be elected throughout Nicaragua. We had patterned our city government in Managua after the system in Washington. We treated Managua as a federal district; and in our capital city, the mayor was appointed.

We would have elections in over 130 municipalities, and this was important to the Liberal Party. The law required that voter registration occur sixty days prior to the election. Thus, we had to do our political homework so as to get the people registered and eligible to vote. We had four Sundays on which Nicaraguans could register. Although there were deadly problems confronting the country, on the four Sundays of registration, I went to Teotecacinte, Nueva Segovia, Jalapa, Esteli, Leon, Chinandega, Blufield, Puerto Cabezas, and to different municipalities in Managua. The purpose of these visits was to inspire people to register and to show them that our political party and our elective process were functioning.

While we were following the democratic process, those in the opposition party were urging people not to register and the U.S. government was assisting them in this effort. Even so, at the end of the fourth Sunday, we felt a successful registration drive had been accomplished.

In December, 1977 the pressure from the United States took a different turn. The White House knew, and the State Department knew, that Nicaragua needed money for many projects. At that time, we had several important projects pending in BID and the World Bank. These projects had to be voted upon before funding could be made. The United States voted openly against Nicaragua and funding for these projects failed to pass. I couldn't cope with this kind of opposition from the United States.

The financial pressure went even further. Plans had been made and engineering studies had been completed on a much-needed highway around the center of Managua. In this instance, Jack Anderson stepped in and wrote a column in which he criticized U.S. assistance in funding for this highway. He told his readers that most of this highway would run through property which was owned by the Somoza family and that we would derive great financial benefit from it. His column must be the Bible for the State Department, the White House, and certain members of Congress, because U.S. assistance was cancelled.

The truth is that a portion of the proposed highway did run through Somoza property, which had been acquired by members of the Somoza family twenty years or more before the earthquake. But a large majority of the thoroughfare would have gone through the property of other landowners. The thinking out of Washington was clear to me. They wanted the people of Nicaragua to know that I was looked upon with disfavor by the Carter Administration.

These events told me that I should have a conference with

U.S. Ambassador Solaun, and I did. I explained to him, as gently and as politely as possible, the importance to Nicaragua of the many projects under consideration. The message met a brick wall. The State Department had thoroughly briefed him on what his attitude toward me and my government should be. He never gave an inch, and the meeting served no useful purpose at all.

It was apparent to me that a lot of things were rapidly coming to a head. The preliminary studies had been completed on the dam project which was so important to Nicaragua. We had been in touch with the French, Canadians, and the Brazilians concerning financing of the Copalar Dam project. These talks had gone well and it appeared certain we would have funding for this much-needed hydroelectric facility. Once more, in steps the United States. When the U.S. learned that financing would be available, a campaign was started, through *La Prensa*, against my financial advisor, Rodriguez Feliu. This attack against a capable man was unwarranted and, as a result, he was the recipient of uncalled-for abuse. Through U.S. intervention and pressure, funding for this project was withdrawn.

Since I was unable to have a meaningful conversation with the U.S. Ambassador, I thought it might be helpful if friends of the Ambassador, who were also my trusted friends, went to talk to him. I thought they might be more convincing than I had been and, if not, they could get a true reading on the official U.S. attitude toward me. Many of these personal connections did go and visit with the Ambassador. They came back with news which I had hoped I wouldn't hear. The message was always the same, "Mr. President, these people and the United States are disposed to overthrow you."

All of my life I had tried to be realistic. That is, meet realism face to face. In every life there is adversity, but how we face that adversity, when it does come, shows the true character of a man or woman. With reference to the developing U.S. attitude toward me, I had to accept the situation. It was discouraging, and I could only hope that somehow I could get through to them the fact that I was a true friend and we faced a common enemy. I was realistic about the danger of my position, but hoped that a way could be found to improve that position.

Chamorro was killed on January 10, 1978. Shortly thereafter the leaders of the Conservative Party came to me with a proposal. They proposed that the municipal elections, scheduled for February 8, 1978, be postponed. They maintained that the political climate in the country was very unstable and that they could not be ready for an election so soon after Chamorro's death. Constitutionally, it was impossible to postpone the elections. We could have put off the election in the municipalities of Managua, the home of Chamorro, but there was no election for mayor in that city. However, I could not see having the election in the rest of the country postponed, and legally it was impossible. The Conservative Party used the event of Chamorro's death to try to bypass the Constitution of the country.

I broke my back to maintain the Constitution and our constitutional form of government in Nicaragua. This was our guarantee of justice in the country. I believe my faith in the Constitution resulted from the civic teaching and training I received in the United States.

If you talked to my most outspoken adversaries in Nicaragua, they would tell you that I was "Mr. Constitution." Whenever a political solution to a problem was proposed and that proposal violated the Constitution, my answer was always an emphatic "no." It was widely accepted, in both parties, that I adhered strictly to the Constitution. This is another thing that makes it difficult for me to understand the anti-Somoza attitude which developed in Washington.

On February 8, 1978, we held the municipal elections throughout Nicaragua. It was an overwhelming victory for the Liberal Party. In an open election, we won in every municipality in Nicaragua.

After the elections of '78, the pressing problem continued to be our relationship with the United States. I needed the United States and I thought the United States needed me. Again I received a call from the U.S. Ambassador. He said he wanted to visit with me and I invited him to lunch. I did my best to convince him that the U.S. needed me and my constitutional government. It was a visit in which many of our problems were discussed. Then, in a cynical manner, he looked at me and said:

"You know, there are some countries who want to overthrow you." My retort was, "What will it take to get them off my back?" He replied: "I think if you shorten your term of office, you will get them off your back." I looked at him in astonishment and said: "Are you trying to say I should resign?" His answer was a simple "Yes." This was a disturbing conversation.

I then pointed out to the Ambassador that I was duly elected to the presidency in an open, fair, and observed election. I reminded him that my election had been officially recognized by all the countries in Central America, and that I couldn't see the reasoning behind his views. I told him that possibly some kind of political arrangement could be made but that I didn't plan to resign.

My ire was rather obvious at that point and I decided it was time for frankness. I looked at him squarely in the eye and said: "Mr. Ambassador, whose brainchild is that? Your government's? Because I want to know officially!" He denied that such was the official position of the United States and remarked that it was just a personal thought of his. Based upon the previous conversations which my friends had with the Ambassador, I was sure he was lying to me.

In retrospect, I went too far in my efforts to convince the United States that they should be working with me and not against me. Due to our long history of cooperation and mutual confidence, I continued to conduct my affairs in a manner which I thought would please the United States. The hope was always there that the U.S. would finally see the light. Another indication of my yielding to the desires of the U.S. relates to the "famous twelve" episode.

There were twelve men in Managua, of business, political, and religious backgrounds, who decided they wanted to oppose me openly. Their decision to take such action was made toward the middle of 1978. It wasn't the opposition factor which disturbed me. In reality, those men were preaching subversion, and this did disturb me. Also, I was upset because the international press always referred to these twelve men as "solid citizens" and "leading businessmen in Nicaragua." In truth, they were actually Sandinistas. We had intelligence information on all of them and we knew of their activities. To the press, however, they were knights in shining armor.

After making subversive pronouncements, they suspected they might be arrested and incarcerated. Therefore, they decided to take refuge in Costa Rica. From that safe haven, they stepped up their campaign against me. I was ridiculed and attacked in advertisements, leaflets, and by other means. These twelve also had an excellent source through which they could attack me and that was the press. Their every word was given wide distribution. But they went too far. They wrote and signed a manifesto in which they called for an armed uprising against me. They told the people of Nicaragua that the only solution was to take up arms and overthrow the constitutionally elected government. In my books, that's treason.

The government of Nicaragua took legal action against these men and they were enjoined. This meant that if they returned to Nicaragua, they would be charged and tried for their subversive activities. The legal action, on the part of our government, caused a furor in the U.S. Embassy in Nicaragua. Immediately, the Embassy came to the defense of these men. Alan Riding, of the *New York Times*, took up the cause of the twelve and wrote highly critical articles about the action our government had taken.

If the Nicaraguan government had suddenly issued an order to arrest all Americans in Nicaragua, I don't think the U.S. Embassy would have been more irritated. Ambassador Solaun talked to different members of the Cabinet and applied as much pressure as was possible to get our legal order lifted.

This constant pressure on the part of the U.S. Embassy had its effect. The government of Nicaragua issued an announcement to the effect that since these men had made their subversive statements outside Nicaragua, no crime had been committed and they could, therefore, return. The order to enjoin had been nullified.

They did return, and a lot of money was spent to get a large airport crowd to welcome the "famous twelve." Our security people at the airport estimated that 5,000 people turned out to greet them. In this instance, the press estimate of the crowd was just the reverse from the estimates they placed on the crowds who attended my rallies. Alan Riding, for example, estimated the crowd at the airport to be in the order of 100,000 people.

These twelve then went to Managua and Massaya, where
they made subversive speeches. In subsequent weeks they went
to Leon, Chinandega, Esteli, and Jinotega. In all of these
speeches, the theme was the same — evoking the violent
overthrow of my government. My associates asked me what
these twelve men were trying to do. I told them that the men
were preparing the country for a revolution. That's exactly
what they were doing. This subversive activity brought no
response from the U.S. Embassy.

My Cabinet and I knew that if we touched one of them, the
U.S. Embassy would come down on us with full force. As a
favor to the United States, we permitted these men to return.
Had we stood firm against the U.S. pressure, we would have
been better off.

Sometime in early February, 1978 the U.S. Ambassador
called on me. I don't have the exact date because my date book,
schedule of events, and list of callers were all left in Managua.
The Sandinistas have those and I'm sure it has provided
interesting reading for them. So, Ambassador Solaun came to
see me and once again we went over the same problems.

Generally speaking, the Ambassador was expressing dissat-
isfaction with my government, and I was endeavoring to find
out what it would take to satisfy the United States. Even
Solaun would have to admit that I was always trying. I was
never recalcitrant in my demeanor or spoken words.

At that meeting, I remember asking the Ambassador what
kind of action I would have to take to create a different
attitude in Washington. In calm voice and manner he told me
the United States might be satisfied if I announced that I
would get out of politics in 1981, and resign from the Army. My
concern, and this concern possessed me, was for my country and
the people of Nicaragua. If I lost in this battle with the
Sandinistas, I knew the Communists would have Nicaragua.
So, I told the Ambassador that his proposal met with my approval
and that I didn't object to making such a public statement.

I remember thinking that now, perhaps, I have some meaningful dialogue going with the United States and that we had
established a common base from which we could work. I was
not exactly in a state of euphoria, but I was happy that this
meeting had proved to be productive.

Shortly thereafter, my supporters decided to have a political rally in Managua to demonstrate to the world their solid support of me and my government. During my many years in government I had attended countless rallies, but none impressed me so much as this one. The attacks upon me were coming from everywhere, the United States, Venezuela, Panama, Costa Rica, and the international press. Contrary to the opinion held by many in the States, the people of Nicaragua are not stupid. They knew what was going on. Their feeling, though, was that my fight was their fight. And that was true, because I was fighting for them. This, then, was to be a demonstration of support for me, and it was some demonstration.

If you are familiar with Managua, you know that the Hotel Inter-Continental sits on a small hill overlooking what once was Old Managua. In front of the hotel is a large vacant area of about eight acres. That's where the rally was held.

On the day of February 26, 1978, I drove into that area and that scene shall be with me always. This was no longer a vacant area. Some 150,000 people were gathered there, and they were not inactive. They were jumping, screaming, and waving banners all over the place. As a man in government without problems, such a demonstration of support would be moving. As a man in government with an abundance of difficulties, such a show of support would bring tears to your eyes. That's the way I felt, as I entered that sea of people.

From a news standpoint, the rally was thoroughly covered. Press people had come from other Central American countries; the international press group and television were well represented. To me, the magnitude of press representation indicated curiosity. They wanted to see how many people would turn out for a besieged president, and they wanted to hear what that president had to say.

In the first category, the press did not give an accurate counting of the people who attended the rally. That was not unusual, because their estimates of people attending my public rallies were generally reduced about fifty percent. The message I delivered that day was significant, but it received scant notice. In my opinion, that speech was probably the most important one I had ever delivered. It represented an official statement of political change for me, my party, and Nicaragua.

I quote from the text of that speech:

"Consequently, I will firmly conduct the presidency of Nicaragua with patriotic deliberation until May 1, 1981. A date on which I will then hand over the presidency to the Nicaraguan who will be elected by the popular vote of the people of Nicaragua. On that date, I will go to my home and I will retire as Chief of the Armed Forces of Nicaragua, in order that our country may have a democratic evolution and that our armed institution will evolve to the benefit and welfare of all the people of Nicaragua."

My decision had been made, and I had announced this decision before 150,000 of my loyal supporters and to the international news media. Now this was February 26, 1978, some eighteen months before my government was toppled. I was once again naïve in my thinking. I thought this was the announcement that would make Carter and the State Department happy. I thought this news would bring joy to the international press. I was mistaken.

The U.S. Ambassador had told me that his government would be satisfied if I announced that I would serve out my term, resign from the Army, and quit politics. That's exactly what I did. If Ambassador Solaun had written my speech, he couldn't have stated my decision with more clarity. Yet, that wasn't enough.

Once more I had run up against a brick wall, the kind that Carter and the State Department, with evil intent, can construct.

Chapter Eight

PEDRO JOAQUIN CHAMORRO

In a small country, such as Nicaragua, becoming well known is not difficult. To the contrary, in a nation as large as the United States, a man may be governor of his state and not be known at all in the other forty-nine states. Pedro Joaquin Chamorro was well known throughout Nicaragua. As I have previously shown, his name was recognized in most of the other nations of Central America and he had many important contacts throughout the Western Hemisphere. These contacts were primarily with the news media and, generally speaking, they were contacts created by his devotion to Leftist causes.

He was my enemy, and he wanted the world to know it. As publisher and editor of *La Prensa*, the opposition newspaper in Nicaragua, he had a vehicle which enabled him regularly to attack me, my family, my government, and everything for which we stood. Having benefit of freedom of the press, he could, when he felt so inclined, put his printer's ink to work for all kinds of vitriolic smears. He was so imbued with his hatred of me that he often went beyond the limits permitted any reputable journalist. If it served his purpose, he misrepresented facts, distorted truths to suit his own fancy, and printed lies. Such was the journalistic nature of Pedro Joaquin Chamorro.

In his boundless ambition to denigrate the name of Somoza, he saw the Sandinistas as a movement which could serve his purpose. Also, he had a penchant for Leftist-leaning people and Leftist-leaning causes. At an early date, he began a relationship with the Sandinistas that was to last until his death.

He had friends of importance, but many of these were

friends of his because they were enemies of mine. It is doubtful that Jack Anderson, for example, could have identified Pedro Joaquin Chamorro had it not been for Anderson's contact with Carlos Andres Perez, who was Chamorro's friend for many years. When Perez became President of Venezuela, Chamorro's contacts and acquaintances expanded greatly.

There is no doubt that Chamorro was in a conspiracy to overthrow my government. He was in the middle of the Sandinista movement, and he was also aiding conspiratorial efforts in Washington, D.C. We learned that a man by the name of Flynn, who was a staff member for Congressman Edward Koch of New York, was in contact with Chamorro in an effort to get sensationalism published. All of this was to be used against me. Then I began to put the puzzle together — Chamorro, with WOLA, with Koch through Flynn and Mark Schneider, and with Senator Edward Kennedy, represented conspiracy.

As my troubles mounted in Nicaragua, Chamorro became more brazen. No one could accuse this man of being timid, but as my difficulty increased his confidence grew. He became one of the key Sandinistas and this Communist-led group looked upon Chamorro as a man who could help their cause immensely. He liked to think that the Sandinistas looked upon him as a hero, but I don't believe that was ever the case. He was a disciple and he could be useful to the Left. With his newspaper and with his contacts, Chamorro did yeoman's service for the Sandinistas.

It's a contradiction of terms, but Chamorro was, at one and the same time, my enemy and my ally. He held deep hatred for me and wanted to see me crucified. Therefore, he was my enemy. His constant surveillance of my administration served as a reminder that public servants should not get out of line. Further, his daily attacks upon me proved conclusively that freedom of the press in Nicaragua was a fait accompli. Therefore, he was an ally.

My relationship with Chamorro began long before I became President. We went all the way through grammar school together, but even as small boys there was a conflict. As youngsters, we had many fights, but in our boyish fisticuffs, Chamorro never bested me. I always won. Psychologically, I think, the results of those early encounters stayed with him all of his life. When, in adult life, my name was mentioned or he thought of me, I think it triggered a mental response, and that response was hostility.

As a young man, he was implicated in the printing of leaflets in which my father came in for four-letter-word abuse. His family thought it best if young Chamorro went off to Mexico for a period of time, and he did. It was in Mexico that he received his first Sandinista-type training. He swallowed the Leftist philosophy, hook, line, and sinker. He returned to Nicaragua a confirmed radical and was convinced that the United States was the scourge of the earth. That anti-U.S. sentiment was to stay with him always.

There were others in Nicaragua who had deep animosity for me, but Chamorro won the "hate Somoza" contest hands down. Attention is devoted to him because his death would serve as a catalyst for the Sandinistas, the Chamorro followers, and those who just didn't like me. His death would inflame the international press and they would retaliate against me.

I remember the day well. It was the morning of January 10, 1978. I had completed my exercise routine, taken a shower, and was preparing for the day's duties. A telephone call came and I was advised that Pedro Joaquin Chamorro had been shot and killed. This was startling news. Although disastrous things had been happening to me, I wasn't prepared for this. I recall saying aloud: "Oh my God, we're going to have another Bogotaso in Managua."

For those who may not remember, Bogotaso is the name given the strife and violence which occurred in Bogotá, Colombia, in 1948. This rampage took place after the Liberal leader, Jorge E. Gaitan, was assassinated. It just so happened that this assassination occurred while the Inter-American Conference was being held in Bogotá, Colombia. I was in Bogotá at the time as a representative of my government, and I saw the city literally torn apart. A mass of humanity stormed from one section of the city to another, burning, looting, and pillaging. With the confirmation of Chamorro's death, I thought Managua was in for a Bogotaso.

I knew, too, that I would be blamed. After all, we were enemies and everyone knew it. His newspaper, *La Prensa*, had been used as a weapon against me, and his vitriolics were always right on the front page for everyone to read. When the news spread, and it would quickly do so, I could foresee mobs gathering in the street, searching for something or someone upon which they could apply vengeance. With this in mind, I thought it best if the police and Army personnel stayed off the streets. Anyone representing the government, I thought, would be an immediate target. So I ordered the police and Army personnel to remain in their barracks. This would avoid bloodshed.

My next thought turned to the perpetrator of the crime. Who could have committed this murder? I knew one thing for certain: No one connected with me or my administration had been involved. Even though Chamorro was a leader with the Sandinistas, my people knew he represented the opposition press and that he was not to be harmed. I had been so concerned about his safety that I recall thinking this man should have security protection. But, then, I knew Chamorro would not accept anything from me. These random thoughts were running through my mind when the first reports started coming in.

The demonstrations had started and they would continue on through the wake and the funeral. Buildings and commercial entities near *La Prensa* were really in for it. Photographs of the demonstrations and violence were flashed around the world. They were carried in most newspapers in the United States. Some of the demonstrators were carrying "Down with Somoza" signs, and these were always photographed. Also, some of the demonstrations were very well orchestrated. In many instances the mob was led by known Communists and they would give the signals for the anti-government and anti-Somoza chants. When television cameras and news photographers were filming, the mob would become very active and very vocal. Through photographs, these known Sandinstas could be identified.

This was not the first time that a death in Nicaragua had stirred the people to extreme emotional fervor. On July 23, 1959, I recall, some students in Leon were killed. This was unfortunate, as violence of this kind always is. In the incident, a simple misinterpretation of orders caused the shooting. After those deaths, there were protest demonstrations in thirteen cities in Nicaragua. After Chamorro's death, there were demonstrations in three cities, so it could have been a lot worse.

I ordered an immediate investigation, with no holds barred. I wanted to know, as quickly as possible, who was responsible and who was involved.

As things happened, I received an important break within two hours after the murder. I was standing by awaiting any news that might develop, when I received a telephone call from Luis Pallais Debayle. He is a cousin of mine and was editor of *Novedades*, the Somoza family newspaper. Luis told me he had some very important information to relate to me and it couldn't be relayed over the telephone. I told him to come to my home as quickly as possible. He also told me that he was going to bring a reporter with him, and I told Luis to bring him along.

After they arrived, Luis said I want you to hear what this reporter has to say. The reporter then told his story. He said that a few days past, a man, who happened to be married to one of his relatives, had come to his office at *Novedades* and told him that he wanted to talk to Luis Pallais. Naturally, the reporter stated, I asked him why he wanted to talk to Luis Pallais. The man said he wanted to get political protection from Luis Pallais. The reporter was surprised and asked why in the world would he want political protection. The man then said: "Because I'm going to kill Pedro Joaquin Chamorro." The reporter then told the man, "You are crazy. Luis Pallais would never give you political protection for that." The reporter then told the man not to bother him with such nonsense, and that Luis Pallais was not in Nicaragua. I then wanted to know the identity of the man. The reporter replied: "Mr. President, his name is [*Silvio*] Peña and he is married to my wife's sister."

With this information, I called the Chief of Police and gave an order to pick up Peña and to do so with all haste. Peña was then picked up at his home; and his car, which was parked in front of the house, fitted the described murder car to a "T".

Peña was then subjected to intense interrogation, and within a short period of time he blurted out the whole story. The international press never gave us credit, but, in my opinion, much credit was due. Within two hours from the time of the crime, we had the murderer and we had a confession.

Peña's story was that he had killed Chamorro under the instructions and payment of a Dr. Pedro Ramos, who managed the Plasma Pheresis Centro Americana plant in Managua. In other words, Peña was admitting to being a hired killer for Ramos.

It was a public fact that Dr. Ramos had litigation pending against Pedro Joaquin Chamorro for defamation of character. The pieces began to fall in place and the whole story unraveled. Chamorro must have been bitter because he didn't have a piece of the plasma plant which Ramos ran. Previously, two other men had endeavored to establish a plasma plant and they had solicited the assistance of Chamorro. As a result of that assistance, Chamorro was to receive a piece of the business. I was privy to a letter which verified that arrangement. Well, those two men failed in their effort and Dr. Ramos was successful. This meant that Chamorro would not have a piece of the business and he was bitter.

After Chamorro was killed, he was taken to the hospital where he was prepared for burial. From the hospital, he was taken to his home where a wake was held. From his home, the body was taken to the *La Prensa* building for another wake. In every one of those moves there were hundreds or thousands of people destroying property as they marched along. The crowd would move from one side of the street to the other, so that nothing was missed for destruction.

Since the polemic between Chamorro and Ramos and his blood bank operation was well known and had broken wide open a few weeks before the killing of Chamorro, the agitators decided they wanted to kill all the Cubans and foreigners who worked at the blood bank. There wasn't much logic to their thinking but, then, what mob has any logic at all? The way these people rationalized was that Chamorro's latest enemy was Ramos, so let's kill all the people associated with Ramos.

The Cubans and other foreigners who worked for Ramos became very frightened, and they should have been. All of these people then made a hasty trip to the U.S. Embassy where they sought protection. The mob had destroyed the plasma plant, the dwellings of the Cubans, and now they wanted the people.

The next thing I knew Ambassador Solaun was calling for an urgent appointment. Naturally, I told him to come over. This time he was asking me for a favor. Things were always different when the Ambassador wanted something from me.

He pleaded with me to approve a plan to move all the Cuban Americans to the United States. He had a problem on his hands and I knew it. I was amicable with the Ambassador and told him that posed no real problem and to proceed with his plan. So, they were all shipped out.

If one would examine the public record of *La Prensa*, it could be readily ascertained that Pedro Joaquin Chamorro thought he was the kingpin of Managua. He honestly believed that, through *La Prensa*, he could wipe the streets clean with anyone. When he directed his venom at Dr. Ramos, he chose the wrong person. Dr. Ramos became bitter as a result of the defamation which Chamorro had heaped upon him. Ramos thought his best course of action was through the courts, so he sued Chamorro. Ramos didn't know that when you sued Chamorro, he got worse. By directing more and more abuse to the plaintiff, in matters of litigation, Chamorro believed the subject of his constant public diatribe would drop the litigation. I sued Chamorro on two occasions so I was familiar with his tactics. The previously used tactics didn't work on Ramos.

Chamorro didn't understand that Ramos, being Cuban, had been brought up under a different code of ethics than had Chamorro. Obviously, he was more volatile and, apparently, concluded that "personal satisfaction" was his only recourse. At that point, he most probably decided to hire Silvio Peña to kill Chamorro.

Peña decided he needed some assistance in killing Chamorro, so he hired three accomplices. In his confession, Peña named these men and they were shortly apprehended. All alleged participants, with the exception of Ramos, were in custody. We were to learn later that Dr. Ramos had gone to Miami prior to the actual murder. So far as I know, he still resides there.

Fundamentally, the legal structure and the judicial system of Nicaragua were based upon the Napoleonic Code. This code is well known in the legal fraternity and in the viewpoint of many U.S. lawyers, this system is more cumbersome and liberal than the judicial system in the U.S.

With reference to the interrogation of the accused killers, my administration and I faced a crucial decision. The manner of interrogation and the rights of the accused were clearly defined in the legal code which Nicaragua followed. If we

made public the interrogation of these accused killers and if
we permitted all elements of the news media to be present and
participate in the interrogation of these men, we would be in
violation of the Napoleonic Code. If we didn't permit open
interrogation, members of the news media and a lot of people
would think that Peña was saying what I, or someone in my
government, had advised him to say. For me this was a
dilemma of some magnitude.

My government and I were already under attack by the news
media, and their first inclination was that, through some
means, I was involved in the death of Chamorro. It became
evident to me that the interrogation of these men had to be
open and with no restrictions to the press. So the defense
requirements, as prescribed by our respected criminal code,
were set aside. I wanted every reporter, every radio commenta-
tor, all interested parties and, through them, the people of
Nicaragua to know the truth.

For three complete days and a good part of the nights,
Nicaraguans were glued to radios and televisions. Peña and his
accomplices were made available to some fifty members of
the press, radio and television. These members of the news
media could ask whatever question they chose to ask. For sheer
drama, no "soap opera" ever produced could compare to those
three days in Managua. Each accused cried, and each man
confessed. Not one single detail of this crime was left unex-
plored. It was clearly established that Peña and his accomplices
had committed premeditated murder.

The perpetrators of this crime had followed Chamorro from
his home on that morning. As Chamorro approached an inter-
section in the desolate part of Managua, these men pulled up in
front of him. The killers then got out of their car, approached
Chamorro, and blasted him with a shotgun.

All of these details were given on radio and television.
People stayed up until two or three o'clock in the morning
listening and viewing. These defendants were interrogated by
the presiding judge, the news media, and even interested
parties. So far as I know, this type of interrogation had never
occurred before.

When it was all over, the people of Nicaragua were convinced, through the facts, that the true killers of Pedro

Joaquin Chamorro were in the hands of the law — except the newspaper *La Prensa* and the Chamorro family. I regretted circumventing the Napoleonic Code, but for me there was no other choice.

The family of Chamorro, and particularly Mrs. Chamorro, would never openly admit that Peña and his accomplices committed the murder. Mrs. Chamorro said "the system" killed her husband. In reality what killed Chamorro was his extreme attack on Dr. Ramos, a Cuban and naturalized U.S. citizen.

The Cuban reference brings to mind something which happened long before Chamorro was killed. Some years ago I decided that some exceptional officers in the Army should be permitted, if they so desired, to continue with their higher education. I inaugurated a program whereby they could obtain Masters of Business Administration degrees at the Instituto Centro Americano de Administracion de Empresas. Some of our most distinguished officers availed themselves of this opportunity.

While attending this advanced study course, one of our officers became a friend of the son of Pedro Joaquin Chamorro. In their visits, I was discussed many times and the young officer suggested that young Pedro Joaquin should come to see me. Well, he did come to see me and we had a good visit. One of his complaints against the government went back to housing construction after the earthquake. He maintained that new, expensive homes were constructed for the affluent and that this was discrimination. I explained to him that the middle class had to have housing just the same as the poor and that special credit arrangements had been made for the housing to which he referred.

I told him that nothing was given to those people. They obtained credit and they would have to meet their financial obligations on those homes. I further explained to him that much of this money was obtained through savings and loan associations for just such housing construction. Young Pedro Joaquin was obsessed with the idea that everyone who had a new house had stolen it. Many others shared that view. To some degree, I think my explanation made sense to Chamorro's son.

As I reflect on that visit and that conversation; I gave Pedro Joaquin advice which could have saved his father's life. I told him to tell his father that he could attack me, my family, and my politics but to use caution with those Cubans. I explained to him that, temperamentally, the Cubans were quite different from Nicaraguans and that his father should be careful about attacking them. The young man thanked me and left my house.

I later learned that Dr. Ramos and Carlos Andres Perez had been roommates in Cuba. It's intriguing to note that Perez and Chamorro were allies and that the former roommate of Perez had Chamorro killed.

It is intriguing to note, also, that Chamorro, although barely deceased, played a significant role in a political power play to unseat the government of Nicaragua. Inasmuch as this episode is tied directly to Chamorro's death, it should be related.

Prior to the assassination of Pedro Joaquin Chamorro, the opposition in Nicaragua began maneuvering to place me on the road of no return.

This plan began with the formation of a committee which, incidentally, was put together hurriedly. Ostensibly, this committee was to serve as a mediation team between the government and the opposition. The opposition meant the Conservative Party leadership, other minority parties, and those business people who opposed me and the government. The committee was comprised of Bishop Bravo of Managua; Bishop Salazar of Leon; Robelo, who was until recently in the junta; a lawyer by the name of Dr. Guandique; and the Bishop from Jugalpa, Monsignor Vega.

The committee spokesman called and requested an audience. I told him that I would be happy to meet with the group and an appointment was made for the early part of January, 1978.

The committee came and we had a long visit. Their contention was that the political problems in Nicaragua had worsened and there was a need for the government to solve the problem. Their voices, their demeanor, and the suggestions which were being made, convinced me that they were trying to get me in a corner. They wanted me in a position that, regardless of what I did, it would inure to their benefit and justify violence.

I told them that I appreciated their effort in a worthwhile cause, but that there were some things they should consider. First, I pointed out that we had an election coming up on the first Sunday in February, and that election should receive first consideration. If the people of Managua received word that this committee and I were having talks, they might assume that some kind of political deal was being made and, consequently, the people might decide they didn't want to go to the polls and vote. I stated further, that in the past, there had been all sorts of rumors and stories about political deals in Nicaragua; and that such a rumor at this time could be very upsetting. Therefore, I suggested, we should reconvene the meeting after the election.

The committee was taken by surprise. They didn't expect that I would use the sacrosanctity of an election to thwart their plans. We had already received word that these people had been working to organize a national strike against the government. This deviously planned meeting with me was to serve a purpose for them. They wanted to be able to report to their people that I had assumed an intransigent position and that it was impossible to work with me. This, of course, would have been another reason for calling a national strike.

These people could not show that I had done anything to hurt them. I had lived up to my word in every respect and had not reneged on anything. Therefore, they had to find some justification for the action they wanted to take. I did not give them that justification. When they left my office, I remember thinking that, at least, I had another month of peace. I was wrong about that, because between that meeting and the election, Pedro Joaquin Chamorro was assassinated. I did not anticipate that tragic event.

Immediately, the Chamber of Commerce of Managua denounced the government. In the statement released by the Chamber it was stated that there was no justice in Nicaragua. They gave no consideration to the fact that within two hours we had the assassin under arrest and would shortly apprehend his accomplices. It mattered not that all of these men confessed in public and that each was given a lie detector test to affirm his confession. What they wanted was an excuse to demonstrate against the government and Chamorro's death was that excuse.

The Chamber, without hesitation, called a general strike for the entire country. At the time the strike was called, I was at my beach home, but I realized this could be a serious matter and that some effort should be made to get the strike called off. So, I sent word to the Chamber of Commerce that I thought we should have a meeting. To my surprise, the Chamber adopted an impertinent attitude. They sent me a nasty telegram and said they would not meet with me. To me, this was a very unusual attitude on the part of the major merchants in Managua. I knew then that more was involved in this situation than an emotional issue.

The strike was ordered after Chamorro's death. Certain members of the Chamber of Commerce began making telephone calls to get all the merchants to close their doors. So the strike was on. Very early we noticed that crowds were gathering in front of the stores. It was significant to me that the workers didn't want to go on strike, they wanted to work.

When I observed that this was an owners' strike and, in reality, a lockout, I knew that those who called the strike had no force. The working people were not with them.

On the second day of the strike, my aide, Max Kelly, came to my office and said: "Mr. President, you better do something about this strike, because it's going to snowball." I told Max that I was aware that the strike could gather momentum, but I said to him: "Max, hadn't you really rather know just how strong these people are? If we make any effort to break up this strike, we don't know what we have." Max agreed with me and I told him we would just have to stand the heat. I knew that if two or three things worked, the strike would end.

I decided we should make a census in Managua to determine just how effective the strike was. We used our government facilities to take a complete census of every business in Managua. We found that out of five thousand business houses in Managua, 50 percent of them were open and doing business. We learned that all of the larger business enterprises were closed and that the smaller merchants had kept their stores and shops open. This same pattern was followed in Granada, Leon, Esteli, and Chinandega.

Government officials from many places in Nicaragua called to ask me what I was going to do about the strike. My response to all of these people was the same: "Nothing, it's their right to close their shops because it's their property." I pointed out that those facilities which provided public service would be required to stay open because that was the law.

This strike was not without bitterness. Many of the smaller shop owners were threatened, some had their businesses bombed and burned, and some were attacked. But in the end the striking owners, who had been urged by the Chamber of Commerce to take that course of action, were defeated. The strike lasted approximately two weeks.

Those striking business people didn't understand that Managua was not a sophisticated society. The residents of Managua had survived an earthquake and they knew how to obtain the necessities of life. The open markets, where fruits, vegetables, and all sorts of things could be obtained, were doing a thriving business. The small, out of the way stores were selling like crazy. The larger store owners didn't understand that they were only hurting themselves. Toward the end of the strike, some of those who had their front door closed were actually selling out of the back door.

The Chamber of Commerce, the committee which came to see me, and the opposition party misread the mood of the people in Nicaragua. These people were in no mood to overthrow the government. The combined opposition forces saw, in the death of Chamorro, what they believed to be an ideal time to force a change in government. While their opposition rallies were drawing only 10,000 people in a city of 600,000, rallies supporting the government would draw as many as 150,000. That should have told these people something, but it didn't.

The assassination of Chamorro threw the opposition coalition off schedule. They obviously planned to use their mediating committee and the demands of this committee as a means of discrediting the government of Nicaragua. Using the committee, they would show that I was not responsive to the will of the people and, thus, the government should be changed. As part of the package, they were making plans for a nationwide strike. Chamorro's death caused the group to make their move before they were fully prepared. Prepared or not, the move would have failed. The people of Nicaragua were behind me and the government. The opposition learned this the hard way.

After the strike was over and after the election on February 8, 1978, I contacted the committee and advised them that I was ready to meet with them again. I was advised that they didn't want to meet with me and, naturally, I wanted to know why not. Their answer was: "It's too late." They were really saying that I had whipped them, and that a meeting at that point would serve no purpose for them. They simply didn't have the support of the people and they knew it.

Even in death, Pedro Joaquin Chamorro played a role in the political life of Nicaragua. The opposition coalition believed his death would assist in implementing their plans to gain control of the government. They overestimated Chamorro's followers, so the strike failed and the plan went awry.

With reference to Chamorro, my conscience is clear. I wanted his killers caught and they were. When I left Nicaragua, they were all still in jail. And, as I mentioned earlier, Ramos is in Miami.

The ghost of Chamorro was to haunt me until I left my country. Immediately after his death, the international press blamed me. Even with the confessed killers in jail and even with all the evidence presented which included the arms that were used to kill Chamorro, a confirming lie detector test, and the testimony of others who had been approached by Peña to assist him in the murder, the Chamorro family, through *La Prensa*, and the biased news media, continued to implicate me. Most of them barely touched on the incarceration of the confessed killers. The people of Nicaragua knew the truth, but the outside world never got the word.

Pedro Joaquin Chamorro, newspaper publisher and a leader with the Sandinistas, died from the blast of a shotgun at the age of 53.

Chapter Nine

THE OAS AND DECEIT

After we had repelled the October, 1977 Sandinista attacks on Massaya, San Carlos, and the Honduran border, we had cleaning-up operations to do in those areas. As a result of these operations, we had patrols all along the border between Costa Rica and Nicaragua. We asked our local commanders in those border areas to request that Costa Rica notify them when Costa Ricans would be coming across the border. In such a manner, our commanders would have advance notice and they could give proper attention to the Costa Ricans who would be crossing the border.

The Minister of Security for Costa Rica, a Mr. Mario Charpentier, decided to take approximately twenty-five news people on a boat trip down the Rio Frio, in order to show them that there was no military operation on the Costa Rican side of the border. As this boat, with Charpentier and the newsmen aboard, approached the Nicaraguan border, one of our military planes appeared on the Nicaraguan side and spotted the boat heading for San Carlos. The pilot of the plane signalled for the boat to head for the local checking point, but the signal was not heeded. Either Charpentier was not aware of our border crossing directives, or he chose to ignore them.

After the boat failed to heed the signals given by the pilot, the Nicaraguan airforce officer then fired two warning rockets. Of course these rockets did not hit the boat because they were meant only as a warning. The boat, with Charpentier and his guests, returned immediately to Costa Rica.

The propaganda which resulted from that incident was

unbelievable. The Costa Rican news media claimed that they were attacked and that Nicaragua had used violence against them.

Costa Rica requested a hearing before the Organization of American States and the hearing was granted. The OAS decided it should send a peace commission to investigate the incident. Nicaragua gladly acceded to the OAS request. We saw the OAS as a significant organization and one which was a guarantor of peace in the area. We wanted the peace commission to come because we believed it would give the commission an excellent opportunity to see what was really going on in Nicaragua.

The commission came and promptly began their fact-finding duties. After their study was completed, the formal report was issued. The findings of the commission indicated the rockets had been fired from Nicaraguan soil but they had landed on Costa Rican territory. At that point, the OAS fact-finding commission condemned Nicaragua as the aggressor.

From that moment forward, I felt the United States was out to get my neck. A member of that committee was the U.S. Deputy Ambassador to the OAS, Robert White. Incidentally, this is the same Robert White who is now U.S. Ambassador to El Salvador. This is the same Ambassador White who issued a statement of great comfort to the Communist Party in May, 1980. From his important position of U.S. Ambassador to El Salvador, he told the world that the problems in El Salvador were being created by the "Right," and if those people thought that because they were anti-Communist the United States would help them, they were badly mistaken.

It was obvious to me that Ambassador White was completely biased against Nicaragua. With White on the commission, it was impossible for Nicaragua to get a fair hearing. So far as Nicaragua was concerned, his position would never change. Even so, we were happy that the OAS had taken a position under the article of The Peaceful Resolution of Conflicts in Latin America.

As conditions progressively worsened for Nicaragua, we went back to the OAS. We were a founding member of that organization and we felt it our duty to inform the organization of outside intervention in the domestic affairs of Nicaragua.

By this time, the OAS delegate from Venezuela had assumed a strong anti-Nicaraguan posture. He continually heaped verbal abuse against me, my family, and Nicaragua. His harsh and abusive language was unprecedented in the OAS. Until this day, no other member of the OAS has been subjected to the verbal diatribe such as the Venezuelan ambassador leveled against me and my country.

As was I, most of the delegates were flabbergasted. In much of his language, the Venezuelan attempted to use cute wording. Many of us wondered, and some aloud, where were the serenity, the seriousness, and the solemnity of this organization? Especially since this was a very serious matter. This was not a fight between two small countries. A principle of importance was involved and the reputation of the OAS was on the line.

It was clear, then, that Venezuela was violently opposed to Nicaragua. That country was out to get us. It was obvious that no one was ready to defend the principles of the organization and the rights of other members, namely the rights of Nicaragua.

We tried to explain to the OAS that we were having regular raids into Nicaragua from bases in Costa Rica. How true this was. People were coming across the border raiding, stealing, and burning farms. After the acts of violence and terrorism, the perpetrators would make a hasty retreat to their sanctuary in Costa Rica.

The evidence presented, the documentation afforded fellow OAS members, and our expressed fear and concern all went for naught. We concluded that this was not a judicial endeavor but that it represented political machinations. And it must be unmistakably understood that the moving force in those political maneuvers was the United States. Venezuela took her clue from Uncle Sam.

I need not remind anyone that the Ayatollah Khomeini, in his flagrant violation of international law, could easily have learned his lesson from Jimmy Carter. It is most regrettable that innocent U.S. citizens must suffer at the hands of a religious fanatic. However, Jimmy Carter set the example and, therefore, Khomeini probably feels he is beyond the sanctions of international law.

Because the United States violated the very precepts of the

OAS, our ambassador in Washington, Sevilla Sacasa, had a direct confrontation with Ambassador White. In no uncertain terms, Sacasa told White what he thought about his abominable behavior and the attitude of the United States. Ambassador Sacasa was dean of the entire diplomatic corps in Washington and wasn't afraid to speak his mind. White reported the conversation to his superiors in the State Department and, as a result, the United States considered a formal protest. Apparently, though, the State Department was well aware of the biased U.S. attitude, because nothing further was said.

After the border incident to which I referred, Costa Rica had a change in presidents. In May, 1978 Daniel Oduber stepped down and Rodrigo Carazo stepped in. It was my thinking that I should do everything within my power to get along with the Carazo Administration. I didn't want trouble out of Costa Rica, and I didn't want Costa Rica to cause trouble for Nicaragua. On three different occasions, I sent my Foreign Minister to visit with Carazo. I wanted to establish a meaningful dialogue with my neighbor to the south. On one occasion, Carazo sent his Foreign Minister to visit me and I took him to lunch at my beach home.

I had good relations with Oduber and hoped to establish good relations with Carazo. Even though, in the not too distant past, he had made a rather damaging statement about the Somozas.

Just before Carazo became a candidate for the presidency in Costa Rica, he had visited Nicaragua. He was there to address a business administration class. During that address Carazo said: "The presidents of Costa Rica have always been elected due to the money which the Somozas had given them for their elections." That comment should have told me more than it did. It wasn't the truth and was designed, I think, to hurt me. Carazo was probably surprised that I didn't retaliate with a remark which could have been damaging to him.

Our efforts for good neighbor relations with Carazo and Costa Rica failed. The Sandinistas continued their raids into Nicaragua, with the knowledge that they had a safe haven in Costa Rica.

Now, back to our meeting in the OAS. Nicaragua wanted to

have a permanent peace commission with military attachés assigned to Nicaragua and Costa Rica. If you can imagine, Costa Rica said she would not accept military attachés because she had no army. That was a ridiculous answer. The military attachés were not going to be there to fight. They were going to be in both countries to observe. It just didn't make sense to me. It occurred to me, however, that Carazo probably didn't want them because, to a great degree, the military people were removed from politics and they could recognize guerrilla activity if they saw it. Well, naturally, Carazo didn't want that. He wanted no military personnel but he did want people who were politically motivated. After the objection from Costa Rica was received, the OAS, in total compliance, decided to send only civilian observers.

The OAS observer team sounded fine to Nicaragua until we saw the makeup of the observer team. We wanted people who could be neutral and impartial, and they proposed anti-Nicaragua people who were also against me personally. One of the delegates on this team of observers was to be from Jamaica, a Socialist country; a delegate from Panama, already our known enemy; a delegate from Colombia, who was later dismissed by his own government for writing a favorable report on Nicaragua; a delegate from Paraguay; and a delegate from one of the small Caribbean nations — I think it was Grenada. I knew that Paraguay would be fair, so the observer team stacked up three to two before it ever came to Nicaragua.

Nevertheless, the team was sent. Early during their stay, they requested to see the controversial border area in Costa Rica. We knew this was the Sandinista sanctuary area from which the terrorists could stage their raids into Nicaragua. Naturally, we thought the team should see the area. Carazo and the Costa Ricans said, "No, you can't see that area because it's our military reservation." Now this is the same Costa Rica that didn't want military observers because she had no army. Yet for some strange reason, she had a military reservation area.

Here again, we found the international cards stacked against us. These cards were being shuffled by Venezuela and dealt by the United States. The kibitzers were members of the international news media. Nicaragua happened to be an unfortunate player in a game in which she had no way of

winning. The shuffler, the dealer, a majority of the players in
that deadly game, and the kibitzers were determined to play by
their own rules. And these rules violated all ground rules, all
guidelines, and all requirements which had been previously
established. What I'm emphatically stating is that these participants thought it was "fun and games" if they did irreparable
harm to accepted international law, so long as Nicaragua bore
the brunt of the international lawbreaking procedure. This
was our untenable position. It was a sad day for Nicaragua.

The American public should be aware of these important
international transgressions of the past, so they may better
understand events of today. It appears they have been treated
like so many sheep. When Carter and his administration ring
the bell, or send the sheep dogs out to bark, the American
public is expected automatically to change its course. With
Nicaragua, Mr. Carter violated every precept of international
law and, in so doing, played a significant role in turning my
country over to the Communists. In Iran, the shoe is on the
other foot, and Mr. Carter doesn't know what to tell the
American people. He rings the sheep bell and he sends out the
sheep dogs, but the American public is not as obedient as he
expected them to be. It is obvious that Mr. Carter created this
mess, and it's just as obvious that he started with Nicaragua.

There is one big difference in this international lawbreaking game. Mr. Khomeini has the Soviets dealing the cards and
stating the rules. Those unfortunate American hostages, who
happen to be pawns in this particular game, will be released
when the Soviet Union relays its message to the shuffler, and
the shuffler happens to be the Palestine Liberation Organization (PLO). Nicaragua was in an OAS game in which there was
no way to win. I know how Mr. Carter felt when he was advised
about the rules of the game in Iran.

So far as the OAS observer team was concerned, I first
thought it would be most beneficial to have them in Nicaragua.
Albeit, I recognized that certain members of the OAS, such as
Venezuela and the United States, were against us. I knew that
other members were fair and took seriously their responsibility
in that organization. I felt the presence of the OAS in
Nicaragua would give us an opportunity to demonstrate to all
that we were abiding by the law. My government and I wanted

these people to know that we were doing everything in our power to maintain peace and avoid a bloody conflict. In this OAS mission, it was of paramount importance that it be made clear to the world that we were on the receiving end of a revolution being exported from Costa Rica.

The violation of international law was never more apparent. It occurred to me that, based on the actions of the OAS in Nicaragua, one member nation could never again have the due respect of another nation. Each nation, henceforth, could follow its own course and forget international law. It didn't occur to many of these member nations that they might one day be under attack from an outside force and need the protection of an international judicial body.

We had the OAS observers but the violent raids continued. The havoc wrought by these Costa Rican-based terrorists ran into the millions of dollars. The steers and cattle stolen in Nicaragua would be sold at the public market in Costa Rica. I remember on one occasion these same Sandinista terrorists stole one thousand steers from a rancher in Nicaragua and ran them across the border into Costa Rica. One of my friends in Liberia, Costa Rica, advised me that the steers were being sold on the public market.

The steers could all be identified by this rancher's brand, so there was no question about rightful ownership. A formal complaint was filed with the judiciary in Costa Rica, but nothing happened. The Nicaraguan rancher never received any money or restitution of any kind for his stolen cattle. It was our understanding that the Costa Rican Minister of the Interior, Mr. Chavania Brilles, was involved with the Sandinistas in their cattle-stealing business. That would indicate this highly illegal operation had approval in high governmental places.

So, we had the OAS. We were stuck with them and we knew their decision would be against us. The power of the United States and Venezuela was too much. With an unfavorable report coming from the OAS observer team, would the enemies of Nicaragua have enough votes to take sanctions against us? That's strange, isn't it? We weren't talking about sanctions against the international lawbreaker, Costa Rica, but against the offended nation, Nicaragua.

It was necessary for us to begin counting heads. We knew it would take a two-thirds vote to impose sanctions. Since Communist Cuba was not a member, that left twenty member nations. We needed to know how we stood with all of them.

I remember it was like walking on eggshells. We had to be cautious so as not to offend anyone. The most amazing thing of all was that we had to be particularly cautious in our relationship with Costa Rica. The Sandinista raiders could rob, plunder, burn, and pillage but we couldn't pursue them across the border. That would have been a "no no."

It reminded me of the Korean War. There the Red Chinese could cross the 38th Parallel with impunity. They could bomb, strafe, and kill U.S. military men, and then make a mad flight for the Yalu River. If the American combat pilots could catch them before they reached the Yalu, the Communist pilots were open for attack. Then a life-and-death aerial battle would ensue. However, once the Communist pilots were beyond the Yalu, they were safe. The political restrictions placed upon the American pilots forced them to turn back when that particular geographical point was reached. In other words, they were denied a necessary military stratagem — "hot pursuit." This was a unilateral restriction. The Communists could do whatever they chose to do.

This was exactly our situation in Nicaragua. The Communist terrorists could kill our citizens, burn our homes, rob our people, steal our cattle, and then flee to the safety of Costa Rica. We were denied the privilege of hot pursuit. Had we chased these revolutionaries onto Costa Rican soil, there would have been absolute revulsion on the part of the international press. Consequently, even our friends in the OAS would have turned against us, and sanctions against Nicaragua would have been passed.

Once more, Nicaragua was abiding by international law. Those who opposed us were not. There were many times when I wanted to engage in hot pursuit of the enemy, and seek out and destroy them. I had to keep telling myself to exercise restraint, exercise restraint.

In looking back, there is serious doubt in my mind that I chose the right course. If we had destroyed the Communists on the Costa Rican border, our nation would most likely still be intact. To be sure, we would have been blasted from "hell to breakfast" by the United States, Venezuela, Panama, Costa Rica, the international press, and even those friendly nations who supported us. As it turned out, being a law-abiding country didn't pay off. We were blasted anyway, and we lost our country to the Communists.

The agony of that experience will never fade from my mind. I recall sitting in my office in a state of disbelief and incredulity. I was forced to stand by while all of this international maneuvering against Nicaragua was transpiring. The Carter Administration and the Perez Administration were, in order to achieve their desired results, applying the ultimate in international pressure. They were seeking sanctions against Nicaragua, and they were lining up support. On my part, it was time for some serious calculating.

In the beginning there were twenty-one members of the Organization of American States. Cuba was voted out and that left a membership of twenty nations. These same member nations were signatory to the Rio Treaty. This was a mutual defense treaty signed in Rio de Janeiro. In our time of turmoil, the mutual defense pact didn't seem to mean too much. Neither did the mutual defense treaty which had been signed with the United States.

I knew it took a two-thirds vote to impose sanctions. It was important to know how many votes we could muster. It appeared to us that we could count on Mexico. After all, Mexico voted for Cuba in the sanction move against that country. It also appeared that we could count on Haiti, Ecuador, Bolivia, Guatemala, El Salvador, Honduras, Brazil, Argentina, Paraguay, and Chile. My count showed the possibility that we had eleven votes. I had to consider the fact, though, that Venezuela might persuade, through economic means, Bolivia and Ecuador to vote against Nicaragua. That, of course would still leave nine votes. In being as realistic as was possible, we were confident we had the votes to sustain our position.

Prior to the vote, it was necessary to send delegations to the various member nations. This was expensive and it was time-consuming. These countries needed the facts and it was our responsibility to present our case. To me, though, it seemed to be an unnecessary waste of valuable manpower and badly-needed money. To me, there seemed to be a hint of insanity about the entire procedure. I thought, this situation reminds me of the times when I went to my farm and would try to demonstrate and explain something new. Invariably the Spanish phrase "cosa de loco" would come out. Literally translated, that simply means "crazy thing." Well, to me, the sanctions to move against my country were truly crazy things.

All this time, Cuban-trained terrorists were on the offensive in Nicaragua. All this time the raids continued from Costa Rica, and invading elements from other countries were being identified. But the news reports coming out of Nicaragua gave no attention and no space to the attacks being made on the government of Nicaragua. To the contrary, it seemed the news agencies, the news correspondents, and the television networks were all competing to see who could come up with the most vicious anti-Somoza story.

Venezuela was not to be left out. She was demanding to know why evil things were going on in Nicaragua. Venezuela's questions were always asked in a manner that could leave only one answer. The question presumed the answer. In reality, all of the questions out of Venezuela were positive statements to the effect that my government and I were doing evil things. The raving and ranting never stopped. Then the quotes from Venezuela would be picked up by the wire services and spread all over. The Venezuelans were having quite a ball, and at the expense of Nicaragua.

The OAS entanglement and suspense were not over. The episode in which I found myself had been traumatic. The heavy drama was yet to come.

Inasmuch as a vast majority of the people in the Western Hemisphere barely recognize the identity of the OAS, perhaps it would be well to explain the formation of the Organization of American States and some of its important articles, as they relate to the difficult position in which Nicaragua found herself.

The Conference of American States preceded the Organization of American States. The Conference was a loosely knit organization which met at intervals of time to discuss, primarily, the various problems of Latin America. It could have been called a regional American Organization. The Conference of American States had no legal foundation and, therefore, lacked direction.

Some fifty-eight years after this regional organization was established, the Charter of the Organization of American States was adopted in Bogotá, Colombia. The birth of the OAS was in Bogotá and the year was 1948.

In the beginning there were twenty-one member nations. Those nations and the dates of their ratification are as follows:

Member Nations	Dates of Ratification
Argentina	April 10, 1956
Bolivia	October 18, 1950
Brazil	March 13, 1950
Chile	June 5, 1953
Colombia	December 13, 1951
Costa Rica	November 16, 1948
Cuba	July 16, 1952
Dominican Republic	April 22, 1949
Ecuador	December 28, 1950
El Salvador	September 11, 1950
Guatemala	April 6, 1955
Haiti	March 28, 1951
Honduras	February 7, 1950
Mexico	November 23, 1948
Nicaragua	July 26, 1950
Panama	March 22, 1951
Paraguay	May 3, 1950
Peru	February 12, 1954
United States	June 19, 1951
Uruguay	September 1, 1955
Venezuela	December 29, 1951

The foregoing represented the original makeup of the OAS. Later, Barbados, Jamaica, Surinam, Grenada, Trinidad, and Tobago were admitted. After Castro came into power in Cuba, that country was expelled.

For the original Charter, signed in Bogotá in 1948, to become effective, two-thirds of the nations had to deposit ratification. When Colombia deposited its ratification on December

13, 1951, the Charter of the Organization of American States became effective. The Charter was registered with the Secretariat of the United Nations on January 16, 1952.

Now let's take a close look at some of the noble-sounding language set forth in the Charter of the OAS. In Chapter 1, Article 1 under *Nature And Purposes* you will find the following language:

> The American States establish by this Charter the international organization that they have developed to achieve an order of peace and justice, to promote their solidarity, to strengthen their collaboration, and *to defend their sovereignty, their territorial integrity, and their independence* . . . .

No one can argue with that language. During Nicaragua's time of crisis, Article 1 was mentioned many times. But there is more — much more. One of the principles on which the OAS was founded is set forth in Article 2, subsection "C":

> To provide for common action on the part of those States *in the event of aggression.*

Oh, how we were to plead our case under this article. We were being attacked, but no one would listen.

In Chapter II, Article 3, the *Principles* of the OAS are defined. I talked about these principles so much, I could recite them in my sleep. Let me now do so while awake, with my own strong emphasis added where appropriate. Consider the following and recall how these international principles were violated in Nicaragua:

> a) *International law* is the standard of conduct of States in their reciprocal relations;
>
> b) *International Order* consists essentially of *respect for the personality, sovereignty, and independence of States, and the faithful fulfillment of obligations derived from treaties and other sources of international law*;
>
> c) Good faith shall govern the relations between States.
>
> d) The solidarity of the American States and the high aims which are sought through it require the political organizations of those States on the basis of the *effective exercise of representative democracy*;
>
> e) *The American States condemn war of aggression: victory does not give rights*;

f) *An act of aggression against one American State is an act of aggression against all other American States.*

To Nicaragua those principles, so clearly stated, meant respect for, and adherence to, international law.

In Chapter IV, once again international law is stressed.

Article 10

Every American State has the duty to respect the rights enjoyed by every other State *in accordance with international law.*

Article 11

The fundamental rights of States may not be impaired in any manner whatsoever.

Article 17

Respect for and the faithful observance of treaties constitute standards for the development of peaceful relations among States. International treaties and agreements should be public.

Article 18

No State or group of States has the right to intervene, directly or indirectly, for any reason whatever, in the internal or external affairs of any other State. The foregoing principle prohibits not only armed force but also any other form of interference or attempted threats against the personality of the State or against its political, economic, and cultural elements.

Article 19

No State may use or encourage the use of coercive measures of an economic or political character in order to force the sovereign will of another State and obtain from it advantages of any kind.

Article 20

The territory of a State is inviolable, it may not be the object, even temporarily, of military occupation or any other measures of force taken by another State, directly or indirectly, on any grounds whatever. NO territorial acquisitions or special advantages obtained either by force or by other means of coercion shall be recognized.

There should be no doubt whatsoever about the intent of those articles. Those who drafted the Charter wanted it absolutely understood that acts of aggression would not be tolerated by the OAS. That theme is expressed repeatedly, because aggression against a member State represented violation of international law. Under *Collective Security*, Chapter VI, observe the language:

Article 27

Every act of aggression by a State against the territorial integrity or

the inviolability of the territory or against the sovereignty of political
independence of an American State shall be considered an act of
aggression against the other American States.

Article 28

*If the inviolability or the integrity or the sovereignty or political
independence of any American State should be affected by an armed
attack or by an act of aggression that is not an armed attack, or by
extracontinental conflict, or by conflict between two or more American
States,* or by any other fact or situation that might endanger the peace
of America, the American States, in furtherance of the principles of
continental solidarity or collective self-defense, shall apply the measures and procedures established in the special treaties on the subject.

In all, there are 150 articles in the Charter. The articles to
which I have referred should be sufficient to substantiate the
fact that international law was observed by Nicaragua. Our
government fervently followed the dictates of the OAS Charter. The same cannot be said for Venezuela, Panama, Costa
Rica, and the United States. Those governments were in clear
violation of article after article.

There was constant aggression, militarily, economically, and
politically, against Nicaragua. Member States, namely Costa
Rica and Panama, were directly involved in the military
aggression, while the United States was indirectly involved in
each form of aggression against the Sovereign State of Nicaragua. Any interpretation of the Charter and existing treaties
would unequivocally demonstrate that Nicaragua was the offended State.

Out of the sad experience with the OAS, one overriding
factor emerged — international politics prevailed and not
international law.

Chapter Ten

THE LETTER

As of July, 1978, conditions had not improved. No matter how hard I tried, it seemed there was no way to please the United States. With Venezuela, Panama, and Costa Rica, my position had deteriorated. This is to say that they were assisting the Sandinista terrorists even more than they had in the past. We were also aware of the fact that Fidel Castro had accelerated his program of aggression against Nicaragua, because more arms, ammunition, and Cuban-trained personnel were arriving.

Then I had a call from Ambassador Solaun. He wanted to see me and, as usual, I told him to come on over. The thought occurred to me, though, that here comes bad news again. In times past, I looked forward to my visits with the U.S. Ambassador, but that was no longer the case. I thought, perhaps the Pavlovian theory is working on me. The bell rings and I want to regurgitate.

The Ambassador came in and we exchanged pleasantries. His demeanor seemed different that day. He was civil and seemed to be in a good mood. He said: "Mr. President, I have a letter for you from the White House. President Carter has written you a personal letter." He handed me the letter and then added, "You understand, of course, that the contents of this letter must not be made public."

The Ambassador's last statement was an outside curve. The contents of that letter, if publicly known, could assist me greatly in warding off my other enemies. I was not interested in a collector's item and, without being able to use the letter publicly, that's what it was. To prove my point, that letter from President Carter to me is reproduced herein and in its exact context.

I thanked the Ambassador for delivering the letter and he departed.

I had tried diligently to establish a working relationship with Perez. It will be recalled that Perez, when all the presidents of Central America were his guests in Caracas, made a special point to ask me about Pedro Joaquin Chamorro. At that time, I assured Perez that I didn't want anything to happen to Chamorro. After Chamorro was assassinated, I sent my Vice Minister of Foreign Affairs to see President Perez. As a favor to him, I thought he should have a complete report on the circumstances surrounding the death of his friend, Chamorro. Also, I wanted him to know that the perpetrators of the crime had been arrested and their confessions obtained. I'm not sure he appreciated this friendly gesture, but I felt it should be done.

With the letter from Mr. Carter in hand, I thought it wise to send my Vice Minister of Foreign Affairs back to see Perez again. Just by having the letter from Carter, I thought I had a stronger base from which to operate. A secret meeting was arranged for my Vice Minister and President Perez. The purpose of which was to arrange, at an early date, a meeting between Perez and myself.

Prior to the minister's trip to Venezuela, I had solicited the assistance of an old Venezuelan friend who had considerable influence with Perez. This was Miguel Angel Capriles, the owner of various newspapers. I felt my relationship with him was solid and if he could assist me, he would.

Under a previous administration in Venezuela, Capriles had been exiled from Venezuela, and my government granted him asylum in Nicaragua. He was treated well in Managua and during his stay, we extended him every courtesy. Therefore, I felt comfortable in asking him for assistance.

When the Vice Minister of Foreign Affairs returned to Managua, his report was not too favorable. He said he had been treated rather badly by Perez, and that Perez didn't have good things to say about me. He reported that Perez didn't see him until midnight and that it was obvious he had been drinking heavily. During the entire meeting, Perez was boisterous and conducted himself in an arrogant manner. My minister reported that Perez was so contentious and overbearing that he was personally offended. I told my minister that this was the nature of Perez and that he shouldn't be offended. One had to know the background of Perez to understand him, and I knew his background.

Nevertheless Perez told my minister he would see me. A date was set and Perez said he would send a pilot to Managua to fly my airplane to the designated meeting place.

The pilot arrived from Venezuela and we took off at the appointed hour. We flew directly to Curacao, where we spent the night. With me, I took my Foreign Minister, my aide, and a dear friend, Manolo Rebozo, who is a Cuban American. Knowing Perez, I felt the need for corroboration, so Manolo was on this trip to serve as a witness to whatever might transpire.

Parenthetically, my close associates and advisors in Nicaragua did not want me to make this trip. They felt I might never return. They, too, were aware of plots and schemes which had occurred in the Perez Administration. They thought, and with some justification, that Perez might have me killed. It was something about which to be concerned, but this trip had to be made. The very life of Nicaragua could depend upon the outcome of this trip. There was no other choice. I had to go.

After overnighting in Curacao, we took off the next morning for the rendezvous spot. As I look back on those events, the entire affair had an air of mystery. We really weren't sure where we were going. The pilot was given certain headings and then these would be changed. Finally we landed on an island, but I knew the existence of this island and recognized it. It happened to be the island where the former Venezuelan president, General Perez Jimenez, entertained. This was the General's fun spot. It was the island of Orchilla.

We landed at 8:55 A.M. and about three minutes later a Learjet arrived. Out of the plane stepped Carlos Andres Perez, the Venezuelan Foreign Minister, and my friend, Miguel Angel Capriles. Greetings were exchanged and, at that point, everything seemed cordial enough. I didn't show it but I recall experiencing an emotional surge. There I was tendering my hand in friendship to a man who wanted to cut my head off. Such a circumstance is sufficient cause for emotion.

From the ramp, where our planes were parked, to the small house where we were to meet was some distance, but it was within walking distance. From previous visits, I knew that Perez liked to walk rapidly and he did on that day. It's strange how one can recall small, insignificant matters totally unrelated to some event of great importance. That walk was thus insignificant, but I remember it well. It was as though Perez wanted to walk so fast that I couldn't keep pace with him. I remember thinking that it was good that I had lost so much weight and that I was in good condition. For some unexplainable reason, there was tension in that walk. Perhaps my subconscious was telling me that this walk was symbolic of things to come.

We entered the small house, sat down, and we talked. I recall thinking that if there was one super-selling effort left in me, now was the time to perform. I began by pointing out to Perez that I was conscious of the fact that he was against me but that his anti-Somoza feeling should be something of the past. With feeling and sincerity, I told him that I didn't want my country and the people of Nicaragua to suffer as a result of that past animosity, and that was the reason I wanted to see him.

For three hours, I gave him an accurate evaluation of the situation in Nicaragua. I wanted Perez to understand that at stake was far more than Somoza and his political future. So details were given as to the strength of the Sandinistas, the source of their training and equipment, the number of Cuban-trained Communists involved, and the influence being put forth by the Communists to take over Nicaragua.

I then told the president of Venezuela that at least some of the things I was doing in Nicaragua were pleasing to President Carter. Without revealing the details of the letter, it was disclosed that a letter had been received from Carter and in that letter he expressed the opinion that I was doing a good job. Perez came back with an unyielding retort: "I don't care what Carter says. Our position is firm and you have to go." This statement was as strong as one president can make to another president. In essence, he was telling me that he was going to have my head and that he had the power to take it. I thought back to those days when he was secretary to Betancourt, an avowed Communist, and I was aide to my father. This was his time for revenge and he was going to make the most of it.

I pointed out to him that I was elected by the people of my country just as he was elected by the people of Venezuela. Further, I stated there was absolutely no need to go through a violent situation and suggested that he have his friends come talk to me. The handwriting on the wall was becoming legible, and I felt there surely must be some way to negotiate. Perez said to me: "I think it's too late to negotiate." I came back with "Mr. President, it's never too late to talk and negotiate." He then stated that he would talk to various other Nicaraguan leaders and see if they would accept the idea of negotiation.

In thinking about negotiations, I recalled a previous conversation I had with Miguel Angel. In trying to set the meeting up with Perez, I endeavored to reach him in Caracas. I found, however, that he was in New York, so I called him there. When I talked to him, he said, "You know, General, we can arrange certain things. We can offer you the safety of your family and your property, with a guarantee of those safeguards from Venezuela, Mexico, and Colombia." He was telling me that I could trade the presidency for my safety and the money I had in Nicaragua. I didn't express myself on the telephone but I knew the validity of those guarantees.

That same topic came up at lunch on the island of Orchilla. The idea was the same that Miguel Angel had suggested — guaranteed safety for the Somoza family, guaranteed property rights, with the provision that I vacate the presidency. Had we pursued this idea, it would have been necessary for me and my family to leave Nicaragua. Our safety could not have been guaranteed in Nicaragua. However, I believe the Perez group would have raised the money to purchase my holdings in Nicaragua. Since most of my money was invested in Nicaragua, I would have been far better off financially than I am now.

Contrary to what the press reported, the most significant portion of my wealth was in Nicaragua, not elsewhere. If I had been concerned only with the power of money, I would have taken their proposal. However, all of us have values and these values vary from individual to individual. For me, there was one intrinsic value which was more important than anything else. I had to keep the Communists from taking Nicaragua. All those present at the lunch heard the discussion.

The luncheon conversation with Perez was rather weird. This was my first opportunity to explore this man's political thinking. He was, I determined, a shallow man who really didn't understand the functions of government. To his way of thinking, free elections in Latin America were a facade. He expressed an opinion that the Liberal Party in Nicaragua was not really a popular party and that the elections were controlled. I found that, in reality, he knew very little about Nicaragua and that most of his information was incorrect. At that point I remember thinking, this man has been spending too much time talking to Jimmy Carter.

At one point in the conversation, I remember Perez telling me that he knew what my problem was. He said: "You know, Somoza, your problem is that you are a soft dictator, and soft dictators can't get the job done. In Latin America," he continued, "the only successful dictators are the hard ones." I couldn't believe what I was hearing. I don't know what he expected me to say but I let the conversation drop.

It became apparent that Perez saw himself as the kingpin of Latin America. His influence with Carter was greater than that of any other president, and on that claim I had to give him a positive mark. He felt this same influence reached all of Latin America and Europe, and on that claim I had to give him a negative mark.

Another point became evident, he was not a well-informed man. Most of his knowledge was empirical, and that knowledge was limited. He seemed to resent those who had university training and education. That, I thought, is a defense mechanism because Perez only finished high school.

As we worked our way through lunch I thought, Mr. Carter has justification for being ignorant in Latin American affairs. After all, his lead man and chief advisor is the man sitting at the head of the table.

When we were returning to Managua, my minister and I had a serious and depressing conversation. It was his opinion that I did not convince Perez to withdraw his effort to overthrow me. I concurred in that opinion. I returned to Nicaragua a sad man.

On the plane I began to contemplate on a part of my conversation with Perez. Toward the latter part of our meeting he said to me: "I want it understood that everything which is said here is secret." I agreed with that request and told him I would honor his desire for secrecy. It then occurred to me that Perez was placing a lot of confidence in me. The Venezuelan elections were to be held shortly and if word leaked out about our meeting, Perez and his party could be damaged. People in Venezuela would then say that he was a two-faced double-crosser, because his public posture had been strongly anti-Somoza. Regardless of his public explanation, the open knowledge of our meeting at Orchilla would have done severe damage to his political party. In that sense, I had to admire the man for exposing himself to political danger. On the other hand, he knew that even as disappointed as I was, our meeting would remain a secret with me.

When the meeting was terminated, we walked back to our plane and headed back home on a, seemingly, long, long trip. As soon as we were airborne, my thoughts turned toward the purpose of the unproductive meeting with President Perez. Much time, effort, and money had been expended for one reason — THE LETTER.

The letter from President Carter came at a time when I needed encouragement, and particularly from the United States. I accepted this letter in good faith and presumed it had been written on a good-faith basis. Long ago I should have learned that when dealing with Mr. Carter, good faith, logic, and reasoning had no meaning at all.

I thought so much of the letter and its significance that I had sent my Foreign Minister to arrange a meeting with Carlos Andres Perez. I thought so much of the letter that in a time of strife and mounting problems, I went to Venezuela to see Perez. Now, I was on my way back to Nicaragua and I had time to take a retrospective view of that letter and what it really meant.

After reading the letter for the first time, my immediate impression was one of satisfaction. I thought, "At least, Mr. Carter is going to get off my back." That presumption was totally erroneous. As I flew back to my troubled country, the real meaning of the letter hit me. I recalled that President Perez showed no emotion at all when I told him I had received a friendly letter from President Carter.

In retrospect, I could now see that Perez probably knew the

contents of the letter before I ever arrived on the island of
Orchilla for our secret meeting. Otherwise, he would have been
most curious about the contents of the letter. As has been
related, he evidenced no interest in my communication from
Carter and quickly advised me that his position had not
changed — I "had to go." Again, my hindsight vision was
excellent. I could now see that Perez and, most likely, all of the
other conspiratorial countries had knowledge of Mr. Carter's
letter before I ever received it.

In reality, this White House letter was a ruse and ploy. When
the letter was written, it was anticipated that, as a result of the
friendly tone, I would cooperate with those forces which were
determined to destroy me and the government of Nicaragua.
This is not an opinion or a prejudiced conclusion, it's a fact.

The deceit of Mr. Carter is unbelievable. He wrote me a nice
letter on June 30, 1978 which, in essence, outlined the favorable
conditions in Nicaragua and, to his way of thinking, the good
work I was doing. Then on July 23, 1978, the *Washington Post*
quoted the Carter Administration as saying:

"We told Somoza that if he reimposes the state of siege,
closes opposition papers, or arrests opposition political leaders,
the U.S. Ambassador will be recalled and we might break
relations. We are not intriguing against any opposition faction.
The fact is, we're against Somoza."

It would be well to take a look at that famous letter which
Mr. Carter had Ambassador Solaun deliver to me.

THE WHITE HOUSE
Washington
June 30, 1978

Dear Mr. President:

I read your statements to the press on June 19 with great interest and
appreciation. The steps toward respecting human rights that you are
considering are important and heartening signs; and, as they are
translated into actions, will mark a major advance for your nation in
answering some of the criticisms recently aimed at the Nicaraguan
government.

I am pleased to learn of your willingness to cooperate with the Inter-
American Commission on Human Rights. I believe that multilateral

institutions can be a most appropriate and effective means of protecting human rights and alleviating concerns expressed about them. I sincerely hope that your government can rapidly reach agreement with the Commission on a date for their visit.

The Commission will be favorably impressed by your decision to allow the members of the so-called "Group of Twelve" to return to peaceful lives in Nicaragua. The freedoms of movement and of expression that are at stake in this case are among the central human rights that the Commission seeks to protect.

You have spoken about a possible amnesty for Nicaraguans being held in jail for political reasons. I urge you to take the promising steps you have suggested; they would serve to improve the image abroad of the human rights situation in Nicaragua.

I was also encouraged to hear your suggestions for a reform of the electoral system in order to ensure fair and free elections in which all political parties could compete fairly. This step is essential to the functioning of a democracy.

I would also like to take this opportunity to encourage you to sign and ratify the American Convention of Human Rights. I have signed this agreement and am working hard to have my country ratify the Convention.

I look forward to hearing of the implementation of your decisions and appreciate very much your announcement of these constructive actions. I hope that you will continue to communicate fully with my Ambassador, Mauricio Solaun, who enjoys my complete confidence.

Sincerely,

JIMMY CARTER (Signature)

His Excellency
General Anastasio Somoza Debayle
President of the Republic of Nicaragua
Managua

So that Mr. Carter cannot accuse me of misquoting or distorting the context, the complete letter is herein reproduced.

If possible, place yourself in my position at the time Mr. Carter's letter was received. With knowledge of the broad-based attack upon me and the government of Nicaragua, the resulting emotional sensation would be one of satisfaction. It would have to be concluded that this was a nice, friendly letter from the President of the United States. On closer scrutiny, however, the communication assumes the characteristics of an "epistle from Euripides."

It is quite obvious but it should be pointed out that in this one letter, Mr. Carter mentions "human rights" six times. That was his vehicle for the destruction of me and the government and he would ride this phony issue until the day the Marxists took over Nicaragua. It is now recognized that on human rights, Carter's creation of calamity, Nicaragua fared as well, if not better, than any country in Latin America. It just so happened that Mr. Carter and his coterie of Leftists were determined to depose me and the government of Nicaragua, and the issue of Human Rights served their purpose.

I was somewhat surprised that he praised me for permitting the "Group of Twelve," as he put it, to "return to peaceful lives in Nicaragua." That subversive group was permitted to return to Nicaragua due to the immense pressure from the United States. Mr. Carter knew they were preaching armed revolution and, yet, he and the State Department placed me in a position where I had to permit their return. It has now been publicly revealed that the "Group of Twelve" was actually part and parcel of the Sandinista movement. I knew that in 1978 but there was no way I could convince the State Department of the U.S. or President Carter.

When I first read the letter, I should have paid closer attention to the following sentence: "You have spoken about a possible amnesty for Nicaraguans being held in jail for political reasons." Again, deviousness rears its ugly head. Mr. Carter is referring to people who were tried in an open court of law and were convicted for various felonies. The human rights people called them "political prisoners," not I. If Mr. Carter had checked with the citizens of Nicaragua, he would have learned that the government didn't throw people in jail for political beliefs. In my desire to get along with the United States, I had agreed to consider amnesty for certain of those people who *they* said were political prisoners.

It will be recalled that this was exactly the same position Mr. Carter took with the Shah of Iran. He forced the Shah to release from prison convicted Communist subversives. Those released prisoners led the movement that destroyed not only the Shah, but Iran as well.

In the quiet atmosphere of my home office, I reread Mr. Carter's letter and I recalled that, according to the media and the human rights people, Nicaragua was holding thousands of political prisoners. What a monstrous lie that was. When the Communist terrorists captured the National Palace and demanded the release of all political prisoners, they could come up with only fifty-nine people. The record will reveal that all of those were convicted felons — with some being admitted murderers. But Mr. Carter, the U.S. State Department, and the Human Rights Commission wanted amnesty granted to all those criminals. Mr. Carter made that very clear in his letter to me.

So what did the letter really mean? From a productive viewpoint, it meant nothing, just nothing at all. From a duplicity viewpoint, it had significant meaning. While praising my efforts to satisfy the United States, Mr. Carter was stepping up his attack against me and the government of Nicaragua.

On the airplane, my Foreign Minister and I discussed the value of Mr. Carter's communication, and we concluded that the letter which brought an ephemeral ray of hope was, in reality, designed to give us a false sense of security. We then discussed the entire meeting with Perez — from the beginning to the end.

After agreeing that we had not convinced Perez, my minister and I then came to the realization that plans had to be changed. We were then realistic in our appraisal of the difficulties we faced. Our enemies would not let up. Instead, we felt their efforts to destroy me and my government would soon be accelerated. To both of us, the imponderable question was, how do we face all of these enemies alone?

For a few minutes, I was quiet and pensive. My companions on the airplane did not disturb me. They could see I was in deep thought. I knew what they were thinking, because their faces revealed their thoughts. They were thinking the General has been in tight spots before and he has always come out of it, so surely he will find a solution. My associates had this kind of trust and faith in me.

My thoughts, for those few quiet minutes, turned to history. I speculated as to how many presidents, or how many leaders of the many nations in the world, had found themselves in an apparently inextricable trap but, somehow, emerged successfully. I recalled my history at West Point and thought of the Athenian Republic.

Athens was a Greek City State whose allies, in her hour of need, had deserted. As the massive Persian Army, led by Darius, the great Persian King and army general, approached Athens they expected the city to surrender. Darius underestimated the will and ingenuity of the Athenians. So, on the plain of Marathon, in 490 B.C., the tiny Athenian Army met and defeated the mighty Army from Persia. Thoughts of the battle of Marathon had always inspired me and that moment when I needed it, inspiration came again.

I looked up at my companions and said, "I have a plan." In reality, it wasn't a great plan but it was the only course I thought we could take. The plan involved a change in our approach to military preparedness. Prior to that time, Nicaragua had allocated only ten percent of her budget to the military and police. That was one reason Nicaragua kept her financial house in order and had excellent progress. We were not spending an extraordinary amount of our national income on defense. Well, this was indeed an emergency and, facing our enemies alone, we would have to start a crash military preparedness program and that would take money. The plan was outlined and all agreed it was the thing to do. History discloses that Nicaragua did not have her Marathon. However, the Greeks did not have the misfortune of facing Cuba, Russia, Panama, Costa Rica, Venezuela, and the United States at the same time.

At any rate, the plane trip back to Nicaragua set in motion a plan. We may not have convinced Perez, but we convinced ourselves of what we had to do.

I learned later that Perez had double-crossed me. He had my word that I would divulge nothing which happened at the meeting, nor would I reveal that such a meeting had been held. I kept the word. For Perez, though, the secrecy agreement was unilateral. Which really meant that he could tell about the meeting but I couldn't. From a source inside the State Depart-

ment, I learned that my plane had hardly become airborne
when Perez dashed off a message to President Carter. In this
secret message, he not only related details of the meeting but
gave President Carter a totally erroneous report. He said that I
was adamant, intransigent, and impossible to deal with. He
indicated to Carter that he tried to find a common ground
from which a compromise could be effected, but with Somoza
there was no way to compromise. This should serve as a caveat
to all those who think presidents will not lie. This is an example
of duplicity, double-dealing, and back-stabbing at the highest
level of government. Carlos Andres Perez, President of Venezuela and Carter's man in the South, proved to be a double-
crosser and a liar.

Chapter Eleven

TERRORISM IN MANAGUA — PHASE TWO

After I returned from the trip to the island of Orchilla, a meeting was set up with our intelligence people. They wanted me to go over a report they had. This report indicated that a group of terrorists were going to take the Ruben Dario Theater. The terrorists, according to the report, had selected the night of a special celebration and the theater was due to be filled to capacity. We had received similar warnings in the past, but this one had the earmarks of being authentic.

The security forces were deployed and we were prepared. But nothing happened. Either the terrorists were alerted to our knowledge of their plan, or they simply called it off.

We were certain there would be another attempt to seize hostages, similar to the tactics employed at Chema Castillo's home. It's impossible to safeguard everyone, but we took every possible precaution to neutralize the terrorists.

Our principal preoccupation was the safety of the Congress. As a measure of safety, we assigned a detail of ten men to guard Congress. These were special police and they had received counter-terrorist instructions. Even so, there might have been some confusion attendant to the regular routine. Just prior to August 22, 1978, we changed our military and police commander for the city of Managua. When this happens, the new commander always inaugurates a few changes which, to his way of thinking, create more efficiency and better police control. At any rate, on the morning of August 22nd everything seemed to be moving in a normal manner.

At approximately 8:30 A.M. I was seated at my desk going

over some reports when I heard what sounded like automatic weapon fire. For a moment I felt a little jumpy but, in those days, we all were. A few moments later a call came in with the report that shots were being fired in the National Palace.

This report caused me immediate concern. The security of this particular building was most important. The National Palace housed many prestigious functions of our government. Included in these were the Senate, the Congress, the Ministry of Finance, the Ministry of the Interior, and the office of the Comptroller General. Within moments I had confirmed that a fire-fight was indeed going on in the National Palace. This could mean only one thing — the terrorists had struck again. Only this time they would not have forty-five people; there would be far, far more.

My first reactions were instinctive. It was as though I had undergone special training for this specific attack. My office was not a scene of chaos where ten telephones were ringing and aides and staff members were running over each other. There were no loud voices. The movies have a way of depicting such emergencies and the movie version and reality didn't match. I knew whom to call and I knew the military people who would be needed. Calls were put through and within moments, the key people for this emergency were on their way to my office. One old movie line did come to me, "This is no drill."

As I think back to that dismal morning, we could have stopped the Sandinistas in their tracks. Fate, destiny, or, if you choose, luck ruled otherwise. At the exact same time of the attack on the Palace, a group of our Special Forces was actually driving around the National Palace enroute to the firing range. These men were capable and they were tough. If given the opportunity, they could have taken the terrorists. The group did stop and got out of the truck to see if they could be of assistance. Due to the confusion, they were advised to leave the situation to the local police. So a Special Forces team, which could have liquidated the terrorists, left the scene.

To an outsider and one removed from the scene, it might appear that our guards for the National Palace were not alert and, apparently, were taking their responsibility too lightly. Such was not the case.

For the terrorists, the decoy technique worked perfectly. In all, there were fourteen terrorists involved. They had dressed themselves in the training uniform used by our Army. In appearance, you couldn't tell one of theirs from one of ours. They carried American-made arms which had been obtained in Costa Rica. Among these were M-1 rifles, semi-automatics, and automatic weapons. Additionally, they had, through some means or other, acquired a truck similar to ours and had painted it exactly like the Army trucks of Nicaragua.

With those uniforms, those weapons, and that truck with numbers on the side, their disguise was perfect. To the guards at the National Palace, they looked like the real thing. Further, these guards had been witnessing the movement of many troops through that area. These troops were on their way to the southern area where much fighting was in progress. Therefore, it was not unusual for these guards to see a truck loaded with soldiers moving around the National Palace. Also, there is no way you can personally know all the men in an army of seven thousand soldiers. Putting all these factors together, it spelled disaster for those inside the Palace and death for the guards.

The terrorists were well trained. Their plan had been formulated with attention to every detail, and each man knew what he was supposed to do. They dismounted from the truck and formed up sharply. Then, in columns of twos, they briskly walked to the main entrance of the National Palace. Many observers were later to say they thought these were Special Forces men on an assigned mission. As this group approached the main entrance, the guards asked them what they were doing there. Their reply was short and deadly — a burst of concentrated fire. Once more, gunfire and death opened a door in Managua for the terrorists. This time, however, it was a much larger door.

After they were inside the Palace, they proceeded to close all the doors. In order to obviate a counterattack by our forces, the terrorists entered the House of Representatives, ordered all members to put their hands in the air, and pushed them in front of all windows. This way the congressmen would serve as human shields for the killers. When I think of their barbaric behavior, it reminds me of the horrible stories of the Middle Ages. In that age, it was not unusual for humans to be sacrificed. To those sadistic militants, the value of a life was nothing.

When the fire-fight terminated and the terrorists had control of the Palace, I received a telephone call from Luis Pallais Debayle, my first cousin and presiding officer of the Congress. He told me they had been overpowered by the terrorists and that, as he talked, a gun was being held to his head. While Luis was talking to me, I could hear other voices in the background. I remember very well hearing the voice of Eden Pastora, known as "Commander Cero," screaming out orders. He was in command of this operation, and he was directing his people to shoot anyone who didn't obey orders immediately. I also remember the voice of Dora Maria Tellez, the only woman in that room, telling Pastora to calm down. Those voices I could hear while Luis Pallais was talking to me.

Luis Pallais then informed me that the terrorists wanted all of the Bishops who were in Managua at that time to come to the Palace and act as mediators.

We started searching for the Bishops. It occurred to me, however, that the terrorists now wanted to include Bishops other than Obando Bravo. The reason was quite obvious. In the previous hostage confrontation, Bravo had been singled out by the terrorists because they felt he was one of them, he assisted them, and he identified with their revolutionary movement. This time, though, they wanted to take some of the heat off Bravo, so they asked that all Bishops in Managua serve as mediators. As things happened, there were three Bishops in a meeting in Managua, Monsignor Salazar from Leon, Monsignor Lopez Fittoria from Granada, and Monsignor Obando Bravo from Managua.

Contact was made with all the Bishops, as well as the Red Cross. The first order of business was to remove the dead and wounded from the Palace. The Bishops and the Red Cross proceeded with that gruesome task.

The big question in my mind was, how many people were the terrorists holding as hostages? Since the take-over was early in the morning, I knew that hundreds of people would be in the Palace paying their taxes to the Internal Revenue Service. Often, early in the morning there would be as many as a thousand people in the palace attending to their taxes. I had a fairly accurate count of the number of governmental employees, which included members of Congress and their staff people. I knew that number would be approximately five hundred. When a count was finally determined, we learned that the terrorists were holding fifteen hundred people as hostages.

The hostages came from every social and political stratum of Nicaragua. In our Congress, it will be recalled, 40 percent of the representation went to the minority party. So the Conservative Party had almost as many of their people in that building as we did. Then there were all those citizens who were there performing their civic duty. Naturally, there were many women and children being held. To the terrorist kidnappers, this made no difference whatsoever. It was made clear to all that any untoward movement would result in death. Those most in danger, however, were Luis Pallais and the other members of Congress.

One recollection I have of that ordeal relates to the mentality of the Communists. It was proven then, and it holds true today, that the Communists are experts in the use of psychology. Further, the Communists proved to me that not only are they capable in psychological warfare, but they are willing to utilize psychopaths to achieve desired results.

While these events were unfolding, I had time to cogitate on terrorist activity. That day it was Managua, but in which city and in which country would acts of terrorism occur tomorrow? With a hand-in-glove relationship between the Soviet Union and the PLO, no country is safe from terrorist activity. We had to face up to this problem in Managua, and all society, sooner or later, will have to meet the terrorist threat head-on. The politicians of the world have not been determined enough to find a cure to that social threat.

During the time I was waiting for the Bishops and waiting for the negotiations, I thought what a mammoth control situation we will have. It appeared to me that every government office would require a controlled security entrance. Then I thought, how can you have a controlled situation for every public office and every public meeting? There are theaters, football stadiums, political rallies, social events, and so on ad infinitum.

It was a staggering thought and I had to conclude that it would be physically impossible to provide such controlled security. To the people of Managua, I thought, freedom of movement and freedom of assembly are extremely important, and if terrorist activity continues, these freedoms will be a thing of the past. Fear would possess each individual and their confidence would be driven from them. Frankly, I was appalled at the way these members of the human race could, without one trace of feeling or humanity, shoot their way into the National Palace and then threaten to destroy fifteen hundred people. I couldn't believe that the value of human life had sunk so low.

Not that it brought me any comfort, but it occurred to me that we were not alone in this situation. I had made inquiries and had talked to other people about this horrible menace which stalked the civilized world. Why, for example, were the public offices in West Germany all protected with sandbags in the midst of a peaceful situation? The Germans told me it was part of their way of life and it gave them a modicum of security. Now, what an injustice! The West Germans have security regulations and requirements much tighter than Nicaragua's, and Nicaragua gets clobbered by the press for trying to control terrorism. Don't misunderstand, I like and admire the West Germans. I use this merely as an example of press prejudice.

In our time, the finger of guilt should be pointed straight at the Palestine Liberation Organization and Yasser Arafat. The PLO has trained terrorists to operate around the world and their course of destruction and death is known to all. There are those who now want to paint Arafat with respectability. Nonsense! His trained killers were, and are now, in Nicaragua. *Long before my government fell, the Sandinistas had a formal agreement with the PLO.* Sandinista terrorists trained with Arafat and they came back home to put their training into practice.

What Mr. Carter fails to realize is that no one has given more support to the Ayatollah Khomeini than the PLO and Yasser Arafat. Are Carter and his administration so blind that they cannot see the connection between Khomeini and Arafat? Who was the liaison between Moscow and Khomeini? The answer, of course, is Yasser Arafat. Who directed the entire scenario with the helpless American hostages in Iran? That's easy, Arafat. The PLO represents the epitome of terrorist expertise and, yet, it was this same Mr. Carter who removed the label of "terrorist" from the PLO. That action by Mr. Carter in 1977 made it much less difficult for the PLO officials to visit the United States. The next thing of importance for the PLO was to open an information office in Washington, D.C., and that they did. That made it much easier for the PLO to export terrorism in the Western Hemisphere and, at the same time, the organization could put on a front of respectability.

To take this absurdity further, on October 9, 1978, the *Chicago Sun Times* reported that the United Nations Secretariat was spending $500,000 in a public relations campaign to "create a moderate image for the Palestine Liberation Organization in the United States and other Western countries." Mind you, Arafat represents expert terrorists and killers, and the United Nations will spend $500,000 to improve his image! Further, the U.S. taxpayer will help to foot the bill.

At this point, logical questions would be, why did the PLO and Arafat want to spread terrorism in Nicaragua, and why would the PLO want to overthrow the government of Nicaragua? There are thousands of miles between Palestine and Nicaragua, and the two areas have so little in common. Each area is different socially, economically, religiously, and in mode and style of living. Then why Nicaragua?

The answer lies in the United Nations and it goes a long way back in time. Nicaragua supported Israel from its inception as a nation. Upon Israel's admittance to the United Nations as a bona fide voting member, Nicaragua supported that nation. In so doing, Nicaragua was supporting and upholding international law as represented by the United Nations. This unwavering support of Israel put the PLO and Yasser Arafat squarely on Nicaragua's back.

The PLO played a direct role in training Sandinista terrorists. I suffered and my people suffered from this foreign-supported subversion. I can only speculate as to how much influence these acts of terrorism had on the ultimate fall of my government. As I look back on that fateful August 22, 1978, I realize even more today that we had a hell of a situation on our hands.

The Bishops, Pastora, and his other terrorists began negotiations. The demands were made known and the Bishops reported to us. They demanded the release of fifty-nine prisoners who were in jail, a cash payment of several million dollars, and the publication and broadcast of their own *Manifesto*.

For those who have never had the unfortunate experience of negotiating with Cuban PLO-trained terrorists, the "manifesto" should be of particular interest. To the Marxist terrorists, the publication and dissemination of their ideas assumed great importance. *La Prensa*, the opposition newspaper, carried the *Manifesto* on the front page, and, as will be noted, the banner headline began: WAR REPORT No. 1, OPERATION: "DEATH TO SOMOCISMO."

The *Manifesto* was printed as follows:

WAR REPORT NO. 1
OPERATION: "DEATH TO SOMOCISMO"
CARLOS FONSECA AMADOR
COMMAND "RIGOBERTO LOPEZ PEREZ"
TO THE PEOPLE OF NICARAGUA AND THE WORLD

THE MANEUVERS OF THE NEW SOMOCISMO

The great social, political and economic crisis, which the Nicaraguan society is going through at the present time, is also reflected on the state of uncertainty of the financial bourgeoisie.

The violent process originated on [sic] October 1977 by the FRENTE SANDINISTA DE LIBERACION NACIONAL (F.S.L.N.) brought out into the open the latent political and economic contradictions among the different sectors and classes of the productivity: the industrial bourgeoisie, the business people, the small and medium bourgeoisie, the factory workers, the farm workers, etc. Briefly, all of them had been colliding in one way or another with the economic, political and military structure of the somocismo. Likewise, these social classes and sectors would draw out their own doctrines in the light of such events, however, the financial bourgeoisie was a stranger to this experience, since they never took any action when the opportunity so demanded. Confused by the great number of those new phenomenons [sic], they probably thought the crisis would easily be dodged by the dictatorship.

From all the bourgeoisie groups, only the financial sector had stayed on the fringe of the anti-somocista process. They never proposed a real way out to the crisis and, on the contrary, they sheltered themselves under absolute silence. The contradiction between the financial bourgeoisie and the somocismo structure never reached a critical point, as it occurs in the other sectors; and this is a logical theory that explains the absence of the financial sectors in the anti-somocista process. Besides, this withdrawal relieved them of the responsibility to take sides, and clearly define their interests. This is understandable while the crisis was not affecting them directly yet.

Nevertheless, the situation of the country has turned more difficult for the somocismo each day, raising the crisis to a higher level and causing deep confusion in productivity, financial and commercial areas. The economic interests of the financial capital are already unbalanced and it is in this instance where they try to take advantage by using the progressive activities of the masses in the latter months of the year 1977 and the current year.

It is not coincidence that in the analysis document which was elaborated by the financial bourgeoisie sector, alternatives are formulated in order to facilitate the stabilization of the system. This document of limited circulation, which was denounced by the Group of the "Twelve" in a press conference in Managua, reflects the somocista character of the financial bourgeoisie.

We are not going to consider every judgement expressed thereby; but we will observe what the financial group claims for itself — better say — whatever had not been accomplished in the daily struggle. In the first place, they project a political and economic strategy to remedy the social crisis. On the economic problems, they suggest unfavorable situations . . . . "77-78 has not been the most favorable, but not the worst either" . . . however, on the political situation, they add: ". . . politics, in the first place, and the financial situation of the government together with the lack of attention due to the specific problems in productivity, have worsened the inflationary and unemployment situation that had already been developing, and which are making the present time a very delicate one, since this situation is supportive of possible popular rebellion." . . . Such theory tries to explain a total crisis tied up to the political phenomenon and isolating the economic factor from reality. In trying to make the general crisis look like a purely individual phenomenon they state that: ". . . the government each day has to resort to a greater repression in order to handle the situation, neglecting not only the attention demanded by the economic activity, but also the security of the people, and administrative vigilance,". . . which means that the moment the country is living, is of a struggle between a group of "agitators" and the somocista government. The financial bourgeoisie expresses that they have nothing to do with this conflict and consider themselves as victims of the same when they say it affects their interests . . . . ". . . the present time and its perspectives, do not supply the private sector — better say — the capital, with assurances in order to develop its activities, and much less, program their future . . . ."

The dominant bourgeoisie of the financial capital wishes to put an end to this prevailing situation by intervening directly or indirectly. With this purpose in mind, they plan a strategy which tends to weaken in the first place the presence of the FRENTE SANDINISTA in the activities of the masses. ". . . In the specific situation in which we are living, is it fear of extremists and certain means of communication . . . ? Do we have to please them . . . ? This is one alternative . . . . Do we have to support the government . . . ? That's another alternative. We could also take a patriotic attitude oriented to restore the peace and preserve the moral standards of the Nicaraguans, without limping to authorities. And who could act under such alternative . . . ? Practically only the authentic capitalists of the Private Sector and the Church. The counterpart would be the President of the Republic and the General Staff of the National Guard . . . ."

This leads us to conclude that these men share the thesis that if the FSLN is not destroyed by the somocista National Guard, they could not go on counting on the same force either, since at the end of the battle both forces would come out exhausted from the struggle. And it is here, precisely where the financial bourgeoisie will be present as the only capable establishment to manage the Estate. So, they would become the decisive political force in the present crisis.

But anxiety is one thing, and reality is another. The financial bourgeoisie believes that the strategy which makes them establish an alliance with Somoza puts an end to the existence of the FSLN, in the way that the political contradiction between the "agitator" group and the somocismo decreases as a result of its "pacific" presence. They do not realize that the plans do not represent simple partial reforms but, great social, political and economic transformations of a strong popular content.

The plan of the financial capital represents the reactionary feeling of a bourgeoisie which was born and was developed under Somoza and the somocismo. This explains the fact that they lack their own political parties, with support of the masses, and that they find themselves forced to lean on parties they have things in common with like the Conservative, the Constitutional Movement and in the maneuver, they also try to get the Church involved.

This political strategy of easy fitting confirms the isolation of the financial bourgeoisie in the anti-somocista struggle process.

But applying the plan of alliance with Somoza, with the General Staff of the National Guard, with the more reactionary parties and with the sectors of the Church that are willing to play the game, they will be burying themselves with the dictatorship.

The financial bourgeoisie, as a result, defines itself in its secret document [*the title of which is not given*] as an ally of the somocismo; and the people of the country and other anti-somocista sectors should unmask and crash it.

To conclude we only need to point out the fallacy of the United States through their Embassy in Managua. We can prove that the document denounced by the Group of "The Twelve" is the work of the Yankee strategists that desperately look for a way out with the great capital, the General Staff of the National Guard, the Clergy, some reactionary parties and Somoza.

The declarations after the denouncing of "The Twelve" come to give shape to what until that moment fell in the field of speculation. Church pronouncements in their Episcopal Conference, in their Presbyterial Counsel, and in their Archbishop Obando Bravo, point out that: "The ruler could, as an option within the politics of mutual concessions, promote with his retirement the formation of that national government, which when obtained the support of all, would prevent Nicaragua from falling into an absence of power and anarchy which is always a threat during the changing process."

Declarations made by Eduardo Montealegre Callejas, President of the Group BANIC; and Alfredo Pellas, head of the group Bank of America; of William Baez Sacasa, of INDE, through "The Voice of the United States," all supporting the position of the Church should be added up to the proposals that a few days before Ramiro Sacasa Guerrero, (ex-Minister of Somoza, chief of the Constitutional Liberal Movement and cousin of Somoza) had made in a public meeting opening up the possibility of dialogue with the tyrant, as long as he removed his brother and his son from their posts as heads of the National Guard.

On the other hand, the words of Luis Pallais Debayle affirming that the dialogue has already been started and the insistent attitude of Somoza to talk and negotiate are evident proofs of a REAL dialogue in which, in the first place, the most representative elements of the great capital requested the tyrant to resign. As it is obvious . . . the people of the country are not, nor will be considered, since it is to those people they want to impose a SOMOCISMO WITHOUT SOMOZA.

The FRENTE SANDINISTA DE LIBERACION NACIONAL denounces to the people of Nicaragua and the world, the alliance of the most reactionary sectors of the Yankee government, the great Nicaraguan capital, the General Staff of the National Guard and the tyrant Anastasio Somoza who intend to negate through dialogue or coup, the heroic struggle of the Sandino people.

The FRENTE SANDINISTA, calls all the democratic and revolutionary forces to fight for the installation of a real democratic popular government, in which all the Nicaraguans will be given participation without sectarianism of any kind.

THE GUARD AND SOMOZA ARE THE SAME THING
NO TO DIALOGUE, YES TO THE UNITY OF ALL ANTI-SOMOCISTA FORCES
NO TO COUP — YES TO THE COMBAT OF THE ANTI-SOMO-CISTA FORCES
LONG LIVE THE POPULAR DEMOCRATIC GOVERNMENT
Free Country or Death.

For the National Direction of FRENTE SANDINISTA DE LIB-
ERACION NATIONAL (F.S.L.N.)
Daniel Ortega Saavedra, Victor Tirado Lopez, Humberto Ortega
Saavedra.
Someplace in Nicaragua. August 1978.

Other significant portions of the *Manifesto* are as follows:

By this time, sectors of the capital, businessmen, and industrial
people planned a national strike on the back of the people. They
thought that with a protest of such magnitude, the overthrow or
resignation of the tyrant was almost certain and as a result they would
be in charge of the anti-somocista process, damaging the great influence of the sandinista masses.

The FRENTE SANDINISTA of SELIM CHIBLE EDMUNDO
PEREZ, FILEMON RIVERA, ROBERTO HUEMBES and CARLOS
REYNA calls the working classes to increment the daily struggle, to
make arms from every tool they have on hand, to give death to the ears
of the neighborhoods, to execute the National Guards who live or visit
the neighborhoods and whom we know have participated in aggressive
acts against the people, to build barricades, throw bombs to the patrols
of the Guards, all in all, punish at all times the criminal forces of
Somoza.

On the other hand, the anti-somocista struggle process has counted
on the participation of the wealthy people of the Conservative Party
who at all times, have sold themselves to Somoza; on the newly rich
people of the Social-Christian Party who have been begging Somoza
for legalization of their party, and on the old rich people of the
Constitutionalistic Liberal Party who endorse the dialogue with Somoza. The other rich people like the business people, industrialists and the
great financial capital, until a few months ago, did not have a major
participation in the anti-somocista struggle. It wasn't until after the
offensive of October 1977 that these forces — with the exception of
the financial capital — were all in favor of the dialogue with the
tyrant.

As the somocista crisis worsens, the financial sector itself becomes
against Somoza. And, we see coincident positions among these sectors
which look for a non-violent way out and demand the tyrant for his
resignation.

These men want a way out in which the National Guard would be the
lifesaving element. In reality, they do not trust the people but the
Guards and they indicate so in their declarations published in the
newspapers of the country and broadcast by the radio. Mr. Alfredo
Pellas as well as Eduardo Montealegre Callejas are worried about their
own interests and say nothing about the people. They say, they do not
agree with Somoza and propose as a solution to negotiate the resignation

of the tyrant, without mentioning the Somocista National Guard. Now, in order to keep talking, we want to make clear that we do not oppose the participation of the financial capital, of the commercial capital, of the industrial capital, and of all the types of capitals that could exist in our country, in the anti-somocista struggle. We agree on their participation — what we do not agree on is in letting them be the ones to set the conditions on the resignation of Somoza. It was they who have for a long time supported Somoza with an accomplice silence which — in their sectarianism — made them deny support even to Pedro Joaquin Chamorro, surely, can't come now and try to impose formulas to protect their own interests forgetting the popular interests.

The FRENTE SANDINISTA publicly acknowledges the support that Venezuela, Panama, Mexico, Costa Rica and Cuba have rendered to us in the struggle of our country. We want to mention the liberal sectors of the Government of the United States, who have made their voices heard condemning the somocista tyranny and protesting against the support the U.S. Government has given to the somocismo.

This was the *Manifesto* which appeared in all the newspapers in Nicaragua, and was given on all radio and television stations. Its wording and content follow the Communist line. And I repeat, Pedro Joaquin Chamorro, on a daily basis, said worse things about me and the government than were enunciated in the *Manifesto*.

It should be noted that two names are given prominence in the headline of this manifesto, Carlos Fonseca Amador and Rigoberto Lopez Perez. Carlos Fonseca Amador, it will be recalled, was the Soviet-trained Communist who stole the name Sandinista and was later killed in a battle with the Guardia Nacional. Rigoberto Lopez Perez was the man who assassinated my father.

The last paragraph of the *Manifesto* should be of particular interest. This *Manifesto* was published on August 24, 1978, and yet Mr. Carter maintained, even after the Marxist victory, that he had no knowledge of foreign participation in the overthrow of the government of Nicaragua. Not only does the revolutionaries' *Manifesto* publicly acknowledge the support that was rendered by Venezuela, Panama, Costa Rica, and Cuba, but it also gives thanks to "the liberal sectors of the Government of the United States . . . ."

When the package for release of the hostages was presented, I was really rather surprised. I thought they would ask for more. I thought they would ask for my resignation. In retrospect, I think they were more interested in the release of the prisoners than anything else. Next in importance was the worldwide news coverage they would receive. They did command the attention of the worldwide news media. Around the Inter-Continental Hotel it seemed as though an international press convention was being held. At that point, I think money was third in importance. Let's take a closer look at these demands.

The prisoners, whose release was demanded, were all convicted felons. Each one of them had been tried in an open court of law and found guilty. Their crimes ranged from murder to assault with a deadly weapon. The fact that the terrorists could come up with only fifty-nine names should have surprised the world. According to so many press reports and the Sandinistas, we had thousands of political prisoners. I tried to explain the magnitude of that lie but until the terrorists submitted their written list, I was not successful. All of the prisoners named were alive and in good health. This is also contrary to certain press reports and claims by the Sandinistas. Remember, my government had been accused of torturing and killing political prisoners. That was one more ploy used by the Communists and my other political enemies to inflame public opinion against me.

Now that the Communists are in control of Nicaragua, there should be no political prisoners and there should not be torturing and killing. On this one issue, Dan Rather, Mike Wallace, Alan Riding, and Karen De Young should have had a field day. As I have already shown, some three thousand men, women, and children of Nicaragua have been tortured and killed since the Sandinistas assumed power. These crimes are a matter of record but the "bleeding heart" press says nothing. Additionally, over eight thousand men and women are political prisoners. Their number is so great that many are exposed to the elements and all of them are on a starvation diet. What a difference!

We knew the terrorists would ask for much more money than they expected to receive. When negotiations reached the money stage, we simply advised them that we had $500,000 on hand and if that wouldn't suffice, negotiations would have to be delayed. Pastora replied that his men were exhausted from lack of sleep and he would take the money.

The demand for publication of their "manifesto" came as no surprise. In compliance with their demand, every newspaper, every radio station, and every television station ran the document. Much of the document dealt with a personal attack upon me, my family, and people in my government. It bothered me not one whit for this information to be disseminated. The manifesto did reveal that these terrorists were Communists and I was happy for the people of Nicaragua to know their true identity.

With reference to air transportation out of the country, terrorist group number two had an entirely different approach than terrorist group number one. This group had apparently made travel arrangements in advance. Is that surprising? We were advised to contact Omar Torrijos and Carlos Andres Perez for their transportation. They didn't want to go to Cuba because they had graduated from Castro's level of cuisine. No, this time they wanted Panama and Venezuela and, apparently, Omar and Carlos Andres knew, without any instructions, what kind of plane to send for their compatriots — the terrorist killers of Managua.

In the personalities that were negotiating, there were four components. These components were Luis Pallais, my first cousin and a hostage, the terrorists, the Bishops, and me. Luis was, at all times, with the hostages in the Palace, and he was under the constant threat of death. I had always admired Luis Pallais but never more than during that crisis. He had been wounded in the head by gunfire when the terrorists burst into the House chamber. Additionally, he was being constantly pressured because he was my first cousin. He is a man of courage. Then there were the Bishops who shuttled between my office and the terrorist-held Palace.

Since 40 percent of the Nicaraguan Congress was made up by members of the Conservative Party, I felt certain the leadership of their party would want to join my political party in condemning the terrorists who were holding the National Palace. I then talked to the Conservative Party leadership and pointed out, as forcefully as I could, the need for political unity. In this crisis I knew the country needed to show a solid political front. Before talking to these leaders, I tried to think of one valid reason why they wouldn't agree to my proposal, and not one reason came to mind. So, I was surprised when they indicated to me that they wanted to think about it. What was there to think about? Communist terrorists were holding the entire Congress and one thousand citizens as hostages, and they wanted to think about condemning such criminal activity. I thought then, there is more to this than meets the eye.

What I didn't know, but later learned, was that these leaders left my office and went straight to the U.S. Embassy. Out of that meeting in the U.S. Embassy came their reply. On the recommendation of the U.S. Embassy, the Conservative Party refused to join the Liberal Party in condemning the terrorists.

It seems unbelievable that such a thing could happen, but it did. To me, it indicated a lack of wisdom on the part of the opposition party, and it was evidence that the U.S. would do nothing to assist the government of Nicaragua. Actually, it was evidence that the U.S. was aiding the other side — the wrong side.

When a situation arises such as the one with which we were confronted, two theories are generally advanced as solutions to the problem. Those criteria were applicable to the thinking which existed in Managua.

It should be understood that in our Army we had an abundance of leadership and courage. That statement is unequivocal, and it applied to the lowest grade of the enlisted category as well as to our outstanding group of officers. Some of the toughest and most capable officers I have ever known served in the Guardia Nacional of Nicaragua. When the terrorists succeeded in taking the National Palace and killing the guards, it was only natural that these fighting men wanted to retaliate.

One problem about which I never had to concern myself was finding volunteers for a dangerous mission. The problem I had was offending some officer or enlisted man by not selecting him for a hazardous assignment. So with the terrorists holding the Palace, there was an immediate move by a segment of the Army to storm the Palace and kill all the terrorists. Plans, strategy, and individual assignments were being discussed before I was aware of it. That's how eager they were. Even though many of them knew they would be killed they wanted permission to storm the Palace. That was one theory as to how we should handle the terrorists.

The other theory stood by negotiation as the proper solution. It has been my philosophy that the first consideration should be the lives of those being held against their will. With that in mind, proceed to consider all options. If the attack route is chosen, what would be the risk to the captives as well as your own men? In other words, which side holds the strategic advantage? Then, too, the mentality of the terrorists must be given consideration. Would they actually kill the hostages at the first sign of military aggression? If your conclusion happened to be in the affirmative, you would be condemning hundreds to death by permitting a military assault. I was convinced that the terrorists would attempt to kill every member of the Nicaraguan Congress at the first hint of an assault. I knew their mentality and I knew what kind of terrorist training they had received. With all the members of Congress crowded in one room and with wild-eyed terrorists holding hand grenades and automatic weapons at the ready position, an attack by my troops would mean death.

I was not alone in these deliberations. We had a meeting of the Cabinet, a meeting of the General Staff, and a meeting with the political leaders of the Liberal Party. I solicited the views of each person because, in this delicate matter, I wanted input from all of these people.

I requested that the military submit their plan. I wanted to know their plan of action. But there was one critical element that would positively determine which theory prevailed. How much time? I had to know how much time would elapse from that first moment of attack until the National Palace could be secured. I was told a minimum time of twenty minutes. That did it. Direct military action would not be attempted. I knew that within twenty minutes, all members of Congress would be dead and that casualties among those poor one thousand souls, who just happened to be there, would be extremely high. The only answer was to negotiate. When that decision was announced, I remember, General Jose Ivan Allegrett and Major Mike Echanis stormed out of my office in anger. They wanted to lead the charge. These military men were afraid of nothing. With twelve to fourteen men they were going to take the Palace and, you know, they would have done it. Others were upset with my decision. But my conscience is clear.

I, alone, would have been held responsible for the deaths of all those people. Most of them had been my personal friends for years and years. Then there were the families. Those dear people would never have forgiven me for not having exercised restraint and good judgement. And in the final analysis, who amongst all our people could ever have confidence in a man, or believe in a man, who gave no consideration to the value of a human life? For the remainder of my days, I shall live with the thought that I chose the correct theory and I did the right thing.

Negotiations moved along smoothly. Pastora and the other terrorists were concerned about time, just as we were. We knew the terrorists had been without sleep for several nights and they were edgy and jumpy. At that point, my main concern was that one of our people might make a wrong move and the slaughter would begin. Therefore, it was important that we expedite negotiations.

Agreement was reached on all points. A time had been set for departure from the National Palace, a bus and driver had been designated to carry the terrorists and the accompanying hostages to the airport; the $500,000 was counted and would change hands at the airport; the criminals would be released from the Tipitapa jail at an appointed hour and taken by bus to the rendezvous point at the airport; Luis Pallais, the Minister of the Interior, and other hostages would be released at the airport; the planes from Panama and Venezuela would be parked at the end of the take-off runway and, when boarded by the terrorists and the released criminals, would quickly take off. Those were the details.

Each part of the negotiated agreement fell into place. All buses, with hostages, terrorists, and criminals, departed at the appointed time. They drove to the airport without incident. At the end of the take-off runway were parked the planes from Torrijos and Perez. Torrijos had sent an Electra and Perez had sent a C-130. The C-130 is a huge airplane, so ample air transportation had been arranged. Luis Pallais and the other hostages were released, the money changed hands, and a motley group of Communists and convicted criminals went aboard the planes. In a few minutes the planes were airborne and we had come to the end of another living nightmare.

This chapter of Managua terrorism had begun at approximately 8:30 A.M. on August 22, 1978. The planes left for Panama and Venezuela at 10:00 A.M. on August 24, 1978.

The terrorists and criminals received a hero's welcome in Panama and Venezuela. They were wined, dined, and feted as celebrities. Pastora, the leader of the Communist terrorists, was honored with a special meeting with President Carlos Andres Perez.

When it was all over, I experienced a letdown. I had not slept and I was running on nervous energy. But I wanted to think: What did it all mean? What we had just been through in Managua, I thought, represented a complete breakdown of international law and order. I knew that so long as terrorists, airline highjackers, and international law violators had a safe haven, these crimes would continue. The fact that the Managua terrorists had two countries which welcomed them made me angry inside. Cuba, of course, would have made three countries, but Cuba takes criminals from anywhere. Panama and Venezuela were looked upon as civilized countries and, yet, they not only welcomed the terrorists, they aided and abetted a criminal cause.

So long as we have this kind of international behavior, there will be acts of terrorism. Only when there is no safe port, only when there is no haven in which criminals can find sanctuary, will acts of terrorism cease. On August 22, 1978 it was Managua, Nicaragua. I remember thinking that tomorrow it could be New York, Rome, or Buenos Aires. A sad commentary, I thought, on our international code of justice.

Chapter Twelve

THE BAY OF PIGS — A FIASCO

Basically, I have limited my discussion of events and activities to that period dating from the Managua earthquake on December 23, 1972 until the present. In this endeavor, there must be one exception and that exception is the fiasco at the Bay of Pigs in Cuba. I direct attention to that military operation due to the fact that so much misinformation has been printed about it, and because that abortive effort relates directly to the ultimate Communist take-over in Nicaragua.

Nicaragua was directly involved in this military endeavor at the behest of the United States. The participation of Nicaragua should not be surprising, when the record is examined. It was well known in Washington and all of Latin America that the Somozas were staunch anti-Communists. My father, my brother, Luis, and I took part directly, indirectly, and openly to defeat Communism in Central America. These anti-Communist activities were conducted in collaboration with the United States and always with the approval of the United States. This is not an allegation, but a matter of fact and record.

Our concern over the success of Castro in Cuba is well documented. Leaders in the government of Nicaragua knew he was a Marxist long before that fact was recognized by the United States. At that time, my brother, Luis, was President of Nicaragua and I was Chief of the Army. We had sounded warnings about Castro, but those warnings went unheeded.

It was not surprising, then, that in 1959 a man from the United States, who went by the name of Colonel Robertson, came to my office to see me. He told me there was an operation in the wind to overthrow Castro. We discussed the idea thoroughly, and he then asked me for my opinion. I explained to the Colonel that I was Chief of the Army and would need to discuss such an important matter with the other leaders in government. We did have a serious discussion on the matter and came to the conclusion that such an undertaking was in keeping with our philosophy, and that we should agree to assist the United States in its effort to overthrow the Communist regime in Cuba. Furthermore, even at that early date we could foresee difficulty with Cuba.

Shortly after Castro came to power, Ché Guevara had sent wave after wave of guerrillas to Nicaragua. We captured these men and later released them.

Our conclusion to assist the U.S. was based on the fact that we recognized the evils of Communism, and unless we assisted our friend, the United States, we could expect nothing but trouble from Castro. Our decision, then, was in the best interest of Nicaragua, our people, and the United States of America. When those interests were served, we concluded, it had to be the right decision.

Colonel Robertson was an impressive individual. He stood about three inches over six feet, was an ex-combat marine who had fought in the Pacific during World War II, and was half Cherokee Indian. The Colonel had a military bearing and exuded confidence. When I gave him our decision, he was pleased but self-restrained. Thereupon, he took his leave and headed back to the U.S.

In a short time, the Colonel was back in Nicaragua and in my office. He told me he had given my favorable report to the appropriate people and they wanted to know how we planned to assist in the Cuban invasion. I told him that Nicaragua would serve as a staging point for the invasion forces. With that point clear, we proceeded with a discussion of plans.

As a military condition, I stipulated that the plans should go no further unless it was agreed that the Cuban airforce was knocked out before the actual invasion began. Unless this military step was taken, I knew the invasion force would not have a chance. With my own eyes I had witnessed the effect of air control in the Costa Rican revolution of 1955. I saw an entire battalion completely bottled up because they did not have air support. With an invasion from the sea, it was essential that the enemy be deprived of air support. Colonel Robertson agreed with my evaluation and departed for the United States.

The Colonel was doing a lot of flying because he was back in Nicaragua in a few days. He reported to me, and advised me that President Eisenhower agreed with my evaluation. Eisenhower was now well aware of the Cuban threat to the Western Hemisphere and was kept informed on each phase of the military planning.

Since this operation had to be kept absolutely secret, the appropriate site was most important. It had to be a location removed from cities or towns. Actually, it had to be a place virtually uninhabited, and yet possess port and air facilities. There aren't too many places in the world which could meet all of those requirements. In Nicaragua, we had just such a location — Puerto Cabezas.

There was much work to be done. There was an airfield at Puerto Cabezas, but it was not in good condition. Therefore the airfield received priority attention. Our time was limited and we had to work fast. The success of the operation depended on secrecy so none of those working at Puerto Cabezas were permitted to leave during one week before the launching. Naturally, they didn't know about the planned military operation against Cuba, but we couldn't take any risks in that regard. In a military sense, they were confined to base. We prepared Puerto Cabezas for the influx of men, aircraft, and ships, and it was accomplished with total secrecy. Not one word leaked out. I was proud of our people.

We were up against another problem and that was time. Within a period of forty-eight hours, all troops, airplanes, and ships had to assemble, regroup, receive assignments, and move out as an invasion force. It was timed to the minute. This small dot on the map, Puerto Cabezas, had assumed importance. Not only was it the rendezvous point for the invasion force, but the surprise air attack on the Cuban airforce was to be launched from Puerto Cabezas, whose code name in this operation was "Happy Valley."

While all of this was going on, I remember thinking that there wasn't another country in all of Latin America which would have accommodated the United States to such a degree.

This knowledge gave me a sense of pride. It meant two things: One, we shared a common ideology; and two, Nicaragua had unchallenged faith in the United States of America.

Between the time of my first visit with Colonel Robertson and the actual invasion attempt, the United States had a national election. Richard M. Nixon was defeated for the presidency by John F. Kennedy. As I stated previously, Nicaragua had good relations with Republican administrations and Democratic administrations. I knew the Nixon faction but I didn't know the Kennedy group. It was suggested that I go to New York and meet Mr. Joseph Kennedy, the patriarch of the Kennedy clan.

I remember the visit as though it were yesterday. We met in Mr. Kennedy's apartment at Grand Central Station. It was an amiable visit, and I liked him. Mr. Kennedy was not loquacious. I think taciturn would more aptly describe him. To me, he seemed down to earth and not at all pretentious. I wanted to establish a good relationship with the Kennedys and, more than that, I wanted them to be briefed on Central America. Mr. Kennedy was interested in everything I had to say, and he assured me that his son, John, would receive the benefit of that briefing.

I thanked him for the time he had given me and for his understanding. Then, with an air of complete confidence, he looked at me and said: "You know, General, my son is going to win this election and I extend to you an invitation to the inauguration." At that time I wasn't sure he was correct in his prognostication, but after that first Tuesday in November, 1960, I remember thinking, Joe Kennedy knows his politics.

In January, 1961, I did go to Washington for the inauguration of John F. Kennedy as President of the United States. However, that was not my real reason for going. The inauguration was a pretext. I went to Washington to have a personal visit with Allen Dulles, head of the CIA.

The visit with Dulles lasted for one and one-half hours, and, in my opinion, it was mutually productive. I had to get the answers to several questions, and, if anyone knew these answers, it would be Mr. Dulles. I wanted to determine if the Bay of Pigs operation was still on. With a new administration, I could not be certain if the plans of the Eisenhower Administration would be carried to fruition. I wanted to know if President Kennedy had been well briefed on the operation, and if sufficient air power would be provided to knock out the Cuban airforce.

When these questions were posed, Mr. Dulles said: "Excuse me for just a moment." He then went to the extreme end of his office where there was a telephone. He made a telephone call and was back in a few minutes. Dulles said to me: "I have just checked with the White House and everything is set." I told him that was fine, but I had to be sure. Mr. Dulles sat silent for a moment and I could readily see that he was in deep thought. I can see him now. He had a pipe in his hand and had his chair turned at an angle. I was observing every move he made, and he appeared to have decided on what he wanted to say to me.

He placed the pipe on the desk, rotated his chair so that we were facing each other, and said: "Now, General, what is it that you want out of this?" My response was: "Nothing, Mr. Dulles, not a damn thing." Then, I pointed out to him that Nicaragua had always enjoyed an excellent relationship with the United States and that that relationship meant much to me and my country. Some of the new breed of Liberals with the new administration had already started making snide remarks about my brother, Luis, and the government of Nicaragua, so I thought that it was a propitious time to get that matter resolved. So I said: "Mr. Dulles, you could do one thing. You can tell those Liberals to get off my back and get off the back of Luis Somoza's government."

Mr. Dulles had treated me well and I was satisfied with the meeting. I returned to Nicaragua and gave a full report to Luis. Everyone seemed pleased with the results of my trip to Washington. Upon returning to Nicaragua, I had another invitation and this one pleased me greatly. Chiang Kai-shek had invited me to visit with him in Taiwan. I happily accepted that invitation. The trip would take me to Taiwan, Japan, Korea, Hong Kong, India, Iran, Israel, and Italy.

Parenthetically, at the time Mr. Carter was planting peanuts in Georgia, I was doing a lot of goodwill work for the United States and the Western world. Wherever I went on that trip, I was to carry the message of the West. I set out on that extended trip the day the invasion force left Puerto Cabezas for Cuba.

Back at Puerto Cabezas, everything was in a state of

readiness. I had personally inspected the facilities and was pleased with what I saw. This was around April 1, 1961, and I felt it was time to advise the political leaders of Puerto Cabezas about the coming event. I told them that in approximately one week we would have a rendezvous of foreigners at Puerto Cabezas and that I wanted everyone to "stay put." I explained to these political leaders that Puerto Cabezas would serve as the jumping-off point for an invasion of Cuba. I wish Americans today could have a view of those enthusiastic Nicaraguans. They were proud, through and through, to be partners with the United States on such an important mission.

As the time approached for the arrival of the invasion troops, I felt tense and excited. The only way you could reach Puerto Cabezas was by air or sea, and nothing was moving in or out. It was sealed off from the outside world, and, so far as I was concerned, there would be no foul-ups. There were none.

Then they started to arrive by air, and the excitement mounted. These Cubans were on a mission of destiny and they felt it. One thousand and three hundred men arrived, all well trained, well equipped and, to say the least, all eager to get on with the mission. The troop-carrying planes landed, one after the other, and in the darkness of night. It was closely coordinated, because then the ships began arriving in Puerto Cabezas. The combination of airplanes dropping out of the sky on tiny Puerto Cabezas, the arrival of ships in the harbor, and a knowledge of the importance of this mission made chills run up and down your spine. You could feel it with all the people who were there.

To add another dimension of excitement, the bombers started arriving. Sixteen or seventeen B-26s arrived. These were the planes which would knock out the Cuban airforce — on the ground.

Also, there were tons of ammunition, rockets, and bombs. It seemed incredible that all those arms, weapons of war, and needed supplies could be assembled in one week. But it was done, and in total secrecy. Mr. Castro had no idea as to what was happening in Nicaragua.

It was important to me to be at Puerto Cabezas and make a final inspection. As I viewed the materials and visited with the men, my thoughts turned to the Normandy invasion. This, I thought, was no Normandy but to Latin America and the Western Hemisphere it could be just as important. I knew the threat of a Communist Cuba and, to me, Castro represented the same evil force as did Hitler. In the beginning no one took Hitler seriously, but Normandy was exemplification of what happens when an evil man is taken too lightly. To a lesser degree, the same could be said of the invasion force gathered at Puerto Cabezas, Nicaragua. Only at that jumping-off point, it was Castro who was misjudged and taken too lightly.

While at Puerto Cabezas, I had a conference with the three leaders of the invasion force. The military commander was San Roman, the political leader was Artime, and the Navy commander was Garcia. Each commander was prepared for this mission and each realized the danger involved. They all recognized that without control of the air, the mission was doomed. However, they had been assured of U.S. air support, so they were confident of success. I went down to the docks and visited with the troops there. They were eager to move out.

Then I went back to the briefing room for final consultation with the American advisors. All of the Americans were using assumed names. My concern was the same as it was when I first talked to Colonel Robertson — knocking out the Cuban airforce. I asked the Americans how they were going to get those 1,350 men off the beach with sixteen old, worn-out airplanes. I pointed out to them that these airplanes would only fly at 250 knots, and unless the Cuban airforce was knocked out, they would be facing jet fighters. Also, the plan was to take the bombers into the Bay of Pigs in four different attack groups. The fallacy in the planning, I stated, was that there would be only four airplanes at the battle scene at any one given time. I told the Americans in no uncertain terms that unless the U.S. Navy came through with jet-fighter coverage, as promised, the mission would be a horrible failure. After that last briefing session, I went back and told Luis that the planning was bad and I didn't think the invasion would be successful.

The next day I took off for Los Angeles on the first leg of my trip to Taiwan and the other countries. That was the same day the invasion troops boarded the ships in Puerto Cabezas for their ill-fated mission.

I was in Los Angeles when the first reports started coming in. The first reports stated that there had been an uprising in the Cuban airforce. That erroneous report most likely came about because the invasion aircraft were painted with the Cuban insignia. The news reports went on to say there was a revolution in Cuba. I was sweating blood and had a "gut feeling" that things had gone wrong.

The rest is history. The bombers actually did a pretty fair job in their surprise attacks, but Cuban jets did get airborne and they made mincemeat out of those slow, cumbersome bombers. In the meantime, the U.S. aircraft carriers stood off Cuba and never launched their fighters. One fighter squadron, VA-34, known as the "Blue Blasters," did get airborne but was prohibited from engaging the enemy. It has been reported that some of those American combat pilots were actually in tears. All was in readiness, but at the last moment, orders came from the White House to cancel fighter support for the invading Cubans. Only President Kennedy and his brother, Bobby, knew why this decision was made. It was a U.S.-planned and U.S.-financed operation and, in the end, it was a U.S. decision that led to disaster for the invasion force and permitted Castro to remain in power.

The Bay of Pigs is an excellent spot for an invasion, provided you have air support. Without control of the air, it's a place waiting for a disaster to happen. It's a narrow inlet which, militarily speaking, provides flank coverage. That is, of course, if you have air support. On each flank there is a small rise in the terrain and without air support, this gave a tremendous advantage to the repelling forces. So the invasion force was landed and tried desperately to move inland. But as soon as the airpower disappeared, Castro's forces moved in with tanks, mortars, machine guns, rockets — the whole show. The invading force was trapped and they couldn't move. The last thing they wanted to do was surrender, but they had no other choice. Castro took some eleven hundred prisoners. With proper air support, those men could have succeeded. Without it, they were sitting ducks. As all this news came to me, I thought of my January visit with Allen Dulles when I was told that everything was "go," and that the U.S. would support this mission all the way. It was a promise made and a promise broken.

On the day of the Bay of Pigs invasion, fate played an unusual role. When Castro was coming to power, a Nicaraguan pilot, Lt. Ulloa, deserted the Nicaraguan airforce and joined Castro. It was this same Lt. Ulloa who sank the invasion ship *Rio Escondido*. As it happened, that was the ship carrying all of the ammunition for the invasion force.

In this abortive mission, incomprehensible things happened. The first air strike took off for Cuba from Puerto Cabezas, then the second strike took off, but the third strike group was halted. Some of our Nicaraguan military leaders rushed in and wanted to know "why in the hell the third strike group was not taking off." The Americans reported the order had come from Washington because the administration wanted "to test public opinion." My God, men were dying and the future of much of Latin America hung in the balance, and Washington wanted to test public opinion!

Since the situation had become so desperate for the invading force, Nicaragua decided it should send its small force of P-51s to the aid of the beleaguered Cubans. The P-51 has a limited range, and it would be impossible to fly to Cuba and return to Nicaragua without refueling. Permission was requested from the United States to fly from Cuba to Key West and refuel. It was assumed that an automatic "yes" would be forthcoming. We were wrong. The reply came back, "Request denied." That was unbelievable.

By that time, I was in Taiwan. It was confirmed that the invasion had failed and for one reason: no fighter coverage. I sent Allen Dulles an urgent message in which I stated that the invasion had failed but that Castro should not be permitted to get off the hook. Dulles responded but it was a noncommittal response.

After Taiwan, I went on to India and, while there, had a long visit with Jawaharlal Nehru, Mrs. Indira Gandhi's father. I remember our conversation quite well. I asked Nehru why he was interfering in the affairs of the Western Hemisphere. He had castigated the United States for participating in the Bay of Pigs invasion, and I thought he was off base with such criticism. I felt it was my patriotic duty to defend the U.S. and speak up for Western ideology. I must have impressed Nehru, because later Luis went to see him and Nehru said to Luis: "Oh yes, you are the brother of that outspoken young man who came to see me." It wasn't just India. In each country on that long journey I stood foursquare for the United States of America.

When I returned to Nicaragua, the Bay of Pigs fiasco was still in the news, and particularly so in Nicaragua. One thing for certain, Castro had not forgotten my participation and until this day he hasn't. By that time, his arrogant personality was being expressed in volatile language. I was the butt of many of his vitriolic obscenities. Often times he said, "Somoza is a son of a bitch, and I'll see him dead." He made a serious threat but, I'm sorry to say, he made good his threat. He didn't kill me, but he played a significant role in killing my country. To me, that's the same thing.

The eleven hundred prisoners taken at the Bay of Pigs were put in Castro's Communist jails. And the horrible tortures carried out on some of them were adequately publicized. But just one month after the invasion Castro himself started a movement to have them all ransomed, by offering to set them free for five hundred bulldozers of the Caterpillar type, then worth twenty-eight million dollars. This led to crosscurrents of activity in the United States more tragic and confusing than had been the invasion itself. To start it off, a group of Cuban refugees formed a Cuban Families Committee, which did succeed in getting sixty of the most severely wounded prisoners released eventually on its promise to pay Castro $2,925,000.

But President Kennedy, apparently for political reasons, was determined to have all of these prisoners released by some more powerful and prominent civilian committee. This had to be done while he maintained the fiction that the U.S. government could have nothing to do with paying to Castro anything that looked like an indemnity; while he, President Kennedy, still maintained absolute control, through his brother Robert (the U.S. Attorney General), over all negotiations; and while Castro was constantly increasing his price. The final result was a supreme effort during December of 1962 to complete the performance by Christmas. It now called for a very solid guarantee by a large enough insurance company, backed by a consortium of large banks, for the delivery of some fifty-three million dollars' worth of drugs and medicines.

These drugs were listed and named by Castro in a lengthy memorandum, and calculated by him as to actual value well below the drug companies' bottom published wholesale prices. Provision was also made for a secret but full spot checking of the drugs and medicines in that enormous consignment, by Castro's agents sent over to Miami for that purpose. This was done, the bond was issued, and on Sunday, December 23, 1962, four planeloads of the more than one thousand prisoners had been landed in Florida.

Then Castro played the last card in his hand. He demanded immediate cash payment of the $2,925,000 still owed him, for the sixty wounded prisoners previously released, before he would let go of any more. So Robert Kennedy, awakened at five o'clock Monday morning over this matter, telephoned Richard Cardinal Cushing, Archbishop of Boston, who agreed to put up one million dollars. General Lucius Clay borrowed the remaining $1,925,000 at some bank on his own signature. By Monday afternoon the Canadian Consul's office in Havana was able to assure Castro that those amounts had already been deposited to his account at a bank in Montreal. So, on Christmas Eve, 1962, the last of these prisoners was set down in Florida.

To bring the Bay of Pigs fiasco into proper focus and relate the release of all prisoners to the current situation in Nicaragua, consider this fact: There are eight thousand men and women of the Guardia Nacional behind barbed wire in Nicaragua today. They are political prisoners of a Marxist government; and, as things stand now, most of these men and women will probably die in prison. However, there has been no effort on the part of anyone in the United States to negotiate for their release, and you have eight times the number imprisoned after the Bay of Pigs.

There is a parallel. The United States promised air support for the Bay of Pigs invaders. The air support was withheld and eleven hundred men were captured by a Communist government. In Nicaragua, the United States broke promises, treaties, and all agreements with my country. As a direct result, eight thousand men and women are imprisoned. How ironical that, in the one instance, the United States would successfully bargain for the release of all prisoners, and in the other, refuse even to acknowledge the fact that an entire army is imprisoned by a Communist government.

I can go one step further. If the United States had lived up to her commitment to the Bay of Pigs invaders, there would be no Castro on the scene today, and the Communists would not have Nicaragua.

Surely there is still justice in this world of ours. But as of this moment, if it does exist, it is beyond my scope of vision.

Chapter Thirteen

SEPTEMBER OFFENSIVE

After the terrorists were successful in their capture of the National Palace, had their demands met and were safely ensconced in their havens, there was euphoria in Havana, Caracas, Panama City, San Jose of Costa Rica, and some areas of Washington.

TV viewers in San Jose, for example, were told that my government and I no longer had the popular support of the people. Some of the Sandinista leaders even boasted that Somoza's time could now be counted in hours, because the people would rise up and overthrow the government. They went so far as to say that I could no longer count on the loyalty of the Guardia Nacional.

Perez believed this to be true as did Castro, Carazo, Torrijos, and Carter. All of these national leaders believed the wild stories being spread by the revolutionaries. They mistook compassion for weakness and disunity. They weren't aware of the fact that the people of Nicaragua were still with me and the government. The appraisal of the Communist revolutionaries, and their supporting international factions, was that the government and I had been dealt a fatal psychological blow — a blow from which there was no recovery. Again, how wrong they were.

With the exception of a few in the military, there was unanimity of opinion concerning the action I had taken. People were grateful for the decision I had made, because the lives of the hostages had been spared. Contrary to opinion outside of Nicaragua, the government and I had more solid support among the people of Nicaragua than we had experienced in a long time. Though there had been serious trouble with the revolutionaries in Massaya and, to a lesser degree in Leon, those military conflicts with the Communist-led and Communist-inspired revolutionaries did not shake the confidence of the people of Nicaragua. In each of those instances, the Sandinistas were routed and peace restored.

But there was to be no respite for me, the military, or the government. After Massaya and Leon, the next city to be attacked was Matagalpa. This is the third largest city in Nicaragua and has a population of approximately 45,000 people. If this city were taken, it would be a ripe plum for the revolutionaries.

In command of the police and military in Matagalpa was Colonel Martinez. He is a deeply religious man, and in a predominantly Catholic country, it was rare to find a Protestant. I would say that Martinez is a good soul and that he was loved and respected. He was able to keep law and order and perform the difficult functions of a military commander with a soft hand.

On this particular occasion, Martinez had allowed the subversives to come within two blocks of the Matagalpa central police station. Very quickly the subversives surrounded the police station and commenced heavy firing. We were advised as to the tenuous position of Colonel Martinez and his men, and we decided it was necessary to send a body of men to assist his detachment. He only had about one hundred men under his command and the attacking force had far more than that.

The detachment was comprised of only newly-trained troops. These were all young kids with no experience whatsoever. So three scout cars were loaded with these green troops and they headed for Matagalpa. Their officers were competent but they, too, lacked experience. I also sent General Fernandez, Army Chief of Staff, and the Minister of the Interior. I wanted to be certain that this operation went smoothly and that it was conducted properly.

I was particularly impressed with the great number of media people who covered "The Battle of Matagalpa." They came from all over and, since we had no censorship, they could send out any kind of story they chose to send. And they were free to take photographs and do television taping. Some of their stories absolutely astounded me. For our young, green boys, they could write nothing good. Their praise and plaudits were saved for the subversives who wanted to overthrow the government. They, the supposedly fair-minded men of the news media, put a singular identification on this military conflict which could only inflame public opinion against the Guardia Nacional. They called this "The Children's Uprising." I found this to be unbelievable, because there were no children. There might have been a few teenagers with pistols, but there were no children. In actuality, many of our young troops were mere teenagers but, to their disadvantage with the news media, they wore the combat uniform of their country.

The news media simply refused to face the reality of the situation. Our troops faced hard-core, well-trained men, not boys, who had come to Matagalpa from various parts of the country. To call this a Children's Uprising was the height of absurdity.

In order to thwart their plan for reinforcements, we constantly changed our checkpoints. By so doing, the revolutionaries could never be certain as to where our checkpoints might be. With this technique, we captured many men who were armed and equipped for battle. We captured one of the men who had been trained in Cuba and was responsible for the entire Esteli section. He was moving from Esteli to Matagalpa. In a few days the battle was over. General Fernandez and Colonel Martinez had performed ably. I was proud of the new troops. They conducted themselves like veterans, and after that, they were. Furthermore, we were able to prevent the downtown destruction.

July and, particularly, August had been difficult months for me and for the government. There were moments when I felt it was earthquake time again. As August came to an end, I remember thinking that surely September would be better. The stepped-up recruiting program was going well and these young men were more than willing to fight for their country. Our military commanders were concerned but confident. The people of Nicaragua had demonstrated that they were solidly behind me and the government. So, there was justifiable reason to think that September would be a better month.

Those hopes were soon shattered. On September 8, 1978, we received word that the Sandinistas had obtained tremendous reinforcement and that they were planning something big — like an attack on several cities at once. We didn't know from which direction these attacks might come, but we knew they were on the way. Therefore, our only course of action, at that time, was to put our people on "special alert." At a lonely outpost, manned by only a few men, that wasn't much consolation. We simply had to stand by and wait. And then it came!

On September 9, 1978, at precisely 6:30 P.M., the revolutionary forces simultaneously attacked Matagalpa, Massaya, Leon, Esteli, Chinandega, and Managua. Their plan was designed by military experts, well coordinated, and carried out by seasoned revolutionaries.

The plan for Managua was to knock out the outlying police precincts, the small military guard stations, and then move into the center of the capital city. These attacks were begun.

In Massaya, the principal attack was on the central police station. In this attack there was wanton and uncalled-for destruction of private property. The revolutionaries put the torch to the entire downtown area of Massaya. They then precipitated looting throughout this area. Massaya was to resemble a bombed-out World War II city. As usual, the news media blamed the government forces for this destruction. The accusation was totally false.

The same tactics were applied to Leon, Chinandega, and Esteli. The attacking forces concentrated on government police positions, while fires were set in the public market and downtown areas and the people were encouraged to loot and pillage.

Their plan immediately to overrun the police centers was foiled. They overran only one police center and that was in Monimbo, where Major Gutierrez was killed. The enemy had failed in its initial onslaught.

The next day, September 10th, a large scale attack occurred on the Costa Rican frontier at Peñas Blancas. Three hundred well-armed men crossed the border from their staging area in Costa Rica and attempted to overrun our immigration compound. This was an important point for the revolutionaries, because the custom house, immigration facilities, and of course the Guardia Nacional detachment, were all in Peñas Blancas.

Obviously, the attack from Costa Rica was a key to the entire plan. The rebels had plotted to keep the Guardia Nacional tied down in all of the other areas, while this force moved inward.

I had great concern for all of the areas under attack, but I knew we had first to secure Managua. The attacking elements were repelled and Managua was safe. But with attacks occurring in so many places at the same time, each commander needed reinforcements and we just didn't have them.

The only troops we had available for military disposition were those still in basic training school. Any military commander would agree that you are spread mighty thin, when your troops in training school represent your reserve forces. There was one other unit, and that was the company which served as the Presidential Guard. That was our situation.

I remember one night, during this September crisis, we had a meeting of the General Staff. The Staff were very worried because, militarily speaking, they could not maneuver. Due to the attacks in so many different areas, our troops were simply pinned down. We badly needed additional troops and they were not available. I came up with what I thought might be a temporary solution to our problem.

I called Major Somoza, my son, who was in command at the basic training school for the new recruits. I explained our problem to him, and told him he would have to take the youngsters out of training school to clean out Massaya and Leon. I knew those young men in training were not ready for combat, but there was no other choice. He accepted a difficult assignment and the "training school combat corps" performed admirably. They whipped the rebels in Massaya and Leon!

At the same time, the situation in Chinandega had deteriorated and the commander was in need of assistance. Well, there were no more training recruits available for combat duty, and that left the Presidential Guard company. So I sent Commander Bravo and the Presidential Guard to Chinandega to assist the training school company. In effect, this left the presidential complex without protection. I remember one day Klaus Sengelmann, Minister of Agriculture, and I were discussing the military events. Klaus looked in front of the "bunker," which housed the presidential office, and said:

"You know, Mr. President, there are two old men guarding this entire complex. If the Sandinistas knew this, you would be dead in nothing flat." He was telling the truth, but emergency situations call for emergency actions. Commander Bravo and his excellent company of men, in conjunction with the training school company, wiped out the revolutionaries in Chinandega.

There was still the problem of Esteli and it was a rather serious problem. In command at Esteli was General Fernandez, with an assortment of men from the Guardia Nacional. The Guardia Nacional had been trained as "one man, one unit." This system was patterned after that of the United States Marines. This simply meant that ten men made a squad — no matter from where they came, ten men made a squad and they were trained to function in that manner. General Fernandez may have had an assortment of men from different companies and different areas, but they knew how to fight.

To Fidel Castro, Esteli had become a symbol. It was very important to him that the Sandinistas hold the city. Many of the Cuban-trained guerrillas were in action in Esteli, and that may be one reason he took such a personal interest in that city. To Castro's great disappointment, General Fernandez and the Guardia Nacional were victorious. The victory did not come easily. Fernandez needed additional troops but we didn't have them. Some of the General Staff wanted to send the training recruits into Esteli, but I was against it and pointed out that those kids had done a good job and military responsibility should be spread. It was decided to let General Fernandez do the job and the battle for Esteli lasted two weeks. When Castro learned the big effort in Esteli had failed, he went on the powerful radio station in Havana and raved and ranted. He took the loss at Esteli as a personal defeat.

Radio Havana is something special as a radio station. It is picked up all over Nicaragua and, even in Managua, it is as strong as our local stations. For twenty years we lived under the booming sounds of Radio Havana. Many people in Nicaragua listened to the station, particularly to the diatribes of Castro. That was when they could hear the "evil" things about Somoza. The information about Esteli and the other revolutionary activities in Managua was being fed to Radio Havana out of our "friendly country" to the south — Costa Rica.

Earlier, I had left the men at Peñas Blancas on the Costa Rican border, in a precarious position. As I stated, three hundred men crossed over into Nicaragua from Costa Rica, supposedly a democratic, nonviolent country, where everything is alleged to be open and aboveboard. These men came into Nicaragua armed with bazookas, armed with Belgian anti-tank and antipersonnel grenades, armed with Belgian FM rifles, and armed with mortars. This invading force represented a moving arsenal.

Against the three hundred Costa Rica-based revolutionaries stood twenty-five members of the Guardia Nacional. During the entire international war in which Nicaragua found herself, many gallant stands were made, but none more so than that of the twenty-five who stood at Peñas Blancas. They defeated the three hundred revolutionaries and drove them back into Costa Rica.

Based upon written reports from two men who were with the invading force, there is absolutely no doubt about the complicity of the Costa Rican government, President Carazo, and other high government officials.

In my duties as Military Governor after the devastating earthquake of December, 1972, it will be recalled that some of my difficult long-range decisions earned me the enmity of a sizable segment of the business community in Managua. Thus, those nearsighted capitalists collaborated with the Leftist priests and the Sandinistas. As part of this collaboration, the January strike was called. This was an economic power play in conjunction with the organized Chamorro demonstrations. The combined assault, it was thought, would be sufficient to bring down me and the government. This effort, as I have stated, failed miserably, because the government and I had the support of the people.

The opposition business group took their loss bitterly. After the unsuccessful strike, the group continued to have meetings in which forthcoming strategy was discussed. They were biding their time for the opportune moment, and then another strike would be called. Their thinking seemed to be that if the government couldn't be whipped militarily, it could be brought down by paralyzing business and commerce. All of those misdirected men of affluence now see the results of their irrational behavior but, for them, the time for rectification has long since passed. So after their first failure, they waited for another chance.

The September offensive was the moment for which they had been waiting. It was their thinking that the widespread attack by the revolutionaries might be strong enough to bring down the government. That attack plus another strike, they reasoned, couldn't fail. In their utter stupidity, these men did call another strike. The pattern was identical to the first strike. Many establishments were forced to go along with the strike under threats of reprisals. Numerous establishments, which refused to go along with the strike, were destroyed by bombs or they were burned. The emotional intensity was that great.

In the first strike we were not in the midst of a multi-front military attack. To be sure, there were militant demonstrations and widespread property damage; but at that time we did not face the revolutionaries in an offensive. The second strike, so far as the businessmen were concerned, was called at a propitious moment. This time the combination of economic and military war would surely bring down the government. So, I was faced with two problems, one economic and the other military.

To the surprise of the Sandino collaborators, the second strike was a miserable failure. The small stores stayed open and the fruit and vegetable markets continued to operate. The people of Nicaragua could get food and for those other things, they could wait. Once again, the collaborators underestimated the support I had from the people. Even with the multiple military offensive, the people of Nicaragua remained loyal to their government.

When I think of the September offensive, it brings thoughts of both a military and economic offensive.

The September offensive was over and we had won. The best estimates indicated a ten-to-one casualty ratio. That is, for each one of our casualties, the revolutionary forces suffered ten. In this revolutionary offensive, we faced a well-organized enemy. It took military know-how to plan and coordinate such a multiple offensive. The international force was well armed, and we found they had solved the problem of logistics. Had this been merely a partisan operation, they would have run out of ammunition in a short time. Their offensive lasted for two weeks and they couldn't carry that much ammunition on their backs. No, this sustained supply was coming from Costa Rica through designated routes. Contrary to news media reports, it was not a spontaneous effort. This military action was designed to terminate the government of Nicaragua and bring an end to Somoza.

We had reports, from reliable sources, that the Communist-led Sandinistas were confident they would be successful in one or more of their targeted areas. In that event, they had planned to declare a national status and ask for international recognition. Venezuela, Panama, and Cuba would have recognized such status immediately, with the U.S. following close behind. Perhaps that's another reason the loss at Esteli put Castro on the rampage.

It was evident that the international news media thought this was the end for me and the government. They were on hand en masse. They were gathered, much like vultures, to witness and participate in the final agonizing hours of a governmental death. During this ordeal, I held several news conferences and fielded all questions. I wanted the news media to know that the "Ship of State" was still afloat and that my confidence had not been shaken. I think they got the message.

July 4th is Independence Day in the United States. That equivalency in Nicaragua was September 15th. It was, until the Communist take-over, a day of national celebration. On September 15, 1978, we found ourselves in the middle of a revolutionary attack. Nevertheless, I observed this day in the traditional way. I gave a champagne reception for all accredited diplomats and the usual toasts were exchanged. Some members of the news media thought this was just a show because, they felt certain, my departure was near at hand. Naturally I was concerned but, of more importance, I had confidence in the people of Nicaragua and the Guardia Nacional. They didn't let me down.

In the offensive, it should be stated, most of the leaders who were trained in Cuba, Panama, and by the PLO, made good their escape. When it appeared the Guardia Nacional would win, they followed a well-established routine. They would tell the local Sandinistas they were going for reinforcements and then they would never come back. On foot, they would generally make their way to Costa Rica and Honduras. In one news report out of Costa Rica, these Communist-trained leaders stated they really weren't hurt too much because, by and large, their cadre returned to Costa Rica. We found this to be true, because we were to meet these same people at a later date.

By this time, the international atmosphere had become even worse. This was due to the handiwork of the international news media. I didn't think it was possible for the news media to become more biased, but they did. With each loss by the guerrilla forces, the media became more vitriolic. It appeared these people, who reported to the world, were diligently striving to make up for the military defeats suffered by the guerrillas. In some instances, money was responsible for their determined effort to bring me down. In others, it was dedication to the Leftist cause. Whatever the reason, I received the "poison pen" treatment on a regular basis, and it got progressively worse.

Again, Carlos Andres Perez made his presence known. He knew the location of the defeated invasion forces and he knew their number was increasing daily by so-called volunteers from Cuba, Panama, Venezuela, and Costa Rica. He knew that most of the international force could be found in designated areas of Honduras and Costa Rica. More importantly, he knew they would have to obtain money to survive and stay combat-ready to attack Nicaragua again. So Carlos Andres Perez donated millions of dollars to the International Red Cross. Ostensibly, this money was to take care of the refugees from Nicaragua. Well, there were no refugees from Nicaragua. The misnomer applied to the defeated Sandinistas who had safe haven in Honduras and Costa Rica.

As of today, over 150,000 Nicaraguans have fled their homeland. There are thousands of refugees in each of several countries, with some sixty thousand in the United States alone. Now these are truly refugees, but you don't hear anything about Venezuela donating millions of dollars to the Red Cross to relieve the plight of these poor people. These people are anti-Communist. Perez and the press were reporting that over five thousand people had been killed in the offensive, and that thousands were fleeing the country. Therefore he was, from a public standpoint, justified in sending money for relief purposes. Perez, however, knew better. The casualty figures were in the order of twelve hundred, and that included killed and wounded.

We had won a military victory and we had won an economic victory, because the second business strike failed. In reality, though, it was a hollow victory. International law was being flagrantly violated and no one seemed to be concerned. Costa Rica was the obvious culprit, but her actions were aided and abetted by the United States, Panama, and Venezuela. We had the OAS agreement, we had the mutual defense treaties, and these signed international documents were worth nothing. Torrijos had even stated publicly that he would form an international brigade to fight in Nicaragua. I learned that treaties and pacts have no real force or meaning.

Although I was thoroughly disgusted by the noncompliance with international law, I was convinced that we had finally won. I remember thinking that we now had unequivocal and substantiated evidence of outside aggressors against Nicaragua. No one, not even those with biased opinions against Nicaragua, could dispute the evidence we had compiled against the aggressors. With an ironclad case against the aggressors, I agreed to receive the Human Rights Commission in Nicaragua.

Before the Commission arrived in Managua, I advised the members that they would have my full cooperation. I meant what I said, because I expected the Commission to be fair with Nicaragua.

There were six members of the OAS Human Rights panel, including Tom Farer who represented the United States. Before this panel embarked upon its private investigation, I remember telling the group, "I hope your mission will serve to help all of us American people and that it will not be an interventionist tool sent by a foreign nation." I also reminded the Commission that their presence in Nicaragua came about as a result of my invitation. I merely wanted them to know that no one and no government had forced the invitation.

Later I would recall how prophetic my words to the Commission really were, ". . . and that it will not be an interventionist tool sent by a foreign nation."

In agreeing to receive the Human Rights Commission, I think my logic was sound. The whole world, it seemed, was making

noise about human rights, and I wanted the world to know that
I had nothing to hide. Further, I had the unmistakable evidence
to prove that the rights of our people had been trampled on by
outside aggressor forces. I had been taught to believe that when
conclusions are reached through sound logic, those conclusions
will be correct. Logic has been defined as "the interrelation or
sequence of facts or events when seen as inevitable or pre-
dictable." The facts and events in Nicaragua led to a pre-
dictable and inevitable conclusion. Even with prejudice, I
thought, the Human Rights Commission would grudgingly
come to the correct conclusion. I was to learn that logic, reason,
analytical deduction, and everyday common sense all represented mental capabilities beyond those of the Human Rights
Commission. For the Commission, there was a more compelling
influence, and that was political motivation.

I determined, as so many others have, that the most flagrant
violator of human rights is the Human Rights Commission,
because they totally ignore the time-honored concept of domestic and international law. Their actions and their decisions are
based solely on one precept, and that precept is politics. Mr.
Carter should be proud of his skillful proselytizing. With
assorted inducements, the Human Rights Commission is politically possessed, and it renders political decisions.

The conduct of the Commission in Nicaragua defied all
known rules of judicious behavior. Even members of the
opposition political party, and those businessmen who opposed
me, were amazed at the procedure followed by the Human
Rights Commission in Nicaragua. I was benumbed.

Their first act represented an assembly call for the Sandinistas, Leftists, and subversives. The announcement was
made that the Commission wanted to talk to all those people
who had anything against the government of Nicaragua. These
people were assured that any and all complaints were being
solicited. I thought: What if such a call were put out in the
United States of America? In that case, I felt, half of the
population of the country would show up. In the case of
Nicaragua, a surprising thing happened. As many people came
to testify for the government as came to testify against it.

The Commission was caught in a quandary. What were they
to do with those who came to testify for the government? It

didn't take them long to solve that dilemma. Their decision was shocking. They only wanted to hear those who had something to say against the government. To the chagrin of the Commission, numerous Nicaraguans went before that corrupt political entity to relate their misfortunes at the hands of the guerrillas. These people told of being shot, robbed, beaten, burned out, tortured, and witnessing murders. All crimes committed by the guerrillas. The Commission turned a deaf ear. They wouldn't even listen and, furthermore, none of these heinous crimes were reported by a Commission charged with the responsibility of investigating human rights violations.

On the other hand, the Commission listened to every Tom, Dick, and Harry who had anything to say against the government. They listened and reported the detailed complaints of the guerrillas. They even went into the jails and talked to convicted felons. The Commission didn't ask them why they were in jail, because they weren't interested. Now if you ask a convicted felon if he has a complaint against the government, what do you think he will say? It doesn't take a great intellect to find an answer to that question. They would ask these prisoners if they were mistreated, if they were tortured, and if their rights had been violated. Naturally, the answer given to all these questions was "Oh, yes!"

Government employees told me the Commission members gleefully wrote down full reports on all the inmates. They were particularly joyful when they could find a Sandinista, Leftist, or an inmate who had something evil to say about me. It's almost unbelievable, but they actually prodded people into giving bitter anti-Somoza statements. You can be certain those statements went down in capital letters. That was what the Commission wanted to hear.

The fact that the guerrillas were violating the laws of the land, and violating the rights of the good citizens of Nicaragua, made no difference to the Commission. The fact that convicted criminals had robbed, stolen, or murdered, made no difference to the Commission. The fact that subversives were attempting to overthrow the constitutional government of Nicaragua made no difference to the Commission. The Human Rights Commission completely failed to acknowledge that all of those factions were gross law violators, and, worst of all, that the rights of law-abiding citizens meant nothing to them. Those were the people who were the genuine human rights violators in Nicaragua and, yet, it was their complaints of human rights violations which were taken down and reported. When, in my mind, I review the actions of the Commission I become angry and emotional, because it was the most diabolical miscarriage of justice I have ever witnessed.

The Human Rights Commission of the Organization of American States is used by the Leftists and, in reality, is an arm of subversion. You don't hear about the Human Rights Commission going to Cuba, Jamaica, or any Leftist country. But it's a proven fact that they pounce on anti-Communist countries. The Human Rights Commission is Mr. Carter's baby, and it represents another tool to foster socialistic notions in the Western Hemisphere.

When the Commission members had terminated their social visits with all those who had "anything against the government of Nicaragua," they packed their files and left. There was no question in my mind as to what their findings would be. Mr. Carter must have requested that a "rush order" be placed on the Nicaragua Report because in two weeks the report was out. It was a long report but the findings could be summed up very briefly: Nicaragua is a gross violator of human rights. That's what Carter, Perez, Torrijos, Carazo, and Castro wanted, and that's precisely what they received.

In life, most people are guilty of small transgressions. The transgression of the Human Rights Commission in Nicaragua runs to infinity. If my West Point mathematics still serves me, infinity represents the limit of a function that can be made to become and remain numerically larger than any preassigned value. In layman's language, no matter how far you go, infinity is still beyond that. To me, that represents the magnitude of the transgression committed by the Human Rights Commission. Some day those people are going to meet up with their Creator, and he is going to ask them: "How honest were you in Nicaragua?" Somewhere and somehow those people will have to answer for their greatest transgression, a sin against mankind.

I should have expected a negative Human Rights Commission report. The U.S. had been putting out strong signals for some time. One strong signal came, just prior to the September offensive, when Nicaragua appeared before the International Monetary Fund (IMF) concerning a loan request.

After the earthquake, it will be recalled, Nicaragua was forced to make several syndicated loans. Some of those were short term and some were long term loans. Some of those loans were coming due and we needed standby credit so those loans could be rolled over. We presented a good financial statement and all elements of our financial condition were presented to the IMF. Our primary concern was the short term debt, but standby credit from the IMF would enable us to renew everything for the next five years. Based upon our productive capacity and projected income, our request should have been approved.

With our financial report and projected needs before the group, a routine discussion was held. At a crucial moment, the United States representative to the IMF arose and said, "The situation in Nicaragua is not clear, and this loan request should be left for another date." That was it! Our much-needed financing was dead. I knew then that the U.S. representative was speaking for the White House and the State Department. Yes, that was a signal and a big one.

After we had won the September battle against an invading force, and after we had compiled mountains of unquestionable evidence concerning the Communist-directed offensive, I thought "Surely the United States will now believe our previous reports." The Human Rights Commission proved that the best logic in the world is fallible. Thanks to Mr. Carter, it looked as though we were winning all the battles but losing the war.

Chapter Fourteen

THE NEWS MEDIA AND JACK ANDERSON

Since adulthood, I have read one or more U.S. newspapers daily. Therefore, I should be familiar with the U.S. style, technique, and method of reporting the news. In most of the major newspapers, one can get the news in three different segments. There is straight reporting, and that simply means that a writer covers a story and gives a factual accounting as to what, where, when, and why. Then you have editorial writing wherein a particular publication expresses its own views on a variety of subjects. Next you have the columns which, generally speaking, are written by experienced newsmen who have become fairly well known.

According to basic journalism ethics, the straight reporting should be unbiased and factual. Conversely, the other two segments reflect personal viewpoints and, therefore, these are expected to be biased.

During the past twenty-five years or so, I have observed a change in this generally accepted format. The straight reporting is not so straight anymore and tends to express opinions and ideas. In such reporting a writer can slant a story so as to bring about a desired public reaction. In my opinion, this is not honest reporting. From personal experience, I can attest as to the damage this kind of reporting can do to a government, a cause, or an individual.

Viet Nam and Nicaragua are two prime examples of what slanted reporting of the news can accomplish. The failure of the United States in Viet Nam can, to a large degree, be attributed to the biased news media. The Communists were

- Two female police students were captured. One of them was four months pregnant. They opened her up and pulled the fetus out. According to sworn testimony given to the U.S. House of Representatives and which appears in the February 26, 1980 *Congressional Record*, this group was under the command of an American by the name of Clifford Scott.
- Major Domingo Gutierrez and six of his men were captured. They were placed in a hole, sprayed with gasoline, and burned alive.
- Sergeant Edwin R. Ordonez of the infantry training school was captured and burned alive.
- Dr. Cornelio Hueck, former President of the Congress, was captured at his ranch near Rivas. He was taken to the town square of Tola where he was shot several times in non-vital areas. Then, with the people of the town present, he was placed on a table and, while he was still alive, his heart was cut out.
- Major Pablo Emilio Salazar, better known as "Comandante Bravo," was captured by the Sandinistas in Honduras after the war was over, and tortured to death. His face was beaten beyond recognition, his arms broken, his ears cut off, his genitals severed, strips of his skin peeled from his body and, finally, he was shot in the head.

Several times I have mentioned Commander Bravo, because he was a "soldier's soldier." On August 1, 1979, Commander Bravo testified in Washington, D.C., before a press conference called by Congressman John Murphy of New York. Other former members of the Guardia Nacional gave statements that day as well as numerous civilians. Those Nicaraguans were there to tell the American people of the horrible atrocities being committed by the new Marxist regime.

From the *Congressional Record* of February 26, 1980, pages H1273–1274, I quote Congressman Murphy:

Some members who attended a press conference I held on August 1, 1979, may recall that Pablo Emilio Salazar, popularly known as Comandante Bravo, sat by my side to warn the U.S. Government that we were supporting a regime that was conducting systematic revenge murders not only in Nicaragua but through hit teams sent to other Central American countries. The U.S. Government through the voice of the State Department scoffed at these charges when they were made in August. I would remind members that Comandante Bravo is the same officer whose murder I have just described.

I would also remind members today that Salazar's death can be laid directly at the doorstep of America's misdirected Latin American policies. I would repeat to members Major Salazar's words of warning of August 1 when he said:

"Most, if not all of us, were trained directly or indirectly by the U.S. Armed Forces. Our noble military friends have now turned their backs on us. We defended our government with the same high ideals of duty, honor, and country taught by our American trainers. All of us here today feel betrayed, not by our American comrades, but by Jimmy Carter's policy."

Salazar concluded his August 1 testimony: "We are not asking for compassion, but an opportunity to help you understand that destruction of our democracy is in the hands of the Siberian Bear dressed in colorful Latin clothes."

The foregoing is just an indication of the horrible crimes committed by the new Marxist government in Nicaragua. Verification and complete statements concerning these mentioned crimes can be found in the *Congressional Record* of February 26, 1980.

But the list of those who were raped and murdered goes on and on. Perhaps it should be pointed out that by and large, these heinous crimes were committed *after* the Marxist victory. As I have stated previously, some three thousand men, women, and children of Nicaragua have been slaughtered. These murders continue until this day, and the brutality is unbelievable.

One thing is clear; the human rights standards proclaimed by Mr. Carter do not apply to the Communists. It should be clear to all that his program only applied to anti-Communists. Further, the news media are now content. They no longer direct their attacks upon Nicaragua. For this position, there is an obvious answer. The Communists now control Nicaragua.

The conclusion one has to reach is that the power of the press is awesome. It makes no difference who you are or what you are, if this sector of our professional society wants to destroy you, it can be done. Again, the would-be straight press is not so straight.

I have no quarrel with editorial writing. The editorial page is where the opinions of any newspaper should appear. Being a strong believer in freedom of the press, I strongly defend the right of any newspaper editorially to take a stand on any given issue.

Then how about the columnists? Once more I defend their right to express their views, so long as they stick to the truth. Unfortunately, many columnists become so obsessed with a cause, an idea, or it may even be the destruction of an individual, that they lose sight of truth and objectivity. Then there are a few who are willing to sell their integrity for the almighty dollar. I believe that the lowest rung on the journalistic ladder belongs to that member of the "fourth estate" who is willing to trade the power of his pen for coin of the realm.

One columnist who comes to my mind is a man whose column appears in over 170 newspapers. Obviously, this man has the power and he knows it. That man would be Jack Anderson of Washington, D.C. If you read his column regularly, you will know that I'm not the only man he has sought to destroy. You will also know that I'm not the only person about whom he told vicious lies.

These attacks upon me, my mother, my son, and my entire family were fraught with bitterness. These personal attacks concerned me and I speculated as to why this noted writer would suddenly zero in on the Somozas. For all those years, he had written nothing about me. I decided that some effort should be made to find out why Jack Anderson was out to get me.

Smaller countries, such as Nicaragua, do not have such sophisticated intelligence gathering systems as do the United States and the Soviet Union. At one time the U.S., with its CIA, could give you a briefing on just about any person of importance in the world. Under Carter, its effectiveness has been crippled. Russia, with the KGB, has the intelligence network to furnish a report on anyone and anything. Nevertheless, Nicaragua did have its sources of information and we had the ability to focus on one particular objective and achieve desired intelligence results. With Jack Anderson, this course was taken.

We were to discover a strange triangle. It was an odd triangle, more like an isosceles, because its points went from Nicaragua to Venezuela and thence back to Washington. This meant from

Carlos Andres Perez to Jack Anderson to Pedro Joaquin Chamorro. Now in baseball, Tinkers to Evers to Chance represented something good — a double play. But Perez to Anderson to Chamorro represented something bad — foul play. This was truly an intriguing relationship.

We had information coming from many sources but the revealing source was the Venezuelan Embassy in Washington. From that source, we were advised that the Foreign Ministry of Venezuela had authorized her Embassy in Washington to expend a sizable sum of money in order to "convince" certain influential members of the press that Somoza should be destroyed. The contacts were made. Shortly thereafter I was under attack. And Jack Anderson led the assault.

His mission was twofold. One, he would destroy my support in the U.S. Congress and turn U.S. public opinion against me. Two, with Chamorro and the influence of Chamorro's *La Prensa* in Nicaragua, he would effectively turn my own people against me. It was a good plan and, in the main, it worked. Anderson did have success with the Congress and he played a big role in turning U.S. public opinion against me. However, he and Chamorro failed in Nicaragua. Anderson and Chamorro, the most influential of all Sandinistas in Nicaragua, were convinced that the scurrilous personal attack upon me by Anderson would absolutely destroy me. They were wrong.

After Anderson had begun his personal attack upon me, Chamorro became frightened. He believed, and correctly so, that I would think Anderson's information was coming from him. He vehemently denied that he had anything to do with the stories Anderson had printed. He even said that it was apparent someone had told Jack Anderson a bunch of lies. Mainly, however, Chamorro wanted me to be assured that he had no relationship with Anderson and would never give him any information of any kind. He even ran a story in *La Prensa* in which he denounced the Anderson articles and claimed innocence of any participation.

With this denunciation by Chamorro in mind, it's revealing to note Jack Anderson's comments after Chamorro's death. In his column Anderson said that "Now that he is dead, I want to give notice that Pedro Joaquin Chamorro was a patriot who gave me all the information to write about Somoza."

So that the people of Nicaragua would know what Anderson had printed about me and my family, I got *Novedades*, the other daily in Managua and a paper in which my family had an interest, to run the full text of Jack Anderson's most vicious articles. There it was for all the people of my country to read. It was the only way I knew to fight Anderson — meet him head on. I did that in Nicaragua, but in the United States it was a different matter. I could not fight back. My victory in Nicaragua was a small one. Anderson's victory in the U.S. was a big one.

When you think about it, the alliance of Perez, Chamorro, and Anderson was not unusual. Chamorro and Perez had been close friends since their days in Costa Rica, and the best hatchet man in the business was Jack Anderson. To my way of thinking they represented the "unholy triangle." I have a good idea, but I don't know exactly, how much money Perez spent; but whatever the amount was, he got his money's worth.

At one time, when my father was President, David Davidson represented the government of Nicaragua in Washington. Davidson had an office called Nicaragua Information Center. One day I was visiting Washington and stopped by the office. Seated at the office typewriter was a young man who really knew how to type. When I came in, Davidson said, "Tacho, I want you to meet a friend of mine. This is Jack Anderson, and he works for Drew Pearson." That was a long time ago, but I never forgot it. Like so many historical events that seem to have no meaning at the time, there was no way I could perceive that, at a later date, this man would set out deliberately to destroy me.

With regard to the press, my position has always been the same. Even though, in many instances, I was treated shamefully by this profession, I am for freedom of the press. If we are to have a free society, then we cannot have a government-controlled press. With governmental control, such as that which exists in China, Russia, Cuba, and now Nicaragua, the people are sealed off from the truth. They are permitted to read only that which the government wants them to read. This concept violates a basic freedom and a human right. To play on an old American cliché, there are a few rotten apples in every barrel; and, left unattended, those few apples can spoil the whole

barrel. Unfortunately, there are too many Jack Andersons in
the press barrel. If given a free license to lie and use dastardly
tactics in personal vendettas, the contents of the press barrel
will turn to rot.

To avoid such decay, the press must police itself. Publishers
and editors must zealously guard and teach the precepts of
honest reporting. This institution, particularly, must protect
the freedom it enjoys. I don't think I need to remind those
members of the "fourth estate" that in a totalitarian domain,
freedom of the press is the first category marked for extinc-
tion.

When I refer to the international news media, I make
reference to radio, television, and the printed word. Of these
three media branches, I think television has the greatest impact.
Many journalists and publishers would not agree with me, but
an examination of statistical data in the U.S. supports my
contention.

My assumption would not apply to underdeveloped nations,
where few television sets exist. Nor would it apply to Communist countries, where both television and newspapers are controlled by the state.

Undoubtedly there are more television sets per household in
the United States than any other country on earth. Naturally,
then, television's impact would be greater where there are more
sets to watch. Also, I'm much more familiar with the influence
of this medium in the U.S. From firsthand knowledge, I can
attest as to its impact.

Do the people in the U.S. watch television more than people
in other countries? I think the answer has to be a resounding
yes. A recent survey showed that the average household in the
U.S. has television on for more than six hours each day. That's
incredible. I wonder when people have the time to talk, or read,
or visit with neighbors.

That same survey revealed that 30 percent of the people in
the U.S. get all of their news from television. That is also
astounding. It means that 30 percent of the citizens of the
United States do not read newspapers or periodicals of any kind.
Do the people believe what they see or hear on television? You bet
they do. In another survey in a large midwestern city of the

U.S. this fact was proven. Children were asked the following question: "If you heard one thing on television and your father told you the opposite was true, would you believe what you heard on television or your father? Over 50 percent of the children said they would believe what they heard on TV. I find that to be staggering testimony as to the impact of television. Remember the old cliché: "It must be true because I read it in the newspaper?" You can add another one: "It must be true because I saw it on TV."

Unfortunately, that unseen electronic marvel that pushes the button in the East and gets an immediate controlled response in the West, applies to television. If you don't believe it, switch channels. Try ABC, NBC, and CBS and you will find they cover about the same national and international stories. That in itself is not bad, but there is an inimical feature in such reporting. Each network will carry the same theme and that theme is disruptive. Any time there is an anti-nuclear demonstration, the networks will be there. A demonstration against the military draft will receive good coverage. The anti-Viet Nam war news covered the television screens in the U.S. from beginning to end and shaped the outcome of that debacle. All networks took an anti-Somoza stance and, in some instances, inflamed public opinion against me. I could go on and on.

We come back to the same standards which should apply to newspapers. Let straight reporting be straight. If a television network wants to editorialize, then identify the broadcast as an editorial. Then the people may reach their own conclusions. When only one side of a story is pounded day after day, it's only natural that the viewing public accepts that side of the story as fact.

On Sunday afternoon, *Sixty Minutes* is the most watched network show in the United States. With top ratings, the show commands big money. If you don't believe it, pay for one thirty-second spot. I have watched the show and I am familiar with the format. Generally speaking, the show is not complete unless someone is nailed to the cross. Also, the program will invariably sneak in a touch of propaganda. You can be sure this propaganda is slanted to the Left.

When I was advised that *Sixty Minutes* wanted to interview

me, I certainly had misgivings. I had seen what they could do to a person. I saw them absolutely destroy a mayor from some town in Indiana. The thought of being interviewed by people so adept at crucifixion frightened me.

My policy, however, had been to grant interviews to those who wanted them. I had met some tough ones who were out to get me, and had survived. More than that, I thought I came out on top. I met with the Public Broadcasting people and, it was obvious, some of their questions came straight from the White House. So far as I'm concerned, those people always came out second best. I wanted the people of the United States at least to be exposed to the pro-Nicaraguan government side. Therefore, I granted interviews. During that last year before the Communist take-over, I probably spent half of my time doing interviews. So when we were contacted by *Sixty Minutes*, I felt the proposal should be given serious consideration.

My aides and I discussed the program and evaluated the pros and cons. We reached the conclusion that those people could do me in. However, I wanted so much for the American people to understand the realities of our situation in Nicaragua and to know what the administration in Washington was doing to us, that I agreed to do the program. All arrangements were made and Dan Rather was sent down to do the program. That interview I shall always remember.

Rather tried every conceivable journalistic trick to trip me up on questions. He knew in advance the answers he wanted and come "hell or high water" he was going to find the question to fit his preconceived answer. Well, he never succeeded. From watching the show, one would never know that Dan Rather spent two and one-half hours grilling me. It's difficult to believe, but Rather condensed that entire time to seven minutes. The remainder of the air time was devoted to old footage or other filming which he did in Nicaragua.

I didn't realize what the power of film editing really meant. With that power, Rather cast me in any role he chose. Everything good I said about Nicaragua was deleted. Any reference to Carter's effort to destroy the government of Nicaragua was deleted. Every reference to the Communist activity and Cuba's participation was deleted.

His insistence that there was torture in my government

probably disturbed me the most. We would go over the subject and then we would come back to it again. He just wasn't getting the answers he wanted. Finally he said: "May we visit the security offices of the Nicaraguan government?" He had heard that this was a torture chamber and he believed it. I replied: "Yes, Mr. Rather, you may visit those offices and you may take your camera." Then I added: "You go right now. Take that car and go immediately so that you can't say I rigged it." Well, he did go, and he saw where the people worked and talked to many of them. When the show came on the air, he made no mention of the fact that he had personally visited our security offices and was free to film, talk to people, or do anything he wanted to do. He knew in advance how he wanted to portray me and his predetermined plan was followed.

When Rather left my office, I was convinced he would take me apart. I was right. The show was a disaster. Rather depicted a situation that didn't exist in Nicaragua. That show did irreparable harm to the government of Nicaragua and to me. Such massive misinformation also does harm to the American people. This is one of the risks of freedom of the press.

I always played fair with the press but it was a one-way street. The media did not play fair with me. The tragic and unfortunate death of the newsman, Bill Stewart, is an example of the one-way street to which I refer.

One must understand that the circumstances surrounding the untimely death of this man were not what could be called normal. Nicaragua was in a life-and-death struggle with a highly sophisticated, Communist enemy. In such surroundings, judgement is not always what it should be. The enlisted man who shot Mr. Stewart was stationed at a forward checkpoint and had been under fire and, like so many of the members of the Army, had been on duty too long without sleep.

Mr. Stewart had passed the first checkpoint and proceeded to the second. I think the *Miami Herald* was the only major paper to report the fact that the enlisted man had twice ordered Stewart to halt. These orders were ignored and Stewart was killed. I'm the first one to admit that the enlisted man, literally, made a fatal error. I am not now defending his actions, but I do feel the circumstances of this unfortunate incident should be known.

As all the world knows, this entire tragic episode was taped with a mini-cam television camera. It was never explained that I had the authority to seize the film and, as a matter of fact, this was suggested to me. But I had always played fair with the news media and that time was no different. I permitted the film to be shipped out and the rest is history. Certain stations in the U.S. ran that particular film clip every twenty minutes. The results were devastating.

In the eyes of most Americans, Somoza pulled the trigger that killed Stewart. That was the message the media wanted transmitted, and that was the message that came through. When the news of Stewart's death reached me, I remember placing my head in my hands and saying, "My God, how could this happen!" But the deed was done and there wasn't enough remorse in the world to undo it.

That one tragedy, all documented on film, did more to turn public opinion against me and the government than anything else. Yet, there was a war going on in Nicaragua, and it was a prerogative of the government to censor or have press control. This we never did, and the film showing Stewart's death was released. I believed in freedom of the press and defended that freedom until the end. Had I been a dictator, as so many members of the news media claimed, nothing critical of me or the government of Nicaragua would have gone out of the country. The media were permitted to film, write, and transmit anything and everything — the good and the bad. It is well known that very little, if anything, good was ever transmitted.

The power of television is frightening. I have felt its strength and know firsthand of its destructive capability. In order to remain free, this important communications medium should exercise restraint and fairness. Otherwise, the Leftist cause, which is the cause supported by so many in this field, will one day prevail. If that day should come, then a Dan Rather would not be licensed to shape, form, and mold a story according to his personal preconceived notions. That decision would be made for him, and who knows, in my case it might have been.

Chapter Fifteen

HOW MUCH MORE?

The September, 1978 offensive by the Communist-led guerrillas was a failure. We were faced with a military war and an
economic war, and in each conflict the government was victorious. It was a cleverly designed scheme, but it didn't work. Very
simply put, it didn't work because the people still supported me
and the government.

This was something that Carter, Perez, Torrijos, Carazo, and
Castro could never understand. The masses were for me and
the government, and their faith could not be shaken. Every
conceivable means was attempted to destroy that faith and
every attempt failed.

In a way, perhaps, the political success of the Liberal Party
in Nicaragua could be compared to the Roosevelt years in the
Democratic Party in the United States. If history serves me
correctly, Roosevelt's support came from the masses. In most
instances, big business opposed Roosevelt but he kept getting
reelected. Had he lived, who knows how long he would have
stayed in office?

As has been stated many times, the Liberal Party was
opposed by many of the more affluent people in Nicaragua.
They represented the cornerstone of the Conservative Party.
When election time rolled around, the people voted, by a vast
majority, for the Liberal Party. In the U.S. there is an old
political saying that, "The voice of the people shall be heard."
Well, that applied to Nicaragua. When I ran for President, I
had the support of the people. This democratic process didn't
suit Mr. Carter and his politically dominated followers. If they

couldn't defeat me in a closely watched election, other means
had to be found.

There is irony in all of this. The news media, in the main,
have been inclined to take an opposite political viewpoint from
the so-called vested interest groups. Their sympathy and support have historically gone with the "people." I was the choice
of my people and was opposed by certain special interest
groups. Yet, the media were possessed with the idea that
Somoza must be kicked out of office — one way or another.

I think the most puzzling thing to the media was how a
strong anti-Communist, free enterpriser could have the support of the people. Carlos Andres Perez could never understand
this and neither could Mr. Carter. They didn't understand the
nature of the Nicaraguan people. They were, and still are, anti-
Communist. Furthermore, in every city, town, municipality,
and even in the "campos," I knew people by their first names.
These people believed in me and they believed in the Liberal
Party. As a result of this faith, we won elections.

When I couldn't be defeated at the polls, other means had to
be found to remove me from office. Many of those unpleas-
ant experiences have been related. The September general
strike and the September military offensive represented a bold
move to destroy me and the government of Nicaragua. This
move failed and I still had the people with me. With the
September victory, I thought we had finally won and that my
detractors would also recognize that fact. I underestimated
Jimmy Carter. I didn't underestimate his intelligence and
ability, because those two areas of limitation had been established. But I did underestimate the extent of his connivance.

Approximately one month after our September victory, Mr.
Carter, unilaterally, inaugurated what he termed a "Multi-
National Consultation on Nicaragua." Technically, this group
was called "The O.A.S. Sponsored Commission of Friendly
Cooperation and Conciliation." Mr. Carter enlisted the support
of Mr. William Jorden, a Texan and former ambassador to
Panama, to consult with Venezuela, Panama, Colombia, Costa
Rica, and other countries. This announcement by Carter to
establish multinational consultation came out of the blue
and took me by surprise. I remember thinking that this man
would try anything, no matter how deceitful or how devious.

The other co-conspirators, Venezuela, Panama, and Costa Rica, were delighted that they had another shot at me and my government. With such a power base, the multinational group could make things happen and the group could command the attention of the international news media. Things did begin to happen.

Mr. Carter and Mr. Jorden proposed that Mr. William Rogers be appointed as one of the mediators between the government of Nicaragua and the opposition. I could not believe that Mr. Carter would make such a proposal. My country had been through hell and was still intact. We had defeated the combined forces of the opposition, which included the Communists, and I thought peace should be ours. But not for Mr. Carter and Mr. Jorden. They now wanted William Rogers to serve as a mediator.

To suggest Mr. Rogers was an affront to my intelligence. He had preconceived conclusions on the government of Nicaragua, and these conclusions were all wrong. It was his law firm that petitioned the U.S. government to place an embargo on certain export items from Nicaragua. To have accepted William Rogers as a mediator would have been like saying to Mr. Carter: "Send your fox down to Nicaragua and we'll put him in charge of guarding the chickens." I had been kicked around so much by the Carter Administration that I thought, this is some kind of a soccer match and Somoza is the football. I wanted to tell Mr. Carter what he could do with Mr. Rogers, but I felt that would serve no purpose. It must be understood that Nicaragua is a small Central American country, and it appeared to me that we had been forced to take on the world. Nevertheless, I stood firm on William Rogers and said that he was not acceptable.

In accordance with protocol, I gave Mr. Jorden my reasons for not accepting Rogers. I told him that my understanding of a mediator was one who was impartial and one who could objectively weigh the arguments of two opposing views and render a decision fair to each side. I politely pointed out to him that if I agreed to a mediator and then did not comply with the mediation results, I would be hypocritical. I stated that, in my opinion, Mr. Rogers could not be impartial and, therefore, I could not accept him as a mediator. My objections did not convince Mr. Jorden, and we fought this matter in the U.S. State Department and in the Organization of American States. In the end, however, we didn't get Mr. Rogers.

While this international maneuvering was taking place, I recall thinking that these proceedings are unreal — it isn't really happening. I thought, how could one man, Mr. Carter, unilaterally precipitate such a convulsive situation for Nicaragua? Did he think that Nicaragua was a domain of the United States and that he owned our small country? I meditated on how this man, after all we had been through, could have the unmitigated gall to send a special envoy to consult with me on the problems of Nicaragua and, as a result of this one man's decision, interfere further in the affairs of my country! Suffice it to say we once again were embroiled in international politics. I could only conclude that Mr. Carter had made up his mind that he would not let this small anti-Communist nation come out victorious.

Mr. Jorden made two visits to my office to discuss mediation. On his second visit, he did a rather strange thing. Before departing, he said: "Mr. President, I would like a souvenir from your office." I responded: "Of course, look around and take anything you like." He finally selected an ashtray which had written on it "SOMOZA–PRESIDENT." As I reflect upon his words and actions, I'm convinced they represented more than just a desire to have something from my office. Jorden knew at that time that the United States would not let up in her effort to topple me and the government. In October, 1978, he knew that the U.S. had me in a vice and that the vice would be screwed down until there was no life left in me or Nicaragua. So he wanted a souvenir before the Marxists took over the presidential complex.

When it was determined that William Rogers was totally unacceptable, Mr. Jorden made a new approach. It was his thinking that if I wouldn't accept their choice as a mediator, then I should agree to a multinational mediation team. For me, that came back to the same basic question — which nations? Mr. Jorden already had his nations in mind, and I had mine. He stated that he wanted Colombia, the Dominican Republic, and the United States; and I wanted Guatemala and El Salvador. It should be pointed out, however, that this multinational group would not be called a mediation team. In essence, this was to be a consultation and negotiation group. As proposed, the group would come to Nicaragua, do a study, and then make recommendations as to the "solution" to *our* problem. It just didn't make sense, but that is what the United States wanted. To me, it was like "same song, second verse."

Naturally, I protested the designation of Colombia. That country's attitude toward me and the government of Nicaragua was well known. I had previously been the recipient of vitriolic attacks from Colombia, and that nation's attitude had not changed. Even more supportive of my position in regard to Colombia, was the fact that we had an international dispute with that country. I pointed out to Mr. Jorden that this was a maritime dispute concerning the continental shelf. I said to Mr. Jorden, "What you want to do is give Colombia the right to build a lighthouse, and use Nicaragua as a base upon which to build that lighthouse." I mentioned to him that such action didn't seem quite ethical to me. But Mr. Jorden had his orders from the White House and the U.S. State Department. Therefore, he insisted that Colombia be included in the multinational group bent upon breaking the back of the government of Nicaragua.

Again, Carlos Andres Perez comes upon the scene. Only this time he made a mistake. Perez always wanted to be smart and clever, but he didn't possess the mental equipment to be either. What he had was money and that, as is well known, can make up for sizable mental deficiencies. He had tried so many times to overthrow my government, and he had always failed. Now he was becoming desperate. In his characteristically scheming fashion, he hit upon an idea which he thought would bring about more bad publicity for Nicaragua, and, at the same time, put himself back in the limelight — a position he dearly loved.

Perez pressured the president of Colombia into making a crass error. Obviously, neither Perez nor the Colombian president kept a log on the activities of Mr. Carter's multinational group. Perez had decided the time was right to denounce me and the government of Nicaragua at the United Nations. He pressured the Colombian president into jointly signing a letter of denunciation, and this letter was presented to the UN.

The United States was deeply troubled when this letter was made public. Colombia, their ally in the "get Nicaragua" move, had made a serious mistake. When the U.S. representative came back to see me, I told him it was exactly as I had stated. I said: "Look, this is not an evenhanded business and Colombia has just proved that." Of course, this meant that Colombia was out.

At that time, Guatemala, El Salvador, the Dominican Republic, and the United States were being considered as the multinational group. I called the presidents of Guatemala and El Salvador and suggested they accept this assignment. With Colombia out, I knew that the United States would exert tremendous pressure on El Salvador to condemn my government. I knew this for a fact; it was no guessing game with me. To get El Salvador off the hook, I called the president back and suggested that he reconsider and not accept the invitation. So El Salvador dropped out. That left the U.S., the Dominican Republic, and Guatemala.

There was speculation as to why I agreed to accept the Dominican Republic. There was a very good reason — I thought Nicaragua would be treated fairly and that the Dominican Republic would not yield to U.S. pressure. That assumption was based on the fact that I had known the Foreign Minister, Admiral Jiminez, for several years and our relationship had been good. Mainly, I believed the Admiral to be sound ideologically, and that was always important to me.

I accepted Guatemala because our two countries had many common problems, and I believed Guatemala understood the reason for our difficulty in Nicaragua. The president of Guatemala selected a man by the name of Alfredo Obiols to represent that country. Obiols had been Vice Minister of Economy for Guatemala during the Arana regime.

When Mr. Jorden left Nicaragua, the multinational group was structured. The Dominican Republic, Guatemala, and the United States would send their representatives to Nicaragua to investigate the differences between the government of Nicaragua and the opposition, and make recommendations for a "peaceful solution."

The entire operation had an air of absurdity. It was as though Mr. Carter owned Nicaragua, and since it was his personal property, he could do with that country as he pleased. I found myself in the uncomfortable position of hoping that two small nations could withstand the pressure and power of the United States of America. I knew what the U.S. would do.

It should be understood that the U.S. State Department wanted the multinational group to have the stature of a mediating team. I had opposed the idea from the beginning and I still opposed it. Even though I believed that Guatemala and the Dominican Republic would be fair with Nicaragua, I was well aware of the pressure the U.S. could exert. I anticipated that the cards *might* be stacked against Nicaragua; and that if I had agreed to a mediation status, I would be honorbound to abide by their conclusions and recommendations. Again, it was just a premonition, but I followed my hunch and refused to accept "the good office holders" as a mediation group.

I had a good reason for accepting the negotiating team. It will be recalled that previously, at a Liberal Party Somoza rally of 150,000 people, I had announced that I would step down from the presidency in 1981 and retire from the Army. In accepting the multinational negotiating team, I hoped that, through negotiations with the opposition groups, a peaceful and harmonious solution could be found for the transfer of governmental power in 1981. This procedure, I felt, could give the opposition groups confidence and they could look forward to peaceful elections in 1981. In prenegotiation conversations, I suggested the writing of a new electoral law which would permit all political parties to start their political activities immediately. Under the old election laws, it was difficult for a new party to get started, due to the number of signatures which were required. Well, I wanted to make it easier for these political parties.

There was another reason why I accepted the multinational group. I wanted to show the world that I was not afraid to have the group come to Nicaragua and that I would cooperate in this endeavor.

I knew the countries involved in this negotiating group and then the representatives were named. Ambassador William Bowdler would represent the United States. He had formerly been U.S. Ambassador to El Salvador and Guatemala. Admiral

Jiminez would represent the Dominican Republic. He had
previously been the Minister of Defense under President
Joaquin Balaguer. I considered him to be a good friend of
mine. Ambassador Alfredo Obiols would represent Guatemala.
He had been the Vice Minister of Economy during the Arana
regime, and Nicaragua had had good relations with the Arana
government.

Additionally, when Arana was appointed Guatemala's Ambassador to Nicaragua, prior to the time he became president,
we had provided him with special security. In his term of
office as Commander of Zacapa, he had wiped out the
guerrillas and there were Leftists who still sought revenge. So,
we gave him special protection. I evaluated the personalities of
this group and was rather pleased. Certainly, I had no personality clash with Jiminez or Obiols. As we shall see, it developed
that personalities were not important, and past relationships
were not important. Their presence on this team was, in reality,
of a concomitant nature. They were there to take orders from
their governments and that course they would follow.

The multinational negotiating team arrived in Nicaragua on
October 6, 1978. They were treated cordially and respectfully,
but there was no genuflecting on the part of Nicaragua. My
people and I had our pride and we were not going to be
patronized.

The initial meeting was held, and it was interesting. At the
outset, I stated that, "In my opinion, the only thing wrong on
the Nicaragua scene is the longevity of the name Somoza." I
stated that my government had met all the requirements of a
democracy. Further, I pointed out that we had met and
fulfilled all recognized conditions of a representative government, and that we were proud of the freedoms enjoyed by the
people of Nicaragua. The group expressed the desire to begin
immediately a dialogue with the opposition. I told them that
was fine, and that they could begin such dialogue whenever
they liked. So, the rounds of negotiations started.

I remember thinking that the outcome of those negotiations
could be crucial for me and the entire government. So I decided
to make, as participants, the entire Cabinet, the Board of
Directors of the Liberal Party, the members of the General

Staff of the Nicaraguan Army, and the Liberal Party members in the Congress and the Senate. I wanted all of these people to have complete knowledge of everything that was being said by me, the negotiating team, and the opposition. During the entire time that the negotiating team was in Nicaragua, all of these people were on call.

The negotiation team had its first meeting with the opposition and returned with the first proposal. The first proposal was drastic, and I was rather surprised that the team would bring back such a proposal. The spokesman for the group said he would like to present the opposition proposal and it was this:

"Mr. President, you, your brother, your son, and your family will have to leave Nicaragua." Since this proposal involved all of the people previously mentioned, the Cabinet, etc., I felt they should be advised. After all, if I left, they would suffer the consequences. The presidency of Nicaragua was, at that point, not limited to me. It involved the Cabinet, the Board of Directors of the Liberal Party, the members of the General Staff of the Army, and all of our party members in the Congress and the Senate. By members of the Congress and Senate, I don't mean just the leadership. The entire party membership was included in these consultations.

There was much movement back and forth, but nothing meaningful was happening. At that time, we decided that Nicaragua should name an official negotiating team. This group was comprised of our Foreign Minister, Dr. Julio Quintana, Dr. Orlando Montenegro, who was formerly President of the Congress for many years, and Dr. Alceo Tablada Solis, Secretary General of the Liberal Party. In that group, every phase of our party was represented — the old Liberal Party segment was represented by Dr. Julio Quintana, the new Liberal Party wing by Dr. Orlando Montenegro, and both by the Secretary General who represented the old and the new factions of the party. This group then entered the negotiation picture. These men worked diligently to effectuate a workable compromise with the negotiating team and the opposition forces in Nicaragua.

After my first visit with the multinational negotiating group, I had the feeling that we would not have honest negotiations. Like the OAS team, I felt this group had come to

Nicaragua with preconceived ideas. After my third visit with the team I was sure. One morning Obiols from Guatemala requested to see the Foreign Minister of Nicaragua. He was ushered into that gentleman's office, and appeared to be in a very nervous condition. His hands were shaking as he handed our Foreign Minister a paper. Then Obiols said: "This paper represents what the opposition will accept, and I urge you to accept it." The Foreign Minister read the proposal and said: "That's ridiculous; we can't accept that." It was practically the same proposal, that my family and I would have to leave Nicaragua. Then the minister came to see me. He said: "Mr. President, the actions of Obiols and his presentation of this proposal positively indicate to me that this man, who we thought would be fair, is against us." I recall telling my minister that he couldn't imagine the amount of pressure the United States had put on that man and the government of Guatemala.

We went around and around in these negotiations but we were getting nowhere. However, one point was coming through loud and clear, the negotiating team had come to Nicaragua with instructions to get me out of office. They maneuvered the situation to the extent that I was almost in that proverbial corner. Due to the fact that the future of so many people was involved, I felt it was time to hold a consultation with the Cabinet, the Congress, leaders of the Liberal Party, and members of the General Staff of the Army. I wanted all of these people to know exactly where I stood with the negotiating team and what it would take to satisfy them.

The meeting was called and I spoke to the group. I told them that in the opinion of the negotiating team, with representation from the United States, Guatemala, and the Dominican Republic, there was only one solution to the political problems of Nicaragua. That solution meant that I, my son Tacho, my brother Joe, and our families would have to leave Nicaragua. I explained further that they were also involved in that solution, because after the departure of all the Somozas, they would have to turn the government over to a board consisting of three members, and that the Liberal Party would have one member on that board. Those respected leaders of the government were in a state of shock. They could imagine the opposition making such a preposterous proposal, but it seemed incomprehensible to them that the "good office holders" of the negotiating team could seriously do so.

I felt that all the military commanders should be advised as to the proposal, because they were certainly involved. So I called in the sixteen department commanders for a consultation. I explained to them that we had reached a crucial point in the negotiation process and that they needed to be informed as to the proposal which had been made. I then proceeded to explain to the military commanders what it would take to satisfy the negotiating team. Almost in unison, they said: "Those people are crazy."

It appeared a stalemate had been reached. I thought, however, there is one other possible solution that might satisfy the United States, and I say the United States because that country was calling the shots. That solution would be a plebiscite. I then called another meeting with the Cabinet, Congress, party leaders, and General Staff. The idea was explained to them and they thought it was more than fair.

The proposal was simply this: If I were the winner in an OAS-supervised election, I would reorganize the government, include the opposition party in significant governmental areas, and serve out my duly elected term. If I lost the election, I would resign as President and the opposition, principally the Frente Amplio de Oposicion (FAO), would be in control of the government. I am oversimplifying the detailed plebiscite proposal, but I have stated the "guts" of the movement. To set forth the volume of official correspondence, proposals, and counterproposals, would require a book in itself. Basically, my position was that all the people in Nicaragua should have a say in such an important matter, so the fair approach was to hold an election.

The negotiating team had arrived in Nicaragua on October 6, 1978, and now it was nearing Christmas. The team ostensibly took a Christmas recess so that each representative could return to his respective country and receive further instructions. Then they were to return to Nicaragua and hammer out the details on the plebiscite. The farce of the entire negotiation procedure is illustrated by the fact that the team never reconvened in

Nicaragua again. One member did return and that was the U.S. representative, William Bowdler. That should make it unmistakably clear that one person, Jimmy Carter, was calling all the shots and that the other members were on the multinational negotiating team in name only.

By that time, Ambassador Bowdler of the U.S. was aware of the unity which existed in Nicaragua. He came to visit with me and said: "I want to congratulate you, because you have the party, the Congress, the Army, and the government solidly behind you." I replied: "Mr. Ambassador, this should show you that I'm not telling lies to my people and they know what they are talking about." He then came back with a statement that enunciated perfectly the position of the United States. He said: "Nevertheless, I have instructions from the President of the United States and the Secretary of State of the United States to tell you that you have to leave." With that message of finality, I invited the Ambassador to lunch.

It was not what one could call an enjoyable luncheon. We reviewed the negotiation efforts, and I endeavored to show him the fallacy of the U.S. position. My words had no effect on the Ambassador. He pointed out that the President, the Secretary of State, the Secretary of Defense, and even Mr. Carter's Cabinet had concluded that I must leave. The Ambassador had laid all of his cards out on the table, face up, and I could read them clearly.

In view of all that had transpired, and events that would follow, I have the moral right justifiably to accuse Carter of being sanguinary. I proposed an election as the solution to Nicaragua's problems. Mr. Carter had instructed his representative to negate any moves toward a plebiscite. It was not I who fostered bloodshed. That dubious honor belongs to Mr. Carter.

Before the Christmas recess, I invited my old friend from the Dominican Republic, Admiral Jimenez, over for a visit. Our friendship covered several years, and I always felt we could talk. The discussion was amiable and, once again, I presented Nicaragua's side of an uncalled-for controversy. He listened politely and then said: "General, accept the proposal. That way you can save your property and your money in Nicaragua." I couldn't help but recall, "et tu Brute." I knew then for certain that the U.S. had the Dominican Republic. I knew, too, that I was being set up for a betrayal. If I handed over the government to the opposition forces, which consisted of businessmen, Sandinistas, Communists, and Leftists, and left the country, those opposition forces could do whatever they chose to do with my property. My old friend, Admiral Jiminez, had suddenly developed the characteristics of a chameleon.

The Admiral came back to the proposal, which was simply that my family and I had to leave the country. I was becoming wearisome of this contumacious proposal and said: "Look, Admiral, you people may think this government is a dictatorship, but your proposal has been handed down through every channel of government, as well as the leaders of the party, and not one person has accepted the proposal." Then I told him that we didn't have even a small ripple of support for the proposal. I told him that in my meetings with all of the leaders in the government, the party, and the Army, there was unanimous opposition to the proposal.

I recall telling the Admiral that if twenty or thirty percent of those people had suggested that I accept the proposal, I probably would have done so. If that had happened, there would have been a legitimate reason for leaving. I could then have said: "Gentlemen, we are divided, so I will accept the proposal." But that was not the case. They were not divided. I knew those leaders, and they had the courage of their convictions. If one of them had thought the proposal should have been accepted, he would have spoken up. In the past we had experienced some rough-and-tumble debates, and those people were not reluctant to express their views.

The Admiral took his leave, but he had not changed his mind. I think his inner convictions were with me and my government, but his instructions had already been handed down by *his* government.

When negotiations were at their most hectic level, I made one rational proposal after another. I tried to find some common ground from which we could work. Logically, one of these proposals should have been acceptable. The negotiators seemed to be in a state of confusion, because they knew I was trying to develop a plan which would be fair for the government and the opposition forces.

Apparently this same confusion was applicable to the opposition forces. That group was a conglomeration of Sandinistas, Communists, Leftists, and prominent business people. In that group there was no real cohesion and the leadership was splintered. At that point Alfonso Robelo, who would later become a member of the ruling Marxist junta, and Xavier Chamorro, brother of the deceased Pedro Joaquin Chamorro, became so confused they asked permission to leave the country so they could visit with Carlos Andres Perez in Venezuela. They knew I was making an all-out effort to come up with a workable compromise, and they needed some direction. Thus, they wanted to consult with Perez. With the nation on a virtual war operational basis, the government was carefully scrutinizing those who wanted to leave the country and those who wanted to enter the country.

Prior to Robelo's and Chamorro's request to go to Venezuela, I had sent Luis Pallais Debayle down to talk to Carlos Andres Perez. Knowing of the influence Perez had with Omar Torrijos and Rodrigo Carazo, I felt it was worth the effort. By some miracle, I thought, Luis Pallais might be able to show Perez the soundness of our plebiscite plan. Perez received Luis and they had a long visit in which all the ramifications of my election plan were discussed. To Luis, it appeared that Perez thought the plan had merit and was worth exploring. Ultimately, however, Perez did not perform as we had hoped. He did not push the plebiscite plan.

After considering the request of Robelo and Chamorro, the government decided against granting Robelo permission to travel to Venezuela. He was a leader with the Sandinistas, and I considered him to be subversive. In my opinion, the denial was warranted. When word of the denial reached Ambassador Bowdler of the U.S., he interceded immediately on behalf of Robelo. After Bowdler's strong intervention on behalf of Robelo, I passed the word on to the proper authority to grant Robelo permission to leave the country. Once more, I was endeavoring to please the United States and, also, I wanted to show Bowdler that I was an open-minded man.

Bowdler was a busy man. Between negotiation sessions he went to Costa Rica to visit with Carazo and to Panama to see Torrijos. He wanted their input on the plebiscite plan but mainly, I think, he wanted to assure these men that the U.S. was standing firm on the proposal that I had to leave Nicaragua.

Finally, the opposition forces came up with a counterproposal to my plebiscite plan, and their stipulations were submitted. They wanted the following:

> • **The removal of the Guardia Nacional from wherever they might be stationed in the country, and that the Guardia be confined to barracks during the election.**
> • **The removal of designated policemen from any and all public duties and assignments in the country.**
> • **The importation of three thousand foreigners to man all polling places and that they would determine who was eligible to vote.**
> • **That on election day, I suspend the duties of all the justices of the peace in the entire country and transport them (around six thousand people) to Managua.**
> • **I was to leave the country seventy-two hours before the election and take my brother, Joe, and my son, Tacho, with me.**
> • **That new voting places were to be established throughout the country.**

There were other ridiculous stipulations. Obviously, we could not accept those terms and conditions. The United States may not have learned about Communist promises, but I had learned. As a starter, I knew the moment the Guardia Nacional were confined to quarters, it would be a green light for all the revolutionaries to move in, and they would have. It would have been an open invitation to military disaster, and I knew it. Of course, that could have been the exact reason for the stipulation. But for the brashness of that requirement, we might have successfully negotiated the other stipulations. Even so, the Liberal Party leaders and I agreed to confine to barracks all military personnel except those on the frontiers and those engaged with the enemy.

I use the words "might have" advisedly. Obviously, we could not agree to terms and conditions which would have made it impossible for the Liberal Party to win. In retrospect, I don't believe Mr. Carter and Mr. Bowdler would have agreed to a fair and impartial election. I can see now that even if we had won an election which had been "rigged" against us, the United States would not have honored the results. Therefore, they had

to be certain that the election guidelines would be so con-
stituted that the people supporting me and the Liberal Party
either would not vote, or they would be disqualified.

Think for just a moment: Would Mr. Carter agree to leave
the United States seventy-two hours prior to election time?
Would he agree to changing the boundaries of all those
precincts which he had carried in the previous election? Would
he agree that every mayor in the country who had supported
him would have to leave his city and come to Washington, D.C.
on election day? Would he agree to change the location of every
single voting box he had carried in the previous election? Would
Mr. Carter agree to the importation of thousands of foreigners, from whatever country, to serve as election judges, particularly if he thought that every single election judge would be
against him? There is no way he would agree to such proposals.
And, yet, this is what Mr. Carter and Mr. Bowdler wanted me
to do.

Actually, the Liberal Party and I agreed to so many of their
ridiculous stipulations that it was difficult for them to find
justification for not calling an election.

When we consider the opposition forces (FAO *et al.*), we
must put in that group the U.S.-dominated negotiating team.
The U.S. representative, William Bowdler, was actually assisting the FAO in the preparation of their plebiscite requirements.

The leaders of the Liberal Party, the Nicaraguan negotiating team, and I were aghast at some of the plebiscite
requirements presented by the FAO and the multinational
negotiating team; but, under the stressful conditions which
existed at that time, we decided to go along with most of their
proposals. In answer to those proposals, we submitted a compromise plan. That plan was more than fair and if the
United States and her co-conspirators had been honestly negotiating, the compromise plan would have been accepted. But
it received practically no publicity and the world was not aware
that I was exerting every effort to satisfy the United States
and reach a democratic solution to the problems in Nicaragua.
Much effort went into the preparation of the Act of Compromise in which we detailed those requirements for a free
and honest presidential election.

Anyone reading the compromise proposal will have to admit, regardless of prejudice, that it was a fair and workable plan. In reality, much of the language in our compromise plan was lifted directly from the plan submitted by the negotiating team.

The perfidy of the United States in this negotiating performance is beyond belief. The plebiscite plan was a good one. If the United States, as represented by Jimmy Carter and William Bowdler, truly believed in the democratic process, a supervised and controlled election would have been called. I agreed to abide by the results and if the people of Nicaragua didn't want me to serve out my term of office, I would step down. Mr. Carter, Mr. Vance, and Mr. Bowdler were fearful that, no matter what restrictions they demanded in a free election, I would still win. They simply could not take that chance. So while the Carter negotiating team was in Nicaragua exhibiting to the world their "serious effort" to establish a free election, Mr. Carter was *demanding* that I leave the country and take all of my family with me. It was a total farce, and that's the kindest language I can use.

Based upon the fraudulent actions of the negotiating team and the orders coming from the White House, I could ascertain that, at best, my future was questionable. My great concern was for the Guardia Nacional, government leaders, and members of the Liberal Party. So I called a meeting of the Cabinet to explain fully the possible consequences. I told the Cabinet it was quite clear that the United States wanted to get rid of me; and that they, and the other party leaders, were not the object of contempt. I wanted them to know that if I left, there was a good possibility they could salvage something. The Cabinet, to a man, came right back with the statement that, "We are all in this together, and we can't permit the dissolution of our government and our country."

I don't possess the words to express the feeling and emotion I experienced as I looked in the faces of these loyal friends. Even so, I went further. I said: "Gentlemen, I have enough money to live outside of Nicaragua, but I don't want to subject you to the peril and danger which may come your way — even if we have a peaceful arrangement." I insisted that they do some serious meditating before it was too late to change their minds. There was no hesitation on the part of the Cabinet. They repeated that all of us were in this together. Their faces, their determination, and their loyalty will remain with me always. As a result of their decision, they would suffer and their families would suffer. This knowledge causes me grief and pain and these, also, will be with me always.

While the so-called negotiations were proceeding, Congressman John Murphy of New York had dinner with President Carter. The true purpose of the dinner was to discuss the problems in Nicaragua and, specifically, the plebiscite proposal which I had made. According to Murphy, they discussed Nicaragua for approximately forty-five minutes. In a later conversation with the Congressman from New York, he advised me that it seemed as though Carter's mind was set against Nicaragua and that he simply could not get through to him.

On another occasion, I tried to speak to Mr. Carter personally. I felt if I could talk to the man, there was just a chance he might realize that he was making a horrible mistake on Nicaragua. That conversation never took place. Carter's mind was made up, and he didn't want to talk to me.

My plebiscite proposal had been personally presented to Ambassador Bowdler, with the fervent hope that it would be acceptable to the United States. As it developed, the negotiating team, to their way of thinking, had completed their work. Before leaving Managua, Ambassador Bowdler came to see me. Bowdler said: "Mr. President, this paper which you have given me is unacceptable. I will leave Nicaragua and when, and if, you decide to accept the opposition's offer, I will be at your service." With that, he left. And that was the end of Mr. Carter's brainchild, the multinational consultation. It's interesting to note that neither Obiols nor Jimenez came by to see me. They knew their official attitude toward Nicaragua was wrong. Their countries had yielded to U.S. pressure and their decisions were made for them in advance.

While the negotiations were under way, a surprising source requested an appointment. General Dennis McAuliffe, the Commander in Chief of the Southern Command in Panama, wanted to pay me a visit. My relations with the U.S. military had always been very cordial and I saw no reason to deny the request. To my surprise, the General didn't come alone — he

came with Ambassador Bowdler. Bowdler's presence made it
difficult to talk to General McAuliffe and I thought, that's
precisely the reason Bowdler is accompanying the General.

After an open discussion, General McAuliffe stated that
he thought I should leave Nicaragua. I remember thinking that
Mr. Carter is being devious again. He has selected the last
source where I might have counted on support, the U.S. Army,
and directed that source to tell me that I should leave. The
White House had used the OAS, the State Department, special
envoys, and now the power of the U.S. Army! Mr. Carter was
employing every facility at his command to destroy me and the
government of Nicaragua. Later I learned General McAuliffe
had denied, under oath before a congressional subcommittee,
that he had ever asked me to resign the presidency or to leave
the country.

After General McAuliffe and Ambassador Bowdler left, I
sat and meditated for a time. I thought, who is really responsible for the debacle in which Nicaragua finds herself? There
was only one answer — the United States of America. Sure,
Cuba supplied arms, men and equipment; Venezuela supplied
money; and Costa Rica provided the staging area for invasion
forces. But who placed an embargo on all military supplies to
Nicaragua? It was the United States. With one telephone call,
the United States could have brought about a halt to the
Sandinista operation in Costa Rica. But Carter took the opposite stance. His single-minded and overwhelming purpose had
been to put Nicaragua in the hands of the Communists. He had
aided and abetted all of those destructive forces with the same
basic purpose. His most telling blow was the embargo on arms
and ammunition. If the Guardia Nacional had not been
deprived of those items, the Communists would never have
succeeded. So I remember thinking, who put us in this tenuous
situation? Only one man, Jimmy Carter.

My thoughts went back to the time after my heart attack,
when Daniel Oduber from Costa Rica paid me a visit in
Nicaragua. Remember, that was in 1977 just after Mrs. Jimmy
Carter had been in Costa Rica and was escorted by Mr. Robert
Pastor of the White House. At that early date, Mr. Pastor had
said to Oduber, "When are we going to get that son-of-a-bitch
to the north out of the presidency?" I didn't realize it then, but

the die had already been irrevocably cast. I was targeted. I'm convinced that this attitude on the part of Mr. Carter will, in the future, weigh heavily on the shoulders of the United States. The Nicaraguan experience will cost the U.S. many friends. The sad part is, and most of the people in the United States know this, that the U.S. no longer has many friends to lose.

With the words of General McAuliffe burned into my mind, I felt it was once again necessary to have a consultation with all of our governmental leaders. I wanted them to know that the pressure was mounting and that now Mr. Carter was using the U.S. Army in an effort to get me to leave. They all understood the importance of the Southern Military Command, because in the past we had enjoyed close relations with that command. Even with that information, the position of my people did not change one iota. Their collective thinking was that this move on the part of Mr. Carter represented *extreme intervention.*

After the Christmas interlude, Ambassador Bowdler came to see me on a matter of great importance. Of course, nothing he could have said at that point would have surprised me. Bowdler said: "I have an ultimatum for you from the President of the United States. You, General Jose Somoza, your son, and your families must leave Nicaragua forthwith." That was it. No more negotiations, no more discussions and, truthfully, no more playacting on the part of the Dominican Republic and Guatemala. The Admiral and Obiols had had their instructions from the beginning, and the entire performance had been a charade.

Guatemala, in particular, knew that should Nicaragua fall to the Communists, all Central American countries would be in danger. There were already pronounced problems with the Communists and the Left in Guatemala. I knew their sympathy was with me and the government, but the power and the influence of the United States were too much for Guatemala. Actually, there was no multinational negotiating team. Instead of assuming a deceitful posture, Mr. Carter should have announced that he was sending Ambassador Bowdler to Nicaragua to tell the Somozas that they had to leave the country. Such an announcement would at least have been honest, and it certainly would have saved a lot of money, pain, and agony.

I told Mr. Bowdler that the ultimatum from Mr. Carter was unacceptable; and after that traumatic experience, I truly felt alone. My neighboring countries, with the exception of Costa Rica, wanted to assist Nicaragua. I had talked to all the presidents, even while the negotiating team was in Nicaragua. I knew for certain what their sentiments were. Romero of El Salvador, Lucas of Guatemala, and Paz Garcia of Honduras were already feeling the thrust of the Communists in their countries. I could sense their collective attitude. Each felt that if he took the side of the United States against Nicaragua, then perhaps, just perhaps, the U.S. would come to his assistance when his hour of peril arrived. They didn't understand Mr. Carter. I had even repeated a previous Bowdler conversation to them and the message was devastating. *Bowdler had told me that the Carter policy was to see that all of the Right-wing governments in Central America were replaced, and that Nicaragua would be the first to go.* I was reminded of Benjamin Franklin's retort to John Hancock just prior to the signing of the Declaration of Independence: "We must indeed all hang together or, most assuredly, we shall all hang separately."

How much more would Nicaragua have to take from Mr. Carter? The answer to that question was near at hand.

Chapter Sixteen

THE FINAL ATTACK

The attacks from Costa Rica were becoming more intense. The infiltration from Costa Rica was increasing each day. We pleaded with the OAS to investigate those areas in Costa Rica which provided staging and training for the aggressor forces. Since those who opposed Nicaragua in the OAS had a majority of the votes, the OAS refused to go to those revolutionary headquarter sites. If they happened, by sheer luck, to wander into one of those areas, the Costa Ricans would admonish the OAS observers because, according to the Costa Ricans, they were in a military reservation area and it was dangerous. The OAS observers would meekly apologize for having trespassed and make a hasty retreat. It was, and still is, incomprehensible.

For approximately four and one-half months Nicaragua had been shelled from Costa Rica. It seems unbelievable, but the shelling of Nicaragua was taking place while the negotiation team was in Managua. Most of the shelling was occurring in the Peñas Blancas area which was the Pan American Highway entrance to Nicaragua.

For over four months we were raising our governmental voices to the highest level about the blatant violation of international law. Those persons going through the Peñas Blancas customs post were witness to those violations and were travelling all through Central America and giving reports about being shelled at Peñas Blancas. The United States was aware of this situation, as were other countries in the OAS, but not one country — not even one man — would come forward and say that the law must be upheld.

Now Mr. Carter is crying about the violation of international law. Surely he can remember that he was the one who started all this international law upheaval, and it was started in Nicaragua. Admittedly, Nicaragua is a small nation, but in the eyes of international law that should make no difference. Mr. Carter should recall that the basic concept of a democracy lies in the legal rights of any individual. The United States has always proudly proclaimed that in the eyes of the law, all people are equal — no matter if they are rich and powerful or just poor indigents. That same rule, under international law, applies to all nations — big or small. Well, in Nicaragua we saw a complete breakdown of this fundamental concept. Our national sovereignty was being violated every day, but Mr. Carter said nothing. Not only that, he and his administration took the side of the lawbreakers.

The leaders in my government and I were totally disillusioned. For all those years we had faithfully abided by the rules of international law and then we saw those rules disappear. Mr. Carter set a tragic example for the Western Hemisphere. The United States is the power in this Hemisphere; the United States is the power in the Organization of American States; and yet, Mr. Carter condoned the external aggression against Nicaragua. The example has been established. In the future, it's every nation for itself. Mr. Carter can take credit for this international law transformation.

A perfect example of international lawbreaking relates to a visit I had with President Lucas of Guatemala. I was giving him a report of the revolutionary raids from Costa Rica and bemoaning the fact that the OAS showed no concern whatsoever. Then I began relating the facts about the mortar shelling which had been going on for over four months. He interrupted that report to tell me he knew firsthand about the mortar shelling from Costa Rica. He said, "I had one of my people bring a racehorse from Panama to Guatemala, and when the driver was crossing over to Nicaragua, he was shelled at Peñas Blancas." He stated further that the driver was really frightened because he thought he and the racehorse would be killed.

I found that to be incredible. There was the president of our neighbor to the north, calmly admitting that he had personal knowledge of the aggression against Nicaragua. He knew such action was in violation of the OAS agreement and he knew of the mutual defense treaties. He also knew that such action against Nicaragua was an undisputed violation of international law. Yet, he did nothing and he made no public outcry about this brazen violation. President Lucas also knew that the Costa Rican revolutionary activities were destroying the Central American Common Market. People were simply afraid to ship goods and merchandise through Peñas Blancas, a strategic spot on the Pan American Highway. We discussed that economic problem, so I knew he was cognizant of the situation.

One could propound an interesting question. With this personal knowledge of the gross violations of treaties and agreements, why didn't President Lucas come forward and tell the world what was really happening to Nicaragua? The answer is most likely already discernible. He knew the United States would be extremely upset with Guatemala, if such a pronouncement were made. The negotiating team, a mockery of justice, was in Nicaragua at the time. Mr. Lucas was quite aware of Mr. Carter's sentiments about Nicaragua, and he didn't want to run the risk of bringing down upon his head the ire of the United States. No matter how hard I tried, no matter how much evidence I presented, even if other nations had firsthand knowledge of the transgressions against my country, I always ran up against those familiar U.S. brick walls.

I'm convinced that history will judge Rodrigo Carazo, President of Costa Rica, harshly. As a result of his political nearsightedness, as a result of his inane participation in an international "game" to destroy Nicaragua, his own country will suffer and his own people will suffer. Carazo, knowingly, provided the essential military base of operation for the Communist-led forces. He, knowingly, provided the airport facilities for the Panamanian airplanes bringing arms and ammunition to the revolutionaries. At the time, Carazo was a hero in the eyes of the Communists. Today, however, I'm confident his own people are cognizant of the evil he has brought to all of Central America.

If history judges Carazo harshly, as I'm sure it will, Jimmy Carter will be judged even more harshly. Because he, with one single telephone call, could have halted Carazo's activity in Costa Rica. Had he taken such action, the Communists would not have Nicaragua today. The seeds sown by Mr. Carter and Mr. Carazo will bring forth a crop beyond their control. Unfortunately, all the people in this Hemisphere will pay the price for that fatuous harvest.

In that period from February until June, 1979, I made three trips to Guatemala. On two of those visits, I met with President Lucas of Guatemala and President Romero of El Salvador. On one of the visits I met with Lucas, Romero, and President Policarpo Garcia of Honduras. Also, on one trip I had a private meeting with Calderon Fournier, Foreign Minister of Costa Rica. The purpose of each visit was to provide the other Central American presidents with a detailed briefing on the mounting pressure being applied against Nicaragua. I wanted these men to know that Nicaragua was being invaded by forces from many countries and that, to a degree, I was fighting their battle. Each president was aware that Nicaragua was being attacked, but I wanted them to know the identity of the aggressor forces.

I knew that if any one of those three nations would come to the aid of Nicaragua, the invading forces could be defeated. I used logic, persuasion, and entreaty to convince them that Nicaragua's cause was their cause. To that extent, I was successful. They understood the briefings, they understood that outside aggressor forces were attacking my country and, further, they understood that in Nicaragua we were fighting for ourselves as well as for them. I received their understanding and I received their sympathy, but I did not receive their national support.

An indication of their understanding came from Paz Garcia of Honduras. With all Central American presidents in consultation, he reported that his government had captured a large cache of arms and ammunition destined for the revolutionaries in Nicaragua. Each box of arms and each box of ammunition was stamped *Dominican Republic*. It was determined that these arms were being flown from Liberia, Costa Rica, to a landing strip in the department of Choluteca, Honduras. Now that was just one instance. They were conscious of the fact that men, arms, and ammunition were flooding into Nicaragua and from various sources.

I had requested the visit with Calderon Fournier, Foreign

Minister of Costa Rica. That visit took place in Guatemala. Fournier is a young man about twenty-eight years old, and he had been picked by Rodrigo Carazo to serve as Foreign Minister. I thought, in visiting with him, that one last effort should be made to enlighten Costa Rica as to the disastrous path she was following.

I told Fournier that apparently he and President Carazo didn't know with whom they were dealing. I stated that Costa Rica was deeply involved with the Communists; and that in time the wrath of the Communists would be turned on Costa Rica. I then said, "I'm telling you these facts because you were born in Nicaragua. Your father, Calderon Guardia, was protected by my father and by me and my family. As a friend of your family for many years, I want you to know that what you are doing is something horrendous."

Young Fournier knew that I was telling him the truth, but he couldn't admit it. In a most unconvincing manner, he stated that neither Carazo nor members of his political party had any knowledge of surreptitious activity in Costa Rica.

My final plea was in vain. I had their hearts but I did not have their hands. The pressure from the United States was too great. Though they purchased oil from Venezuela, it was not Perez they feared. Perez influenced Omar Torrijos but not Lucas, Romero, or Paz Garcia. The man they feared was Jimmy Carter, and Mr. Carter had told them, in no uncertain terms, what their posture *had to be* in regard to Nicaragua.

After that last visit, I returned to Managua with the certain conviction that Nicaragua stood alone. I recalled a previous thought in which I pictured Nicaragua as standing on the wrong side of a huge weakened dam and the consequences for Nicaragua, if that dam should not hold. At that time in the not too distant past, I remember thinking that our reinforcement hopes for that dam lay with the United States.

I could now revise that analogy. On the watershed side of that dam, the United States had directed that the gate control valves of all smaller dams be turned to full open. And now I could clearly see an ocean of water descending upon that weakened structure. Oh yes, large cracks were already apparent, and through those cracks poured devastation on Nicaragua.

When the United States gave orders that all the small upstream dams should release their storage, it signified that it would be only a matter of time until the dam would burst and Nicaragua would die an agonizing death. As I went back to Managua, on my last trip from Guatemala, I knew the flood was on its way.

Nevertheless, I returned to Nicaragua determined that I would give my country the best that was within me. I thought of another U.S. idiom, "Where there's a will there's a way." Well, I had the will, but the way seemed beyond my reach. For the Congress, my political party, the Army, and the people of Nicaragua I made a pledge to myself that I would give my all. Miracles had happened before, and there might be one left for Nicaragua. This meant getting on with the business of the country, giving attention to pressing economic problems, and preparing the Army for the revolutionary push that was sure to come.

This was early May, 1979. With a war going on and with revolutionary forces moving in from several directions, it may seem incredible, but it was time to give attention to the planting of the next crop. I then called a meeting of my economic advisors to discuss acreage availability, supplies of insecticides and fertilizers, and the overall agricultural economic outlook. To a large degree, Nicaragua depended upon agricultural exports, and it was important that we proceed with our planting. I had to think about the economy of the country.

It will be recalled that, due to the interference of the United States, we were unable to obtain standby credit from the International Monetary Fund. This meant that our short term and long term notes were overdue. We had not been able to meet the payments on principal and interest which were due on December 31, 1978. Most of these loans had been obtained after the earthquake and they were made for a period of five years.

A New York bank was the holder of one of the larger loans and that bank was demanding payment. So I sent Dr. Incer Muniz to New York to negotiate with the bank. The bank said it would try to renegotiate the loan, but first Nicaragua had to pay the interest which was due. Knowing very well how the banking community worked, I agreed to pay the full amount of interest due up to December 31, 1978. After that, the short term note holders requested that their interest be paid, also. We were told by the short term note holders that once the crops were brought in, they would issue new credit. We not only paid the interest but we paid the principal on all short term loans.

I was trying to save the good name of Nicaragua, get the new crops in with an adequate supply of fertilizer and insecticides, and, at the same time, prepare our country militarily for the onslaught which I knew would be coming.

On May 27, 1979, a revolutionary force infiltrated from Honduras and attacked Jinotega. A military force was dispatched to that city and the guerrillas were defeated. On the heels of the Jinotega attack, a force of one hundred guerrillas came across from Costa Rica near Santa Cruz. Their objective was Nueva Guinea. After we had successfully cleaned up Jinotega, we moved into the Santa Cruz area, and that invading force was wiped out. Shortly thereafter, another force came across from Costa Rica and attacked El Naranjo. Those invading forces were engaged and they, too, were wiped out. We were facing one attacking force after another. One thing was quite apparent, though, the Guardia Nacional, even when greatly outnumbered, could handle the enemy. These scattered attacks were a prelude of what was to come.

In early June, Nicaragua was subjected to a generalized attack in Managua, Massaya, Esteli, Matagalpa, Leon, and Chinandega. This was a widespread assault and it was clear to me that our forces would have to follow a strategic plan. I met with the Army staff and we developed our strategy. It was decided that Managua would receive priority attention. After Managua, we would direct our military attention to the Costa Rican frontier, and then we would move, one stage at a time, to the other cities under attack. We cleaned out Managua, but it took us two weeks to do it. One must understand that our military forces were facing experts. They knew military strategy, they were well equipped, and they, too, had a plan.

In each one of the cities under attack, the invading aggressor forces endeavored to surround the local police center, which also served as a command post for the local Guardia Nacional. Once they had such a center surrounded, then they could direct concentrated firepower on that center.

In Chinandega, the local commander disrupted the strategy,

and was successful in avoiding encirclement. The same cannot be said for Leon. There the police center was completely surrounded. In Esteli, Matagalpa, Rivas, and Massaya the police centers were all surrounded. An attempt was made to surround the police center in Jinotepe, but it failed.

The stage was set. We recognized that this offensive was no minor incursion. We were being attacked in force. Our men displayed courage, initiative and, in army terminology, they fought like hell.

The international invading forces were defeated at El Naranjo. The Guardia Nacional forces at El Naranjo were recalled to Managua to reinforce our troops there. We then received a chilling message. Crossing over from Costa Rica, a country that claimed it was not a staging area for the Communist-led troops, was a virtual army. The message stated that a force of over five thousand troops was pouring across at Peñas Blancas. I thought of "the gallant twenty-five" who had defeated a force of three hundred, and I knew the command post could not hold off an army of five thousand men. This time, the command post could not withstand the invasion force, and Peñas Blancas was overrun. Our brave and daring "Comandante Bravo" was fortunate in that he was able to extricate himself and most of his men. This was after the command post had been surrounded.

By this time, we were using every facility at our command. In the attack on El Naranjo, I recall, we used the *M.S. Managua* ship very efficiently. This was a merchant ship with forty-millimeter Bofors mounted on the top deck. As the invaders came across from Costa Rica, the merchant ship, standing just off the coast, completely neutralized the invaders.

We had a forty-foot Coast Guard ship which was normally stationed in Lake Nicaragua. It was decided to use this small Coast Guard vessel in repelling the invaders. The vessel was operating in the Sapoa River and a forward observer was being used to direct the boat. We were surprised when it was reported that the Coast Guard vessel had exploded. That was the opinion of the forward observer, the only crew member to survive. Later, however, we learned the Coast Guard boat was hit by a 105-millimeter recoilless gun grenade.

When I received the authenticated report that our vessel was sunk by a 105-recoilless grenade weapon, I reported this fact to the OAS. I pointed out to those people that this was prima facie evidence that we were not fighting an internal uprising, as the OAS claimed. I stated that we were fighting organized armies, because only bona fide military units in an organized army possessed such weapons. Of course, this evidence made no difference to the OAS. The enemy had the latest sophisticated weapons, and whoever said that we were fighting a bunch of disorganized kids was nuts. Their weaponry was superior to ours and we didn't have the armament to withstand such offensive fire power.

Each of the cities being attacked was under severe pressure. However, the army which had crossed over from Costa Rica represented the most serious threat. The decision was difficult, but I had to withdraw troops from the various besieged areas and move these troops to the southern battlefield.

At this crucial time, the government of Panama announced that if the revolutionary forces could capture a city in Nicaragua, the government of Panama would immediately recognize the provisional government of the revolutionaries. When that happened there was not one voice of protest out of the OAS. Panama had flagrantly violated international law and this violation went uncensured. I knew then the OAS was finished. No longer could this Western Hemisphere organization command the respect of any nation. Henceforth, it would be an organization in name only. It was as though we were going back in time two hundred years, when there was no international law at all.

At that point, all I knew was to slug it out, and that's what we did. There was fierce fighting in and around Rivas, but the main invading force from Costa Rica was kept fairly close to the southern frontier. The guerrillas took the farm of Dr. Cornelio Hueck, former President of the Nicaraguan Congress, and captured him. Previously, I mentioned the horrible circumstances of his death. Suffice it to say that Dr. Hueck was taken into the town of Tola and there he was publicly sacrificed. The town of Tola was the parochial responsibility of Father Garcia Liviano, a Spanish Communist. It was he who planted the seeds of Communism in the Tola area.

The fighting was heavy in Matagalpa, Esteli, Leon, Massaya, Rivas, and Managua. This represented six departments of the country in which battles were raging.

While we were engaged in these fierce battles, we were expecting a ship from Israel loaded with arms and ammunition. This, incidentally, had been paid for before the ship ever left Israel. Our most monumental problem was the acquisition of arms and ammunition. Mr. Carter had successfully dried up almost every source. We were finally able to complete a transaction with Israel and, we felt, the arrival of that ship could easily turn the tide of the war.

As the ship approached the Atlantic coast of Nicaragua, we received word that the ship would not dock. It was reported that the captain was fearful that something would happen to the ship. After receiving that report, we directed the ship to go to Guatemala. We had obtained permission from the government of Guatemala to unload the ship there. For Nicaragua, a disaster then occurred. The ship, with our lifesaving arms and ammunition, did not proceed to Guatemala — it turned back to Israel. We suspected the reason for the sudden change in shipping plans, and later our suspicions were verified. U.S. intelligence had learned the destination of this ship and they obtained information as to the cargo she carried. Due to extreme pressure applied by the United States, Israel made the decision to return the ship to its home port. Somewhere in Israel there is a large consignment of arms and ammunitions which could have saved Nicaragua.

The United States steadfastly refused to sell Nicaragua anti-tank or anti-personnel grenades which could be fired from a rifle. In combat, that is a devastating weapon, and if one side has the weapon and the other doesn't, the side with the weapon has a distinct advantage. The revolutionaries had Chinese rockets and the Belgian rifle grenades, we had one recourse — the airforce. So we used the airforce to neutralize the enemy.

Anyone who followed the war in Nicaragua will recall that the news media castigated the government forces for bombing the enemy. The media failed to explain that the enemy possessed sophisticated weaponry which we didn't have, and that these weapons were tearing us apart. When I think about those battles and the erroneous reports which were sent all over the world, I get bitter. When Carter says the United States played no part in the death of my government, and when he says he didn't know international law was being violated, he is lying. Everything that happened was reported to the U.S. Embassy and the U.S. Embassy advised the White House and the U.S. State Department. They had all the evidence and all the information.

Why should one Israeli ship, destined for Nicaragua, have assumed such importance to Mr. Carter and the State Department? Through their own intelligence sources, the U.S. knew what was aboard. That ship carried, among other military items, ten thousand anti-tank and anti-personnel grenade rifles with ammunition. With that weapon, we could have matched the Chinese rockets and the Belgian rifle ammunition. That precious cargo could have won the war for the anti-Communist forces of Nicaragua.

When the United States saw that I was going to stick it out and that I was not yielding, that nation spearheaded a drive in the Organization of American States to pass a resolution condemning the government of Nicaragua. Mr. Carter got what he requested. I read the resolution to the people of Nicaragua so they would know precisely what the OAS had said. When that resolution passed, I realized that there would not be a place in the world where Nicaragua could purchase arms and ammunition. By pushing for that particular resolution — and getting it — Mr. Carter had effectively cut off Nicaragua from any possible source of supply.

By then, an avalanche of men, arms, and equipment was pouring into Nicaragua from Costa Rica. Open vans and trucks, loaded with weaponry, were being brazenly driven across the entire length of Costa Rica. Those, of course, were coming from Panama. At the airport in Liberia, Costa Rica, flights were arriving daily from Panama. These were carrying both men and supplies. The perfidy of it all is beyond imagination. Who would believe that during all of this treachery, an OAS observer team was sitting in Costa Rica? Ostensibly, they were there to report any violations of the OAS Charter. But like the three monkeys, "They saw no evil, they heard no evil, and they spoke no evil."

By late June, 1979, I could see the ball game was over. My

chief concern was the welfare of those dedicated and loyal members of the Guardia Nacional and the members of the Liberal Party. It was then that I started a dialogue with U.S. Ambassador Pezzullo concerning some agreement whereby these men and women would not be imprisoned and liquidated.

With the knowledge that we were facing defeat, I directed my thoughts to the basic problems with which we were confronted. Eliminating all the reasons for our perilous predicament, which have been discussed in some detail, at that moment we had two basic problems. First and foremost, we were rapidly running out of ammunition. Unlike the Greek warriors in the battle at Marathon, this was not a battle in which we could use spears, bows and arrows, and our bare hands. Had that been the military situation, we could have won. Contrary to press reports, we had the manpower to win. These men, some sixteen thousand at that point, had the will and determination to win.

When a man is fighting for the preservation of that piece of land on which he was born, when a man is fighting for his home and his family, you can be sure that he will do so with all his might. Those gallant members of the Guardia Nacional didn't need added incentive. But if they did, it came with the proven knowledge that they were fighting men from Panama, Venezuela, Cuba, the United States, Costa Rica, West Germany, and other countries. They were fighting and dying to preserve their homeland against a conglomeration of foreign invaders. Try to put yourself in their position and you will see that the adrenaline in your system automatically increases to maximum proportions. Be assured that those men were willing to fight and they were willing to die for their country.

In those last few days, some sentries were stationed at checkpoints in Managua with no ammunition for their automatic weapons. If it's possible, imagine how they felt. On the other hand, place yourself in the position of the enemy. Assume you are directing the attack against a city in Nicaragua and your intelligence sources reveal that checkpoint sentries have rags stuffed in the loading portion of their weapons instead of clips. Without a doubt, you would know that the army you were facing was running out of ammunition.

Actually, the United States had effectively established a

blockade against Nicaragua. It was bad enough when the U.S. refused to sell us arms and ammunition but when the U.S. was successful in drying up other sources of supply, it was, for Nicaragua, a mortal blow. So, our lack of ammunition was our most basic problem.

When that military position is reached, you grasp at straws. Some of my people had knowledge of supply sources who, for a price, could deliver a limited supply of ammunition. We checked those sources and some ammunition could be purchased. Such purchases are always expensive and, in our case, it took cash and in U.S. currency. That brings me to our second basic problem. The Central Bank was running out of dollars. You can be sure that the Nicaraguan cordoba was not acceptable outside Nicaragua. Inside the country, the rate of exchange was ten cordobas to the dollar. Outside the country you couldn't exchange one hundred "cords" for a dollar. That was our other problem — lack of dollars.

There was one hope for acquiring dollars and that hope rested with our coffee exports. June is normally a big month for the exportation of coffee and that always brought in sizable revenue. We still controlled the ports and we had the capability of moving our export products to the ports. Well, we moved the coffee, but once more we came face to face with the influence of the United States. No shipping company would agree to come into our ports. Ostensibly, this position was taken due to the danger involved, but the enemy had no airforce and the ports were secure. We couldn't export our coffee for only one reason — U.S. political influence. For certain, that meant no more dollars.

There was still one way in which a minimum amount of relief could be achieved. The Somoza family owned a small shipping company — three ships — and these could be utilized. These, however, were highjacked at sea and taken to Panama. There the ships were confiscated by Torrijos and Aristides Royo, the self-avowed Marxist who serves as the puppet president of Panama. These ships represented personal property but Royo saw fit to send these ships back to Nicaragua and turn them over to the Marxist government. One ship which was owned by a Panamanian company was chartered to our shipping company. This ship was highjacked out of Puerto Rico and taken to Cuba. That ship is still being held by the Cuban government. Again, we saw gross violation of international law.

In June we began to see a different approach by the Communists. News releases were coming from the Communist Party in Mexico, Colombia, Panama, and Venezuela. They were announcing to the world that they were going to send international brigades to Nicaragua. This was not an idle threat. Communist forces came from each of these countries and joined in the battle to defeat the government of Nicaragua. Each one of those governments was a member of the OAS. The action by the Communist Party in those countries was a clear violation of the OAS Charter, the mutual defense treaty, and the Neutrality Act. But not one of those governments opposed the pronouncement or the actions of the Communists. I can only conclude that those governments are extremely weak, or they have a deep fear of the Left. Based upon the statement made to me by Perez of Venezuela that he "didn't want to face up to Castro," I believe that fear was the motivational influence.

In early June, 1979, while Nicaragua was fighting for her life, we had one last opportunity to prove the involvement of Panama, Costa Rica, Cuba, and others. Of course, additional proof was not needed, because President Carter and the U.S. State Department had files of evidence to prove the activities of these conspiratorial forces, and the CIA report which proved *direct* involvement.

When my government was invited to participate in the Hearings before the Subcommittee on the Panama Canal, I decided we should accept. I wanted the congressmen on that Subcommittee to see with their own eyes the type of weaponry which was coming into Nicaragua through Costa Rica from Panama. Also, I wanted the Congress to have a detailed account of the international crimes being committed against Nicaragua.

Naturally, we couldn't send all of the captured weapons to Washington, but we sent a wide variety. We could even trace the origin of these weapons and many of them were coming from the United States.

To present our case to this Subcommittee, I selected my

aide, Max Kelly, and Luis Pallais, Vice President of the
Nicaraguan Congress. Incidentally, they were well received by
this important Subcommittee. And at the termination of those
hearings on June 7, 1979, a majority of that Subcommittee was
convinced that Nicaragua had been the victim of international
aggression.

The remarks of Luis Pallais clearly outlined the transgressions of Panama, Costa Rica, and Cuba. Luis is an honorable
and truthful individual. I don't think one member of that
Subcommittee doubted the veracity of his statement. He
touched on many sensitive and significant areas. His formal
statement was as follows (with my emphasis now added).

Mr. Chairman, I welcome the opportunity to meet with this distinguished subcommittee on a matter of such portentous importance to
my country and the world.

*Nicaragua is under a relentless attack by international Communism
led by Cuba and Panama.* Those who refuse to recognize this reality
and see the present crisis and turmoil in Central America only as a
product of national and socioeconomic issues are blind to history and
the evidence so clearly revealed by events.

Let us briefly review some of this evidence. My country, Nicaragua,
has been a victim of 20 years of Soviet-Cuban subversion and terrorism
with the coming to power of Fidel Castro in 1959. From that time
onward, world Communism has sought to overthrow the constitutionally elected and successive governments of Nicaragua to impose Marxism
on the people of Nicaragua, a system our people totally reject.

The Frente Sandinista de Liberacion Nacional (FSLN) terrorist
movement is the principal armed force by which the U.S.S.R.-Cuba are
attempting to achieve this objective. *The Sandinista leaders have been
trained and indoctrinated in Cuba and the Soviet Union.*

Some people have been taken to take special graduate studies by the
Soviet Union, at the Patrice Lumumba University in Moscow.

*The Castro regime has provided weapons, financial and logistical
support and open sanctuary for Sandinistas fleeing Nicaragua after
carrying out terrorist actions.*

Such has been the flagrant involvement of Cuba in this ongoing
campaign *that it has now become politically — and logistically —
expedient for Cuba to move the frontline base of operations to Panama.*

On coming to power in 1959, Fidel Castro immediately targeted two
countries for takeover: Panama and Nicaragua. As a result, *Panama is
today a Marxist enclave* on the isthmus through the treachery of the
present leaders of that nation. The Panamanian people have been
betrayed from within, Mr. Chairman.

Nicaragua has proved to be much more difficult. In August, 1978 the Sandinistas carried out a sneak assault on the National Palace in Managua, killing five and holding almost the entire legislative body and 1,500 ordinary citizens hostage for 45 hours. Following the negotiated release of 59 fellow Sandinista terrorists from prison and a one-half-million-dollar cash ransom, these terrorists were flown as they demanded to Panama. Many shortly reappeared in Cuba.

From that moment, Panama openly has become the continental haven for bloody terrorists and a base for recruiting, reequipping, and training of terrorist forces determined to take over Central America on behalf of Marxist socialism.

Over the intervening months since that August 1978 assault on the National Palace in Managua, *scores of Sandinista terrorists have been flown to sanctuary in Panama aboard Panamanian Air Force aircraft; their leaders flown to other countries in the region including Cuba, and Venezuela* under Carlos Andres Perez, who was President then, as part of the operations to recruit for and reorganize their terrorist operations.

We have read in the press of open meetings with President Carlos Andres Perez and General Torrijos.

On August 30, 1978, Marxist terrorist leaders Eden Pastora and Dora Maria Tellez were flown back to Costa Rica aboard a Panamanian military aircraft to meet with Costa Rican President Rodrigo Carazo.

On September 10, 1978, 22 Sandinistas arrived in Havana, Cuba, from Panama and were met and fêted by high officials from the *Central Committee of the Communist Party of Cuba and Panamanian Ambassador Miguel Brugeras. On September 15, 1978, Panama dispatched four helicopters to Costa Rica to support action against Nicaragua.*

On September 27, 1978, Sandinista leader Tomas Borge arrived in Havana from Panama and reported to Fidel Castro on the terrorist operations in Nicaragua.

Pictures of this meeting were published in the world press.

On the same day, *Jorge Aparicio, former ambassador of Panama to Algiers, confirmed that several former members of Panama's government are among the volunteers enrolled in the Communist international brigades of mercenaries being trained and equipped in Panama.*

On November 28, 1978, the Associated Press reported that, "generally reliable intelligence sources show *Panama as a possible conduit for Cuban-financed aid and weapons in the struggle to overthrow the anti-Communist Government of Nicaragua.*"

December 28, 1978, former Panamanian Vice Minister of Health, Hugo Spadafora, confirmed that 20 experienced Sandinista guerrillas were in Panama the day the U.S. Senate voted on the ratification of the Canal Treaties, prepared to blow up the Canal with Panamanian troops under the command of Gen. Omar Torrijos.

January 18 of this year, Gen. Omar Torrijos, while visiting Carlos Andres Perez, then President of Venezuela, publicly stated, *"There are*

*more arms than men" available for the attack on Nicaragua. He
admitted that Panamanians are fighting the Somoza Government.* This
was also very well covered by the world press, and it was said personally
by Gen. Omar Torrijos.

On March 13, and 16, two vans equipped with false compartments
were intercepted at Peñas Blancas on the Costa Rican-Nicaraguan
border by the Nicaraguan National Guard. Seized were 90 M-1 carbines,
34 FAL rifles, and large quantities of ammunition and material.
Seventy M-1 carbines were traced to Universal Firearms Corp. of
Florida and Johnson Arms of New Jersey, manufacturers of these
weapons, and which had been shipped to Caza y Pesca, S.A., in
Panama, a G-2 Panamanian intelligence front.

Investigations by a U.S. Federal agency, the Bureau of Alcohol,
Tobacco, and Firearms, revealed in an affidavit filed in the Miami
Federal Court on May 1, the complicity of the Panama Government in
the purchase of these arms for the Marxist-Leninist Sandinistas,
similar to what Fidel Castro has in Cuba.

*Panama President Aristides Royo in Washington, D.C., on May 11,
said "*** if I am going to smuggle arms, as a head of government, in my
account we have planes in the Panamanian Air Force."* The use of
Panamanian Air Force aircraft on behalf of the Sandinista terrorists
has for some time now been a well-documented fact.

What is less well known is the direct involvement today of the Fidel
Castro Government of Cuba in the present turmoil in Nicaragua.
Castro has tried to be very careful not to be showing his hand on this
thing, but as Mr. Kelly explained, *it has been proven that these Cuban
arms are now in the hands of the Communists fighting the constitutional government of my country.*

*On May 30, the Nicaraguan Foreign Ministry quoted reliable sources
as reporting the landing of a Cuban aircraft of Russian manufacture, an
Ilyushin 62, in Panama, from which some 200 fully equipped men
disembarked and boarded Panamanian Air Force trucks.*

*On the same day a four-engined aircraft painted yellow with a red
star on its tail was impeded from landing near Siuna in northeast
Nicaragua to give support to Sandinista terrorists attacking U.S.-owned
gold mines. It was later seen at the Rio Hato Air Force Base in Panama,
this same aircraft.*

Nicaraguan intelligence reports that on June 4 a Panamanian Air
Force plane landed at the Liberia Airport in northern Costa Rica and
discharged men and material for the beleaguered Sandinista terrorists
fighting the Nicaraguan National Guard at El Naranjo just across the
border from Nicaragua.

*The flow of automatic weapons from Cuba through Panama to the
Sandinista terrorists has now been fully established.* Over 150 FAL
Belgian-made rifles have been captured from the Sandinistas and
traced by their special characteristics and marking to those originally
sold to the Cuban Government by the Belgian manufacturers.

A quantity of these rifles were taken from the vans intercepted on the Costa Rica-Nicaragua border on March 13 and 16 of this year [*1979*].

We have here with us a member of the Customs Department to explain how these weapons were found in our border. These are the same two vans from which 70 M-1 carbines were found, which had been bought by the Panama Government for the Sandinista terrorists. The conclusive evidence of the origin of these weapons will be given by Mr. Max Kelly in his statement.

Mr. Chairman, the evidence is endless. *The present turmoil in Nicaragua is being provoked by Cuba and Panama with the hypocritical complicity of Costa Rica. Blatant recruiting for the international brigades of mercenaries in the government-backed press in Panama and the wanton use of Costa Rica as a conduit for Cuban-Panamanian-sponsored men and arms to launch, with impunity, repeated attacks against the government and people of Nicaragua, is a matter which should be of the gravest concern to the Government and people of the United States.*

The inordinate size of the Cuban Embassy in Panama and the Soviet Embassy in San Jose, Costa Rica, is totally out of proportion to the existing formal trade and cultural ties in Panama, is yet another clear indication of the extent and penetration of Soviet-Cuban influence in Central America.

At this present time, Mr. Chairman, innocent Nicaraguan blood is being spilled in the fighting now taking place on Nicaragua's borders with Costa Rica. There are no words to express the miserable cynicism of the Costa Rican Government which is in an unnatural alliance with Panama and Cuba, is attempting to overthrow another Central American Government, elected constitutionally by the people of Nicaragua.

The complicity of Panama in the present attempt to destabilize an established and recognized government — a user of the Canal for a major percentage of its foreign trade — raises the critical question of whether the Canal should be entrusted to the current leaders in Panama. I agree with President Somoza who has called Panama's interference in the internal affairs of Nicaragua the height of irresponsibility and has stated that General Torrijos and President Aristides Royo are unfit to operate a canal of such socioeconomic importance to the world. Is it possible that these people will comply with the neutrality provisions of the treaty?

That is a question that must be in the mind not only of the American people, but of other people in Latin America and the world.

In face of this open aggression against Nicaragua, the U.S. State Department is silent. On the other hand, the political and economic aggression by the U.S. State Department against the Government of President Anastasio Somoza is a matter of record.

On November 28, 1978, State Department spokesman *Hodding Carter*, referring to reports that Cuba and other governments had been supplying weapons to the Sandinista National Liberation Front, said, *"We have raised these concerns with Cuba and other governments."* On *May 11, of this year, Panamanian President Royo said in Washington, D.C. that he had received no pressure from the U.S. to stop any kind of aid to the Nicaraguan terrorists.*

Two days ago, on June 4, the U.S. delegate to the Organization of American States stated formally before that body: "We condemn external intervention in the Nicaraguan situation if such be proven."

The conclusive evidence, Mr. Chairman, which we are submitting to this committee today proves that there is an external intervention by Cuba and Panama. Intervention in our affairs is dangerous, because we state very clearly that this is not a problem of the government of Nicaragua. *It is a problem of the Free World — because we feel if ever our government would fall to the Communists, Marxist Sandinistas or defenders of Sandinistas, that it will be only a few days before Central America will follow.*

What will happen to the oil fields in Mexico? Can we have another kick in the belly like Castro? That is something that we, the democrats in the world, should be very much concerned about.

This foreign involvement in Nicaragua is internationalizing the present violence. *Fidel Castro has clearly embarked on reckless adventurism in Central America which will eventually threaten the very security of the United States.*

Mr. Chairman, may I finish on a private note? I was a hostage in August 1978. At gunpoint I transmitted by telephone the demands of the terrorists to our government. Our life was then at stake.

During the long negotiation — this is the picture taken then by one of the reporters. This was during the capture of the Palace. During the long negotiations, I had the opportunity to discuss policy with the terrorist leaders.

I remember that when everything was finished, at 2 o'clock in the morning, the leaders of the group, No. 1 and No. 2 — they are always called by numbers — called me to discuss the political situation in Nicaragua; and I told them that since I had my hands tied, how could I discuss that with them, being a prisoner, so they untied my hands.

Under these discussions, I gave my opinion as to the solution of the political problems in my country, and I told them that the solution should be accomplished through legal, constitutional means, through the dialog we would have, so that Nicaragua could have between negotiations and dialog a proper government and a proper election in 1981, so that the people could choose.

I asked them: Why do you fight? Why don't you leave the guns? Why don't we try to solve these problems by democratic means in terms of a vote?

The answer was very stern and very definite. They said:

"We experienced what happened to [*Dr. Salvador*] Allende in Chile.

He tried to work with the bourgeoisie through elections in a democratic process.

"What happened was that the CIA and the bourgeoisie of the country killed Allende and we failed. The only solution is to fight to the end until we eliminate the National Guard and the military forces of Nicaragua, replaced by social forces of Sandinistas, *and then we will have a situation just like Fidel Castro has in Cuba.*"

I know pretty well I told him that you are talking about the bourgeoisie, and that the strongest bourgeoisie we have in our country in Nicaragua are the farmers, because the farmer likes to have his own piece of land. He is very attached to it. He is very attached to his cows, to his cattle, to his horses, and even to get drunk whenever he wants to.

They answered: "Yes, we know that perfectly well. *That is the reason we will take over and establish a Cuban-type government when we eliminate the Nicaraguan forces of the National Guard.*"

We in Nicaragua have no problem controlling and fighting the guerrillas, but we feel if we have the open connection from Cuba, Panama, and Costa Rica of guerrillas, 100-150 come in every month armed by the Panamanians and by the Cubans and fight in Nicaragua, we are creating a tremendous economic problem in our country; and I believe this situation on a small scale can be compared with the situation in Vietnam, with the only difference that in Vietnam you had as your borders North Vietnam and Communist China and here you have the borders of Costa Rica and Panama.

We believe that the State Department should use its influence through diplomatic channels. *If they stop the smuggling of arms coming from Cuba and Panama we will have no problem eliminating Torrijos and we Nicaraguans can resolve our political problems through dialog and negotiations, and keep our territory free from Communists.*

I was told then in the palace when I was a prisoner and again at the airport when terrorists left Nicaragua, that I was a condemned man in their eyes. I can say to you that I had a report from my country 2 days ago that the Sandinistas have just given me the same treatment they have given to the Shah of Iran. They, the Communists, Marxists, terrorists, have voted and given instructions to any people of Nicaragua that I am a condemned man and I should die if anybody can kill me wherever they can find me.

Since then, I have had several attempts on my life, Mr. Chairman, and I fear them not. However, let me take this opportunity to put in the record: Should they succeed, I hold those who support the Marxist terrorists responsible for my death, which would never happen.

Thank you.

We return now to our main theme, a narration of *The Final Attack.*

Luis Pallais made it very clear that if the arms, ammunition, and men flooding Nicaragua from Panama were stopped, Nicaragua could settle her own problems through dialogue and negotiations. I feel certain the Subcommittee recognized that fact, but for Nicaragua, the die was cast. Even so, we would marshal our forces and do the best we could.

When a nation is in a life-and-death struggle communications are vital. There must be a constant interchange of information. In Nicaragua we had a highly sophisticated system of communications. At no time, while I was in Nicaragua, did I lose contact with my department commanders, not even a small patrol of forty men. We had a nationwide VHF communications network; we had a nationwide CW communications network; we had telegraph and we had the telephone. So we had excellent communications with every section of the country. At all times we knew exactly what was transpiring. I received a complete report at seven o'clock each morning and then I talked personally with every department commander.

As the war intensified, the reports from the department commanders were always the same — we need ammunition. They stressed the fact that the revolutionaries had monstrous firepower and that their own retaliatory fire capability was diminishing. These were distressing reports and there was nothing I could do to alleviate our critical shortage of ammunition. As it turned out, that was the advantage which brought victory to the revolutionaries.

I sadly recall the attack upon the central police headquarters in Leon. The Guardia Nacional and the police were confined to a relatively small and very old building. They were surrounded by the enemy and the old building was being pounded by Chinese RPG rockets, which had been supplied by Cuba. While this was taking place, I was on the telephone with the commander and I could hear the blasts from the rockets. Those men inside the building were going crazy as a result of the explosions. I remember thinking how erroneous the media had been in their reports about the ill-equipped revolutionaries. The revolutionaries had it all — automatic weapons, rockets, grenades, and even anti-tank, anti-personnel grenade rifles. Those surrounded men in Leon knew, because they were on the receiving end of that firepower. From my command post in the "bunker," I could hear and visualize the hell of Leon.

Since all news reports included some mention of the "bunker," it might be well to examine the "bastion of defense" that I occupied. One point should be understood, it was no bastion of defense.

After the earthquake, my office was built by a subsidiary of International Housing Limited. It was built with precast aluminum forms and, thus, it was square shaped. In conjunction with the office complex, a bedroom and kitchen facilities were added for emergency purposes. The construction called for reinforced concrete and all construction was above ground. It was a simple, unostentatious layout. In a friendly manner, the people began calling this square building "the bunker." When we think of a bunker, we automatically identify with an impregnable, below-ground fortress. My bunker was anything but that. It was just an office building. But people in Managua all called it Somoza's bunker and I found myself referring to my office as "the bunker." It was, however, the office of the President and in that time of peril, it was the central command post for all operations.

As our military situation became more serious, I asked all Cabinet members to remain on call at all times. Each morning they came to my office for consultation and a current briefing. As events became critical, I asked the Cabinet members and the Congress to move into the Inter-Continental Hotel, which was only about one hundred meters from the bunker. At that time, Luis Pallais had begun negotiations with the United States. Those negotiations dealt with my leaving the country and what kind of guarantees we could obtain for members of the Guardia Nacional. As a result of these negotiations, we needed the Cabinet and the Congress nearby. Therefore, they moved into the hotel. Also, those leaders of the government needed to be available at all times for consultation on matters relating to different parts of the country.

During the last stages of the war, the headquarters of the training company, which was near my office, became the center for monitoring enemy communications. All of our communications specialists were brought into that center. We heard all enemy radio transmissions and we knew exactly what they were saying and what they were doing. The enemy was using single side band radios. So while attacks were being made

on several cities, we were in communication with our own
commanders and, at the same time, we were monitoring communications of the enemy. As the tragedy of Leon came to me
by telephone, the monitoring center was privy to the orders and
directives of the enemy in that same battle. Later I will devote
special attention to the Leon debacle. So as to understand our
military situation, it might be well to review the entire May
offensive — the plan and how it began.

In the September, 1978 offensive, the International Conspiracy coordinated simultaneous attacks on several cities, as
well as a frontal attack from Costa Rica. In that offensive the
conspiratorial forces were defeated by the Guardia Nacional.
The revolutionaries learned much from that military experience. They learned that we had excellent mobility, and that we
could shift from one attack area to another with speed and
with strength. They learned that our firepower was good and
that they had no match for our mortars. We had a few rifle
grenades in Managua, and they learned about those. The lesson
they learned was costly, but they did learn.

Between the September offensive and the final offensive,
the international revolutionaries upgraded their equipment to
the extent that they had superior firepower and a never-ending
supply of ammunition. In the final offensive, they brought in
French bazookas, Chinese rockets, Belgian anti-tank and anti-
personnel rifle grenades, mortars, and hand grenades. The
final offensive, which began in May, 1979, had purpose and it
had excellent planning and direction.

The purpose of the offensive was to take the life out of the
Nicaraguan government. This offensive was designed to bleed
the country of its manpower, its energy, its transportation
system, its will to fight and, finally, its munitions. They
succeeded in only one phase of this plan and that was a
depletable area — munitions. In the end, our Army was intact,
we had energy, and our will to fight was stronger than ever. But
that was the plot and that's how the offensive began.

The first offensive move by the enemy was the capture of
the Bonanza mine and the Rosita mine. These mines had airstrips, so we decided to move our troops to this area by air
transport. We defeated those groups and pursued them into the
bush.

Next, the enemy moved one hundred men across the Rio San Juan from Costa Rica. These men then moved into the agrarian reform program at Nueva Guinea. We then moved a combat group into that area and wiped out the enemy. Then came the Jinotega attack, which I previously related, and we defeated the revolutionary forces at Jinotega.

But then came the attack on Managua, Massaya, Rivas, Leon, Esteli, Matagalpa, and Chinandega. For all intents and purposes, this was a simultaneous attack. To meet such massive assaults, our forces, our supplies, and our military equipment were spread thin. Contrary to media reports and foreign public opinion, Nicaragua did not have a tremendous military machine. Our military status related directly to the philosophy of the Liberal Party, and for that philosophical approach to the military posture of our country, I must accept most of the responsibility.

On that point, I think a personal observation is necessary. Of first importance to the Liberal Party of Nicaragua was the economic development of the country. Therefore, expenditures for the Guardia Nacional, police security, intrastate police, and arms and ammunition amounted to 10 percent of the national budget. No country in Latin America, and that includes Costa Rica, can match the tight budget of Nicaragua for security purposes. In retrospect, I do not regret that such a policy was followed, because we brought the country to the height of development. But considering the fact that there are so many international pirates and the fact that Leftist forces have been given free rein throughout the world, I regret that Nicaragua did not spend more money on her military establishment.

As I look back on the recent past, there was no reason to believe that Nicaragua should have had fear of external aggression. We had no territorial disputes with any of our neighbors. So it seemed logical to me that the taxpayers' money should be spent in the area of economic development. Actually, Nicaragua had not purchased any sophisticated military machinery since 1957. If, today, the question should be raised as to why we didn't have more sophisticated weaponry and greater supplies of ammunition, the foregoing represents the plain unvarnished truth. And I repeat, for the political decision to limit armament expenditures, I accept the responsibility. My hindsight vision is excellent but my foresight was something less than 20-20. Nicaragua was being attacked by international aggressor forces and that I didn't anticipate.

The final assault had begun. We knew this was a serious attack, so it was decided that we should observe military restraint for two or three days. That would give us time to make an accurate military assessment of the entire offensive operation, and enable us more intelligently to deploy our forces to meet the multiple attacks.

After a careful evaluation, we decided there were two principal areas in which we should counterattack immediately. The first was Managua and the second was on the southern border with Costa Rica. We were successful in both areas. The international invasion force from Costa Rica was driven back into that country. We then left a skeleton group on the southern border and brought the main military body back to Managua. They assisted the government troops in pushing the enemy forces out of Managua, and those forces retreated to Massaya. We then defeated the attack on Massaya.

We were next making preparations to send a force to assist Matagalpa. It was then that we received the shattering news. As I stated previously, an international force of over five thousand men was crossing over from the Costa Rican border. We now realized that the first attack from Costa Rica had been a probing effort. My first action was to attempt contact with the OAS observer team stationed in Costa Rica. I thought that, blind as they have been, they can surely see an aggressor force of five thousand men. I couldn't even get in touch with them, or they already knew of the attack and didn't want to become involved. My efforts with the OAS were to avail me nothing.

We slowed the invading force with airforce rocket fire and with mortars, but we couldn't stop them. Our plans to relieve Matagalpa were thwarted. That relief force had to be sent to the southern frontier. With so many attacks in so many different areas, it was like a military chess game. My moves were determined by the reports I was receiving from the various department commanders. For example, if the commander in Leon told me he was holding his own, it meant I could send troops to a more threatened area.

The top priority of the invading forces became evident quite early. They sought to close the connection between Managua and the various department commanders. They wanted to disrupt railway transportation and the highway system. To a degree, this priority movement was successful. But the invaders failed to take into account that we had seven helicopters and each helicopter could carry fourteen fully-equipped combat troops. We also had the aero cars from Spain and the old reliable DC-3s. The enemy made it difficult to move troops on the ground but we had limited means by which troops could be moved by air. Even though our air transportation was limited, we moved well over one thousand troops to the southern border in one day.

Up to that point, each department commander under attack was holding fast. They asked for only one thing and that was ammunition. We were doing our best to supply them.

In Managua, the government troops were a little slow in dislodging the enemy. Our forces were up against the Chinese rockets, and that presented a problem. Had I exercised greater control on civilian movement in Managua, they would not have been able to bring in all those rockets. But every time I made a move to provide tighter security in Managua, the pressure was put on me from the United States. Mr. Carter interpreted such moves as being in violation of human rights. Had I tightened up on security, the enemy would not have had the rockets, but Mr. Carter and his human rights people would have been coming at me with "hellfire and damnation." I chose to pacify Mr. Carter and that proved to be a serious mistake.

All during the offensive the enemy forces operating in Costa Rica were very active. By this time there were twenty staging and training areas in that country. Their logistical support was everything an invading force desired. If they couldn't move arms and ammunition by land, they would do so by air. Every time it appeared that we had the international invading forces cut off from ammunition and supplies, an airplane would arrive on the scene and drop needed supplies to the surrounded forces. That procedure was followed in the capital city of Managua. From their protected sanctuary in Costa Rica the airplanes, provided and flown by Panamanians, could easily give support to any area in Nicaragua. Often times these planes landed and discharged war supplies and men.

For several years, Nicaragua had been developing airstrips. In our small country we had something over two hundred airstrips. These were constructed so as to develop and give service to remote agricultural areas. It was a great plan for developing unproductive agricultural areas, and we could not foresee that many of these airstrips would be utilized by an invading force.

Once more we were facing a dilemma. Nicaragua depended on her agro-industry. June and July were the months when the crops had to be fumigated, and these airstrips were essential to the crop-dusting planes. If we destroyed the airstrips, we destroyed the crops. We chose to leave the airstrips operational. This decision worked to the disadvantage of our military. On one occasion, a twin engine plane was spotted as it was about to take off, but our airforce destroyed the plane while it was still on the ground. The next day our commander from Leon called and advised me that the airplane had brought in hundreds of rockets. His command post was receiving a pounding from Chinese rockets. As it developed, the enemy was using the airstrips all over the country. The airstrips were meant to be a boon for our agro-industry, but they turned out to be a "bust" for us militarily.

At the beginning of the May offensive the Army had four ancient Sherman tanks, and they were scattered all over Nicaragua. By this time we had none, so we had no armored force at all. These old Sherman tanks had proven useful against the cement block barricades thrown up by the enemy. But the Chinese rockets used by the Sandinistas took care of those old tanks, and in short order.

The revolutionary forces had a standard plan of attack for each one of the beleaguered cities. They would press the attack so as to confine the area in which the police and Guardia Nacional had to operate. This pressure would be maintained until our military unit was surrounded and squeezed into the command post. In essence, our force would be sitting in the middle of a square and the attacking force would direct fire into the center of that square and from all sides. In all of the cities under siege, the downtown area was of adobe or brick construction. When the attacking force occupied the buildings surrounding the command post, they cut squares in the connecting, or common, walls. In this manner, they could move from one building to another without exposing themselves to our people. This was not a technique known to Nicaraguans, and it was obvious that these men had received special guerrilla training. It fit the pattern of the PLO in the Middle East.

In the beginning of this offensive, I was confident that the enemy would finally run out of ammunition. Had I known that in Costa Rica they had an arsenal which was constantly replenished and that they would make use of both land and air to keep the revolutionary forces supplied, I would have urged our department commanders to conserve their ammunition. This offensive went on for over a month and the invading forces were never short of ammunition. The enemy could maintain a constant fire pattern because they had an ammunition and arms depot in Costa Rica. We, on the other hand, had absolutely no source of supply, and the enemy was well aware of our predicament. They also knew that the United States would see to it that no sources of supply would be opened up to us.

As has been shown, many of our department commanders were in dire straits. All the areas under attack had similar problems. The tragic events at Leon could be repeated for most of the other command posts. It's appropriate, I think, to take a closer look at Leon. Besides, Leon has special meaning to me because that was the city in which I was born.

When the attack on Leon began, all of the central part of the city was abandoned by the citizens. Approximately 80 percent of the population of Leon simply moved out. Those who remained represented the lower economic level and they lived some distance from the center of the city. Except for the government defenders of the city and the international invading force, the city was essentially vacated.

The previously described technique was used in Leon. The invading force had superior firepower and greatly outnumbered the government force. With constant pressure, the detachment of some two hundred men was surrounded in the central police headquarters. These two hundred men were confined in a building which contained approximately three thousand square meters. Their firepower consisted of rifles and automatic weapons.

From the adobe and brick buildings which surrounded the police and Guardia Nacional, the enemy poured a constant hail of fire into the police headquarters. The invaders were using the deadly Chinese rockets, against which my men had no defense. When I talked to the department commander on the telephone, I could hear the cries of agony in the background. My heart bled for those men. I searched for reinforcements to send to Leon, but we had none. All available troops had been sent to the southern frontier to battle the army which had come across from Costa Rica.

The commanding officer in Leon, Major General Gonzalo Evertz, was wounded and incapacitated. As so often happens in a crisis, assistance came from an unexpected source. Retired Brigadier General Ariel Arguello had presented himself to General Evertz and volunteered to help. When General Evertz was wounded, the retired Brigadier assumed command. General Arguello had been a good soldier, and had faithfully performed his duties. He was now retired and he didn't have to stay and fight in what was sure to be a losing cause. His young son had also joined him in the battle of Leon.

Since no supporting troops could be sent to Leon, and since it was obvious that these men were in a death trap, the decision was made to evacuate the central police headquarters. The plan was to get out of the building and, if possible, make their way to Height Fortin, a point of high ground overlooking the city. From the time those troops left the building until they reached Fortin, it was a bloodbath. The revolutionaries had the protection of solid walls and the retreating detachment had nothing but "guts and guns." It was indeed a sad predicament. The brave and loyal Brigadier General Arguello was killed and so was his son. Those who made it to Fortin were fortunate. So many of their buddies had fallen along the way — never to rise again.

That was the end of Leon. After that battle, the decision was made to abandon the city totally, and no effort was ever made to retake it.

In my opinion, the defeat at Leon marked the beginning of the destabilization of our military situation. By this time, we had an accurate count on the aggressor forces. Over twenty thousand men were attacking Nicaragua. They were coming from staging areas in Costa Rica and Honduras.

The daily report, which I read at seven o'clock each morning, was always of importance to me. Prior to the May offensive, that portion of the report dealing with our munitions supply received attention, but it did not command my immediate evaluation. As the offensive continued into the fading part of June, that segment of the daily report received my immediate attention. We had an accurate measurement of those munitions which had been expended in our multiple defense effort, and we knew exactly the quantity we had in our munitions depot. One fact was clear, the stock of ammunition in storage was being rapidly depleted. I knew this demand-and-supply situation could go on for just so long. Our central supply had to be replenished.

The rapid depletion of our munitions was, I thought, comparable to the oil shortage in the United States. There, oil is being consumed at a faster rate than reserves are being discovered. That simply means that at some point in time, if the present rate of consumption continues, the United States will have no oil. To meet her current demand for petroleum, the United States augments domestic production with the purchase of foreign oil. If all foreign markets were closed to the United States, the situation would become catastrophic. That's exactly the position in which Nicaragua found itself with regard to munitions. There was one big difference, we had no domestic production and were therefore totally dependent on foreign purchases. When Mr. Carter closed those markets to Nicaragua, it was just a matter of time until we had no munitions at all.

Tragically, the enemy was aware of our munitions problem. They knew that if they could maintain military pressure long enough, our forces would be reduced to using their bare hands and victory would be theirs. Perez and Torrijos and, through them, Castro knew precisely the untenable position of the Nicaraguan forces. They also knew that Mr. Carter would see to it that we did not receive any significant supplies of munitions. The longer the attacks continued, the more confident our enemies became.

It reached the point that our department commanders were calling in and reporting that they had no more ammunition for their mortars. It was my painful duty to tell them to discard their mortars and use their rifles. When you know that your own men are facing Chinese rockets, anti-personnel rifle grenades, mortars, and an assortment of automatic weapons, that's a distressful order to give. But I had no choice.

Our combat airforce consisted of eleven push-pull planes, six T-33 Trainers, and in the last two weeks we received four Skyraiders. To some degree, the airforce could neutralize the sophisticated weaponry of the enemy. However, in the last two weeks we ran out of bombs for the airforce and these planes then proved to be useless. We were simply running out of munitions of all kinds, including mortars, howitzer 105 ammo., and small arms ammunition.

We finally found a source in Europe that agreed to sell us a limited supply of ammunition. When the airplane went to Portugal to pick up the shipment the plane was picketed. This clearly indicated the depth of the International Conspiracy. The Leftist forces knew what kind of plane would be arriving and when it would arrive. This time the button had been punched in Central America and the red light came on in Portugal.

Even with the shortage of ammunition, our men were doing surprisingly well. By that time we had Matagalpa, Esteli, Chenandega, and Massaya stabilized, and Rivas was cleaned out. In Managua, we then had some three thousand men. We were expecting the forces which had taken Leon to move on Managua, and we wanted to be prepared.

As might have been expected, all kinds of suggestions were being made to me. It was strongly suggested to me that I enlist the support of the civilian population. I considered the idea and decided it would be wrong. It would, I thought, put the civilian population in jeopardy, and for the future of Nicaragua it should not be done. Instead I called for volunteers. To these volunteers we had passed out seventeen thousand rifles. Unfortunately, there was little ammunition for the weapons. Until the day I left Nicaragua, volunteers were coming forward. At the time of my departure, we must have had close to twenty thousand men who wanted to fight the enemy. These men were never defeated by the international invaders; they simply did not have the means with which to fight.

I have sympathy for the Guardia Nacional, their families, and the members of the Liberal Party. Those people have endured unbelievable hardships under the Marxist regime. In my conduct of the presidency, I have no remorsefulness. The people of Nicaragua know that I tried to do my job properly. They also understand that our small nation did not have the power or the means to take on the International Conspiracy which destroyed our country.

In the final analysis, the human rights campaign was the human bloodshed campaign. That instrument of Mr. Carter's was responsible for the deaths of thousands of people. And what do they now have in Nicaragua? After the Marxist victory, thousands of innocent people were slaughtered, and this mayhem continues to this very day. The people of Nicaragua now have no rights at all. The jails are full of political prisoners who have committed no crime. So many of these people are in jail merely because they were *accused* of being a Somocista or a member of the Liberal Party!

What happened to those affluent business leaders who opposed me? That is also a tragic story. Now, these are the men who supported the Sandinista movement with time, effort, and money. Repeatedly they were warned that they were supporting Communists, and that a Sandinista victory would mean a Marxist government in Nicaragua. Their answer was always the same: "We can control the Sandinistas." How wrong they were — and what a price they paid for not heeding the advice given by so many. Many of them are now in jail and most of them had their property confiscated by the Marxist government. For those people, support of the Sandinistas cost them everything.

One of my most outspoken critics and a leader in the Broad Opposition Front had been Fernando Aguero. He was a man of means and a substantial property owner in Nicaragua who had given money to the Sandinistas, and was elated with their victory. One day, however, he was advised that all his property was being confiscated by the new government. He was irate. He pointed out to the Marxists that he had always been an enemy of mine and that in no way could he be called a Somocista. He simply couldn't understand why his property was being taken.

The explanation given Mr. Aguero was terse and to the point. He was told, "It's the law," and that's the only explanation he ever received. Aguero is now walking the streets in Miami.

Another bitter foe of mine was Eduardo Montealegre, president of the BANIC Group. He openly criticized me and the government, which was his privilege. But in donating sizable sums of cash to the Sandinistas, he made a serious mistake. He, too, was repeatedly warned that he was supporting a Communist movement. His answer was always, "We can control them." His property was confiscated and Mr. Montealegre is also walking the streets of Miami. Those are only two examples, but I could name thousands.

It will surprise a lot of people but before the Carter Administration came to power, Nicaragua had a total of five thousand policemen and members of the Army. That's all we had and yet we were secure, free, and prosperous. After the human rights expeditions and the subsequent international intervention, it became necessary to increase that number substantially. I should point out that the Nicaraguan soldier was the equal of any soldier in the world. Our military personnel were disciplined, well trained, and they had courage.

Most of our training techniques were patterned after those of the United States. Our military academy was patterned after West Point and it turned out superb officers. In the Nicaragua Military Academy we had a constant flow of cadets from many countries in Latin America.

Over a period of years, we sent over fourteen thousand men through various military training programs in the United States. These included the air school, the ground school, the artillery school, the staff school, and many others. A sizable portion of these U.S.-trained men are now in prison and the rest are wandering around the world. Due to our close association with the U.S., Nicaragua was often referred to as "the little U.S.A." of Central America.

My idea was to expose the maximum number of Nicaraguans to the United States — to the American way of life. This philosophy is contrary to that which exists in Communist-controlled countries. Those countries do not want their people exposed to the way of life in the United States. I wanted the people of our country to understand democracy and freedom. I wanted them to see what a capitalistic society could produce. With such exposure, I felt, we could have an American type of society in Nicaragua. I did my best to create a United States type of atmosphere in Nicaragua, and I was succeeding.

That is why I call the actions of Mr. Carter a *total betrayal.* Today in Nicaragua, the United States does not have a place to hang her hat. There is a Marxist government and this government is not friendly to the United States.

The negotiations with U.S. Ambassador Pezzullo continued. Pezzullo was in regular contact with the opposition leadership, and at intervals he and I would have a session. On one such visit, toward the end, the Ambassador came to my office and said that arrangements had been made for me and my family to go to the United States and that upon my departure, the U.S. would endeavor to keep the Guardia Nacional intact and give special attention to members of the Liberal Party. He told me the United States would grant me a visa, and that a residence visa could be obtained because Mrs. Somoza was a U.S. citizen. Further, he stated that the U.S. would receive me as a Chief of State and that I would be provided security. This was what I had been waiting to hear from the United States.

I then got in touch with my brother, Jose, and my son, Tacho. I explained to them that we were in an impossible situation, and that we were running out of ammunition and there was no more coming. I told them that with our departure, there was a possibility that we could save the Guardia Nacional and the Liberal Party. I explained, also, that due to the unprecedented resolution of the OAS, I had a legitimate reason to resign.

The OAS resolution read like a fairy tale. It called for the complete reposition of my government and identified the government with my name. When I read the resolution and saw they were calling it the Somocista government, I could hardly believe it. When I carefully read the resolution, I thought what little people they were, and what a big man I must be. It seemed unbelievable that those seventeen condemning nations of the OAS would deign to call me by name.

In the entire history of the Organization of American

States, the resolution passed against me and the government of Nicaragua was unprecedented. If the United States could get seventeen member nations to demand my resignation and the replacement of my government, I would be forced to step down. If I refused to adhere to the principles of that resolution Nicaragua would, in essence, become an "international outlaw." It would mean that no member nation of the OAS or the entire United Nations would sell Nicaragua arms and ammunition. As has been pointed out before, the OAS is an arm of the United Nations.

In Washington, D.C. on June 23, 1979, a special meeting of the Organization of American States was called to consider a resolution which called for my resignation and the complete reposition of my government. As was noted earlier, it would take seventeen member nations to pass the resolution; that would represent two-thirds of the voting members. The U.S. did her homework. Before the resolution was even considered, she had fourteen cosponsors and only three additional member nations were needed to destroy me and the government of Nicaragua. As will be noted, these additional votes were obtained and Nicaragua was condemned. Since that document and the vote on the resolution are historically significant, it would be well to review the resolution and the vote. They are as follows:

ORGANIZATION OF THE AMERICAN STATES

OAS/Ser.F/II.17
Doc.40/79 rev.1 corr.1
June 23, 1979
Original: Spanish

RESOLUTION PROJECT

(Proposed by the delegations of Barbados, Bolivia, Colombia, Costa Rica, Ecuador, United States, Grenada, Jamaica, Mexico, Panama, Peru, Dominican Republic, Surinam and Venezuela)

THE SEVENTEENTH CONSULTATION MEETING OF FOREIGN MINISTERS, CONSIDER:
That the people of Nicaragua are suffering at the present time the horrors of a bloody struggle against the armed forces, which is causing

great suffering, and loss of lives and leading the country toward a serious political, social and economic convulsion;

That the inhuman behavior of the ruling dictatorial regime in that country, revealed by the report of the Interamerican Commission for Human Rights, is the fundamental cause of the dramatic situation the Nicaraguan people are going through;

That the spirit of solidarity which inspires the hemispheric relations unavoidably turns the obligation of the American countries to carry on all the efforts available to put an end to the bloodshed and to prevent that this conflict continue disturbing the peace of the continent;

DECLARES:

That the solution of this serious problem belongs exclusively to the Nicaraguan people.

That from the view point of the Seventeenth Consultation Meeting of Foreign Ministers, that solution should be inspired upon the following bases:

1. Immediate and definite replacement of the Somocista regime.

2. Installation in the Nicaraguan territory of a democratic government that involves in its constitution the representatives of the major groups opposed to the Somoza regime that reflect the free will of the people of Nicaragua.

3. Full guarantee of the Human Rights for all the Nicaraguan people without exceptions.

4. Carrying out free elections as early as possible that lead to the establishment of a true democratic government that will guarantee peace, freedom and justice.

RESOLVE:

1. To urge the member states to carry out all the steps within their power to expedite a durable and peaceful solution to the Nicaraguan problem upon the said bases, respecting scrupulously the no intervention principle and abstaining from any action against those bases which are not in keeping with the peaceful and enduring solution of the problem.

2. To undertake their efforts to promote the humanitarian aid to the population and to contribute to the social and economic recovery of the country.

3. To maintain open the Seventeenth Consultation Meeting of Foreign Ministers as long as the present situation continues.

Voting For	*Abstaining*	*Voting Against*
Barbados	Chile	Nicaragua
Bolivia	El Salvador	Paraguay
Brazil	Guatemala	
Colombia	Honduras	

Voting For	Abstaining	Voting Against
Costa Rica		
Ecuador		
Grenada		
Jamaica		
Mexico		
Panama		
Peru		
Dominican Republic		
Suriname		
United States		
Venezuela		
Trinidad and Tobaco		
Haiti		

Had Nicaragua been able to purchase arms and ammunition, we would have continued our fight against the aggressor forces alone. I am confident we could have defeated the enemy. Also, I knew that many member nations of the OAS were sympathetic to Nicaragua and yet, due to U.S. pressure, voted for the resolution. Legally, however, the resolution was binding on the entire membership of the Organization of American States. Therefore, Nicaragua and Somoza were condemned. Actually, the U.S.-motivated resolution banished my government in the family of nations.

I then wrote, in my own handwriting, my resignation as President of Nicaragua for presentation to the Congress. I carried that handwritten resignation in my pocket for seventeen days. During that period, Ambassador Pezzullo was working on the agreement with the revolutionary forces.

I then called a meeting with the Cabinet and the General Staff and explained my decision. I also called as many of the department commanders as I could reach and asked them to come to Managua. Obviously, the Army was very much involved and with Pezzullo, we had even negotiated the new Chief of the Army. General Mejia was selected to take over that position. The idea at that point was to turn over the government to the opposition and fuse the Guardia Nacional with the Sandinistas. If anything could have pleased me at that juncture, it was the fact that the Guardia Nacional would be kept intact. It was for that reason that my resignation was not submitted the day I wrote it. By July 16th, I had the assurances I wanted from the United States.

In trying to follow the OAS resolution, I called in all of the old department commanders and told them they would be replaced. New department commanders were then appointed and I met with all of them. In that meeting I said, "Gentlemen, I'm going to resign, because our government cannot continue with the OAS resolution which was passed. I am taking with me the ministers, the Cabinet, the members of the General Staff, and Liberal Party members of the Congress. By total compliance with this resolution, you people may have a chance." I wanted all of my people to know that I was not leaving because of fear, I was leaving because I had seventeen nations against me in the OAS and they were demanding my resignation.

In my administration, I had always adhered to the Constitution. In that trying and desperate moment, I refused to bypass the Constitution and ignore the proper protocol. If I were going to resign the presidency, I wanted to do so properly and with class. Those tenets had been my trademark, and in that time of personal frustration, I would not abandon those principles.

I called the Congress into session at the Hotel Inter-Continental and told them of my plans to resign and that, in my place, a new President would be named. The members of Congress requested only one thing, and that was, after accepting my resignation and fulfilling their constitutional duties, that they be given the opportunity to get out of the country when I resigned. I gave them my promise on that request, and I kept my word. For ten straight days, I had a Convair 880 fly from Miami to Managua and stand by. Each day the plane would return to Miami and the next day it would make the trip again. That Convair 880 represented transportation out of the country for the Congress.

When Ambassador Pezzullo said that all arrangements had been completed, General Rafael Porras typed my letter of resignation. I signed the letter and it was sent to the Congress. Congress accepted the resignation and named Doctor Francisco Urcuyo Maliaño as the new President. It was all over.

One person with whom I had trouble was my son, Tacho. Due to his sense of loyalty to his men, he felt strongly that he should not leave. On that issue we had a heated argument. If he had stayed, he would have been killed. On top of that, he would have been in violation of the OAS resolution, because he, along with my brother, Joe, was included in that resolution. I had to tell my son that I was speaking for the entire family, and he had no choice in the matter. He would have to leave.

So in the early morning hours of July 17, 1979, the Cabinet, General Staff, department commanders, the Congress, and the Board of Directors for the Liberal Party made their way to the airport. I was able to get all of them out of the country before the new Marxist government began its bloodbath.

Those last few days in Managua deserve special attention. It was a traumatic experience and about each person who departed that night, a touching and emotional story could be written.

Anastasio Somoza on the right, at age 14, with brother Luis, then 16, on the family farm at Santa Rita, Nicaragua in 1940.

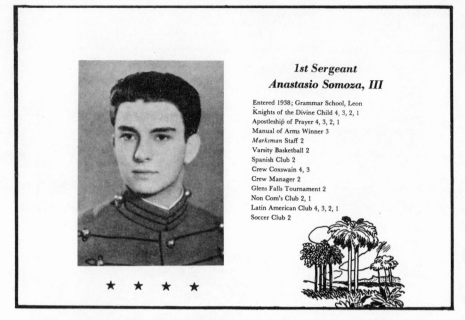

1st Sergeant
Anastasio Somoza, III

Entered 1938; Grammar School, Leon
Knights of the Divine Child 4, 3, 2, 1
Apostleship of Prayer 4, 3, 2, 1
Manual of Arms Winner 3
Marksman Staff 2
Varsity Basketball 2
Spanish Club 2
Crew Coxswain 4, 3
Crew Manager 2
Glens Falls Tournament 2
Non Com's Club 2, 1
Latin American Club 4, 3, 2, 1
Soccer Club 2

Yearbook picture of Anastasio Somoza as upperclassman at La Salle Military Academy, Long Island, New York.

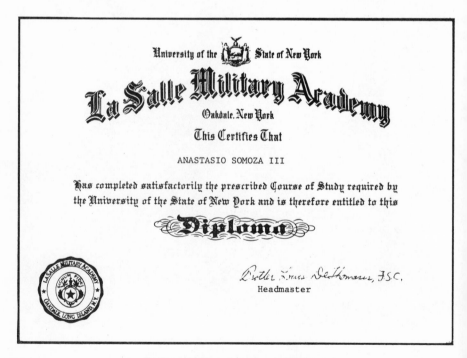

University of the State of New York

La Salle Military Academy

Oakdale, New York

This Certifies That

ANASTASIO SOMOZA III

Has completed satisfactorily the prescribed Course of Study required by the University of the State of New York and is therefore entitled to this

Diploma

Brother Louis DeThomase, F.S.C.
Headmaster

La Salle Military Academy Diploma.

Photograph of Cadet Anastasio Somoza taken at West Point (United States Military Academy, Class of 1946.)

United States Military Academy

Be it known that Cadet *Anastasio Somoza, Jr.* of the *Republic of Nicaragua* having been carefully examined on all the Branches of the **ARTS, SCIENCES** and of **LITERATURE** taught at the United States Military Academy, has been judged worthy to receive the Degree of

Bachelor of Science

In testimony whereof, and by virtue of authority vested in the Academic Board We do confer upon him this Degree.

Given at West Point, in the STATE of New York, this *fourth day of June* in the Year of our Lord One thousand nine hundred and *forty-six, (1946.)*

Superintendent

Commandant of Cadets

Frederick A. Smith, Jr.
Dean of the Academic Board

West Point Diploma of Anastasio Somoza.

General Anastasio Somoza and brother Luis flank Cardinal Spellman. This photograph was given to Somoza by Cardinal Spellman who had inscribed upon it the following message, "General and Mrs. Anastasio Somoza, with a blessing for their families and themselves. Respectfully, F. Cardinal Spellman."

Anastasio Somoza reviewing the "colors" in Korea during 1961.

Scene of terrible destruction caused by Managua earthquake, 12/23/72.

General Somoza reviewing the damage in Managua on 12/24/72.

President Somoza addressing more than seventy-five thousand at a
Nicaraguan political rally during 1978.

Anastasio Somoza meeting the press at Sandia Laboratories in
New Mexico, June, 1978. Pictured here with New Mexico's Governor Jerry Apodaca.

THE WHITE HOUSE

WASHINGTON

June 30, 1978

Dear Mr. President:

I read your statements to the press on
June 19 with great interest and appreciation.
The steps toward respecting human rights that
you are considering are important and heartening
signs; and, as they are translated into actions,
will mark a major advance for your nation in
answering some of the criticisms recently aimed
at the Nicaraguan government.

I am pleased to learn of your willingness to
cooperate with the Inter-American Commission
on Human Rights. I believe that multilateral
institutions can be a most appropriate and
effective means of protecting human rights and
alleviating concerns expressed about them.
I sincerely hope that your government can
rapidly reach agreement with the Commission
on a date for their visit.

The Commission will be favorably impressed
by your decision to allow the members of the
so-called "Group of Twelve" to return to
peaceful lives in Nicaragua. The freedoms
of movement and of expression that are at stake
in this case are among the central human rights
that the Commission seeks to protect.

You have spoken about a possible amnesty for
Nicaraguans being held in jail for political
reasons. I urge you to take the promising
steps you have suggested; they would serve to
improve the image abroad of the human rights
situation in Nicaragua.

President Jimmy Carter's June 30, 1978 letter to President Somoza.

(First page.)

I was also encouraged to hear your suggestions
for a reform of the electoral system in order
to ensure fair and free elections in which all
political parties could compete fairly. This
step is essential to the functioning of a
democracy.

I would also like to take this opportunity to
encourage you to sign and ratify the American
Convention of Human Rights. I have signed this
agreement and am working hard to have my country
ratify the Convention.

I look forward to hearing of the implementation
of your decisions, and appreciate very much
your announcement of these constructive actions.
I hope that you will continue to communicate
fully with my Ambassador, Mauricio Solaun, who
enjoys my complete confidence.

Sincerely,

Jimmy Carter

His Excellency
General Anastasio Somoza Debayle
President of the Republic of Nicaragua
Managua

Second page of President Carter's letter.

A. SOMOZA

GENERAL DE DIVISION G.N.

Junio 29, 1979

Honorable Congreso Nacional
Pueblo De Nicaragua

Consultados los Gobiernos que verdaderamente tienen interés de pacificar al país, he decidido acatar la exposición de la Organización de los Estados Americanos y por este medio renuncio a la presidencia a la cual fui electo popularmente. Mi renuncia es irrevocable.

He luchado contra el comunismo, y creo que cuando surjan las verdades, me darán la razón en la historia.

[firma] A. Somoza

APARTADO 4659, TELEFONOS: 26861-3
MANAGUA, D.N. NICARAGUA

Photocopy of President Somoza's handwritten letter of resignation.

ON OPPOSITE PAGE ▷

Typed copy of President Somoza's official letter of resignation, above, with English translation below.

PRESIDENCIA DE LA REPÚBLICA

MANAGUA, D.N., NICARAGUA, C.A.

16 DE JULIO DE 1979

HONORABLE CONGRESO NACIONAL
PUEBLO DE NICARAGUA

CONSULTADOS LOS GOBIERNOS QUE VERDADE-
RAMENTE TIENEN INTERES DE PACIFICAR AL PAIS, HE DECIDIDO
ACATAR LA DISPOSICION DE LA ORGANIZACION DE LOS ESTADOS
AMERICANOS Y POR ESTE MEDIO RENUNCIO A LA PRESIDENCIA A
LA CUAL FUI ELECTO POPULARMENTE. MI RENUNCIA ES IRREVO-
CABLE.

HE LUCHADO CONTRA EL COMUNISMO, Y
CREO QUE CUANDO SALGAN LAS VERDADES ME DARAN LA RAZON EN
LA HISTORIA.

PRESIDENTE DE LA REPÚBLICA

English translation of President Somoza's letter of resignation:

Having consulted the governments which are interested in the pacification of the country, I have decided to accept the resolution of the Organization of American States, and by this means, I resign the presidency for which I was popularly elected. My resignation is irrevocable.

I have fought against Communism, and I believe that when the truth is known, history will say I was right.

A. Somoza
President of the Republic

Anastasio Somoza at work in his home office
in Asuncion, Paraguay, May, 1980.

Map showing the final combined Marxist offensive against Nicaragua.

Weapons boards display the type of arms used by the Sandinista guerrillas and pinpoint the sources of these armaments for hearings of the Panama Canal Subcommittee of the U.S. House of Representatives, June 6–7, 1979.

Photo of Major Pablo Emilio Salazar, the courageous
"Comandante Bravo," taken on December 31, 1978.

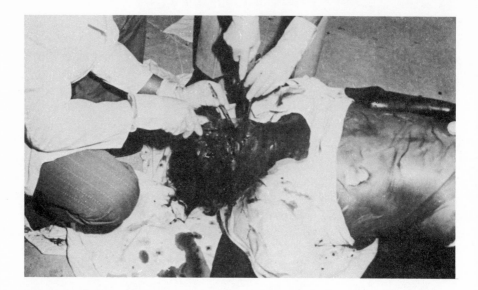

Remains of Comandante Bravo following his assassination in Honduras by a Sandinista "hit team," after their Marxist victory in Nicaragua. Dark lines are deep burns, lighter strips represent peeled skin.

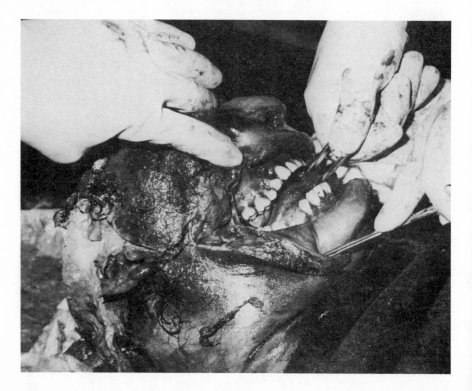

Chapter Seventeen

NICARAGUA NOW — COLOR IT RED

It's easy to say "I told you so," and it's axiomatic that in hindsight we all have 20-20 vision. Perhaps axiomatic is an improper word selection; because Webster defines axiom as follows, "a proposition regarded as a self-evident truth." So far as Nicaragua is concerned, there are still those governments, such as the United States, who refuse to accept the self-evident truth. Which is that Nicaragua is now a Communist state. A large majority of the people in the U.S. and more and more members of the U.S. Congress recognize that fact; but Mr. Carter and the State Department cannot accept it, or they refuse to admit that they misled the American people.

I tried to tell the State Department in Washington, the President, the Congress, and the American people that Cuba, a surrogate of the Soviet Union, was our common enemy and that the Sandinista movement was Communist. There were others who sounded the alarm, but their voices, like mine, were muted.

In Latin America, the common question is, "Why is it that the United States never learns?" This question relates to her inability to learn from experience, that the Communists can't be trusted. A treaty means nothing to the Communists. If it served her purpose, the Soviet Union broke every treaty she ever signed. For recent evidence of that fact, I refer you to the SALT I treaty Russia signed with the United States. To those of this Godless ideology, neither vows, promises, oaths, nor written agreements mean a thing. Their philosophy is to lie, cheat, steal, or kill so long as it furthers the aim and goal of

Communism — which is world domination. These aims and goals are rapidly being achieved.

There are a few leaders in the world who have the courage to stand up against this rampaging red tide, but their numbers are diminishing. As their voices are stilled, the path of Communism becomes easier and easier.

I often speculate as to the reason for the tremendous success of the worldwide Marxist movement. I think of two reasons. One, they have one common ideology. Whereas, in the so-called free nations of the world, there is no common ideology. Each nation follows its own course, apparently oblivious to the common denominator which is applicable to all. That common denominator is individual liberty. Two, the ringmaster of the worldwide Communist movement is the Soviet Union. In the history of the world, there has never been such a dedicated and capable ringmaster as the Soviet Union. Now that covers a lot of territory and includes ringmasters such as Alexander the Great, Genghis Khan, Napoleon Bonaparte, and Adolph Hitler.

In this second category one has to give credit where credit is due. The worldwide success achieved by the Communists is not accidental. Within that diabolical movement, there is strategic intelligence, unmatched political expertise, a spy system second to none, a military machine unequalled in the world today, and the uncanny ability to reach out and take what is desired without creating a worldwide conflagration. Would the free world risk a war with the Soviets to save Hungary, or Czechoslovakia, Poland, or Ethiopia, or Yemen, or Angola, or Iran, or Latvia, or Lithuania, or Korea, or Viet Nam, or Cambodia, or Laos, or China, or Afghanistan, or Nicaragua? The cagey Communists understand the thinking which exists in the U.S. and the free world. In advance, they know that the predicted logic of the "West" will be a resounding NO, because saving this country or that country is not worth running the risk of World War III.

But in the case of Nicaragua, President Carter, Secretary Vance, and their wrecking crew actually assisted the Soviets in taking the country. Being cagey again, the Soviet Union used her puppet, Castro. This way she could not be accused of taking overt action against a nation in the Western Hemisphere. Arms, men, and equipment poured into Nicaragua from Cuba. The shipment of weaponry and equipment followed a circuitous route but the final destination, Nicaragua, was reached.

From the Soviet Union the war goods travelled to Cuba, from Cuba to Panama, from Panama to Costa Rica, and from Costa Rica they went overland through Costa Rica to the Sandinistas in Nicaragua. These shipments were verified, and documented evidence was presented to State Department officials, to members of Congress, and to the Organization of American States. To these important people in Washington and certain leaders in Latin America, I warned that the fall of my government would mean a Communist take-over. That warning went unheeded and today the Communists have an ideal two-ocean base from which to operate in Central America.

With the fall of my government, there was ebullience in Moscow, Havana, and Washington, D.C. The Communists had won, and the free world had lost. As soon as the Army of Nicaragua had capitulated, Cuba started direct flights to the Managua Airport. These flights brought more arms, military equipment, military personnel, and they also brought something else. They brought teachers, hundreds of them, nurses, and doctors. Even then, the United States refused to recognize it for what it was — a Communist victory. Apparently Mr. Carter didn't want to be left out of the picture so he made a move of his own.

Now comes one of the most stupid moves — and he had made many horrendous mistakes — that Carter has ever made. With the U.S. taxpayers' money, he is going to finance the Marxist government in Nicaragua. It's as Lenin said a long time ago, "Americans will sell us the rope with which we will hang them." In this instance, the U.S. is not even selling the rope. It's being given to the Communists. Is there no sanity in the U.S. State Department, and has Carter gone off the deep end?

This financial aid to a proven Marxist government indicates a State Department situation even worse than lunacy. It could indicate that the U.S. now has Communists and Communist sympathizers in most sensitive positions in the State Department. Mr. Carter is in the "deep end" but lacks the wisdom and intelligence to know it. Therefore, he takes the advice of the

State Department and gives U.S. dollars to the enemy. And now, mind you, he is not giving them just a token amount.

After the Communists had won in Nicaragua and were still in the stage of euphoric celebration, Mr. Carter sent $3.5 million in food and medical supplies to the Marxists. Then the State Department notified the U.S. Congress that it was taking $8 million of foreign aid money, previously destined to some other area, and sending this money to the Communist government in Nicaragua. That's not all. Not by $75 million it isn't.

It should be mentioned that Mr. Carter, in his big push to get an additional $75 million for the Marxist government in Nicaragua, called on Mr. Viron Vaky for assistance. Mr. Vaky held the prestigious position of Assistant Secretary of State for Inter-American Affairs. It should be remembered that this is the same Mr. Vaky who previously was caught in a lie about misuse of earthquake aid to Nicaragua. Mr. Carter thought the House Foreign Affairs Committee, which was considering Mr. Carter's request for the $75 million, could use some of Mr. Vaky's expert testimony.

In his plea for additional economic aid appropriation, Mr. Vaky, with a straight face, told the Committee that he was "pleased that the Nicaraguan government has re-established an open press." Perhaps in Vaky's opinion it's "open" because the press is now Communist controlled. In properly assessing Mr. Vaky's opinions on Nicaragua, it would be well to consider the fact that before he was transferred to this esteemed position in Washington, Mr. Vaky was stationed in Venezuela, where he and Carlos Andres Perez became close friends. That association, in itself, should explain Mr. Vaky's attitude toward Nicaragua today.

During the first week of March, 1978, the House of Representatives passed a $75 million aid bill for Nicaragua. The Senate had already passed the bill. Mr. Carter insisted on having this aid and he got it. In the governmental structure of the United States, the House of Representatives is closest to the people. In assessing the mood of the House toward the Communist threat in Central America, I thought surely this legislation will not pass. But it did — by five votes.

Carter has been told by the rebel leadership that "We are Marxists." The State Department knows full well, as Carter

should, that Tomás Borge, the Communuist strongman of
Nicaragua, is a close friend of Fidel Castro. He trained in
Cuba, and he has promised to make Nicaragua a Central
American bastion for Communism. The same can be said of
Moises Hassan. My God, the ruling junta is Marxist and every
single position of power is held by a well-known Marxist or
Socialist. It isn't that the Communists in Nicaragua are trying
to disguise their true political identity. Quite to the contrary.
They have told the United States and the world: "We are
Marxists." Carter has taken the position that these are "good
ol' boys" in Nicaragua and we need to give them some money
— a lot of it. Doesn't the United States ever learn?

Shortly after the Marxist government took over in Nicaragua, Carter and the State Department decided they needed
legislative assistance, if they were to get the money they
wanted for the Communist government. So, Senator Edward
Zorinsky, Democrat from Nebraska and Chairman of the
Senate Foreign Relations Committee's Western Hemisphere
Affairs Subcommittee, was sent to Nicaragua on a special
Airforce jet to make a personal inspection. This was a fact-
finding mission. The Senator stayed three days and came back
to the United States convinced that Tomás Borge, Hassan, and
the other Marxists were OK, and that they should have
immediate financial aid. The three-day experience, with every
minute being controlled by the Marxists, really impressed the
Senator from Nebraska. He even suggested that President
Carter "seriously consider" providing military assistance.

Through my own intelligence sources, I know when Senator
Zorinsky was in Nicaragua and I know the people he saw. I find
it difficult to believe that a supposedly intelligent man, who
holds such a high office in the United States government,
could be so easily "snowed."

When he returned to Washington, the "erudite" Senator was
asked about the more than eight thousand political prisoners
being held by the Marxists. These are people who have been
imprisoned after the Marxist take-over. He assured the press
and his colleagues in the Senate that Tomás Borge, the friend
of Castro's, had promised him that the new government
already had a plan devised to release one hundred of these
prisoners each day. That was a lie, and Borge knew it was a lie.

I wonder if the Senator knows that none of these political prisoners were released and that they are now being tried for political crimes. Each man will most likely receive the maximum sentence of thirty years at hard labor. For most of these men, the only crime they committed was being loyal to the Guardia Nacional in which they served. Thus far, only three hundred men have been tried. At the rate the revolutionary tribunal is going, most of these men will die in prison before they are ever tried, not to mention serving a long prison term.

But President Carter and the State Department had their expert and he came through for them. Carter, the State Department, and Senator Zorinsky were all privy to relevant U.S. intelligence information. It revealed that the main objective of the new Communist government was to construct a major support base in Nicaragua which could support the Communist movement throughout Central America. Senator Zorinsky and the State Department had an answer to this shocking evidence that represented the ultimate in pretended naïveté. The answer:

"The best thing we can do is steer clear of trying to put a particular ideological stamp or imprint on this government."

It doesn't take any secret intelligence effort to obtain a copy of the October 17, 1979 issue of *Barricada* — formerly the Somoza-owned newspaper, *Novedades.* This newspaper is now the official voice of the Sandinistas! On its masthead is a photograph of General Sandino. The headline of that particular issue is as follows: OCTOBER REAFFIRMS THAT THE ROAD OF THE REVOLUTION IS THE ARMED FIGHT. Above that headline was a large photograph of V.I. Lenin and his famous quote, in celebration of the 62nd anniversary of the great Communist revolution of October, 1917.

How could anyone be so naïve as to misunderstand those words? For Senator Zorinsky, I will accept naïveté. For Carter and the State Department, I maintain they were collaborating with the Communists and knew exactly what they were doing. They saw, as I did, the leaflets which appeared in Honduras two days after the Communist victory in Nicaragua. In this leaflet, Tomás Borge said he would join forces "with the revolutionary organizations of other Latin and Central American countries." To make the message absolutely clear, on the cover of this piece of propaganda there is a photograph of Tomás Borge and Fidel Castro which was taken in Havana.

No longer can we afford the luxury of silence. In revealing truths as I am so sincerely trying to do, in speaking of events which heretofore have been whispered but not spoken or written publicly, I realize fully well that I place myself in even more jeopardy. But the people of the United States and the free world must know what is happening, events that sooner or later will affect them.

With my many years in government, with my military training and background, with my close association with governmental leaders throughout the world, and with intelligence information, I come to one startling conclusion: There is a planned and deliberate conspiracy in the United States of America to destroy that Republican form of government. I know that this is being done in the name of peace. Peace to me, the good people of Nicaragua, the solid American citizen and freedom-loving people everywhere, means the absence of armed hostility. To the dedicated Communist, peace has a diametrically opposite meaning. To the Communists, peace clearly means that point in time or space when and where there will be no opposition to Communism.

So if a Communist shoots you with a high-powered rifle, don't worry about it. It was done in the name of peace and with a peaceful rifle. If you are shipped off to a slave labor camp in the cold of Siberia, don't be too concerned, because it's all in the name of peace. Or, if you happen to be one of those in a barbed-wire compound in Nicaragua, exposed to the elements and slowly starving, just remember you are there to further the cause of peace. To the average American businessman, the dutiful homemaker in Mexico City, or the serious student at the University of Madrid, the foregoing may appear to be an overstatement. Sadly, though, it's true. This is the underlying theme of the worldwide Communist effort.

Mr. Carter and the State Department take the position that by giving the new government money, it may keep the new regime from falling into the hands of the Communists. That's wishful thinking and they know it.

The exodus from Nicaragua is astounding. Thousands upon

thousands are fleeing the country. They found, to their horror, that indeed the Sandinistas were Communists. Those business leaders who maintained they could control the Sandinistas have fled the country, or they are striving to leave. Many of those misguided individuals were placed in jail. The Sandinistas decided they had been robbing the people. These businessmen learned, to their regret, that you can't do business with the Communists and that the Cubans are taking over.

A former United Nations official, who now resides in Panama, reported that there are now nine thousand Cubans in Nicaragua. This, of course, includes doctors, nurses, teachers, technical people, and the military. Most of the Cubans are in Managua. This means the Cuban influence is quite evident.

From a population viewpoint, let's draw a parallel. If one million Russians were abruptly deposited in the United States, with most of them placed in Washington, D.C., it would be comparable to what has happened in Nicaragua. In that event, you couldn't turn a corner in Washington without bumping into a Russian. In Nicaragua today, that's the situation with the Cubans. They are everywhere, and their presence is felt in every phase of life; in all economic, social, and military activities. And if Cuban actions of the past can be used as a criterion, their numbers in Nicaragua will continue to increase.

Any realistic appraisal of Nicaragua today will reveal a Marxist government. That may not be clear to Mr. Carter, but it is to the rest of the world; even to President Rodrigo Carazo, the Sandinista supporter in Costa Rica.

Other nations who blindly supported the Sandinistas have now had an opportunity to view the makeup of this revolutionary government. They have found that most of the high-level assignments have gone to known Communists or, at best, Socialists. Some of these are as follows:

- Tomás Borge, Minister of the Interior and an avowed Communist who trained in Cuba and is a personal friend of Fidel Castro;
- Jamie Wheelock, Minister of Agriculture, who received guerrilla training in Cuba and is a Communist;
- Henry Ruiz, Minister of Planning, who received special education in Moscow and is a Communist;

- Humberto Ortega Saavedra, Minister of Defense, who graduated from Patrice Lumumba University in Moscow and is a Communist.

The most gross appointment I have saved until last, because a single line would not suffice. This was the appointment of Nora Astorga to be special prosecutor for the new Marxist government against the political prisoners, which includes eight thousand former members of the Army. These men and women are being tried at this time, and they are subject to thirty years' imprisonment at hard labor. Thus far, some three hundred have been tried and very few have been found innocent. I repeat, Nora Astorga is the chief prosecutor and I would like for her name to be remembered. She is a young woman known to all adults and most children in Nicaragua.

Astorga became famous — infamous would be a better word — by setting a sexual trap for General Reynaldo Perez Vega, my number two man in the military, and participating in his atrocious murder.

Unfortunately for General Vega, he had been having an affair with this young woman for some time. For this relationship he would pay with his life. On the night of the murder, General Vega went to Astorga's house and, on the allegation by Astorga that she had no liquor, he sent his driver and bodyguard away to get some. This, of course, was planned. General Vega had no way of knowing that secluded in the house was a group of Sandinista cohorts of Astorga's. What happened to Vega should not happen to any human being. First, he was beaten into a bloody pulp. Then his eyes were gouged out, his throat cut, his body burned with cigarettes, and as a final act of torture, his genitals were cut off and stuffed in his mouth. Attending doctors estimated it took several hours for the General to die.

This murderess now dispenses justice in Nicaragua. This female vampire now sits in judgement of those eight thousand surviving members of the Guardia Nacional of their country.

There were countless other vicious atrocities, but I thought Nora Astorga deserved special attention. It may be recalled that this is the same Nora who came in for special praise by Karen De Young of the *Washington Post*.

Now, these appointed ministers are separate and apart from the Communist junta. The original members were: Sergio Ramirez, Violeta Chamorro, Alfonso Robelo, Daniel Ortega, and Moises Hassan. Chamorro and Robelo have recently resigned.

These people rule Nicaragua with an iron fist. All basic freedoms have been removed from the political, economic, and social scene. And this is only the beginning.

Freedom of the press has always been a basic philosophical belief I hold. In Nicaragua today, even the Chamorro family cannot print the news as they see it. Neither do they have editorial liberty. The February 15, 1980 issue of *American Relations* explained this matter quite well, and I quote:

> The condition of the press [*referring to Nicaragua*] is similarly dismal. The only television station is operated by the government and it takes an unwavering Marxist line, as does the leading radio station. There are several other smaller radio stations and these are sometimes cautiously critical of the government, but there is nothing like the criticism that was permitted under the Somoza regime.

The publication continues:

> *Novedades*, the former pro-Somoza newspaper, has become *Barricada*. This official publication of the Sandinista government manifests a consistently Marxist editorial policy. The editor of *Barricada* is Carlos Fernando Chamorro, son of the late Pedro Joaquin Chamorro, editor of the opposition paper *La Prensa*. Chamorro appears to be a committed Marxist.

Today in Nicaragua you read what the government wants you to read, and on television you see what they want you to see. One of the first directives from the ruling Marxist junta was to establish block control in every city. This followed the exact plan laid out by Fidel Castro in Cuba. Block captains are appointed and they report on the coming and going of individuals. Further, if they suspect that something suspicious is going on in any home or that a weapon may be hidden, they have the authority to search the premises without a search warrant.

Periodically, through unnamed sources, I receive clippings from *Barricada* and *La Prensa*. It's with remorse and sadness that I read this material, but I want to know what is happening to the people of Nicaragua. One issue of *La Prensa* carried a detailed outline of the block captain system, how it works, and what is expected of the block captains. To appreciate fully the individual liberty and freedom which existed in Nicaragua prior to the Marxist take-over, one should thoroughly digest the Sandinista Defense Committee's directive in *La Prensa*:

The counter-revolutionaries are becoming a threat to our revolution. They are organizing and are harassing our militia, our army, and our military personnel. That is precisely why we at the CDS must assume the control and the vigilance of the counter-revolutionaries. As well as informing the security agencies. The CDS must be the eyes and the ears of the revolution. They must at this time be its principal defenders. This control must be carried out as follows:

1. It is necessary to have a map of the suburb where you live.

2. A census must be taken to determine who lives in your block. Each block must make a list of its neighbors.

3. If a counter-revolutionary individual lives in that block, we will do the following:

   A. Locate his house
   B. Make a file
   C. Have constant vigilance of the identified element to know all his movements.

4. All the members of the CDS must carry out this vigilance and for that purpose it is important that they establish posts in each block. All night there must be watches by turns, each car that goes by, take down the make, color and license number. Every time the dog barks, see who goes by and where he is going. Keep watch to know which neighbor arrives late, if he carried packages or is with friends. Watch those houses where cars arrive late at night and take down all details. When you see someone who doesn't belong in that section, watch him and follow him so that we know what he is doing. We must not let even one movement go by, since it could be the counter-revolutionaries.

5. Regarding the authorization of travelling, migration papers, there must be verification that the person who must approve departures is the person in charge of the Sandinista Block Committee.

6. All persons must carry a letter from his old Sandinista Block Committee to the new CDS of where he will be living.

7. Be alert to the following:

   A. If you have a Somocista neighbor: accuse him.
   B. If you see a strange movement in your block: watch it!
   C. Carry out your night watches to watch for counter-revolution!

SANDINISTA DEFENSE COMMITTEE (CDS)

MANAGUA, D.N. September 29, 1979.

The foregoing represents the conditions under which the people of Nicaragua live. These people have been accustomed to free movement, free thinking, and free individual activity. Those freedoms no longer exist. Neighbor spies upon neighbor and there is constant fear. There is always the possibility that you will be falsely accused. Then what? You are presumed guilty until you can prove yourself innocent. Furthermore, if the block captain doesn't like you or suspects that you are unfriendly to the Communist government, any food rations which are due you and your family can be cut off. The Communists know very well that if you control a man's food supply, you pretty well have him under your control.

The Marxists wasted no time in starting their indoctrination program for the students. To date, some two thousand Cuban teachers have been brought to Nicaragua from Cuba. The education program is also working in reverse. Nicaraguan students are being transported to Cuba for indoctrination and training. The parents have little, if anything, to say about this fateful decision. Normally, the students are not permitted to correspond with their parents but if they do, all letters are censored. This human tragedy goes on day by day and with each passing day, more governmental restrictions are levied upon the people.

When it comes to Cuba and Fidel Castro, Mr. Carter and his State Department have consistently used blindfolds and ear-plugs. I told the proper U.S. authorities on many occasions that Cuba was our common enemy. They refused to listen. I presented documented proof and they refused to believe what they saw. I detailed the Communist plans for the take-over of Nicaragua and they refused to understand. On numerous occasions I specifically warned of Communist aims and objectives for all of Latin America, and still they weren't concerned.

I went so far as to explain that through a cleverly designed education and indoctrination program, Cuba, under the guidance of the Soviet Union, was training young boys and girls as the future revolutionaries and leaders' for Africa and Latin America. I recall discussing the inherent dangers of such an educational program. The reaction was always the same — one of expressed disbelief or non-interest. I wanted the United States to understand that in Cuba we both faced a mortal

enemy and that Cuba wanted, and if unopposed would ultimately get, far more than Nicaragua.

To illustrate my point, I used the Isle of Youth as an
example. This small island lies about 250 kilometers south of
Havana and it has been converted into a virtual Communist
educational fortress. At that time I estimated that some ten
thousand African students were on the Isle of Youth receiving
indoctrination. That estimate has now been proven incorrect.
There are over fifteen thousand African students on that
island. They come from the Congo, Ethiopia, Mozambique,
Namibia, Sao Tome, Angola, and the western Sahara. Published reports now positively show that the only students on this
island who are not of African origin are from Nicaragua.

My intelligence sources knew the function of this island,
and I felt sure the White House and the State Department had
the same information. They must have known, as I did, that
thousands more students were on the mainland receiving the
same indoctrination program. I used all of my intelligence and
verbal skills to convince the United States that what was
happening in Cuba was no short-term ideological briefing. I
desperately wanted those representatives of Mr. Carter to know
that this was for the long pull and that Cuba was playing "for
keeps."

I can now take a retrospective view, and with that view come
to a shocking conclusion. Had I taken Ambassador Bowdler,
Ambassador Pezzullo, or any of the other Carter representatives to the Isle of Youth, it would not have changed their
minds. Had they heard the opening promulgation by those
thousands of students, it would have been interpreted, at least
for public consumption in the U.S., as teen-age fervor. I have
long believed that when the unvarnished truth is presented to
the people of the United States, they will understand and they
will perform in accordance with the dictates of truth. The
people of the United States would understand the daily chant
given by those thousands of students on the Isle of Youth:

"Long live Communism. Long live the Soviet Union. Long
live proletarian internationalism."

Those words do not defy comprehension. The sentences are
short and the words easily understood. Unless, of course, you
refuse to face the reality of those rabid enunciations. I faced

that reality several years ago, when young men returning from Cuba were interrogated. I learned of Castro's indoctrination program and then I saw that same dogma being taught by certain Jesuit priests in my own country. I saw young minds being twisted and turned. I saw the results of conversion to Communism.

To the Carter team, my warnings, my positive proof and, finally, my pleas went unheeded. Their collaboration with Costa Rica, Panama, and Venezuela meant the United States of America, the staunch defender of individual liberty and international law, was collaborating with Fidel Castro. Had the U.S. stood firm and honored her treaty commitments to the Republic of Nicaragua, students of my country would not be on the Isle of Youth today, chanting: "Long live Communism. Long live the Soviet Union."

Under my administration, workers were permitted to organize and had collective bargaining. If they chose to do so, they could go on strike. In a recent news article I read that the Communist government had issued a stern warning against strikes of any kind and stated that if a strike were called, the strikers would face the Army. We all know what that means and so do the people of Nicaragua. Under Communist rule, strikes are simply not permitted.

During the spring of 1978, anti-government and anti-Somoza sentiment became more apparent. This anti-government attitude manifested itself in two particular areas, the Catholic churches and the high schools of Nicaragua. Contrary to public opinion outside Nicaragua, these activities against the government and against me were possible because we had fluidity of freedom in Nicaragua. In a controlled state, such anti-government activities would not have been permitted.

It was my belief that individual liberty would shape the country into a more virile, free, and democratic society. It was my conviction, and still is, that freedom of expression was vital to our country. The record will show that our people enjoyed this freedom, and they exercised it.

On any given Sunday, one could go to certain Catholic churches in Managua and hear anti-Somoza, anti-government sermons. The priests used the pulpit to disseminate anti-government news — and opinions. If they wanted to print and distribute messages to those who never attended church, they could do it. If they wanted to broadcast those anti-government messages, they could do it. In many cases, I actually assisted them in their technology.

These people were free, and I respected their right to think freely and to express themselves. After all, we lived in a democratic society and if a majority of the people didn't like their government, they could vote for a change. The thing that irked the international press and those outside governmental leaders who didn't like me, was the fact that the Liberal Party had the support of a vast majority of Nicaraguans. The record will also show that this support *did not* come by force. Our elections were held in accordance with constitutional requirements and were free. The sanctity of the ballot box was guaranteed. I respected the right of a person to oppose me.

We began to receive reports that there was trouble in some of the high schools. Students bent upon disorder would intercept other students and threaten them if they attended class. If that didn't work, the problem students would go to class themselves and attempt to disrupt the routine. On the part of the students, this was a form of protest against the government.

I met with all the high school principals and it was a real give-and-take session. These were the men and women closest to the problem source and their ideas and expressions were needed. One of the principals analyzed the problem quite clearly. He stood up and said: "Mr. President, about seven percent, or less, of the boys are causing all the trouble." He went on to point out that each high school had its leaders and these leaders, upon completion of a particular disruption plan, would go to the university to get new instructions. I knew of the Leftist activity at the university, and then I knew that their sphere of influence had reached down into the high schools.

One might ask, why did I permit such anti-government activities from the university and high school students? The only answer I could give is that was the way we interpreted freedom in Nicaragua. With the Communists now in control of Nicaragua, you can be sure that freedom is not interpreted in the same manner.

Perhaps the point I want to make is that a large majority of our citizens did not support these anti-government groups. It was my philosophy that those opposition forces had to be able to express themselves. This they were permitted to do. I believed that suppression of freedom was not the answer to expressed opposition. I still hold to that belief.

Those were internal problems, and through the democratic process of government we could have handled those problems. The answer was not in throwing those students in jail. The answer was not in banishing those priests who opposed me and the government. The answer, I felt, was to let everyone express themselves and then let the voters decide whom they wanted to lead the government, and what political party could best serve Nicaragua.

Due to external interference in the domestic affairs of Nicaragua, this political process was nullified. The crime committed against the people of Nicaragua was naked, external aggression and violence. Nicaragua had always been able to conduct its internal affairs in an orderly and just manner. But when other nations, such as the United States, Panama, Costa Rica, Venezuela, and Cuba, decide they will impose their will on the domestic affairs of a country such as Nicaragua, that country is doomed. An international crime was committed against Nicaragua. What crime? I repeat, with external aggression and violence, a free nation was destroyed.

You can't blame the people of Nicaragua for fleeing their homeland. Those fortunate people who live in an atmosphere of freedom, of stability, of family tradition, and in a governmental clime conducive to that inward satisfaction which comes from permanency, cannot begin to understand the trauma which loss of home and country can mean. Yet, some 150,000 Nicaraguans have fled their country and most of them believe they will never return. They left their homes, their property, their family possessions, and everything. Most of them left the country with one small bag.

Try, if you can, to relate to such a drastic decision. To draw a parallel, it's as though some 15,750,000 people in the United States decided they could not live under conditions which had been thrust upon them, and left their homeland forever. To illustrate the parallel further, in this exodus you would find most of the country's doctors, lawyers, businessmen, engineers, scientists, and those with technical know-how. After the Communists took Nicaragua, that is what happened.

Even if President Carter, ex-Secretary Vance, and Ambassador William Bowdler fail to recognize a Communist government when they see one, the same can't be said of the Central American presidents. Of course, they are all being threatened by Castro's Cuba and Mr. Carter is not. To his way of thinking, everything in the United States is still safe and secure, because the Communists are still eighty miles away.

The Conference of Central American Presidents had scheduled their annual meeting for 1980 in Managua. All of the presidents, including Rodrigo Carazo of Costa Rica, decided they didn't want to attend such a meeting in Nicaragua. So the presidents of Guatemala, El Salvador, Costa Rica, and Honduras understand the threat of the Communist government in Nicaragua, even if Mr. Carter does not.

It's interesting to note that President Carazo gave vital support to the Sandinista cause. He provided sanctuary, plus staging areas, and permitted military hardware and men to be transshipped across Costa Rica to the Sandinistas. Without Carazo's support, it's doubtful that the Communists would have succeeded. I take Carazo to be a weak president and, in my opinion, he yielded to pressure from the White House, the U.S. State Department, and the Venezuelan government. It's a little late but Carazo, like Carter, is discovering that the Russians are not the "good guys in white hats." He recently berated the Soviet Union for meddling in Costa Rican affairs.

For several years, the Soviet Union Embassy in Costa Rica has been used as a KGB (Russian intelligence) center. Costa Rica is a small country, about the size of West Virginia, and has a population of approximately two million people. Yet the Russian Embassy staff in San Jose is almost large enough to serve a country as large as the United States. One must understand, however, that Costa Rica was the only country in all of Central America which would permit Russia to operate an embassy. The Russian Embassy was opened in 1971.

For this benevolence on the part of Costa Rica, thanks and recognition must go to her former president, Don Pepe Figueres. For the establishment of diplomatic relations with the Soviet

Union and the opening of a Russian Embassy in Costa Rica, it is reported that Figueres received $500,000. Some reports indicated that he received as much as $5,000,000, but I think those figures are exaggerated. I hope "Don Pepe" enjoyed the money because he did untold damage to all of Central America.

The Prime Minister of Spain, Adolfo Suarez, recently paid a visit to various Latin American countries. He was scheduled to stop in Nicaragua; but, with the obvious Communist government in Nicaragua, he cancelled that visit.

All of this suggests one thing; the rest of the world recognizes the new government for what it really is — Communist. Then how is it that Mr. Carter and his administration fail to see the Communist threat to all of Central America, the Caribbean, Mexico and, in reality, all of Latin America? Not only does he fail to see but he pours millions upon millions of U.S. taxpayers' dollars down a Communist rathole. The absurdity of it all is beyond me.

Carter has gone so far as to announce that he does not believe the Caribbean area is vital to United States interests. This reminds me of the time when the then Secretary of State for the U.S., Dean Acheson, announced that South Korea was not an area of vital interest to the United States. Remember what occurred? The North Korean Communists took this as their signal to move, and they invaded South Korea. That disastrous U.S. military undertaking should be familiar to everyone.

One thing of which you can be sure, the Soviet Union and Cuba consider the Caribbean as being vital to U.S. interests, even if Mr. Carter does not. The U.S. signal of "non-interest area" added fuel to an already burning fire. The Communists have taken Nicaragua, so you can color my country red.

The Jewel of Central America, as El Salvador has long been called, has reached the point of no return and could fall at any time. In March, 1980, the U.S. sent a "jewel" of a different sort to El Salvador and, in their desperate situation, this was the type of jewel they needed least. Mr. Carter sent them, as the new U.S. Ambassador, Mr. Robert White. This man White is a Leftist and a well-known trouble maker. After he had been confirmed by the U.S. Senate, a confirmation he didn't receive without a fight, he proceeded to El Salvador. Upon arriving, the proverbial "bull in the china closet" assumed his usual didactical posture.

To the surprise of no one who knew him, but to the shock and dismay of the ruling government, Ambassador White announced his sympathy for the Left. He was Carter's selection for a critical area and he was thoroughly briefed by the State Department. One can only conclude that Mr. Carter and the State Department are dedicated to the proposition that the anti-Communist governments shall not win. As of this moment, you could color El Salvador pink because that little country is almost gone.

Honduras, Guatemala, and Costa Rica are rapidly being infiltrated by the Communists. Each day there are more killings in Guatemala. There, again, Jesuit priests can be found in the front of the Communist movement. These political priests seem to be omnipresent. They were effective in Nicaragua, and now they are being effective in Guatemala. I'm not saying these priests are not active in Honduras and Costa Rica, because they are. It's simply that they are devoting more attention to Guatemala at this time.

The people in Guatemala are aware of Mr. Carter's attitude toward Communism in Central America, and they are alarmed. On January 26, 1980, an editorial appeared in *El Imparcial* which accurately described the feeling about Mr. Carter. It began with this headline: WITH FRIENDS LIKE JIMMY CARTER — WHO NEEDS ENEMIES? And I quote the lead-off paragraph:

> Often in the course of the history of our convulsive planet, the stupid, the incapable and the irresponsible mediocre politicians, with pretentions of statesmanship, arrive on the scene to provoke irreversible situations. Such situations produce resulting consequences which are beyond repair affecting generations and the destiny of all humanity.

Of course, the writer is referring to President Carter. The editorial goes on to describe what this man had done to the free world and to his allies. It is pointed out that Carter is handing over the entire Caribbean to the Soviet Union, but with Cuban teachers. The editor said: "Formidable Russia. Poor gringos. Iran, Nicaragua, the Persian Gulf, the Caribbean, two allies, two strategic zones, dismantled by a political incompetent . . . ." That just about says it all, and I believe the writer spoke the truth.

Repeatedly, members of the ruling Communist junta in Nicaragua have proudly proclaimed their Marxist philosophy. The Sandinista leadership have openly admitted their relationship with Cuba. They have not misrepresented themselves. The Cubans have even admitted their role in Latin American subversion. As far back as July 22, 1979, the Cuban position was stated publicly by a Cuban. On that date, the Associated Press carried a story about Ramon Sanchez Parodi, who heads the Cuban Interest Section in Washington. I quote the Associated Press: "Sanchez, who heads the Cuban Interest Section in Washington, admitted for the first time Cuba was helping anti-government movements in Guatemala, El Salvador, Honduras, and Nicaragua, but gave no details." That's plain and simple language. Sanchez made no effort to cover up the fact that Cuba is assisting in the overthrow of these governments. That was after the fall of the Nicaraguan government and I understood perfectly. You can be sure, also, that the presidents of all other Central American nations now understand.

Don't think the administration in Washington didn't know about this, because they did. In a CIA secret document, that isn't so secret anymore, dated May 2, 1979, it was reported to the White House and to the State Department that there was direct intervention by Cuba in Nicaragua, Guatemala, and Honduras. Now, this was some forty days prior to the final Sandinista offensive in Nicaragua. The secret document went on to specify the kind of military hardware which Cuba was delivering to the Sandinistas. Not only that, the method of transporting these war materials was described. The Panama airforce flew the arms from Cuba to Panama. From Panama they went through Costa Rica to the Sandinista camps. We knew this but we weren't aware of the fact that Washington had been given all the details.

Listed below are the salient points of that secret CIA document which the State Department admitted having. To me, the shocker is that the *Chicago Tribune* broke this story on June 27, 1979. My government was not handed over to the Communists until the following July 17th! The *Tribune* was convinced it had dropped a bombshell, and that this story would have to be carried by the "big" news media. The *Tribune's* two-line banner headline across the top of Page One read: CUBA, PANAMA AIDING SOMOZA FOES. Here it is:

1. Since late September, 1979, Cuba has made at least two and possibly three armed shipments to the Nicaraguan guerrillas, using Panamanian air force planes. These shipments included 50-caliber machine guns and Soviet AK-47 automatic rifles. The shipments went first to Panama and then to Nicaragua via Costa Rica.

2. Panama serves as a staging point for Nicaraguan guerrillas. They are sent to Cuba for training via Panama. Then they are sent back to fight in Nicaragua via Panama. An official of one of the three guerrilla factions was quoted as saying that half of his men had been trained in Cuba.

3. Castro has been active in mobilizing support for the Nicaraguan guerrillas in other countries. In February, 1979, he promoted a meeting of Communist Party representatives from all of the Central American countries plus Mexico and Panama. At this meeting, the Communist leaders discussed not only support for the Marxists fighting in Nicaragua, but also plans for future meetings to discuss strategy for revolutionary activity in other Central American countries.

4. In March, 1979, Fidel Castro met personally with the leaders of the three factions of the Nicaraguan guerrillas. At this meeting in Cuba, Castro persuaded them to establish a unified leadership. He promised to give them arms, money, and weapons if they did this.

5. Castro advised the Nicaraguans to downplay their dedication to Marxism *at this time*. This, he counseled, was necessary to lure non-Marxist support for their efforts.

6. Castro even advised the Nicaraguan rebels on battlefield tactics, counseling them to concentrate on hit-and-run tactics and avoid frontal attacks on the Nicaraguan National Guard.

Now, the news media had this story but they chose to ignore it. Primarily, I think, because it proved every contention I had made. Therefore, most of the people in the United States didn't even know about the story. The important thing, though, is that Mr. Carter knew about it and Mr. Cyrus Vance knew about it.

With this knowledge, why did Mr. Carter lie to the American people on national television? With a straight face he said that the U.S. was not involved in the overthrow of the Nicaraguan government. That was a bald-faced lie, and you will see that it was. He went further and said that to his knowledge, Cuba was not directly involved in the overthrow of the Nicaraguan government. That was an even bigger lie.

I have never purported to be a fan of the former U.S. Ambassador to the UN, Mr. Andrew Young. It is my judgement that Mr. Young gave solace and comfort to the Communist movement everywhere. On one point, however, he gets an understanding ear from me. Apparently Mr. Young lied to President Carter about a clandestine meeting he attended while he was still the U.S. Ambassador to the UN. So Mr. Young was dismissed from his post. Word was given to the press that Mr. Carter would fire any of his appointees who were guilty of lying. If that transgression is grounds for dismissal, Mr. Carter should have resigned a long time ago. That's one thing on which he gets a very excellent mark. In his association with Mr. Carter, Mr. Young should have learned that it's not "Do as I do, but do as I say."

The CIA also revealed that fifty members of the Fuerzas Populares de Liberacion (FPL), a Communist organization in El Salvador, had received four months of intensive military and ideological training in Cuba. These are the leaders of the Communist movement in El Salvador today.

The story received rather extensive coverage in *La Nacion* of Buenos Aires, Argentina on March 10, 1980. It was still considered top-rate news at that time.

Mr. Carter says the Caribbean is not an area of vital interest to the United States. Somehow, I doubt that many Americans would agree with that statement. Leaders of other nations with whom I have talked personally find it difficult to believe that the President of the United States would make such a statement. There is one nation in Europe which takes an opposite viewpoint from Mr. Carter and that's France.

As basic geography teaches us, France is thousands of miles removed from the Caribbean. Whereas the United States lies next door to that area. But France has a vested interest in the Caribbean. The island of Martinique in the West Indies happens to come under French rule. In some areas it's considered to be an overseas department of France. There is trouble in Martinique, and France recognizes the source of that trouble.

To be sure, that source is Cuba. Apparently, though, France

is not going to give up without a fight. On March 14, 1980, the *Buenos Aires Herald* ran a Reuters story relating to the Martinique situation and the story was accorded considerable space. The headline read: FRANCE BLAMES CUBA FOR UNREST IN MARTINIQUE. Hurrah for France! At least some nations have the courage to face up to Cuba and tell it like it is. Paul Dijoud, the state secretary for French overseas departments and territories, had this to say:

> International Communism is on the march in the Caribbean and Cuba is the Central American staging post for Soviet action. France plans to halt this penetration together with the West and free nations.

Martinique is a small island with approximately 450,000 people. According to today's U.S. standards, the island is of no strategic importance and, therefore, should not be an area of vital interest. France feels differently, and obviously Cuba and the Soviet Union do too, because they want Martinique.

At a time when it appears that all the other nations in the world tremble in front of the Soviet bear, France is exhibiting courage. Recently, President Gisçard d'Estaing of France took a strong stance against the Soviets. In essence he said that if it appeared the Russians would overrun Western Europe, and that includes France, he would not hesitate in using atomic weapons or anything else France might have in her arsenal. The French President must understand the Soviet mentality, because that's the only language to which the Soviets pay any attention.

France now says she will take a position against Cuba in the Caribbean. There was only one part of Mr. Dijoud's statement that concerned me and that was, "together with the West. . . ." If West means, as I think it does, the United States, then Mr. Dijoud had better examine the record. The U.S. will not assist France, if it means taking on Castro. Castro is Cuba, and Cuba is Soviet Russia. If the French have a confrontation with Castro they might find themselves, as I did, being opposed by the U.S.

For verification of Carter's strange relationship with Cuba, let's examine an official document. In his testimony before the U.S. House of Representatives Subcommittee on June 7,

1979, General Gordon Sumner, former Chairman of the Inter-American Defense Board, disclosed just how far the Carter Administration would go in order to protect Fidel Castro and his crony, Omar Torrijos.

This part of his testimony relates to an incident which occurred in Managua in 1977, when the combined Joint Chiefs of Staff were holding their conference in Nicaragua. General Sumner reported:

> At the meeting in Managua, just prior to my meeting with General Torrijos, I had prepared a one-page statement. I was there as an observer. The Conference of the American Armies is a very powerful political forum in Latin America. The armies run Latin America, not the airforce or the navy, but the armies. They always invite the chairman to be there.
>
> I prepared a one-page statement which I cleared with the Joint Chiefs of Staff. The night before the meeting was to convene, I gave the senior American delegate, General Kerwin, the Vice Chief of Staff of the U.S. Army, my statement. He told me that I could not use the statement; and the statement was a very simple explanation of what the Cubans were doing in Africa, and the implications of their action in Africa for this hemisphere; and I was, in effect — but not in effect — I was flat muzzled. I was told "you cannot use that statement."
>
> I told General Kerwin that I did not want to get into a confrontation with him. As it turned out, one of the other chiefs of a delegation, chief of the army, I believe it was the Brazilian, asked me a question which allowed me then to give the statement, but I could not *go in* and give that statement. It was the policy of the Government at that time, the U.S. Government, not to mention Cuban intervention in Africa. *"Do not, for God's sake, mention anything about Fidel Castro"*; and this to me was just unacceptable. And it was that particular incident, along with a string of other things that have happened, that made me decide I could no longer be a part of the administration . . . .

That statement by General Sumner was made in November, 1977. On that same trip to Central America the distinguished General was to hear Torrijos expound on the virtues of Fidel Castro and state unequivocally that he was assisting and would continue to assist the revolutionary Sandinistas in Nicaragua. It was as though Torrijos felt that with Castro for a friend, he didn't need anyone else. At that point in time, the Carter Administration had already given the Panama Canal to Torrijos, but the U.S. Congress had not passed implementation legislation. Even though Torrijos had to have that legislation passed, he brazenly admitted he would violate the OAS Charter and exert every effort to help the revolutionaries in Nicaragua. Torrijos was never really a very intelligent person, but he was intelligent enough to know he had nothing to fear from the Carter Administration.

I recalled again the conversation with my friend from Costa Rica in which he stated the "man on the street" in San Jose believed the United States was afraid to assist Nicaragua because they, the U.S., felt that Castro could defeat them. Then I thought again about the words of Carlos Andres Perez, President of Venezuela, "I don't want to face up to Castro." And now came this from one of the most outstanding generals in the entire U.S. Army: "Do not, for God's sake, mention anything about Fidel Castro."

If France believes the United States will assist her in any anti-Castro operation, I would strongly urge the French leaders to examine the Carter record.

The Martinique situation is just one more example of the global desires of the Communists. This small island should not be of great importance, but to the Soviets and Cuba it is. For that matter, how could diminutive El Salvador be of importance? To "Them," it is of importance and that's what counts.

In the Soviets' long-range planning, one must not overlook Mexico. For some time, Mexico felt she was secure from Communist subversion. That reasoning was based on a false premise and President Lopez Portillo should now be aware of the threat. Trouble has already started and Mexico can expect a dramatic increase in protests, demonstrations, and violence. The pattern is always the same.

Nicaragua was the first target in Central America. To their way of thinking, and mine, Nicaragua represented the toughest nut to crack. If Nicaragua, with its strong and reliable ties with the U.S.A., could be taken, then logic dictated that the other Central American nations would fall like dominoes. The strategy was sound and it's working.

Think ahead for just a moment. What country borders on Guatemala, and what country has recently developed oil reserves comparable to those found in the Middle East? Certainly, the answer is Mexico. You can be absolutely sure that Mexico's huge reserves of oil and gas represent a tempting morsel to the Soviets. Mexico is not to be excluded and is projected as part of the Soviet Union's Western Hemispheric bloc.

If Mr. Carter feels secure because the Communists are still eighty miles away, how will he feel when they are just across the Rio Grande? Based upon the previous logic shown by his administration, the President would tell the American people to pray for a big rain.

Today, Nicaragua is a Communist nation. The proud and anti-Communist people of my country are suffering, and the suffering will not abate. For them, there is no tomorrow. The tomorrow was yesterday. So get your map of Central America and color Nicaragua red. Better make it blood red, too!

Chapter Eighteen

THE TAPES

I had been advised that for some time the U.S. State Department had taped certain conversations which I held with the U.S. government. This caused me no concern, because I was always very candid with the U.S. So far as I was concerned they could have broadcast my conversations. In many instances, this was very nearly the case. Often the subjects of my conversations had a way of mysteriously appearing in the *Washington Post.* Even though, as a rule, those conversations were of a confidential nature, it bothered me not that information would be "leaked" to the press.

In those last few days before my government fell to the Marxists, many crucial conversations were occurring with the U.S. representatives. It was then that I decided to do something which I had never done before — tape the conversations. My feeling at the time was that I wanted a word-for-word record of everything said by both sides. Those sides were the United States of America and the duly elected government of Nicaragua. In the past, I have alluded to those taped conversations, but this is the first time they have been reduced to writing and reproduced.

My premonition was that discussions in those crucial meetings would be distorted, misrepresented, and falsely reported. That premonition proved to be correct. After each session in which the United States was determining the future of Nicaragua, the U.S. representative would report to Washington. Washington contacted the other conspiratorial countries and presented their version of the completed session. Then I would receive a feedback on what Washington had reported. Often times I was shocked at the U.S. version, but, most of all, I was disappointed in the ethics of the Carter Administration. They had me in a corner and they knew it. They could present their views to their associate nations, but I could say nothing. There was no way in which I could publicly present Nicaragua's side of those sessions.

Consequently, there were rumors in Managua as to what was transpiring in those sessions. These were ugly rumors which indicated I was "selling out" the people of Nicaragua and the Guardia Nacional. There were times when the press published reports of those meetings, and, as we learned, their information came from the U.S. participant.

Historically, these tapes are meaningful. To me, however, they assume tremendous personal importance. They reveal that throughout those agonizing sessions with the U.S., I pushed for two things: preservation of the Guardia Nacional and a U.S. guarantee that the people of Nicaragua would not be handed over to the Communists. In order to achieve these two vital objectives, I offered to resign the presidency and leave the country immediately. That was as early as June 27, 1979. This was what the U.S. demanded but, as is shown, the U.S. wanted to delay my resignation. Those members of the news media who were in Managua at that time should find that fact, as well as many others, most significant.

If my resignation had been accepted on June 29, 1979, the day I wrote it, much bloodshed could have been avoided. More importantly, the Guardia Nacional would not have been without ammunition. It should be obvious to any reader that the "resignation green light" was given by the U.S. when the Guardia Nacional no longer possessed warmaking capabilities. By July 16, 1979, those staunch anti-Communist men of the Army were without the means to combat the aggressor forces.

Even so, the tapes prove my contention that before departing Nicaragua, I had a U.S. guarantee that the Guardia Nacional would be preserved and that the people of Nicaragua would not be subjected to a Marxist government.

After reading the tapes, there should be no doubt that the Carter Administration contrived to hand Nicaragua over to the Sandinistas and, in this contrivance, used deceit, duplicity, and outright lies. Read the tapes and reach your own conclusion.

TAPE 1

[*The following conversation took place in November, 1978 between President Somoza, U.S. Ambassador William Jorden, and Mauricio Solaun.*]

Jorden: Well, I am very happy to be here; visit with you, share some ideas, report on my recent activities which have been rather hectic. You can imagine — I am in country "X" one day and in another country the next day, but it has been rather interesting . . . I think productive.

Somoza: I have a comment to make. You have ended up at the end of the circle, right here.

Jorden: I wanted to tour the territory and see what was going on, and get some viewpoints and ideas, before visiting with you.

Solaun: I wonder, Mr. President, if it would be possible for Ambassador Jorden to talk privately with you.

Somoza: Certainly.

Solaun: Fine, excuse me. [*He leaves the room.*]

Jorden: It's been wild. Because I started in Panama and I went to Costa Rica. I went to Honduras, Salvador, Venezuela, Colombia, Guatemala, back to Panama, and [*am*] now finally in the heartland. Well, I just want to assure you that I come as a representative of my President and my Secretary of State.

Somoza: I would like to tell you that I welcome you. I have seen a lot of people who have used my case as propaganda, and they thought I was going to receive you in a very unfriendly manner. I want to assure you, and Mr. Vance, and the President that I understand these things in politics.

Jorden: I want you to know just that I come in total friendship.

Somoza: I look at you that way.

Jorden: I am not the kind of man who likes to play games. I have been in diplomacy for a good long time, and I have developed a reputation over the years of being an atypical diplomat. I believe in being candid, frank, and I believe in honesty; and that can sometimes cause me problems. But it's the only way I know how to play the game; so be it. I don't know how you wish to proceed, Mr. President.

Somoza: I'd like to hear what you have to say.

Jorden: I could . . . let me just lay out the situation as we see it and follow the instructions which are designed to guide me, reflecting not my views but the considered views and analysis of my government — and when I say that, I mean all of the government.

I think there is a unifying view, except [*for*] certain members of Congress, but [*among*] the executive branch, the State Department, the Defense Department, and a significant number on Capitol Hill as well. At the outset, of course, my main interest is to restore order in this part of the world and to help your country to get back on the path of economic progress — and as I say, we would like to give an appraisal of how it looks to us.

Our feeling is that Nicaragua, as a result of events in the recent past, is gradually becoming dangerously polarized, and that —

Somoza: When you say polarized, Mr. Ambassador, what do you mean?

Jorden: In the sense of the Nicaraguan government and the opposition being increasingly at odds and the opposition being increasingly critical of the government and pulling into separate camps, rather than the smooth spectrum of political opinion which exists in some places but doesn't exist in others. We can see this tendency, the poles developing.

I'm talking of polarization, of course. I am not talking about the Sandinistas where there is obviously a polarization, but other elements in the society, political and economical. We are terribly concerned that everything you have built up, and your brother before you, is in danger of being destroyed. And that means the political structure, institutions. The economic prospects don't look to us to be very good. We gather that commercial activity has gradually come to a halt. There has been a flight of capital — I don't know exactly what the figures are — and the foreign exchange reserves are dangerously low, and our information is that there is no very good prospect for new investments until the situation is calm, and people . . .

We understand that the motives of certain elements of the opposition are not all that disinterested and patriotic, and everyone has personal and selfish interests. But obviously the opposition to your government is widespread, and again, we understand that the Sandinistas are only one small element; and if it were only the Sandinistas, the situation would be manageable, but it has developed into something quite different. We believe that the situation at this present moment . . . We don't see that . . . The actions that you have taken have ended the violence for the moment, but we are persuaded it is a temporary thing. I have very good reason to know that the Sandinistas are active. They are getting support, they are recruiting people, and it is only a matter of time before they start again. So, I don't see that the developments of the last month have ended that threat, but in any case you know as much or more than I do about this thing . . .

We know there have been efforts towards a dialogue in the past, but the cold fact, as we see it right now, is that no dialogue can be negotiated or can emerge solely within Nicaraguan society. We believe that some outside assistance — some friendly, good offices, some encouragement of both parties to reach some kind of agreement — can be healthy, useful, constructive, and that without some kind of outside influence it's not very likely to happen.

I think, very frankly, I think that the opposition elements in this picture are afraid. I think they have to have the confidence to face up to you and be on a man-to-man basis, and, if there is some kind of middleman, someone offering of good offices, that it would make it easier perhaps for them to state their views. Frankly, without that we are afraid they are going to hold back, and just call you names without getting into the process of solving the problem. So, in any case, with all the things that we have seen, sharing the views of others who have watched it very carefully, it is our judgement that we are in something of a downward spiral. There will be moments when it looks better, but I think it will go downward again and the situation will just gradually get to the point where perhaps total chaos could occur . . . which would be . . .

In any case, what we want to do is help you and our other Nicaraguan friends to establish this situation, work towards solutions, towards answers, in a totally friendly and cooperative way. I am not talking of any kind of an imposed solution, Mr. President. We are friends, we want to work together, we want to make some suggestions and perhaps serve as a kind of bridge at the outset so that Nicaraguan elements can gradually pull together; and in the final analysis, the only solution that will last will be the Nicaraguan solution. It's just that at the current stage, that perhaps a useful role could be played as a friend, with others perhaps, in providing a catalytic agent to get this process started, and see where we come out.

For that reason my mission was to talk to other governments about that; and we now have the agreement of other governments that will join us in this effort, if they are wanted, by selecting distinguished representatives of each government to take part as a conciliator, mediator, or what anyone wants to call it. I don't think that the names are important, except that we understand that it is not the intention to try to impose any solution . . .

The countries that have agreed to participate in this effort are, so far: the United States, the Dominican Republic, Honduras, Colombia, and possibly Guatemala. President Lucas said he would appoint a representative but he wanted to think about it a little bit. I think that if this move is welcomed by you, I think he will very quickly name a representative.

I can't speak for the other governments. You understand, I have been mostly on the road for the past five days — I don't really know what has happened in terms of selection. I believe some people have already been selected, but the United States designate for this purpose will be William Rogers, who is a distinguished lawyer and former Assistant Secretary of State for Latin America. I don't know if you know Bill, but —

Somoza: I know him, but he is not acceptable for us. He has stated biased opinions about the Somoza family.

Jorden: He has? I'll convey that. Let me just check these notes to make sure I have covered all the territory. Well, this group of distinguished representatives will come to Nicaragua, will meet with you, and they will then meet with the opposition groups and get their points of view, positions — encourage them to appoint a group to act, perhaps — and then go back and forth, and really try to minimize differences, and perhaps reach a point where these opposition groups and the government are sitting down talking to each other about a solution that would be acceptable to all principal elements of the society. That's the kind of process. I don't think we can be too specific because it's a rather unique exercise.

Somoza: The only one in America.

Jorden: We are trying to develop an imaginative approach to what we see is a real problem, so there will be a lot of trial and error and it will be up to everyone concerned to make the differences clear and try to minimize them. At least, that's the general approach that we have developed. They wanted me to make clear that this process should not, in advance, be subject to any preconditions by any of the parties. *We don't want the opposition to tell us that the only thing that can solve this problem is for President Somoza to leave. That's unacceptable, unacceptable. We don't believe anyone should lay down fixed conditions. You know, if this isn't done, I won't play ball!* I think that the concerns that you have, and they are very real and specific, should be discussed with this group.

The problem is just not internal. There are external elements in it. These folks will have to deal with other governments that, for one reason or another, whatever that may be, have not remained neutral; and they will have to be discouraged from using force to inject themselves into this situation. I am thinking now of Venezuela, and Panama, and Costa Rica. My private feeling is that Costa Rica is sort of caught in the middle with no real force to deal with the situation. In any case, there are external problems.

Well, they reminded me that you have said in the past that the choice is either you, Somoza, or chaos, and we don't believe that those are the only alternatives.

Somoza: *I have never said the choice is Somoza or chaos.*

Jorden: Well, I don't know where they have got that. I apologize for raising it, if you haven't said it.

Somoza: *No, I haven't said it.*

Jorden: In any case, as I have said earlier, we are terribly concerned that the Nicaraguan situation, which has already spilled over into neighboring countries . . . unless something is done to correct the situation and work towards a solution, I think that it does clearly play into the hands of Communists and Castro. I think that they are hoping that this will be a situation that they can use and establish a base in the mainland and go from there. All of your neighbors, as you know, are deeply concerned about what could happen because they recognize that if anything serious happens to Nicaragua then they may be next, so they are concerned. I cannot sit down at this moment with you, Mr. President, and say what the final formula is going to be. That's a job for the negotiators and the mediators . . .

This is a sensitive point, but I have to be honest. *The possibility of your departure from office before 1981 is one of the possibilities that has to be considered.* I am not saying it has to be done, I am saying it has to be considered. *Since other elements have made such an issue of your immediate departure then at least that matter could not be off limits as a subject of possible discussion.* Whether it is necessary, or how it might be arranged, is quite a different matter. *That's a matter for you and your people to decide.*

In any case, we do want you to understand that your views will carry tremendous weight, and your views will receive every consideration in this process by everybody. What we would like to work towards is a solution that is dignified and smooth, as graceful as possible. *You know, your country and mine have been very close for a great many years. We have worked together in many things.* When there have been problems, we have tried to help. With the [*Managua*] earthquake . . . in the same spirit . . .

Somoza: I would like to tell you something, Ambassador

Jorden, and you will excuse me for saying this, it is painful for me to say it, *but I don't trust the United States anymore.*

Jorden: I am sorry to hear that.

Somoza: I am telling you from a West Pointer's viewpoint. I have gotten my lickings from your administration in the past, straightforward. This time it has been a game. I don't feel I have the right to ask a man like you, with your trajectory, for advice, for instance. I have gone to the highest level in the United States government. I have a letter from the President of the United States for the good gestures that I made, and what is it getting me? So, let me state that —

Jorden: Do you mind if I take some notes so I can report accurately?

Somoza: No, please do.
I don't doubt that I have opposition in Nicaragua, because we have had in the past opposition. I am trying to accommodate the opposition, except the Communists, of course, and I am going to tell you that I consider that this situation which I am in — the main party responsible for this situation is the United States government. This happened after Mr. Carter took power. I haven't turned against the United States, but I have reasons to turn against the United States. They have treated me like an enemy.

Jorden: I wonder if I could ask in what way, Mr. President, you know, because I am not a Nicaraguan specialist.

Somoza: Sure, I'll tell you. Carter gets inaugurated and the munitions boys put a complete embargo on all guns sold to Nicaragua.

Jorden: That was in 1977.

Somoza: Yes, in 1977.
You have a man who is in the human rights section, Mark Schneider, who was constantly trying to get Ted Kennedy to go

against me publicly . . . Now, this man was connected with the
FSLN who were fighting in the mountains and who were the
Communist FSLN. You have got Social Christians, you have got
Conservatives, you have got Liberal independents running in
the FSLN, but *the real FSLN is in Cuba.* They left from
Havana, and some went from Panama to Cuba.

Jorden: *A lot of them have had their training in Cuba,
military and ideological.*

Somoza: Absolutely.

Jorden: *That I know.*

Somoza: So, what has happened? These people thought that
with the attitude of the Carter Administration, they would have
"Carte Blanche" to do as they pleased.

I have played ball with the administration. I am a political
animal. I have not lost everything, I have played ball. I have said,
all right, if Mr. Carter wants a political victory I am going to
provide it. That's politics, survival is politics. I went to all the
extremes to please these people and I haven't been able to do so. I
went to New York and I had a meeting with the ex-Secretary of
Defense of your country, Clark Clifford, and I said, "Mr.
Clifford, I cannot get into the administration. I have done every
damn possible thing to satisfy these people and I am not able to
do a damn thing."

Now, by December of 1977 the administration had suspended the FMS credits to Nicaragua, suspended the signing of
aid. It had given instructions for all of the U.S. delegates to vote
against Nicaragua in the IDB, in the World Bank, and of course
in the Export Import Bank. They had given instructions for the
delegation of the United Nations to bear down hard on the
Nicaraguan delegation.

Jorden: Bear down hard to do what?

Somoza: You know, to combat us in every way.

There were four leaks in the State Department that encouraged Jack Anderson to publish some ridiculous articles and they

started about the attitude of [*then U.S. Ambassador*] Turner Shelton. And, to them, my name was mud — and it all was started by the United States State Department. Look, only a guy who has been through the mill at West Point has the patience to stand all this crap. Turner Shelton got his satisfaction three months ago. Jack Anderson said, "I am sorry that we said such a thing about you." . . . Oh, yes . . .

My record with the United States politicians has been so good that when they tried to halt the military aid to Nicaragua, the Congress voted to keep me in the aid bill. Finally they were withholding all of these credits in the IDB and the World Bank and AID and I talked to my friends in the Congress. Then they began talking to the administration and they went to see Mr. [*Warren*] Christopher, and they told Mr. Christopher that the treatment of Nicaragua on the basis of human rights was not just. Why should they give other countries, who had far worse records than ours, money and withhold it from Nicaragua?

Even [*Congressman*] Jim Wright from Texas had to intervene and notify Christopher that if he didn't allocate the money he was going to lobby to wreck the foreign aid bill. So, finally, they came around. In the meantime, I got this letter from the President which outlines all the steps I've taken to try to satisfy the opposition here and make this a workable government of democracy.

Jorden: *This is a good letter.*

Somoza: That letter made me feel that I was making headway with the administration, so I tried my damndest to see if I could neutralize my enemies. By this time one of my strongest enemies was Carlos Andres Perez, so I made a date to go see him, and I talked to him for six hours. I explained to him that the time to organize this country from now until 1981 was short. He said, "I don't think you will have the time." I told him, "You, who are backing my enemies, tell them to talk to me. I will talk to them." So, let's say I haven't wasted any moment to try and make peace.

Now, the country was in political turmoil after the assassination of Chamorro, and I decided to let the people demonstrate. I didn't want to have bloodshed on my hands because my archenemy was killed. There were people accusing me of having

[*had*] him killed. So, I said let them demonstrate to let them get
the steam off. So we let them demonstrate for eight months.
They had been making barricades, and they decided to go into
this shooting match. The newspapers said it's too late, unless you
resign there is going to be a war here.

I tried to make negotiations with them prior to the assassination of Chamorro. After the assassination, they were very adamant. They put everything on Chamorro's head. They didn't
want to talk. So, right now we have a situation which I think is
very delicate and I am, shall we say, taking undue risk in han-
dling this situation. Because on the other side, there is no one
who has a following to hold the country together. We have to go
to an election — a popular one-man, one-vote election.

Jorden: Is there any possibility, Mr. President, of rather
than one person trying to hold it together, rather some kind of
group that would represent different elements, your own party
and others?

Somoza: Yes, if we had a leader in the Liberal Party. We have
leaders in the Army. I would say we have a possibility, but right
now I am the leader of the Liberal Party and I am the leader of
the Army. So, I told the opposition this: "You people have two
jobs to do: You have to look for a new President, and you have
to look for a new Army leader." I told it point-blank to their
faces, to the most responsible opposition leaders. So, I think I
have proven that I am a leader of the Army with this situation
— don't you think so, Ambassador?

Jorden: *I think that's correct.*

Somoza: I think the Liberals have stood fast. The Liberal
Party has stood fast. I haven't had any renouncements or anything like that. And we have had plenty of reasons for people to
quit the party; because they have been menaced, and threatened, their houses have been burned, etc.

I didn't want to ruin my relationship with the White House. I
figured if I got my nose bloody the White House would look and
say, "Hey, what's happening to Somoza?" So now, since the
inception, since the discord that that guy Schneider had with

Mr. Shelton, the political officer here has sent in reports that have been 100 percent against the established regime in Nicaragua.

I grant you that, among the educated people and the well-to-do people, I might have the lowest popularity that I have had — but not among the common people. If the common people were not with this regime, Mr. Ambassador, I wouldn't be talking to you now. When a man can produce a rally of 150,000 people after the turmoil we have had, and the assassination of Chamorro and all of the XYZ, he must have some backing. These people came out under the harassment of the opposition, shooting, throwing tacks into the road, throwing kerosene cans into the buses, etc.

When I can rally 150,000 people, Mr. Ambassador, I am not quitting. And, that's not the only proof I have given to your observers here. On Labor Day, the 1st of May, I had around 75,000 people at a rally, and on the day of the Liberal Party we had 40,000 people, and between all those days there was a lot of violence in this country to scare the hell out of everybody. Now, I grant you that when you look at the rank and file of the well-to-do people, you will find that historically, they have been against the Liberal Party.

You must understand, Mr. Ambassador, that your damned U.S. Embassy has been nothing but a messenger center for the opposition. They even received orders from Washington to scan out the Army to see who was against Somoza. This was done to see who could be counted on in a coup. You would remember a retired Brazilian general by the name of Maura. He was a translator for Eisenhower, Kennedy, and Johnson. That should make him dependable, don't you agree? Well, he visited with the U.S. Embassy and came back with the report that they were ready to overthrow me and the government.

Jorden: Look, if there were a decision to overthrow you, I should know about it. If I thought these people were playing games, I wouldn't have accepted this assignment.

Somoza: All right, now about this guy Mark Schneider —

Jorden: *Mark Schneider is a horse's ass, but he doesn't* make American foreign policy. He weighs in and he argues his point of view and he gets some things done which shouldn't be done, but when it comes to the real thing —

Somoza: But, he is causing serious problems.

Jorden: He is making problems, I agree with that.

Somoza: You have this entire continent right now in an upheaval.

Jorden: How well I know that.

Somoza: Because this guy has been insisting on so many ridiculous things?

Jorden: *I think you have a tendency to exaggerate the importance of this one guy, because the human rights issue is bigger than Mark Schneider. He is riding it, he is using it, and he is pushing it in ways you and I would disagree on sharply.*

Somoza: I want you to know that I'm doing my utmost to accommodate the United States without losing my pants.

[*End of meeting.*]

TAPE 2

[*The following conversation took place on December 21, 1978 between President Somoza, U.S. Ambassador William Bowdler, and General Dennis McAuliffe, Commander of the U.S. Southern Command in Panama. The General had telephoned President Somoza and asked for an interview. The Commission they refer to is the OAS — sponsored Commission of Friendly Cooperation and Conciliation.*]

Somoza: When did you come in, General?

McAuliffe: Just this morning, a few hours ago. I wanted to talk to you about the situation here in your country and Central America.

Bowdler: Mr. President, I am here because our government is very much concerned about the impasse that we seem to have reached in negotiations. My government wants me to express that concern to you.

Your people have taken a position that makes it very, very difficult to negotiate. We just don't think that insisting as they have done on the FAO [*Broad Opposition Front*] adopting a position which is foreign, and that it cannot follow, is a reasonable position. Particularly in light of the fact that the plebiscite would be internationally supervised. And if you were to win this, you would have a firm pledge from the FAO that they would accept this and act as a responsible, constructive opposition. We feel that such is more than one might expect from the outcome of this. We are very much concerned over the outlook of these negotiations. We have worked for two and one-half months and we appreciate the action you have taken as facilitating the climate for these talks.

Somoza: Our position, Mr. Ambassador, is that we make the plebiscite as fair as possible. Our position has been that the FAO take part in the future government and let the Congress elect somebody. Furthermore, they wanted me to leave the country. I was the one who proposed a plebiscite as a solution to the political problems in Nicaragua.

My viewpoint, Mr. Ambassador, is that I am for the democratic ideals. I see a serious threat from the Left. They are militant, and with each passing day they become stronger. That's why I want to see a consolidation of democratic forces against the Left, and that's what I'm trying to do. That's why I proposed to bring the FAO into the government, even if I win the plebiscite.

Bowdler: Mr. President, the reality of the situation is that you have three forces in Nicaragua: your government, the moderate opposition which you call the FAO, and what you identify as the Sandinistas, or the extreme Left. The moderate opposition doesn't want to team up with the Left.

Somoza: Mr. Ambassador, don't think that I haven't spent a great deal of effort in trying to accommodate the FAO. I have bent over backwards trying to please those people. Nobody in this country has received the concessions those people have received. I know this is a political situation but the way you propose the election is not the way the Nicaraguan people understand. The Nicaraguan people have always been cognizant of the way their government functions. I'm not trying to give you a previous answer to the proposal, but I'm trying to be as objective as possible. The FAO is a victim of its own viciousness. Look, we have had thousands of people killed in Nicaragua and this doesn't seem to concern the FAO.

I want to assure you that I'm not thinking of my own personal welfare, but the welfare of Nicaragua. If we are to find a peaceful solution to the situation in Nicaragua, the Conservatives, the moderates, and the Liberals will have to combine forces against the Left, and that's what I want to do. That's why I proposed that the FAO participate in the government. If I win, these people who don't like Somoza will be part of the government.

Bowdler: If you win, Mr. President, you will have the satisfaction of knowing that you have won a supervised election and the pledge of the FAO that they will cooperate with you and accept the results.

Somoza: I told you that our position vis-à-vis your government is very, very difficult because *we have felt the dislike of this U.S. administration* for my government. I'm very concerned because *you people are trying to set up an electoral system in Nicaragua which is not recognized worldwide and one you don't even follow in your own country.* The election system you people are recommending is one that is foreign to the people of Nicaragua.

Bowdler: Well, it's a very special circumstance, as you know. The problem here is one of confidence. The people have lost confidence in the democratic process of Nicaragua. The [OAS] international Commission [of *Friendly Cooperation and Conciliation.*] has suggested a procedure as a way of conducting the plebiscite which would give confidence to the people in the country as well as international opinion. So far as the

election is concerned, I think the FAO will accept something
along this line. I think it's a fair and reasonable proposal.

Somoza: I assure you that I am looking for a peaceful
solution. We have tried to be fair in every way, but every
suggestion we make is not good enough for the Commission.

Bowdler: So far as the Commission is concerned, this is not
the time to follow the constitutional provisions of Nicaragua.
It is not the appropriate time for that, it is not necessary, and
*the main issue here, in all candor, is your presence in the
government.* I say this in no spirit of personal animosity, as we
have discussed in the past, and —

Somoza: Mr. Ambassador, I know politics, and I understand that I have to be laid on the table. If someone has the
idea that that box over there is no good, then thought has to be
given to changing it. That's why I arrived at the idea that an
election should be held. Let the people decide if that box over
there should stay where it is or be removed. However, you
refuse to accept our ideas as to how the plebiscite should be
held.

Bowdler: Mr. President, you told us in our first meeting
that the main issue was the name Somoza.

Somoza: Absolutely, it is.

Bowdler: That's the problem.

McAuliffe: Mr. President, I am here for a very specific
reason, and it is to convey to you the very serious concern of the
military and the Joint Chiefs of Staff that I stand for.
Within the past month I have met with all the principal
members of the Joint Chiefs of Staff, during which we spent
considerable time talking about Nicaragua and Central America. You may have read that the Chairman of the Joint Chiefs
of Staff visited me in Panama last week and we discussed
Nicaragua. I want you to know that every member of the Joint
Chiefs of Staff is concerned about the instability, the poten-

tial for violence which exists here in Nicaragua. It is of military significance that we maintain peace and stability in Central America.

Now, we have all been closely following the activities of Ambassador Bowdler and the other members of the negotiating team. We all support the plebiscite idea and hope that it will bring peace to Nicaragua and that it will assure peace in the other countries of Central America. The reason that I'm here at this precise moment, Mr. President, is that we perceive that the cooperation you have given to the negotiating team is no longer evident.

Somoza: Let me say something to you briefly. I was asked by Ambassador Jorden to leave the presidency. I told Ambassador Jorden that I felt my vacating the presidency was not the solution. I tried to explain to him the special circumstances which exist in Nicaragua. I have seen this country deceased, and I believe I played a significant role in bringing it back up to where it is now. Now we have political trouble. So I proposed the plebiscite. I am all for the plebiscite. There are certain things which we respect here in Nicaragua; I'm not sure but what you people have taught these things to us. So this is the way we handle our political matters.

With all due respect to the Commission, these are certain things which they don't want to accept. It seems they always listen to the other side — the side that has no real popular backing. If the plebiscite is organized along traditional lines which the people of Nicaragua understand, there will be no problem. But the problem is that they want to move us out of our position and completely take over the election procedure. This is something I cannot understand. It's as though you were holding an election in the United States and your destiny would be decided through an electoral process controlled and directed by foreigners. There is another thing, General, the dominant party in Nicaragua is the Liberal Party, and the Somozas are simply figures in that political party. The Liberal Party is something you feel and hear throughout the country. Even if the Somozas are removed, the Liberal Party stays. Please be assured that I am aware of the gravity of the situation. I want you to accept my viewpoint as one of honesty and sincerity.

McAuliffe: *We on the military side of the United States recognize that we have had strong and very effective friendship with the military officers of this country and with you in particular. We do not want to throw that over, so to speak.*

Somoza: I don't think you should, General.

McAuliffe: No. *But we do recognize, as the Ambassador has said, that the situation has changed. Speaking very frankly, Mr. President, it is our view that peace will not come to Nicaragua until you have removed yourself from the presidency and the scene.**

Somoza: General, don't you understand what I'm doing? I'm laying myself wide open by proposing a free and supervised election. I thought this was the agreed-upon solution, follow the democratic process. We want to do what is best for Nicaragua. I'm not telling you anything out of school, but the people of Nicaragua know what is going on. They know who the enemy is. I told the Ambassador in our first meeting that the problem is the confidence of the people in the results of the election. He understands, without a doubt, that *I am for a free election and that I am for an election which will be supervised by the Organization of American States. Now they want to impose restrictions which would not be acceptable anywhere in the world.*

Bowdler: Mr. President, I think that what the OAS Commission has proposed is as fair as we could hope for under the circumstances which exist today in Nicaragua. You have had OAS observers in the past, but there is no confidence in that type of supervision. We need the type of arrangement suggested by the Commission so that the FAO will have confidence in the election. If you win the election, you remain as President and install various elements of the opposition party

---

*It should be noted that on June 6–7, 1979, General Dennis McAuliffe gave sworn testimony to a U.S. congressional subcommittee during the Panama Canal hearings that he had never asked me to resign the presidency or leave the country. This question was put to General McAuliffe at two points during the hearings, and he lied to the subcommittee each time.

in your government. *If you lose, you step aside, but the Liberal Party will remain and so will the Guardia Nacional.*

Somoza: General, if we are proceeding on the basis that we hate Somoza and he must go, then we have no game. If you believe and maintain that Somoza is a political risk if he wins that election, then we have nothing. If, even with the restrictions of the Commission, the Liberal Party and Somoza should win the election, then how do we substantiate the information you have given that I am the key issue?

McAuliffe: *That is exactly the way we see it, Mr. President. We see that should you win the election and remain in office, you will continue to attract more and more guerrillas, more terrorists from neighboring countries.* This will continue to be a source —

Somoza: What I'm trying to tell you, General, is that *we are fighting people who are not anti-Somoza, but people who have a different ideology than yours and mine. It seems impossible for me to get this point across to the United States.*

Bowdler: Mr. President, there are a lot of people in this country who don't sympathize with those boys with the gun, and —

Somoza: And they don't sympathize with me, either.

Bowdler: No, they do not sympathize with you, either. There is opposition to you.

Somoza: I have never taken the position that I didn't have opposition. I'm doing my best to understand what the General is telling me. What he has actually outlined to me is that if I turn right, I hit the wall; if I go forward, I hit the wall; if I turn left, I hit the wall.

McAuliffe: *I'm not here to narrow the political outcome. I'm just telling you that from the way we look at the situation, your presence in Nicaragua is a symbolic thing and as long as* you remain in Nicaragua, you will attract terrorists and violence. This was very apparent last September when there was an upheaval.

Somoza: My God, General, I'm greatly concerned about this thing and I think about it every night and day. I just don't want the Communists to take over Nicaragua.

McAuliffe: We are also concerned, and if you follow the plan suggested by the United States, the Leftists and Communists will not take over and we will have a moderate government. What I'm saying, Mr. President, is that we [*will*] have a moderate government that does not have the name Somoza.

Somoza: By way of information for you, General, because it's apparent you were not informed as to what I have said and announced to the world: *In accordance with U.S. wishes, I said to a huge rally that at the end of my term in 1981, I would remove myself from the political scene and would retire from the Army. That statement was made last February.* Then I contacted the opposition and said, "Let's talk." They won't talk. There has been a tremendous amount of intransigence on the part of the political opposition.

I'm going to be quite frank with you. *This obvious intransigence has been supported and pushed along by people in your government who led the political opposition to believe that your government could overthrow me.* For me, this was a hard pill to swallow. After all, I have had a very open and clean relationship with the United States. The first indication I got was when Ambassador Jorden came down. And even the Ambassador here said, Why don't you have an early departure from the presidency? To me, they were playing along with your administration on the Human Rights issue. *They were getting no reading from the democratic people but from only the Leftists.*

I know what that State Department wants — and that's for me to quit. I can go two ways and one of those is an election. *But what you people propose is a type of election that would cause a revolt if it were held in the United States!*

Bowdler: Mr. President, this is a very special situation that exists today in Nicaragua. It involves one figure, one name, and one issue. The Commission thinks its [*election*] plan is fair.

Somoza: Mr. Ambassador, you have one distinct advantage over me. I am speaking as the Head of State and whatever stand I take with reference to the election will be used against me.

Bowdler: How can you say it will be used against you?

Somoza: Let's face reality, Mr. Ambassador, the idea is to get Somoza out of the government, one way or another. So I must talk to my people and the Liberal Party leaders about this meeting. [*Here all speaking at once.*]

McAuliffe: Mr. President, I want to assure you that the Guardia Nacional will play an important role in any future government of the country. We think the Guardia has the capability, certainly the officers are very well trained, and their attitudes are excellent. They will be able to assure peace and tranquility in the country. Sometimes you read in the newspapers of the other Central American countries that the Guardia will have to be neutralized. *Well, we want you to know that the Guardia will play an important role in maintaining not only law and order, but stability and the strength to defend the country if necessary.*

Somoza: General, that sounds good but there is one problem. *All of the campaign directed against me by your government has also been directed against the Guardia Nacional.*

Bowdler: Would you repeat that, that our campaign has been against the Guardia Nacional?

Somoza: *Absolutely. Your government has charged that the Guardia Nacional has been in violation of human rights in Nicaragua,* and that's a big issue. Whether I stay or go, it is important that something be done about that feeling, because it is wrong. What I'm telling you is a fact, and I felt you should know about the charges made by some of the people in your government. *I think you should know also that members of the Guardia Nacional now think they are being attacked by your government.*

Bowdler: I'm glad we have this information.

McAuliffe: Perhaps the makeup, complexion, and image of the Guardia Nacional should be changed. Separate the police force from the Guardia. My military people here have been working on that problem with your people.

Somoza: Yes, we have been cooperating with your people on this matter. You know, the name Somoza has not always been bad with your government.

McAuliffe: Perhaps we should also remove the name Somoza from any connection with the Guardia.

Somoza: That could be. It could be.

[*Tape ran out.*]

TAPE 3

[*The following conversation took place at 16:30 P.M. on June 27, 1979. The occasion was the first of two meetings attended by President Somoza, U.S. Ambassador Pezzullo, U.S. Congressman John Murphy (D.-New York), Luis Pallais (Vice President of the Nicaraguan Congress and cousin of President Somoza), and Nicaraguan Foreign Minister Dr. Julio Quintana.*]

Somoza: I brought the Foreign Minister with me. I thought you had the other companions with you, but I had rather listen to you in English; me being a Latin from Manhattan, I had rather listen to the things in your language because I can understand them just as well as in Spanish. I have asked Congressman Murphy to be here because I believe that it is necessary for me and for him to be witness to this — I welcome you, Mr. Ambassador, to Nicaragua.

Pezzullo: Thank you, we met a long time ago. We met in '73 after the earthquake. I came down for a short visit and we had breakfast together, you were gracious enough to invite me for breakfast.

Somoza: Yes, I don't remember, Mr. Pezzullo, but anyway you are welcome.

Pezzullo: Thank you, I appreciate that very much. Well, let me state the positions my government has taken after very serious and thoughtful consideration. It is nothing we take lightly, *it was done at the top.* I don't believe there has been an issue I know of in recent times that has gotten the type of setting that this one has, and it was done with the care which is outstanding . . . Nothing was done lightly, nothing was done for the sake of expedience . . . It was all done on the basis of our long relationship; a long feeling of friendship with you, the government, the people . . . This is nothing we look back upon without the best feeling. In fact, the United States believes that it has more involvement in this country over the years than it has with the most . . . [*and that*] is very important.

I want to emphasize that I think the results we ended up with . . . the conclusion we drew up after all these studies and after the experience of the negotiations, the mediation effort of last year, is that we have come to a point here which obeys certain priorities; and, as we have stated, and the Secretary stated yesterday before the Congress, *we don't see a solution without your departure, we don't see the beginning of a solution without your departure.* That is a tough position to take but we do it after a careful study and with a great desire to see this thing come to an . . . to see this thing come to an end, to see this country settle back into something resembling peace, and we offered a proposal to your minister that Secretary Christopher . . . later I repeated it to . . . Pallais so there would be no misunderstanding.

What we thought was necessary was your resignation . . . through a means of turning over the government to the Congress; the Congress then, through a quick action, appointing a successor to your constitutional position which would immediately bring a ceasefire, a beginning of a political dialogue, which would give an opportunity for the forces in this country to seek a total solution and hopefully preserve as many institutions as are preservable. We would like to see the institutions which are worth preserving, preserved. We would like to see a security force of some sort emerge from this with the capacity to keep order . . . We know that you are concerned with that too, you invested a lifetime into it; we are not unmindful of that. We don't want to see chaos in this country and we don't want to see something we will all be unhappy with. We think that without something of that nature . . . without a statesmanlike act on your part, we are going to be caught in something which is going down . . . . That's essentially where we came out, and it is done without rancor, but it is done not —

Somoza: I don't see it in your face, Mr. Pezzullo.

Pezzullo: You don't see what?

Somoza: Rancor in your face.

Pezzullo: I am a man that feels passion, but not hate. I would honestly not have taken on this assignment if it was something that I personally felt was unethical or cheap. You are a complicated country . . . and represent a broad spectrum of people, as you well know . . . but we are not doing this in an attempt to want to cheap-shot you. I think the hope of this is that you can leave in dignity, you have made . . . that's basically where we would like to see it go.

Somoza: I was told there would be no room for negotiation — that my point of view would be listened to. I don't pretend to negotiate, but I would like to give you my point of view if it is possible.

Pezzullo: Sure, that's what I am here for.

Somoza: I am sorry that I have made you wait so long. We are ready to accommodate the United States' desire and we think also that we must put out of this discussion personal matters. *We want certain guarantees that will insure that this* *country will not be taken over by the Communists — that's the most principal thing.* The other thing is that since we are good friends — because today we heard on a news station a report that was adverse to me, to my name, my family, my tradition, nevertheless that is part of life — we are good friends with the United States, and we should be treated as such.

Pezzullo: *We are not against you.*

Somoza: *But your administration is against us. We have never been against you — we admire and respect your ideals, etc., through circumstances of life; we, we would like to be able to have the facilities which are due to a good friend. Right now it is embarrassing for you to be good friends with the Somozas, because you made it so. However, we think that nobody in the world will ever forgive you for having chastised us.*

Now, there are certain basic things which I [*would*] like to discuss with you. One, which is basic for your national interest — not for mine — your national interest, is: *What are you going to do with the National Guard of Nicaragua?* I don't need to know, but after you have spent thirty years educating all of these officers, *I don't think it is fair for them to be thrown to the wolves.* Mr. Ambassador, let me say this to you: These men who are actually fighting today are not babies. They are people that you brought from the common houses of Managua, Nicaragua, and made them gentlemen and good people through the education of the United States — right now the U.S. is going against these people! So you have to take into account: Why are these people not obedient to the U.S. now — what should be the natural course of events? Well, very simply: because *they were educated to fight for what they think is democracy, representative government, and against Communism; and they have been doing this,* and in doing this they have been called violators of human rights.

So when you broke with me, you broke with a man who was fighting for your cause indirectly, and these people have felt themselves alienated because they have been fighting Communism, just like you taught them at Fort Gulick and Fort Benning and Leavenworth. Now you talk about them turning against me, how can they turn against me in the face of the

enemy, the common enemy? We have gone through all of this
— so I think that they, in a very decent manner, need a chance.
*I am willing to sacrifice myself — whatever pride I might have
— if the U.S. is willing to protect the lives of these men and the
Guard.* I am not interested in influencing the events in Nicaragua; I have been President twice and certainly *I don't want
this to be a bloodshed.*

Pezzullo: We agree on that.

Somoza: *For your national interest, these people in the
Guard represent a democratic government and the right to
capitalism. On the other side, they represent the Cubans . . .*
You have . . . I don't have to tell you.

Pezzullo: How do we preserve the Guard?

Somoza: By giving them the logistics they need to make
themselves felt in the country — that's all.

Pezzullo: I don't think this is the moment to talk . . . I
don't think it is fair to you . . . you miss the key point . . .
the reason we are where we are now, or where you are . . . this
country . . . is not because [of] the withdrawal of U.S. support. I don't believe that's the issue. The issue is that a series of
forces have been drawn which we tried to address with you very
seriously last year. We made a major effort to work out and
look at it, and spare a lot of bloodshed. *We are not abandoning
the Guard,* and that is not an unfair thing to say. We have been
training these people, as you say, to reach this point, and for
their sake this was not our interest. Our interest is in preparing
a professional guard that could serve this country and could
serve this country loyally and patriotically under any circumstances. It's the political issues that . . .
I thought we could get by without this. I really don't see that
we are going to help one another and I really want to help you. I
say that honestly; I don't come here to try to bargain or make
something out of or make a case worse than it is. The truth of
the matter is, we are at a period that I think the U.S. can help in
a small way. Our ability to help is being withdrawn . . .

This thing, it is getting to a point where it is getting out of control. We are willing to do what we can to preserve the Guard . . . I appreciate your thoughts about that because I think you can play a role in that, we are not going to come in here with the wherewithall to do it now . . . we yesterday . . . we are not going to do that . . . we couldn't even if, if tomorrow we made the decision to come in here with everything you needed to combat subversion, which I don't think you can anymore. I don't think we could get that through our Congress — I know we wouldn't get it through our Congress. We are talking about the impossible — not that we turned against you — the circumstances have reached the point where it is impossible to go on that way. We do want to preserve the Guard, we would like to see a force emerge here that can stabilize the country, we might never see that happen.

That's why we are coming to you. We think the proper position we can take, we are talking to you very honestly . . . we can walk away like some of the other Hemisphere countries, just close up shop and walk away, but we just don't do things that way. We are going to stick it out, and try to be helpful — without breaking relations or cutting the money — we don't do that, and we take an awful lot of abuse, don't think we don't, and do that manfully. We don't ask excuses, we do it. I think it is unfair really, to put us in the position of your enemy, we are not . . . we are not your enemy. Let's get out of this thing gracefully, if — I am not sure we can, anymore — with our best efforts on both sides.

Somoza: It is my belief that we can . . . *Let me say this, Mr. Ambassador: Ever since the Carter Administration put an embargo on arms and . . . shipments to Nicaragua, they gave the green light for all these people to start organizing for this revolution. You know very well that the Nicaraguans have always looked to the U.S. for their inspiration for good or for wrong.*

Pezzullo: *That's true.*

Somoza: And they have had enough time since 1977 to organize, and people otherwise would never get into a revolution . . . . This is part of history, but I want to tell you that I did my best to try to change the administration's viewpoint, and perhaps part of the problem right now is because I opened myself to have the forces, that you now say are uncontrollable, demonstrate and show themselves. I figured that was the only way to get recognition from the Carter Administration, but it did no good. The more they demonstrated, the more violence they showed.

The Carter Administration never showed a positive attitude towards my government; I am a politician.

Pezzullo: And a good one.

Somoza: I am a politician; I understand the game. Some you lose, some you win.

Pezzullo: You won most.

Somoza: True, but I am also man enough to understand what's going on. That's why I say the Carter Administration is trying to do me in.

When Mrs. Carter went to visit Costa Rica and President [*Daniel*] Oduber . . . he [*Oduber*] had a very long talk with Bob Pastor [*a White House advisor to President Carter*]. Bob Pastor asked President Oduber, When do we get rid of that son of a bitch up North? And President Oduber, who is my friend, personally flew to Montelimar to tell me what Pastor had said . . . and to tell me how he had to explain to Robert Pastor that really I wasn't a son of a bitch, that I had done a lot of things in this country and I put the country up to the modern state of things. The next thing, I went up to New York last June . . . I talked to the ex-Secretary of Defense for [*Lyndon*] Johnson, Clark Clifford, I said: "Clark, I want you to help me in this situation." He said: "It would be useless if I take your money. I could talk to the President but it wouldn't do any good."

Then you closed off the credits, you voted actively [*in the United States Congress*] against Nicaraguan credits in the multinational situations, and if it had not been for the action of certain congressmen we wouldn't have gotten anything reinstated. So, let's not bullshit ourselves, Mr. Ambassador, I am talking to a professional. You have to do your dirty work, and I have to do mine.

Pezzullo: Let me just be —

Somoza: So let's not, shall we say, try to hide . . . I don't want to get into an argument with you because, my dear friend, I was practically brought up in the U.S., I have nothing against the people of the U.S. I want you to understand and know that this administration has done the most to do me in. Now, it's because I believe in the American system that I asked Ambassador Jorden to integrate this Commission that came in September, and it's because I believe in your system that we are talking, and I don't think all of you are bad people. Let's face it, and this is why we are talking. But I want to . . . I am not trying to negotiate, you see, my position now is a very simple one: With your administration all the guerrilla leaders are no longer afraid, and the Carter Administration gives them support.

Pezzullo: Not true. We still recognize this country.

Somoza: I don't want to, as I said, to put any conditions. You recognize this country then . . . I move the part of the government that you don't like, and you give this government its due backing.

Pezzullo: Let me illustrate something, I think we could make the case . . . I am not going to argue with you, there are elements in every administration that say things they shouldn't say, there are things that look one way and I couldn't persuade you even if I made the arguments. I am not that closely associated with what happened in the last couple of years. This administration, which came in on a human rights platform, had to take a different attitude than the Ford Administration did and it went after not only Nicaragua . . . Your country really was not pushed as hard as the country I just came from — which was Uruguay, they cut — the amendment cut off the thing, off completely in 1976, so I come from a country where I have heard this for the last two years, I am not apologizing, I am just telling you the reality of the situation; the truth is —

Somoza: Yes, and we have been cut in the Congress.

Pezzullo: If anything, you had stronger voices in Congress than any country in Latin America. But the point is, when this program began a lot of countries felt it. Uruguay, Chile . . . for God's sake, Chile got it a hell of a lot worse than you got. I think the whole [*President Salvador*] Allende problem ended up looking worse in the American eyes than it should have, but that's history. I can understand that — you can understand that — you can understand that the truth of the matter is, it's not only the Carter Administration. I was in the OAS this last week and let me tell you, there is no sympathy there . . . there is no feeling there for you. It's not as if we are saying your administration has to be removed and something drastic has to be done — no, this whole Hemisphere is there, with very, very few exceptions — and it is not because —

Somoza: Mr. Ambassador, I am aware of that, and it is because I am aware that we are talking. Within my realism I want to give you my points of view. My points of view are the institutionality of the Guardia Nacional. If you recognize the government that comes out of my demise, it would satisfy me very much, because I would know then that you would do your utmost to help them . . . I am not trying to delay this, understand me . . . I feel that if my demise is necessary, as I consider necessary, . . . I am being very honest, it should give the people in the government a chance, so let's get down to the hard facts, Ambassador. One, to . . . don't force me to resign and walk through the bush. Because if you don't give me an alternative to go where I think my other country is, the U.S., my alternative is to resign and go to the bush. And then you have a Sandino again, all over again, and this poor goddamn country will never have peace.

So I need guarantees for the people that are close with me. I have thrown many people out of their natural habitat because of the U.S., fighting for your cause, and I think I will get some of that back, so let's talk like friends. I threw a goddamn

Communist out of Guatemala in 1964, I personally worked on
that, and so did I do the same thing with the Cuban Bay of
Pigs. So I . . . look . . . I am broad-minded enough to open
up, but I also would like the great U.S. to be quite clear what
they can guarantee to me or not. Because, unless I get a
guarantee, Ambassador . . . I am talking about a fair deal,
just a right to life. The human rights that I might have, I would
go to the bush. Now, I am practically in your hands, so now
administer your puritan justice on this matter. Let's talk very
frankly . . . You know, you and I have practically the same
background; I grew up in New York with Jack, since I was ten
years old.

Pezzullo: I grew up in Staten Island . . .
We have not done this lightly; by good people, not children,
good people; professionals as good as we have got, they're not
the best in the world but that's all we have got. If we can
guarantee something for you, we will; we honestly will. There is
no guarantee to give . . . . What we have got right now is a
situation where if we don't break this circle somewhere, and the
circle is a simple one, the arms will keep coming in and there is
no way of shutting it off unless we have a political cut. I think
we can put something together to prevent the country being less
destabilized.
You have become — because of circumstances, because of
history — become the core of the problem, and you know that.
Now, unless you settle that, you don't have a chance of dealing
with the rest because you focus the problem, and without
focusing the problem, it is difficult to put the other parts
together again. The Guardia, in a good measure, becomes your
captive, is victimized because of its being with you. It's not
because you want to victimize it, but because it is part of you
— so much a part of you, you spent your life with it. So you've
got to rupture that.
Now rupturing it, everybody recognizes it very well. There
are all kinds of destabilizing elements involved. Nobody wants
to see a Russian here . . . bloodshed. A Leftist victory, who
knows if that will ever come, but who the hell wants to see this
country turn into a bloodshed? Nobody wants to see that. If
you rupture that Guard by your going out and taking it with

you, that's a possibility. We see that, but there is no way to guarantee that. If you guarantee it, then the Guard gets hurt, because it's still too associated to you. We do have to have a cut. You have to have a point at which you leave, as I mentioned before, and we try to put that Guard together the best we can, to hold and have a ceasefire here . . . and put in place some stability and then try to build . . . this thing again. But you can't . . . there is no way of guaranteeing, because if you walked out, just to take that possibility, you walking out and us going in with a major assistance effort to the Guard, it's still associated in the minds of these people here as your Guard. You would be right back where you were before, because then you have gotten into a situation where you are still engaged in a civil war.

You have got to jump over the gap with that Guard and the whole political process . . . and it is very dangerous, and we know it, but we don't see any other alternative. We have talked about bringing in a new Guard leadership — we talked about looking into the ranks for people who have quality, and trying to inspire them to hold and be loyal to a transition government, and waiting for the right moment where we can come in as much as we can.

We have had a long history together, and that's why we would like to see it, if we can, end in a nice, graceful way and still try to play a role. But there is no easy fix. There is no . . . in this one. If the arms don't stop coming in, the war continues. If we don't make the cut . . . We have got a chance of stopping that, if we make the cut. The question is, how do we reach this through that forced period? We hope to put some stability into this darn thing and come in and try to help. Give the new forces a chance to stabilize. I won't believe, and it's a guess, we don't know, how many of these people are running around calling themselves Sandinistas are really all that rabid Communists . . . how many of these kids that have reached the explosive point are just joining in.

Somoza: Mr. Ambassador . . . The U.S. called me and I agreed to have the bombers leave here and knock the hell out of the installations in Cuba, like a Pearl Harbor deal. I am going to answer you: All the leaders who are now fighting in Esteli, in Chinandega, in Matagalpa, in Masaya, in Diriamba, in Rivas, are men that we have fought for eighteen years and were trained in Cuba.

Pezzullo: *I buy that, I agree,* but where does this insurrection come from, why do you have people willing to join this thing?

Somoza: *Because, Mr. Ambassador, the U.S. gave the green light,* but we won't get into that. My viewpoint is that you have half of that army which is fighting us pro-democratic, and it is going to be dominated by non-democratic forces. But I have to explain to you what you are playing up to . . . but I wanted to explain that to you. Now it alleviates my situation if I leave, and you keep relations with this government.

Pezzullo: We are not thinking about breaking relations . . . What we proposed was *that you step aside* and *turn the government over to somebody in the Congress* which is in Article 7–167 of the Constitution.

Somoza: *I am doing that.* I have asked the Congress to convene tomorrow or Friday.

Pezzullo: But that is only the first stage. The second stage has got to be to move to put something in which there is a break with your government.

Somoza: You are proposing a coup d'état.

Pezzullo: We are proposing a break.

Somoza: A coup d'état.

Pezzullo: It's . . . in effect it is a break, because if you don't break that circle right there, you don't get anyplace, you . . .
That's our position.

Somoza: All right, where do you propose to make that break?

Pezzullo: We haven't been able to put all that together yet.

Somoza: Oh.

Pezzullo: But we will. I don't know if it will work, I really don't know if it will work.

Somoza: What happens if there is a military coup?

Pezzullo: Against what? It won't solve anything, and if you turn over the government tomorrow to Congress [*words indistinguishable*] . . . that you can do it. You are jumping faster, nothing is going to happen, nothing is going to change. A military coup? . . . We are trying to get to the core of it.

Somoza: All right, what is the core?

Pezzullo: Well, the core is to make the break. That's what we have explained to . . . To make the break, now, it is a hell of a mess. Just sitting here talking to you about it is strange enough. We are talking about a break.

Somoza: Mr. Pezzullo, I am a practical man, I am not a cynic, but I am a practical man. I have to figure your approach is serious because *I am determined to try to save this country from the hands of Communism.*

Pezzullo: I am sure you are, and I think you can understand our interest in the same direction.
Do you know Brazil? A military-dominated country. Brazil plays very sharp poker, very sharp poker. When they ante . . . we stay in the pot. We would like to stay in the pot. We would like to help —

Somoza: I am going to say this to you, Ambassador Pezzullo, I want you to help because all these people are indirectly fighting for your people. Outside of personal interest, out of some nine hundred officers we have, eight hundred or so belong to your schools. I mean, the solution is the goddamndest thing you have ever seen in your life, and OK, I can sacrifice myself. I am fifty-some odd years old, but you have a lot of good people here, and really great thinking people.

Pezzullo: I agree . . . I can't tell you we have it all together . . . we would like to be able to put something else together where at least we would have a balance of forces, that the junta doesn't dominate the thing. I fear one thing . . . that the junta comes into power, and if we put the best light on them, with a military force made up of militants and Sandinistas . . . you might have kangaroo courts . . .

Somoza: . . . The other thing which is very interesting, Mr. Pezzullo, is that Mrs. Chamorro and Robelo are the only two so-called moderates, and the rest are known Communists.

Pezzullo: We know their backgrounds pretty well. I have never met any of them. The only chance that we see —

Somoza: The only chance that you see is *for me to leave,* to leave you room to maneuver within Nicaragua. That's what you are really asking me.

Pezzullo: We have got to work down this thing. If we do it at all. If it doesn't work.

Somoza: The other thing, of course, is the . . . the news is out that you are down here.

Pezzullo: Oh, yeah.

Somoza: According to that, you are here to ask me to resign.

Pezzullo: That's right, but let's be realistic, you know, if we can't do that, then we don't have the capacity to make any of the other moves, you see. In other words, we do deliver up something and say here is something, we can do this, and let's bring peace here. The way you could help . . . help yourself and help us . . . it is going to be a new Nicaragua, and I wouldn't want to keep you. I don't know where in the hell it's going to go. You know this country better than we do, but it is going to shape in a different way, but chances are, if . . . this way that you would have a society with private enterprise . . . if it goes the other way . . .

They know the whole damn thing would go. They would come and sweet-talk to us that they are nice people, and so on, but give them five years and they would nationalize banks, and so on; we see all that. Maybe that's unrealistic, but that's where we come out.

Somoza: No, I think you have a point. There is a saying here, "Muerto el perro se acaba la rabia": If I remove myself from this country maybe the rabies will go away.

Pezzullo: What we are afraid of, has gone the other way already, and that you can't get . . . in other words, there is so much blood. They have got so much taste of blood in their mouth. I think this country would appeal to . . . if you were out of the picture, and they have got a chance to go back to work, start building their lives, I think then people would look back upon this period and say Somoza did wonderful things to them. *You might be able to come back.*

The point is, if you left with a certain amount of dignity and you left with class, I think that's the touch. If you walk out of here, I mean, it might make you feel better, but if you walk out of here and went after the States, and *after the Carter Administration, talk to Reagan and coo up to the Reagan campaign, it might make you feel better, but it wouldn't help you.* And I am not speaking partisan, because I don't give a damn if it is a Republican or a Democrat in there because I am going to retire in a couple of years anyway. It doesn't matter to me, but that's the truth. *The American people wouldn't like it, they really wouldn't.*

Somoza: They shouldn't make me mix into their internal politics.

Pezzullo: I think if you walked in there with a nice tone to your approach —

Somoza: My dear friend, I am a giant to be talking to you

right now after I have had the Hemisphere clobber me.
Whether they like it or not, *I must have some loyalties in
Nicaragua.*

Pezzullo: *I don't know how you keep this thing going. I don't
know how the Guard stays. I admire you, I admire that. It's
been chewed up.*

Somoza: Oh, yeah, now the other thing of course is that
fact that even if I decide to, the . . . is right here. Because
these people are going to get more logistics. They will keep on
coming.

Pezzullo: That's the sad truth . . . What we are afraid of
is that, if you start getting more and more countries recognizing
this junta, it's going to be impossible. Then we are out of
business. We will be out of business very quickly. I don't know
what Peru will vote. Brazil is watching this. If we can't play a
card very fast, this is going to go out of our hands.

Somoza: What do you call fast?

Pezzullo: I think we have got to put it together in three or
four days to a week. I think if we wait more than that the whole
goddamn thing can come down on our heads. I don't think the
administration will hold off more than that. I think they
would pull me out of here, and say, Come on, let's get out and
save our ass. I mean, we have a lot of people . . . I am worried
about their asses too . . . sitting in the goddamn compound.
Because this thing can turn and it can be the Americans who
did it. We are an easy target. They would overrun us in five
minutes. I can't do that, so if you want to sit down and talk this
thing through and work it through right now, I'll play straight
with you.

Somoza: I do want to.

Pezzullo: All right, let's do it, will you? You need a day —

Somoza: *Supposing I leave tomorrow.*

Pezzullo: *I don't want you to leave tomorrow.* I've just got to get organized a little bit. [*I have got to*] talk to a few people.

Somoza: Let's say, three o'clock tomorrow.

Pezzullo: Let's do it — all right — *please don't move too precipitously,* let's keep the thing.

Somoza: My dear friend, we have been victorious. We have gotten licked a couple of times, but this time I am not going to move without having my back well protected, so you are my protection.

Pezzullo: Let's do it with grace.

Somoza: Right!

[*End of meeting.*]

TAPE 4

[*The following conversation took place on June 28, 1979. The occasion was the second of two meetings attended by President Somoza, U.S. Ambassador Pezzullo, Nicaraguan Foreign Minister Dr. Julio Quintana, U.S. Congressman John Murphy (D-New York), and Luis Pallais (Vice President of the Nicaraguan Congress and cousin to President Somoza.*]

Somoza: *What I am trying to tell you is that I have been a good ally of the U.S. and its people and its government; I am not fighting for myself, I am fighting for my people here . . .* The circumstances have made a lot of governments gang up on these people, who now are under the circumstances that there are a lot of governments sitting outside of Nicaragua trying to gang up on these people; and if I am the rabid animal, all right, I will remove myself. *But I will not allow my people to be slaughtered, and this is something I want you to take seriously. I am ready to go and I am also ready for you, the U.S., to stand up for the people who have for thirty-five years helped you get that extra cut in your tie.* If it hadn't been the Somozas, we are just an incidence, it's the Nicaraguan people, and it's the

vulgarity of these other people, now. I am not delaying anything, I am not making any problem, *I am ready to go*, but *I am
not putting* [up with] *any conditions, because if I have to put up
with any conditions, I will not speak with you.*

Pezzullo: My conditions are very few.

Somoza: *Except you must remember that the Nicaraguan
people are the friends of the U.S., and you must protect them.
You are asking me to surrender unconditionally. I am ready to,
the only thing I have is the moral voice to tell you, don't*
sacrifice people who have been your tools in your hands and
props in your foreign policy. This is my contention, I have no
personal interest whatsoever.

Pezzullo: OK. I think that is a fair statement, and think
what we proposed is without any great —

Somoza: *From now on every drop of blood that's going to be
shed in Nicaragua is going to be the responsibility of the U.S.*

Pezzullo: We don't accept that, we just don't accept that.
You talk about no conditions, and then the next word —

Somoza: If you don't accept that, I want to know that.

Pezzullo: It seems to me we will waste time —

Somoza: Look, Ambassador, I am only trying to clarify
things, because I have my conscience to live with, and I am not
a man who is without a conscience. I think I have done what is
best for my country. All right, you don't take the responsibility.

Pezzullo: The point is, number one, we spoke yesterday
about the leaving, the quality of the leaving, and the precision
with which we plan it, that has to include a certain approach —
a certain way it could be done. If you are going to tell me now
that every drop of blood that's spilled is the responsibility of
the U.S. you are casting this thing in a way which is going to be
difficult later on. I can see that, I want to be honest with you

because I don't think if I said that to Washington . . . they first of all wouldn't take it well, I don't think it is what you mean, and I certainly don't expect that to be the condition under which we proceed.

We have got to proceed accepting, as we did last night, that we have reached the critical condition, the critical situation which we tried to avoid last year through the mediation effort, with a very honest attempt. With the mediation effort, we tried to avoid the very thing we are facing today. You know, in history [*it is*] very seldom you have an opportunity to have that period when you can make the decision to avoid conflict —

Somoza: I did my damndest.

Pezzullo: We didn't come away feeling that, we didn't feel it. I wasn't involved, but I am just telling what —

Somoza: Right.

Pezzullo: We were trying to really help.

Somoza: Let me say this, Ambassador . . . I mean . . . I have all the moral guts to talk to you and to all the world, because I did my best to avoid this.

Pezzullo: Let me go back in history a moment, because I think it is important to talk about the Liberal Party; I think this is an institution that does have strength. When we were at the point in the discussion last year on the plebiscite issue — which, after all, was going to be an issue having to do with popular expression of will, because we were facing this — what we saw was an imminent clash.

It was your idea. *The plebiscite idea was yours, we took it out of your own Liberal Party presentation.* We accepted it even though, at the time, the FAO and their group were very skeptical. They thought it was a device to avoid the issue. We went through that, we went through it very carefully. We put in a great deal of effort to test just the thing you are saying, mainly the popular willingness in this country, and eventually we failed them.

I think the only way we are ever going to see the Liberal Party re-emerge — and I am sure it will, because it didn't come out of dust, it came out of some expression of the Nicaraguan people — is to put back into interplay the political process that allows them to reappear in a different guise without you, but with their force. And that will come. It may not come in a year, it may come in four years, but if it's there, it will come back.

Somoza: Ambassador, let me tell you this: *When Ambassador Bowdler told me frankly,* like two New Yorkers spoke to each other, he said: *The President and Secretary Vance want you to leave, and they are giving you the chance to nominate the Cabinet, and to nominate the government and the Guardia people that you can leave. And I told Mr. Bowdler, who is also an old hand in this business, I said, Mr. Ambassador, I cannot do that because I am not going to leave the people without the popular backing in this country. There is going to be a vacuum of power and then you are going to have a take-over by the Communists, who are armed, so I would suggest that we go to a plebiscite, and we count up who has the most strength. If I don't have it, I go; if I have it, I stay and I make the government of reconciliation. Then they came back with ideas where I was going to play a naïve man, where an international commission was going to organize, print, count, and scrutinize the votation.*

Now, you must realize that I am not a child and neither is the Liberal Party a child. When they saw those conditions they said they would not accept them, and that's why we never got to the plebiscite. Without registry, a new concept of having . . . something that was never contemplated in the history of Nicaragua, now . . . I went to the Commander of the Army, the Congress, and to the Supreme Court; to the Junta Nacional y Legal of the Liberal Party, to the Cabinet, to the autonomous agencies, and I put all of this up to them: and all of them, 100 percent, said we would not accept those conditions.

So I wanted you to know that I am not an absolute ruler. I have consulted the base. I am not Trujillo, I am Anastasio Somoza, who was educated by the Christian Brothers and by the teachers at West Point, who knows that every day of the battle you go down to your soldiers and talk to them about what's going on. And *I have had the moral responsibility to go* out there and say to them: . . . *Gentlemen, I am ready to go if you think that's the solution; and they said No, you are not going to go.* So I am not talking here without a moral cause. *I am talking here with the backing of all the people and I want you to understand that* . . . otherwise I wouldn't have lasted ten days.

Mr. Pezzullo, do you think I am stupid? I am far from it. *Mr. Bowdler told me, the President and the Secretary of State said that you have to go, and so did Jorden, William Jorden, say the same thing.* I can read, and I mean not between the lines, but on the front page. *I said all right, if I have to go, let's go organized, let's go to a plebiscite* . . .

All right, Mr. Ambassador, outside of my feelings of how I feel about Cyrus Vance and Jimmy Carter, I have my feelings towards the American people, and I think Cyrus Vance and Jimmy Carter are wrong. *And I have an obligation towards the American people.* I don't know, maybe I am more patriotic than what you think, about the interest of my democratic feelings. *If I didn't think what is going on was not correct, I would have left a long time ago. I think your whole policy is wrong.*

What I am trying to tell you is that I proposed a plebiscite and it was put in such a way that the people of Nicaragua did not accept it. So, you are not facing now only Anastasio Somoza, Mr. Ambassador, you are facing the Liberal Party, you are facing the Cabinet, you are facing the Congress, and you are facing the Army commanders. Now, this is something that I wanted to explain to you because I want you to understand the gravity of the situation and also the weight of the situation. No man could stand one week after the OAS resolution and be Head of State like I am, unless those people have already cast their vote. I would be out, and this is what's going on in Nicaragua. Now, I realize that if I win the war I can't do a damn thing for my people, so I am ready to go, but I want you to understand what kind of forces you have still in your favor. The Sandinistas don't have all the people in Nicaragua . . . forget it.

Pezzullo: I thought we had agreed on that point.

Somoza: Look, what I am trying to do, Mr. Ambassador, I am trying to illustrate —

Pezzullo: I think it is very useful and it is a key point, there is no question. The key point is that *the political forces have been so polarized, because of the circumstances; your person has done that.*

Somoza: *And I am glad that I have done it, because most of the time the U.S. is naïve about the appreciation of things. I have dealt with you people in many circumstances, and I have had to disagree with you in many instances.* This is why I am still disagreeing with you in certain things, and you look at things very nicely [*from*] behind a desk. *But we down here in the middle of things, we understand what is going on.* I don't pretend to guide you people but I pretend to let you know what I feel so you might get an idea of what is going to go.

I am not fighting my going, but I am trying to inject to you certain realities which — I hope that you can get them to your account. Listen, I *am not trying* to *delay.* I *am ready to go now,* but before I go, you have got to listen to me and you have to take into account what I have to say. I mean, I can go tomorrow, to the bush, or I can go to the U.S., which is going to be more painful to me, but I want you to understand that the situation in Nicaragua is far from being what you people have read in the papers; otherwise we wouldn't be here.

Pezzullo: I really think in that regard you do us a disservice.

Somoza: In what?

Pezzullo: I don't think we are all that naïve about the reality of the situation here. The reality is . . . I think I said . . .

Somoza: Mr. Ambassador.

Pezzullo: Yes?

Somoza: This is the time for friends to become frank and I have no misgivings in telling you what I think, so please explain to me where I am wrong. I am a rational man and want to know.

Pezzullo: I know that.

Somoza: If I am all screwed up, I want to be proven that I am all screwed up, so let's get down to brass tacks. This is what we call here "el derecho del berreo": You have me not yet "checkmate," you have me checked.

Pezzullo: We don't want you checked or checkmated.

Somoza: All right, but I feel myself being checkmated.

Pezzullo: Checkmated by circumstances beyond everybody's control, and probably even beyond your control.

Somoza: Most probably.

Pezzullo: Forces in history are not all that simple to follow, they sort of converge all of a sudden, and I think your . . . these things that converge . . . time has caught up.

Somoza: *My dear friend, that's why I am saying to you: I am ready to leave.*

Pezzullo: That's what happened. I don't think it is Jimmy Carter, or Secretary Vance, and it is not Pezzullo and it is not any of us: It's the circumstances having come to a point . . . there is a break point.

Now, the question is, how do we do whatever we can to preserve the possibility of these institutions surviving? We said this the first time we talked about it. This is exactly what Warren Christopher said to me; what I said to Luis Pallais a week before. That is a true and honest reflection of our concern.

We want to see the change occur despite the tragic proportions of what has happened, the suffering that's going on here. Not only the victims, the violence, the poor people who are without work, without food, and so on. It's gross.

We are concerned about these things. We don't want to see the thing engulf either, in a bloodletting by a group of Marxist ideologists sweeping through and having kangaroo courts, as I mentioned, and killing off people indiscriminately. We don't want to see that. In fact, that's exactly what we are trying to avoid, and we are not alone in that, despite even some of the supporters. I was reading something today, that Pepe Figueres condemned the Sandinistas for some executions. He and another group of people came out and condemned it very vigorously as a senseless act. Despite they being wrong or you being wrong, it doesn't matter. Nobody wants to see that.

What we would like to do is have you leave with a dignified exit, while there is still time. Try to put in . . . force enough pressure on the situation to allow this thing to go back into a democratic form. We would like to see the institution survive.

Somoza: The only guarantee is me and my people.

Pezzullo: That's right. We talked about how we could preserve some segments of the Guardia. I'm sure that it is not just swept aside or falls apart with your departure. When you go, there is a chance to put something viable in its place quickly, and get into a transition government that we can get international support for, and put in the kind of resources that prevent going to the Left. *Your Liberal Party will survive, your Guardia will survive — under a different name, probably, but the elements of that Guardia* [will] *stay there. It may be a different conformation, it may be different services or something like that, it doesn't matter, but they as people will survive.* If we let the damn thing go further, I think we are all out of business.

We are very vulnerable. Don't think that the U.S. is playing with full confidence. We were fighting about a Hemisphere that thought that all we were trying to do was to impose another version of Somocismo. They didn't even want to talk to us, they thought that that was our device. They still think it, they still think that, so we have headaches; maybe we are crazy.

Somoza: No, you are not crazy.

Pezzullo: We get headaches, and we don't always come out with the same conclusion as somebody looking at it from your point of view, but it is being done with great sincerity.

Somoza: *You are not crazy, you are looking after your sheik.*

Pezzullo: We don't have any sheik. What we would like to see is this country come together. We would like to see Nicaragua prosper; you know what I mean.

Somoza: I would like for you to talk to the Central Americans and let them make a statement of their interest.

Pezzullo: But we *have to start with your going*, what I would like to be able to devise with you.

Somoza: You know, Mr. Ambassador, you are like making love to me, and —

Pezzullo: But you buy what I said, I mean —

Somoza: Yes, I do, I do, for God's sake, yes, and I don't feel resentful about what is going on because in the overall business, *I have been able to identify the enemy*, which was not quite identified in September. In September it was total anti-Somocismo, and then after September the things came out, and we identified the enemy as being: one, the Communists; two, the moderates; and three, the Baptist [*Jimmy Carter*]. So right now we have the enemy identified.
Now, you might think I am a goddamn . . . *but I want the future of my children to be assured that it's not going to be a Communist world*. That's what I am fighting for.

Pezzullo: I told you sincerely: We would like to be helpful, we really would!

Somoza: *I am ready.*

Pezzullo: The real thing . . . we have got to stop thinking in terms of the process we go through.

Somoza: All right, why don't you make out a sketch.

Pezzullo: What I will do, what I would like to do for you is to make out a sketch and come tomorrow to see you, and we will sit down and try to make that in some sort of focus. The panorama, or the procedure, you understand. We talked about the procedure, the steps we will go through, the timing of it all.

Somoza: You have to get the Conservatives to come into Congress —

Pezzullo: Do you think you can get that going?

Quintana: I don't think so, many are in Miami.

Pezzullo: Maybe we are going to have to jump over that step.

Somoza: Maybe.

Pezzullo: What is the other constitutional possibility? Can't you resign, and assign a minister? Let me put it this way: Suppose you are incapacitated, or removed because of natural causes.

Somoza: The Minister of Gobernacion would ask Congress to meet. Congress, then, would elect a member of Congress.

Pezzullo: So you go through the same process.

Somoza: Yes.

Pezzullo: Well, what is your guess as to when you could get a quorum? — because that is the key in terms of timing.

Quintana: May I speak in Spanish?

Somoza: Yes, of course.

Quintana: I mean, we send the citations, but because of these events, some deputies have gone to the U.S., some because of fear, others for precautions . . . The Conservatives can . . . some of them, for example Chamorro Coronel and Fernando Zelaya, have spoken with the Department of State.

Pezzullo: Not recently.

Quintana: Not recently, about eight months ago; but these are people that have been close to the Department of State. We need these Conservatives, part of them at least, to come to Congress to have a quorum.

Pezzullo: And where are they, do you know?

Quintana: Some of them are here; others are in Miami and it's difficult to bring them, but the Embassy knows where they are, because they have [*all*] been in touch with you sometime.

Pezzullo: How many members were missing?

Quintana: I mean, I don't know how many members were missing, but we don't have a quorum today. Besides, I believe the Embassy has the moral strength to help resolve this problem . . . We need the Embassy to help these friends come to the sessions —

Somoza: Ambassador, I want you to understand that I understand that the Somoza regime is a stigma, it's got a big, big, long tail. Now, if you guys are going to replace us with somebody who is your friend, I beg you to replace us with men who'll go along with you. I pose no conditions; I am terribly disgusted that all these FAO leaders just took off and left the country, and I haven't put any of them in jail.

Pezzullo: I thought you put a few in jail, that's why they left the country.

Somoza: How many do I have in jail?

Pezzullo: There are two you should let go.

Somoza: Who?

Pezzullo: Joaquin and that other fellow. Part of the problem . . . [*is*] a lot of history that is co-optive, and the problem is to put all this into a stable environment again. It's going to be difficult.

Somoza: The man that's going to be elected after I leave will have to make a call to all the forces in Nicaragua —

Pezzullo: I think you are right, that's exactly what the call has got to be.

Somoza: After that they are going to —

Pezzullo: You will be a thing of the past.

Somoza: I am already a spent round.

Pezzullo: In two years you will be thinking on how you will come back.

Quintana: [*laugh*] I agree with you.

Pezzullo: In eighteen months you are not going to sit on the beach.

Somoza: Let me say this to you, Mr. Ambassador: I love my people, and it is going to be them who are going to decide what's going to happen here . . . This is part of the strength I have had . . . so I am ready to settle this matter.

Pezzullo: OK. Let me come back tomorrow and we will sit down and talk details; we will set bench marks . . . It's good to do business with a good chess player.

[*End of meeting.*]

TAPE 5

[*The following conversation took place on June 29, 1979. Present at this meeting were President Somoza, his son Tacho, U.S. Ambassador Pezzullo, U.S. Congressman John Murphy (D-New York), Luis Pallais, Nicaraguan Foreign Minister Dr. Julio Quintana, and General Samuel Genie.*]

Pezzullo: Well, I'm sorry about the mix-up today. I heard about this thing. It was sloppy work. We should have been a little more careful. You people have been very helpful and cooperative on these evacuation flights.

Somoza: Yeah, I mean, I was very distressed because people up in Montelimar knew that plane was coming.

Pezzullo: Oh, yeah.

Somoza: But it worked out.

Pezzullo: It worked out. I want to thank you; as I said, it was sloppy, sloppy staff work, so . . . Well, let me tell you that Washington is very pleased with what they think is the beginning of the process now of thinking through the very thing we are concerned about. That the aftermath be one which is carefully tailored and gives every bit of possible preservation to the structure.

Somoza: Right.

Pezzullo: And this I can assure you is exactly what our concerns are and exactly where we will be going. And we'd like to have you understand that as we get this in place, *then we will be coming to you in terms of having you put together the more specific scenario of the whole thing,* because it has got to fit into place in a very carefully designed way, so that it doesn't fly off somewhere and cause problems. So that's where we are in our own corporation. So the scenario I planned, which I plan to bring in, which I told Washington I'd like to present, they said to hold off until we have a few more things positioned right so we can do it carefully and with more exactness.

Somoza: I appreciate that, Mr. Ambassador, however, *time is now working against us because there are a lot of people talking about my possible resignation;* the *Miami Herald,* etc.

Pezzullo: But do they have something in, I, I see that —

Genie: *They had a story yesterday morning, first page, even*

*with giving complete details which were supposed to be written
by a wire service belonging to them, where they gave the whole
picture exactly.*

Somoza: What am I going to do, just tell them another lie?

Pezzullo: Well, I had the press in today and they started
with me and I told them, "Look, I know you've got jobs to do,"
but they wanted to know what we talked about; that is not an
area I am going to discuss. I respect the confidentiality of what
I discuss and they are not going to hear anything from me.

Now, I've seen what the [*Washington*] *Post* and the *New
York Times* . . . uh, I recognize that fact and it is a condition,
I don't know where it happened from or how it happened, but
it's a condition we are going to have to deal with. One thing that
gives me — even though it's not a good condition, I must say —
one thing that gives me a little confidence out of it is that
perhaps it is needed in the atmospherics of this whole thing, to
pave the way. If I would have had control of it, I would have
kept that thing completely controlled, and quiet, but it's out.
But it may have a positive aspect to it, because it will look a
little bit more carefully, carefully drawn.

The fact of the matter is, it puts you in a position of when
you don't do it, showing that there is control, there is a posture
on your part which is still dictated by your actions. If you are
not being driven after this, you are making your own decisions,
governing your own welfare and your own future, and that's
the way I would — if I were you, that's what I would tell the
press. "Nobody's going to tell me what to do. I am going to
make these decisions on the basis of my own best judgement. I
was hoping we could start going on a timing basis quickly, you
know, I think we still will." It will just take; see, one of our
problems is that the Secretary [*of State*] and the [*U.S.*]
President are in Tokyo. They're just coming back, so I think it
will all be together very quickly, and I'll be pushing them very
hard to get things in order.

Somoza: *I guess you understand that right now my life is
worth nothing, and the longer I stick around here, it will be
worth less.*

Pezzullo: *Well, that's your life . . .* you know, whoever is thinking that way, his life isn't worth anything either. *Because this structure will hold and the Guardia will survive, not in the same form, but it will survive.* If we all play our cards well, which is one of the things I wanted to talk to you about. The, what I think the office you call the Guardia should be thinking about now is that post-period, and their role in that post-period, and their survivability in that post-period. *Because they are disciplined officers who made a commitment to defend their country, and to defend and protect the interests of Nicaragua, and to preserve their order. And that's the discipline they have to draw on.*

You've been, you've dedicated a good part of your life to building that kind of discipline and your departing the scene unquestionably is going to leave a vacuum that is not going to be easy to fill. But, if right now that word is coming down from your level, that their commitment, their discipline, and their adaptability in the days ahead is going to permit them to continue on as a security force in this country, that is the best message you can give them. Because that will be . . . that will be the key, their ability to hold under new leadership, during this period, and give us all a chance to create the conditions to permit them to go on to another stage without being chewed up. And I think chances for us to do that are very good, very good.

Tacho: Mr. Ambassador, I think — may I?

Somoza: Sure, go ahead, you're —

Tacho: I've been in the firing line with the people that are under stress at this stage; and my best, my very best observation on the subject, is that in that post-period what you would need here, as the United States, would be almost an immediate injection of officers that have served here and have had contacts with the Guardia Nacional and have had relationships. Because, unquestionably, in certain strata of the Army — basically coming from the top major colonels right now, down to those that are the senior lieutenant colonels right now, in the strata of which 70 to 80 percent are at their retirement positions at this moment — their leadership has always come directly from above. Either through the President or through the advice they have received from the Milgroup commanders here who've had in the past, before Colonel Matthews, a very close relationship with those officers.

You'll find a larger amount of initiative in the sense of making decisions, not consulting them to the top as the others have in the groups that are the senior lieutenant colonels, going on down. They are more used to a different style of leadership in La Guardia and they have had a little more leeway in their decisionmaking.

I interject that and I would say that to cover that vacuum, to cover that vacuum that will exist if most people in the government have to leave, I would make the suggestion to have a team of officers ready to come in, either to the defense attaché's office or to the, as a Milgroup, to the new government of whatever. Because I know that they will be looking towards this as a possibility of sounding out or finding buts.

I know this has been sort of traditional in a certain way, but I think that it's an idea that you should play with, put it in your scenario; because, to be very, very frank with you, the leadership as it exists now emanates from three different people you see; from the President, or from yours truly, or from General Jose Somoza. And in that large strata, as I said, the top people. The others would be able to organize themselves a lot faster and to get on the job a lot quicker, because they have that, they've had that, that experience. I wanted to interject that.

Pezzullo: I think that's very helpful. I am sincere in saying that your help in this is going to be crucial. I really believe, I think you both love that Guardia as much as you do, General; as much as you love anything else, it's been your baby. So you can help us very much during this period.

Somoza: *Mr. Ambassador, let me say this, because of the structure of the Guardia Nacional, I was not ready to do anything but to go.* The Guardia Nacional of Nicaragua has accepted one way or the other the elections in Nicaragua. You know, it wasn't easy for me to receive the word from Ambassador Bowdler, to get off the pot and do this and that. But knowing the structure of the Guardia Nacional, I think you will have to work very hard after I leave to get back the confidence of these people. *And these people, Mr. Ambassador, mainly are not fighting for Somoza, they are fighting the enemy they have fought for the last eighteen years, Communist Castroites. That's why you have not had any success in getting these people to turn on me, even in the overtures the United States has made.*

So the officers, the defections we've had in the Army —

Pezzullo: Wait, wait a minute, what overtures?

Somoza: Well, I understand that when you say that, when you agree that I should leave, that that's an overture for the Army.

Pezzullo: Oh but, please, please, we have never done that element. We have never sought to undercut you. I ought to know.

Somoza: You have done that publicly, which is, it is a, shall we say, a way of doing it. *What I am trying to tell you, Mr. Ambassador, is that these people are quite aware of who their enemy is. That's why they are fighting like dogs and cats.* Now that is something you should have — I mean, I've discussed with the officers the position of the United States, and they said, "Well, the United States is wrong, 'cause we know who our enemy is." But, I want to bring that up to you so that you understand that you have a dedicated group of people.

Someday, I'm going to have to die. But, thinking about my departure (I say will, I [*will*] for other intended purposes die.), what are these officers going to do? *But mainly, Mr. Ambassador, these men are fighting against Communism. They are not fighting for the Somoza regime. They have been trained from A to Z by U.S. officers.* Philosophically, these people are democratic.

Mr. Ambassador, politically, for me, what I have now nobody's going to take away, politically. As you said yesterday, I might come back stronger.

Pezzullo: I wouldn't discount it.

* * *

Tacho: What we have to make sure is, that whatever happens in this damned country, people within a couple of years, people can go out and vote for what the hell they want.

Pezzullo: That's, that's the key.

Tacho: Because that's the only way there's peace in this damned country.

Pezzullo: And we've got to work hard at it.

Tacho: And let me say this, Mr. Ambassador, somehow or another, OK, they go out and vote, but you're always gonna find those people of the same Frente. But by that time you won't have that stigma to be able to —

Pezzullo: Well, that's the thing. The thing is, that you always have a lunatic. You have them in every country, at every time. What prevents that lunatic from turning a country into an armed camp is the question. Usually it comes from some condition that allows that thing to fester.

Tacho: After a couple of years of when this thing calms down . . . that's what's going to happen. The pressure has to go down, back to normal.

Pezzullo: Once these extremists are put in a situation where there are other forces of play they are going to be the minority. They won't represent more than five or six percent.

Somoza: They've got some muscle now because Castro has backed them and some of the Conservatives' kids back them. The Communists never have any amount of people like these people.

Pezzullo: No. It comes to a head like a boil. Well, as I said, I'll be back to you as soon as we have this thing better entrained. Be patient and if there's anything we can do during the interim, please feel free to call on me anytime. I'm sitting, doing nothing else.

Tacho: Dodging bullets at night and dodging the guns. By the way, apparently it's peaceful out at your side of the strip.

Pezzullo: Yeah, it's quiet.

Murphy: We're worried that Las Piedrecitas might be mistaken for La Loma.

Somoza: Yes.

Tacho: I know, the top marine told me he's worried about it. But you know, Mr. Ambassador, I . . . hell, I'm the youngest guy in this room and, supposedly, the one people say has the most to lose, but I feel in my heart, and this is why I told the General, that all my . . . whatever I can do to give a hand. *That whatever happens for as long as the U.S. makes sure that elections can take place in this country, that no half-assed, crazy son of a bitch is going to come in here and prevent the situation.* Then whatever stepping down can be done, can only be picked up again.

Pezzullo: That's where we are.

Tacho: *I just hope that you people can, I really hope that you people can stand the initial pressure when you start in a situation that will guarantee the ability to every little guy to be able to grow up free.* Because there is the fact that some guy, just because he has the education, this or that, wants to make sure that that last Indio and that last Barrio doesn't get to vote.

If you can prevent that, Mr. Ambassador, you'll get the backing of everybody. But if you just let those who have the money, the intellectual pull and the technocrats do it, you're gone. Because there are too many Indians in this country.

Pezzullo: OK, Luis, we'll see you.

Tacho: Nice to see you . . . see you, sir. Hey, Jack, take care.

[End of meeting.]

TAPE 6

[The following conversation took place in July, 1979, between President Somoza and U.S. Ambassador Pezzullo.]

Somoza: I want to say this to you, and I'm not saying this as an explanation for me to stay. I'm making this explanation so that you may better understand the way my side has handled this problem. And, as you said the other day, perhaps in two years I'll be back. Well, I probably won't be back, but the Liberal Party will.

Pezzullo: You may be right, you may be very right.

Somoza: Through all of this I have been true to myself. I never wanted to cheat myself and I never wanted to cheat my people. We have been honest. I have had a Catholic education and was always taught to tell the truth, be true to yourself. Besides the Catholic education, the formal military education I received made me even more conscious of the importance of the truth.

If I were a two-bit soldier, I would have been gone from Nicaragua a long time ago. But I think the government and I have the right to be doing what we are doing, because this government was duly elected by the people. After the tremendous stress of the earthquake, the Liberal Party and the Somozas pulled this country out of the shambles which remained. That's why they elected me, and I was elected with a huge majority. Also, there was no one else to lead the Liberal Party and I had to accept the candidacy. It was not easy to stabilize the country after the earthquake, but we did it.

What I'm afraid of, Mr. Ambassador, is that you and the United States will fight on the other side, the wrong side.

Pezzullo: I'm sure that I really haven't been here long enough to talk to the other side. I haven't had that much experience here. I think they are at the point where, unfortunately, we don't have time to do those things. I hope history treats you, treats you well in this matter. I'm concerned very much. I hope this thing sorts out so we don't see more bloodshed. It's one of those things that's not easy to put together. But, I'm hopeful we can do something very quickly and get this process moving and move on to another stage as fast as possible.

Somoza: *Yes, because outside of my personal feelings, I don't want this country to go Communist.*

We have over 200,000 people in this country who are property owners. An average first-degree family connection amounts to about six people. So, if you multiply six times 200,000, you come up with 1.2 million people who have ties to property ownership, and that's over 50 percent of the total population ownership. And you can be sure those 1.2 million affect another 800,000 people. In reality, we have some two million people, from babies all the way to old men, who are attached to property.

Now, this is a count that your people don't understand. There will be no peace here, Mr. Ambassador, if there is a Leftist take-over, because our people are not willing to give up their land. I don't care what you call it, they are not willing to give up their land.

For example, in one agrarian reform settlement area, one thousand recruits came in, voluntarily. In another area, which three years ago was the center of guerrilla activity, four hundred recruits came in. In what was supposed to be the heart of "Sandino land," some seven hundred recruits volunteered. You, yourself, could ask these young men, why did you volunteer for the Guardia Nacional, and they would tell you they are defending their home and their property. *Philosophically, then, you are working against one of the fundamental principles which made your country great, and that is the ownership of property.*

Pezzullo: No, we're not, you know —

Somoza: There is much political fiction about myself. Due to this political fiction and because we are losing so many lives, that is why *I told you the first day that I'm ready to go.* But I plead with you, don't let these people suffer. When I go, goddamn it, take all the sanctions away and give these people a chance. Even all these people with fancy ways, these business-men who are now in Miami, they are all property owners.

Pezzullo: I know, they are sitting up there complaining. I realize that. They're not here.

Somoza: But anyway, that is the motivation to save the structure of Nicaragua. What are you doing about . . . [*tape snapped*].
    . . . Contrary to what your government believes and con-trary to press reports, my family and I have taken unproductive land in remote areas, and we have made that land productive. We started the first irrigated rice fields, and now many people are in that business. In many ventures we don't make much money; but the important thing is that we have created jobs.

Pezzullo: I realize, I realize that you have investments in that area. I think that some day when this is all over, you and I have to sit down and talk about this period. But, that's not the key thing here. For whatever reason, sometimes in history you get a confluence of forces that works in strange ways, and that's what's happening here. This confluence of forces comes to the point where you have a crisis. Ah, even the death of Chamorro, there is a flash point for this thing. The fact that his murder was never completely worked out, nobody discov-ered who the guilty parties were, and we were fed a lot of —

Somoza: Mr. Ambassador, we do know and that murder has already been cleared —

Pezzullo: But it's not accepted — that's what I'm saying. It is clear, but it is not accepted. People don't think it's true.

Somoza: They don't accept it for political reasons.

Pezzullo: *I agree. I'm not disagreeing with you.* I'm saying that these things happen. If Joaquin Chamorro didn't die, I think the situation would not have deteriorated. I think —

Somoza: That's true.

Pezzullo: It's a series of things that happened that caused this whole situation; bad luck, circumstance, timing.

Somoza: Like the killing of the newspaper man.

Pezzullo: We were flooded with telephone calls. People were saying, Why don't you go down there and stop this damned thing? You know, you know the emotions.

Somoza: Yes, I got telegrams saying, "We're declaring war on you."

Pezzullo: You would see this on television, right on television, all day. Well, as I said, someday we can sit down when this is all over, and, over a good Scotch and soda, discuss it.

Somoza: Oh, yes.

Pezzullo: But, let's try our best to bring it to a graceful . . . a graceful ending.

Somoza: Mr. Ambassador, I'm trying to do just that —

Pezzullo: I appreciate, let me say that I appreciate your attitude, and in spite of everything else that has gone on, I appreciate it. I found our discussions to be gentlemanly. We can sit and talk to one another just straight, man to man. I'm very much concerned about everything you've said and I'm telling a lot of people about it, and we'll try to put this into place as soon as we can and I'll be back to you to set a date.

Somoza: All right. What's most important, Mr. Ambassador, and I'm not trying for a comeback because I have been President twice, *is that Nicaragua not fall into the Communists' hands. The national interest of the U.S. will not be served well if the Communists take over this country.*

Pezzullo: *Agreed, agreed.*

Somoza: Mr. Ambassador, you should know that 90 percent

of the entire officer corps of Nicaragua have gone through various United States military schools.

Pezzullo: I know that.

Somoza: *Well, you cannot discount that because of a Somoza —*

Pezzullo: *We will not. We will not. I told you that our interest is in preserving the Guardia Nacional.* Even if the name changes, there will be some, we want this thing to survive as an institution.

Somoza: These people are all democratic people.

Pezzullo: We will. This is our concern. It's easy for us to . . . like the Brazilians, say go home, and sit around and let things go, but we are not doing that.

Somoza: I don't think you should.

Pezzullo: We're working hard at it, and I hope, with a little bit of luck, we can —

Somoza: You must know that I have fear of assassination.

Pezzullo: Well, I agree. Well, you know how to take care of yourself, there's no question. It will be a short time. This is not going on much longer, it can't. So, I don't have to tell you to take care of yourself. We are all in a funny position with this thing. It's very delicate and a lot of people are very serious, but, OK.

Somoza: Understood.

Pezzullo: Keep well.

Somoza: Thank you.

[End of meeting.]

TAPE 7

[*The following conversation took place between President Somoza, his son Tacho, U.S. Ambassador Pezzullo, and Luis Pallais.*]

Pezzullo: Mr. President, I have been asked to come in and get instructions in a talk with you on the basis of decisions in Washington.

To review the situation, as you know, we have been involved the last couple of weeks in an attempt to try to work out the transition arrangements to talk about. There have been a lot of actors in the scene and we have been one of them. We have wanted the negotiations to continue and are still going on; and still discussions are going on. But we felt that it is our duty to come to the point with you and tell you that the longer it continues, in the terms of your staying, the longer it seems to perpetuate the problems. We talked about this before and I think the time is short now, in terms of trying to get things into place. At the same time, we don't want to dictate anything here. We are just coming to you and suggesting to you that this makes more sense, and the sooner the better. But you have to make the decision yourself in terms of whether it makes sense to you. But we have come to that conclusion and we continue to hold our hand out in terms of the offer of the United States. That's about the sum total of it.

It has been some time since I saw you last and I understand the strain on you, and the period of doubt. But we think it is here, and so that's my message to you today. The formula you will exercise in doing it is up to you completely, and all we would like to know is if you intend to do it soon. Then soon we could work out the method of your entry into the United States and so on. We would not want you to fly into the airport and not be properly met and so on. We want to greet you and give you all the courtesies of entry and so on, and we will have to know the time of arrival and where the people will be, and so on.

Somoza: Let me ask you this, Mr. Ambassador, as a bona fide ex-President, will I have diplomatic immunity in the United States or not?

Pezzullo: Well, it's not a question of diplomatic immunity, you will have a —

Somoza: No. No. Remember, not in this period of time. In the other period. That period of time during which I was President from 1967 until 1972.

Pezzullo: Yes, in — terms of diplomatic immunity is, ah, are paid to functionaries. Even when a president, when he really comes from another country, he doesn't have diplomatic immunity. He has the protection of being Chief of State and that's what you will have the minute you walk the first step into the United States. You will have the protection of the United States law.

You will also receive, as I said, the courtesies of the port in which you come in, which means we will facilitate your entry and the people with you. We have not touched on an issue on that, and I have no instructions from Washington about that, but I think we can discuss that and I will be glad to get going with the recommendation. I think it is a thing that you can expect, not for a long period of time, because your status will change, but certainly I think that is something we can do.

Somoza: Unless the initial period —

Pezzullo: Until you get settled in and you can take care of your arrangements yourself. That is all you are able, but the ministers would know as well as I, diplomatic immunity in turn does not apply here —

Somoza: The lawyer just asked me whether the law compensates for that.

Pezzullo: [*It*] will not. For instance, an ambassador has more rights than a citizen. He has diplomatic immunity; you can not arrest him. You could be arrested for crimes, so you wouldn't have that immunity. But you will have all the protections of the law. Same as any other citizen. No difference.

[*At this time, A. Somoza Jr. (Tacho) comes to the meeting.*]

Somoza: And now we have the ball, Tacho. Negotiations have dragged on and on. So long that the United States feels that we have an option to make a decision for ourselves and for the good of our country and the institution. And my answer is that I'm going to consult with our people about the thing and think about it. Then I'll let them know as soon as possible so we can work out some kind of schedule.

Tacho: Did they drag their feet on the other side?

Pezzullo: You know, this seems difficult because there are many actors, and a lot of people are in play. [*To*] stop dragging feet is a series of complicated factors. The amount of people in play is unusual. Here we are not talking about one to one. We are talking about all the actors: The *Venezuelans* have been on this, the *Panamanians*, the *Colombians*, and so on.

So it has been a lot of actors in play and everyone is running around to different places. It doesn't even take place in one spot. But we think the longer it drags on, the less satisfactory it's going to be to you and your own interests.

Pallais: Does that mean in case of the Army, the President has the right to leave the people in the position he feels they should be in the Army?

Pezzullo: *We are leaving that option completely up to him.* He can leave and make whatever decision he wants about the Army. *He can leave under any condition he wants about the Army. That's his business.* We think he has to do some things on the basis of his own appreciation, such as what is best to leave behind.

Tacho: Did you get the information that an American plane has been involved again?

Pezzullo: I heard the one notice on the radio, about the push-pull airplane that went down.

Tacho: That's part of one of the five planes that came down from Texas. We got the names of all the pilots.

Pezzullo: Could you give me that, because I saw the one reported to me and I think somebody gave it to McCoy. One push-pull, as far as I know, [*is*] with the registration of a North American. But the pilot . . . Nobody knows who pilots this . . .

Tacho: Mr. Ambassador, this is a part of a lot of five aircraft coming from Texas to Guatemala, and from Guatemala to Costa Rica. We have the numbers, they are all push-pull.

Pezzullo: Can I send somebody over the . . . I'd like to report that, and . . . if you have the names of the American pilots, and the registration numbers of the whole thing.

Tacho: That was given to General Sanchez. I don't know if General Sanchez has given it to Colonel [*James*] McCoy, but I will give it to you.

Pezzullo: I had one, but I didn't know about all five.

Tacho: If that aircraft that fell is one of the five, with that one you'll find the rest of them. We finally tracked down the Chinese launchers, the RPG-2s that are being used to blast us to bits. They were bought by a Panamanian company in Lisbon, from a Hungarian company in Budapest.

Somoza: It was in the name of Caza & Pesca. Four million dollars' worth of arms have been sold to Caza & Pesca with an export license that was given to them by the Ammunition Board of the [*U.S.*] State Department.

Pezzullo: Was this a deal of the former consul of Miami, for the Panamanian consul?

Somoza: Prior to that, Caza & Pesca bought four million dollars' worth. I am sorry to say that somebody in the State Department Ammunition Board must have been winking at this, because it's impossible for a club to buy four million dollars' worth of rifles.

Pezzullo: I know that the case is under indictment. I know the former Panamanian consul is under indictment. Four million dollars' worth of carbines were bought from the Hialeah Manufacturing Company and the things were getting so stacked up that they decided to smuggle them out.

Tacho: But somebody is being set with that buy of four million dollars' worth of arms. I don't know where we are, and another government is being set up for another revolution. Because it's interesting to easily know the proliferation of American-made shotguns, and they are all practically the same, all exactly the same. We have about fifty of them, and they are all the same. So, I said, wait a minute! We brought them in and they are practically the same and they were not sold here. This type of coincidence is occurring so often.

Pezzullo: Those were probably bootlegged in. Shotguns are sold anywhere.

Tacho: Dominican Republic shells, in this type of coincidence? The Dominican Republic doesn't have shells. You are probably aware that one of the largest traffickers in arms in the Caribbean is the Dominican Republic, and the fact is that the plane that was shot down was carrying those shells. The Minister of the Interior of the Dominican Republic said this.

Pezzullo: In that plane?

Tacho: Yes, in that plane. The people themselves are beginning to wonder about the situation. They went to Jinotepe and performed a proclamation against the wall type of shooting. Had it been an informant or something like that, I could understand that. But they systematically shoot entire families.
There was a captain with a family of four. [*Neither*] the captain nor his family had anything to do with repression of any kind. His duty had been at the airport. They killed his mother, his grandmother, his father, his grandfather, and then they got his two sisters and two brothers. This type of thing occurs wherever the terrorists go. In the last two days they stopped the Red Cross from going into Jinotepe. They did this

because we managed to put the Red Cross in immediately after we left so the Red Cross could observe the situation. We knew this type of thing would happen.

In the heat of battle, I can understand a man being placed against the wall and shot, but the systematic plaza type of executions I cannot understand. In Leon, for example, this type of situation is gathering momentum. There doesn't seem to be too much cooperation amongst the terrorist groups. They use cruel methods. In battle they are like the Red Chinese, and use human wave attacks.

In Costa Rica, we have information that in the southern pockets they are using speed pills to feed these people. They put them up in a screaming line and then say, GO! Then they are shot down like dogs. They are raiding every refugee camp they can find, aided and abetted by Costa Rica officials; give these people two days' training and then throw them into the line.

They had to abandon the people east of Sapoa, Cardenas, and Colon, due to the lack of people they had to put in the front line. With one squad we can wipe out Cardenas in two or three days. This is the military situation. In Tola a Marxist priest, Garcia Leviana, is assisting in setting up propaganda mail inside the city in which they are telling everyone they are going to be shot. Well, this is totally false. We are pulling people out of Tola by dropping leaflets. They have been getting ammunition from a push-pull airplane out of Costa Rica.

Pezzullo: Are these the same push-pulls doing the supplying?

Tacho: As far as we know, Mr. Ambassador, there is another one. However, so far as we know, these push-pulls are from the same lot which was reported to us by the Guatemalan intelligence.

Somoza: You heard of the Red Cross plane hired to bring medicines from Beirut to Costa Rica.

Pezzullo: Yes, it was in the U.S. news and on TV yesterday.

Somoza: The International Red Cross hired the plane to go to Beirut and pick up some medicines for Costa Rica. When the pilot noticed that he was ferrying arms into Costa Rica, he defected.

Pezzullo: Where did the plane end up?

Somoza: That I don't know, but there is a big scandal in the United States.

Pezzullo: I didn't see that. We heard something on the news, but I haven't seen anything.

Tacho: There is definitely a feedback from the people living in cities under terrorist control. This is most disquieting when considering the future government of these terrorists. The system which has been imposed upon these people is not quite like Wall Street. People who have been our enemies before, are now coming out of the cities and saying, "Thank God for you." Under the terrorist system, these people must obtain a pass to go from one block to another, and this is not the Nicaraguan system.

I didn't know if you people at the U.S. Embassy had received this feedback.

Pezzullo: We heard about the zones in Leon, and about the coupons on food, and all that.

Pallais: They are doing the same in Jinotepe. I told the President yesterday that I had information about fifty people being shot in Jinotepe.

Tacho: Nobody is clean on any side, but the terrorists have developed a systematic elimination program and that is why we must try to get the Red Cross in to supervise, because I understand —

Somoza: That's why I allowed the press to go anywhere where our government troops are, in order to stop this abuse. That is why —

Tacho: I told them to go and watch what was going on, because it is my belief that with the press observing, no one will do anything incorrect.

Somoza: All right, Mr. Ambassador . . . .

[End of meeting.]

Those tapes accurately reflect the situation in which I found myself during those last few days. Over and over I advised the United States that I was ready to leave. The tapes reveal that I was advised by Ambassador Pezzullo that I should not make any "precipitous" moves. The United States forced me to stay in Nicaragua until they decided it was time for me to leave. In face of the OAS resolution which had been passed, I knew the longer I stayed, the more difficult it would be for the Guardia Nacional and the people of Nicaragua.

One has to conclude that during those meetings and the unexplainable delay of the United States, the people of Nicaragua, the government, and I were in the hands of the United States. Had I been permitted to leave on June 29th, the Guardia would have been intact, and a Marxist take-over could have been avoided. So far as the Carter Administration was concerned, this was not to be. They played the game until the very end, when there was no alternative. Despite honorable pronouncements and promises of all kinds, Carter and the State Department were determined that the Sandinistas would control the government of Nicaragua.

In retrospect, I think of the two things I requested of the United States — only two. Repeatedly I asked for preservation of the Guardia Nacional, and a commitment from the United States that Nicaragua would not be turned over to the Communists. My word does not have to be accepted in this regard. The United States promised that the Guardia would be preserved, and the United States promised that the Marxists would not take over Nicaragua. The tapes disclose the actual conversations and the commitment I received from the United States.

Recently, in the quiet of my home office, I listened to the tapes again. As I hear those solemn promises from the United States, I feel anger. Every promise made to me, the government, and the people of Nicaragua was broken. Those supposedly crucial sessions went for nought. It occurs to me that in the future, no country will be able to accept the pledge, oath, or promise of the Carter Administration. To be sure, every country in Latin America is aware of the fact that this administration cannot be trusted.

At one time, "The word of the United States was good as its bond." Out of those tapes comes the stark and frightening realization that the "word" of the United States no longer means anything. It's a certainty that other nations will act accordingly.

Chapter Nineteen

A TIME FOR TEARS

During the first part of July, 1979, U.S. Ambassador Pezzullo and I met in the mornings and in the afternoons. These conversations always centered around the status of the Guardia Nacional and the members of the Liberal Party. Mr. Pezzullo knew, and I knew, that we could expect no more ammunition or supplies, not from anywhere. Therefore, the U.S. was insisting that I resign the presidency. It may seem strange to those far removed from these traumatic meetings that I was dealing only with the United States. Venezuela, Panama, Costa Rica, and Cuba were not directly involved in those proceedings. The reason was very simple. The United States was in command of all conspiratorial forces. After our sessions, Pezzullo reported to the combined opposition forces in Nicaragua and the results of those sessions were then passed on to the other international conspirators. Each country had a day-to-day report on the progress Pezzullo was making.

In one of those meetings, Pezzullo had stressed the fact that the entire leadership of the Guardia Nacional would have to be changed. I recognized that fact and was perfectly willing to concede the point, if it meant preservation of the Army. Pezzullo surprised me and said that I would have the right to select the Chief of the Army, the General Staff, and the department commanders. He stated that these decisions were completely up to me. I decided to name General Sanchez as Chief of the Army.

Then, with the agreement that the Guardia Nacional would be preserved and members of the Liberal Party protected, I agreed to resign. On that day, Pezzullo left and advised me that it would take him a little time to work out all the details. It was then that I painfully wrote my resignation in longhand. For seventeen days, I carried that resignation around in my pocket. Those were the longest seventeen days of my life. The days and nights were filled with suspense. I couldn't do anything or say anything that might indicate I had agreed to resign. I knew such knowledge would totally demoralize my own people and that, quite likely, a bloody free-for-all would develop in my own forces to determine who would succeed me.

I felt that I was a pawn between two forces. One of those forces was the group trying to take over the government, and the other force was my own people who were adamantly opposed to any kind of capitulation. With sound reason, I felt there was a strong possibility that I would be assassinated by one force or the other. It was a trying time.

After the ordeal of waiting and waiting, Pezzullo reappeared on Sunday, July 15, 1979. This time, however, he came with a different story. He said that I would not be permitted to name the leadership in the Guardia Nacional. He brought a list which he said had been prepared by the White House and the State Department. This meant the original agreement was off. He told me that my list was not acceptable. For approximately one hour, Pezzullo and I discussed the reasons for the change in the U.S. attitude. He said the White House and the State Department believed it would be better for all concerned if they provided a list of their own.

For Chief of the Army, Pezzullo submitted six names and stated that any one of those would be acceptable to the United States. They were: Col. Francisco Manzano, Col. Gabriel Caceres, Col. Pablo Zamora, Col. Alfredo Juarez, Col. Enrique Bermudez, and Col. Federico Mejia. I sat down with my advisors and we chose Colonel Mejia. That selection proved to be no problem, and I felt Colonel Mejia was a reasonable choice.

I felt a deep sense of loyalty to those men who had served me long and faithfully. I wanted to be honest with them and advise them as to the latest developments. On July 15th I called a meeting of all Cabinet members, the General Staff, and the department commanders. Actually, there were two meetings.

The first was with the Cabinet members. In that meeting I explained to them the precarious condition of our warmaking capability; that we had no more ammunition; and that my resignation was the only way the Guardia Nacional could be preserved. Therefore, I stated that I had decided to submit my resignation to the Congress, and that the Congress would select a new President to negotiate with the revolutionary junta. The Cabinet members were in a state of shock but they had complete faith in my judgement. Though it was eating at their insides, they went along with my decision — to the man.

Next came the meeting which I dreaded the most. It was a situation I had to face, and I was filled with apprehension. This was the meeting with my Army General Staff and the battle commanders. I knew these men. They were tough, intelligent, and dedicated to their country. They had always been loyal to me and I knew that with what I was about to tell them, it would put that loyalty to the sternest test. I went into that session with the feeling that I stood a fifty-fifty chance of not coming out alive. Any one of those combat generals could have decided that a surrender was impossible, and that the only alternative was my assassination. In such a situation, a man has to call on some source of inner strength, and that's what I did. I walked into that room as the Chief of the Army, and assumed the bearing of total confidence. This was the way my generals had always seen me and that night would be no different.

My approach with the battle commanders was somewhat different than my presentation to the Cabinet members. With the generals, I detailed our military situation. Then I stressed the importance of preserving the Guardia Nacional. Next, I dealt with how this could be done. I pointed out that the OAS resolution had closed all doors for the purchase of ammunition and that there was no miracle source available to us. In view of those compelling obstacles, I stated that I had decided to give total compliance to the OAS resolution. This meant I would resign as President and Chief of the Army. It meant that my brother, General Jose Somoza, and my son, Colonel Somoza, would also resign and that all of us would leave Nicaragua. I explained further that the entire Cabinet would resign and that a new government would be formed. Through such action, I stated, they would have a chance of successfully negotiating with the new government and preserving the Guardia Nacional. I stressed the point that, in my opinion, there was no other solution. As I was addressing the generals, I looked each one of them squarely in the eye. They knew that I was sincere and that I was giving them the best judgement at my command. They accepted my decision and, thus, a very risky meeting was terminated.

As I was walking out of that meeting I came face to face with Major Pablo Emilio Salazar, known to all the people of Nicaragua as "Comandante Bravo" of the Southern Command. No one could ask for a better combat leader than Bravo. He was fearless, but he knew when to exercise caution. To him, his men always came first and his combat troops would have followed him to the end of the earth. Ours was an emotional meeting, and it was the last one we would ever have. Bravo said, "Is it true that you have to go?" I told him it was true.

Bravo couldn't understand why I had to leave. Each time he and his men had met the enemy they had soundly defeated them. I explained to him that what we were up against was far bigger than all of Nicaragua, and that we had men fighting in the field with no ammunition. Further, I explained that even if we could get munitions, we had only a small amount of dollars in reserve. As I talked to Bravo, I thought the total responsibility for the situation in which Nicaragua found herself rested with Jimmy Carter. We had sixteen thousand men who were willing to fight, but they had no ammunition; and we had the loyal support of the people, which even the International Conspiracy could not destroy.

Bravo then looked at me and said: "It's final; you are really going to leave?" I could only respond that it was final. At that point, this brave "man's man," and hero in his own right, began weeping. There were no more words for me. I was too choked up to talk. I embraced this gallant man and walked away.

After the revolutionary victory, Bravo and his men made their way by barge to El Salvador. From El Salvador he went to Honduras. It was all over, but the Sandinistas wanted Bravo. A trap was set for him and he was captured. The Sandinistas could not defeat him on the battlefield, but he was captured

under supposedly peaceful conditions and tortured to death
— in exactly the same manner that General Perez Vega was
killed.

Again, it should be noted that a Sandinista "hit" team
captured and tortured to death Comandante Bravo. This was
done after the war was over; and this horrible event took place
in Honduras. Tomás Borge, the Communist Minister of the
Interior for Nicaragua, gloated publicly over this atrocious
murder.

Contrary to what Mr. Carter, the U.S. State Department,
and the media would have you believe, Borge is a vicious
Communist killer. If there is any doubt about that allegation,
take note of his speech to a youth rally held in Managua on
October 17, 1979. Borge's entire speech was broadcast on
Managua Radio Sandino at 1800 hours GMT, and the speech
was monitored.

With reference to the torture death of Comandante Bravo
and Borge's comments about me, his words are as follows:

". . . the truth is that that henchman is now seven feet
underground. He was the coordinator of the Somozist counter-
revolution . . . the truth is that the head of that sector of the
counterrevolution has been cut off. The enemies of our people
will fall one by one, and sooner or later assassin Anastasio
Somoza's turn will come."

Borge exemplifies the new Marxist government in Nicaragua. He has patterned his speech, his Communist techniques,
and his sadistic behavior after his hero and companion, Fidel
Castro.

The media have had this information for some time, and,
yet, for some reason, Borge has remained untouched.

Sunday, July 15, 1979 was a day packed with one emotional
event after another. When the day started, I had serious
misgivings about being alive when the day was over. Could
there be a worse day? The answer is yes, and that would be July
16, 1979 and the early morning hours of the 17th.

A meeting was held with Ambassador Pezzullo on the 16th to
complete my departure plans and discuss arrival arrangements
in the United States. Pezzullo asked me which airport I pre-
ferred and without hesitancy, I said: "Homestead Airforce

Base." That decision came out of my loyalty to the U.S. military. The schedule called for a departure from Managua at 4:00 A.M. on the 17th.

The only person in the government who had advance knowledge of my resignation was General Rafael "Adonis" Porras. He had always been my good "right arm" and I trusted him implicitly. He knew that my written resignation had been in my pocket for some time. On the 16th I called Porras into my office and told him that every act and every final governmental function should be done properly. I handed him the handwritten resignation and asked him to use his best typing skills on that important document. The emotional impact of those staggering events was also getting to General Porras. He must have started a dozen letters before he finally finished one. He brought it to me. I signed it and placed it in my inside coat pocket.

On the 16th I directed General Porras and Luis Pallais to prepare a list of all those who would be flown out of Managua that night. That was a difficult assignment because seating space was limited, as well as baggage space. I had to draw the line somewhere, and the departing group that night would consist of the Cabinet, the General Staff, the department commanders, and very senior military personnel. Pezzullo had directed that no officer above the rank of senior lieutenant colonel would be permitted to remain in Nicaragua. It was his belief that those ranking military people were too close to me. The members of Congress would not leave Nicaragua until they had completed their constitutional duties later on the 17th.

There were so many people I wanted to take with me and simply could not do so. I thought of lifelong friends and associates who would most likely have serious problems with the new government. Leaving some of them behind represented a life-and-death decision. Not one of those devoted friends ever complained. They understood.

On the night of the 16th at approximately eight o'clock, I had my second meeting with the new military commanders. They recognized the seriousness of their situation and the importance of preserving the Army. With them, I reviewed all the points of agreement between me and U.S. Ambassador Pezzullo and reiterated the promise from Pezzullo that the

Guardia Nacional would be preserved. I turned the meeting over to General Mejia, the new head of the Guardia Nacional. General Mejia and the new commanders then began work on Army reorganization plans.

At 10:00 P.M. Luis Pallais Debayle came to my office and I delivered to him my official letter of resignation. As Vice President of the Congress and Chairman of the Liberal Party, his function was to present my letter to the Congress on the morning of the 17th. As to my resignation and their departure time, members of Congress had approximately twelve hours' advance notice. That's not much time to put your house in order and prepare to leave forever!

Things were hectic at the Hotel Inter-Continental. Members of the Cabinet, the Army General Staff, the retired military department commanders, and members of Congress were all housed in that one hotel and waiting to leave. A movement of this kind takes much coordination, so I put Colonel Linarte in charge of that operation. At 11:00 P.M. he had buses and military escorts parked several blocks from the hotel and ready to move out. At 3:00 A.M. the buses rolled up to the main entrance of the hotel and the entire contingent, with the exception of members of Congress, boarded the buses and headed for the airport.

Shortly before four o'clock on the morning of July 17th, I called my personal staff together for a last farewell. This included the cook, the waiters, and presidential orderlies. It was a sad and touching moment. I embraced each one of them and once again tears were flowing. I think most of them felt that we would never see each other again.

A car was waiting in front of the bunker, and we took the car to the top of the hill behind the bunker where a helicopter was waiting. As I sat there in the helicopter waiting for lift-off, I felt the emotions of the past few days welling up inside me. As I took one last look at the lights of Managua, tears started rolling down my cheeks. It wasn't that I was indulging in self-pity, because my thoughts at that moment were about my country. I felt deeply that all the good work we had accomplished in Nicaragua had simply gone up in smoke, due to conspiring foreign forces. In a few minutes the "chopper" touched down at Las Mercedes Airport.

My last words with my son, Tacho, had been harsh, and my admonitions had been expressed in front of the General Staff and the military department commanders. This semi-public reprimand was initiated because my son was insisting on staying in Nicaragua with his men. In his rationalization, he and his men and, for that matter, the entire Army, had not been defeated. Therefore, he concluded that he should stay and fight. In that last conversation, I told him to be at the airport at 4:00 A.M. and that it was imperative for him to be on time. He then let me know that he was a twenty-eight-year-old man and quite conscious of his duties and responsibilities.

When we arrived at the airport, Tacho was not there. At first, I was angry and, as time passed, I became apprehensive. I knew the loyalty he felt for his men. Had he gone against my orders and decided to stay? Had the Sandinistas captured him? They wanted him very badly. Or, could he have been involved in an accident? I knew for certain that we needed to get airborne.

There were many enlisted men at the airport and all of them carried loaded rifles. Their attitude seemed friendly enough, but in a situation like that, one never knows. One of the men came up to me and said: "Chief, I don't have any money. Could you give me some money?" It just so happened that I had two thousand cordobas in my pocket and I gave that to him. By that time, I was becoming quite angry with Tacho. I thought, if he doesn't get here soon, anything could happen.

My son then arrived and he was thirty-five minutes late. I was sharp with him and marched him over to the aircraft in which he was to fly. I still thought he might decide to stay in Nicaragua. So I gave orders to the pilot to taxi out for take-off and that my plane would follow. Shortly, all planes were airborne. In that flight to Homestead Airforce Base, we had a Convair 880, a Learjet, and a Dehavilland 125/600.

On that flight to Miami, many thoughts raced through my mind. Mainly, my thoughts centered on what President Jimmy Carter and the U.S. State Department had done to Nicaragua. In a brief span of time they had absolutely destroyed what it had taken thirty years to build. In one quick easy move they had scuttled fourteen thousand men who had gone through U.S. military schools and were the main bastion of defense against Communism in Central America. I was in agony.

When I left Nicaragua, we still had a mutual defense pact with the United States. The White House and the State Department knew, without any reservations, that the Sandinistas were being supplied with arms, ammunitions, and trained guerrilla leaders from Cuba. They also knew the revolutionaries were receiving munitions, supplies, and men from Panama, Venezuela, Ecuador, the Dominican Republic, Peru, and Colombia. They were well aware that all of this movement of men and warmaking equipment was being brazenly carried out across Costa Rica. How much, then, does a mutual defense pact with the United States mean? Under Mr. Carter, such a pact has no meaning at all.

After we arrived in Miami, the Convair 880 was immediately sent back to Managua. I had promised the members of Congress they would have transportation out of the country, and I wanted no slipups.

Back in Nicaragua, early on the morning of July 17th, the Congress was called into session and Luis Pallais presented my letter of resignation. According to constitutional provisions, my resignation was accepted and the Congress selected a new President, Dr. Francisco Urcuyo. Either in his acceptance speech or in response to a question by the news media, Dr. Urcuyo was quoted as saying he hoped to serve out my unexpired term. That comment caused a furor and repercussions were quick to follow.

We had been at my Miami Beach home a very short time when the telephone rang. It was approximately 11:00 A.M. General Porras answered the call and quickly handed the telephone to me. It was Under Secretary of State Warren Christopher. His message to me was brief but unmistakably clear. Christopher told me that under the terms of the agreement with Ambassador Pezzullo I was welcome in the United States; but that based upon the comments made by the new President, I was no longer welcome. He then made the comment that he was speaking for the highest level at the White House. That, of course, could mean only one man, Jimmy Carter.

Once more, I encountered the treachery of Mr. Carter. I had followed the U.S. plan to the letter. For the future of the

Guardia Nacional and the Liberal Party, I wanted to adhere to every point of the agreement. Total fidelity to Pezzullo's plan had been driven home to all military commanders, General Mejia, and the new General Staff. Then I found that I was being held responsible for a comment made by the new President of Nicaragua, while I was still heading for Miami. Mr. Carter and the State Department were holding me responsible for a matter over which I had no control.

I then thought of a conversation I had with Ambassador Pezzullo in Nicaragua. When he was laying out the terms and conditions relative to my prospective "stay" in the United States, he made a statement which greatly surprised me. The essence of his message was that if I got in touch with Ronald Reagan, the U.S. would send me back to the Marxist government in Nicaragua. That was a meaningful threat. If I were extradited, the very best I could hope for with the Marxist government would be a firing squad.

I recall thinking, "Why Reagan?" I didn't even know the man. And I knew that once I was in the United States, I would not engage in politics of any kind, but would walk softly and assume a low profile. Pezzullo could have told me to avoid John Connally, George Bush, or Gerald Ford, but for some unknown reason he specified Ronald Reagan.

I knew then I would have to be very careful with public statements and simply avoid the press. Someone who wanted to get rid of me could simply accuse me of having talked to Reagan; and the White House would have sufficient reason to arrest me and send me back to Nicaragua.

When I linked the Pezzullo warning with the Christopher comment, I knew my stay in the United States would be brief.

That same afternoon, still July 17th, I began preparations to leave the United States. It appeared to me that Mr. Carter would send me back to the Marxists in Nicaragua. I had been in the U.S. less than six hours. I sent General Porras and an advance party to the Bahamas so that arrangements could be made to go there. After spending less than two days in the United States, I was on my way to Georgetown on the island of Great Exuma.

Most of the government and military people who left Nicaragua on July 17th did so with the feeling they would return. Pezzullo had told me and members of the Cabinet that we would be outside Nicaragua for no more than six months. So most of my people departed with the belief that a new government would be restructured, but that they could return in a given period of time. They never dreamed that Pezzullo's word meant nothing, and that the United States was part and parcel of a plan to install a Marxist government.

Pezzullo had assured me that the Guardia Nacional would remain intact. He pointed out that there would be changes, but the Guardia Nacional had to stay. I didn't leave Nicaragua with the idea that I would be returning, even though Pezzullo said otherwise, but I did leave with the conviction that I had preserved the Army and the Liberal Party. In the previously displayed logic of Mr. Carter, perhaps he and the State Department kept their word: The Guardia Nacional was kept intact because they are all together — in prison.

The new military department commanders, selected by the United States, and the men in the Guardia Nacional were in for a big surprise. The new commanders had been led to believe they would have regular communications with the U.S. Embassy. They were to work together in the reorganization of the Army and in structuring the changes which would be required by the new government. They did have brief consultations with Colonel McCoy and Ambassador Pezzullo, but they were receiving different stories from each of them.

Those commanders possessed a high degree of intelligence, and it didn't take them long to realize that Pezzullo was playing games. On July 19, 1979, forty-eight hours after my resignation, the new U.S.-chosen commanders began leaving the country. They got out the best way they could. Some by air, and some walked through the mountains to Honduras. Their decision to leave was a wise one. Had they stayed, they would have been shot or imprisoned. The entire Guardia Nacional was the victim of a horrendous deceit by Mr. Carter.

In the south, near the Costa Rican border, Commander Bravo saw through the flimsy charade. He made the decision that he should get himself and his men out of Nicaragua. It took ingenuity and determination but he improvised barge transportation. On barges and makeshift boats, he and his men shoved off from San Juan del Sur near Rivas, and made their

way to El Salvador. Part of the Southern Command was not so
fortunate. That detachment was scheduled to meet Bravo at
San Juan del Sur, but they never made it. The commanding
officer refused to leave the area until every outpost had been
notified as to the plans. It was a gallant thing to do but by so
doing, those men missed their rendezvous with Bravo, and they
were all captured. Bravo waited as long as he could, but the
other southern contingent did not make it.

Until the very end, the officers and men of the Army had
complete confidence in the United States. They did not believe
Mr. Carter would be instrumental in delivering Nicaragua to a
Marxist government. My reports from officers and enlisted
men who escaped indicated that, to a man, they believed the
United States would not permit the destruction of the Guardia
Nacional. Most of the officers and men had received training
in the U.S. and they actually felt they were a part of the U.S.
military program. At one point during this military debacle,
there was euphoria in the ranks of the Army. Word was passed
that the U.S. Marines were on their way to Nicaragua to assist
the Guardia Nacional. For a short time, at least, the rumor gave
the men hope.

An army without ammunition cannot fight, and so the
Marxists achieved a tremendous victory in Nicaragua . . . .
However, they used their victory erroneously. Anyone who
followed the International Conspiracy which destroyed Nicaragua should have been intelligent enough to have known that
once the battle was over, it was time to unwind the tensions in
Nicaragua. If they had merely used common sense, something
meaningful could have been made out of the victory. There
was a way to unify Nicaragua, but the Marxists chose to ignore
unification and, instead, created permanent dichotomy.

Unity could have been achieved by advising the Guardia
Nacional to lay down their arms and go home. They could have
said that the war was over and everyone was going to live in
peace. They could have said we are going to punish that guy,
that guy, and that guy, but there will be no punishment for all
others. We are going to confiscate all Somoza property, but the
rights of all other property owners will be honored. They could
have invited those thousands of refugees to return to their

homeland and take part in the rebuilding of Nicaragua in a democratic society.

Instead, they not only confiscated the Somoza property, they confiscated property of our political friends, the property of our commercial friends, the property of anyone who sympathized with me or the Liberal Party, and even the property of those business people who had supported them. Then, they imprisoned eight thousand members of the Guardia Nacional. Next, some fifty thousand civilians who were suspected of supporting me and the Liberal Party were placed in jails scattered throughout the country — Chinandega, Esteli, Leon, Puerto Cabezas, and other cities. Had they chosen the proper route, the millions of dollars which fled the country before the fall of my government would have returned. A vast majority of those 150,000 refugees would have returned. There could have been an atmosphere of unity whereby the economy of the country would have bounced back. That's why I say they used their victory erroneously.

After the Marxists took over the government of Nicaragua, the junta made the charge that I had left with all the money. That lie is still being kicked around by the Marxists. This was another effort to discredit me in the eyes of Nicaraguans and to tarnish further my image outside of Nicaragua.

From a dollar standpoint, the country was broke and I have previously alluded to that fact. The United States was responsible for the dollar shortage in my country, and not Somoza. Mr. Carter saw to it that we could not export our coffee crop, which would have meant a sizable influx of dollars. Mr. Carter saw to it that the U.S. Department of Agriculture shut down beef exports from Nicaragua to the United States, and that U.S. action crossed out another source of dollars. The U.S. Embassy in Nicaragua, under orders from the U.S. State Department, advised Nicaragua businessmen in the opposition party to transfer all dollars out of Nicaragua to the United States. Those conspiratorial actions absolutely decimated the dollar supply in Nicaragua.

The news media gave wide coverage to this blatantly false accusation by the new Marxist government. U.S. government officials knew it was a lie and so did the Marxist junta. Both governmental entities knew that, in the end, we had no dollars with which to purchase ammunition, even if we could find a source which would sell to the government of Nicaragua.

We had cordobas, the official currency of Nicaragua, but we couldn't give those away. There was no way we could purchase ammunition with "cords" and no one would exchange dollars for cordobas.

This was exactly the financial situation encountered by the Marxist government. After my government fell, they could not get credit from the International Monetary Fund. They confiscated property right and left, so none of the "flight capital" was returned. Daniel Ortega, a devout Communist and member of the ruling junta, stated in a speech before the United Nations in September, 1979, that the new Marxist government in Nicaragua would not recognize or repay foreign debts contracted by the Somoza government. With that statement, Ortega discouraged any other banks from making loans to the new government. Their financial problems were further aggravated when the new government nationalized all banks. So the Marxist government has no dollars, no credit, and banks are not willing to lend them money.

The statement that I had absconded with funds was another ruse, another lie by the Communist government of Nicaragua.

Let's face reality. In Nicaragua today there are twelve hundred members of the outstanding officer corps of the Guardia Nacional. There are sixteen thousand first-class infantrymen still alive. The Liberal Party was the dominant political party and, though now declared illegal by the Marxist government, that party is still alive in the hearts of Nicaraguans. The ruling junta should know that the country will have a violent upheaval unless there are free elections and unless those 150,000 refugees are permitted to return in an atmosphere of freedom. Otherwise, there will be no peace in Nicaragua.

For the bloodshed which occurs daily and for the bloodshed which will surely follow, those member nations of the OAS who voted against the Republic of Nicaragua must take full responsibility. Two men, however, were the prime movers in the OAS and they must share the ultimate responsibility. Those men are Carlos Andres Perez of Venezuela and James Earl Carter of the United States.

As a result of their unprecedented actions, many tears were shed in Nicaragua, and some of those tears were mine. Now, tears are shed daily for those eight thousand loyal young men of the Guardia Nacional who languish in prison. Tears are shed daily for the thousands upon thousands of civilians who are incarcerated throughout Nicaragua. If those conspiratorial forces who are responsible for this ongoing miscarriage of justice could witness the horrible conditions in which the families of those men live, even they might shed a tear.

On that early morning of July 17, 1979, as the helicopter took me to the airport in Managua, I hoped that in Nicaragua the time for tears had passed. Unfortunately, it was only the beginning.

Chapter Twenty

BETRAYED

The word betrayed has been defined as, "having been delivered to an enemy by treachery." That definition aptly fits the sordid betrayal of Nicaragua. Our nation was truly delivered into the hands of the Marxist enemy by President Jimmy Carter and his administration. In this treachery, his most active accomplices were Venezuela, Panama, Costa Rica, and Cuba.

I was betrayed by a long-standing and trusted ally. That, in itself, is bad enough. But, more importantly, two million anti-Communist citizens of Nicaragua were neatly placed in a U.S.-designed package and handed to the Communists. To my way of thinking, and there are millions who share this view, that act of treachery was an unforgivable sin.

In the betrayal of Nicaragua, the President of the United States gave credence to the view that eighteen million people living in Guatemala, Honduras, El Salvador, and Costa Rica might also expect betrayal. As noted previously, we have Ambassador William Bowdler's word for that. Actually, then, it isn't merely a "view," because the threat by Mr. Bowdler has already been made.

For me and freedom-loving people everywhere, it's impossible to understand the reason why Nicaragua was betrayed. As to the "how," that's a different story. The record clearly speaks for itself. For all his days, Mr. Carter will have to live with that record on his conscience.

I do not now, nor have I ever engaged in idle accusations. Let's review *how* Nicaragua was betrayed by the Carter Administration.

- After one week in office, Mr. Carter cut off all military assistance to Nicaragua.

- The Carter-appointed U.S Ambassador to Nicaragua was advised that he shouldn't get too close to Somoza, and he promptly began an intimate association with opposition forces, including Sandinistas.

- Clear evidence of betrayal came from Robert Pastor, Mr. Carter's personal representative from the White House, when he asked President Daniel Oduber of Costa Rica, "When are we going to get that son of a bitch to the north out of the presidency?"

- The White House and State Department constantly ignored positive proof that the Sandinista movement was backed by Cuba with men, arms, and equipment.

- Under the guise of the Human Rights Commission, public support was given to the Sandinista movement, while deprecating the democratic government of Nicaragua.

- Through his dominant influence in the Organization of American States, Mr. Carter put unbelievable pressure on member nations to condemn the government of Nicaragua.

- By Executive Decree, Mr. Carter prohibited the sales of military hardware to Nicaragua.

- Mr. Carter's representative on the International Monetary Fund twice blocked badly needed standby credit for Nicaragua. These acts represented economic betrayal of an ally.

- When financing for Nicaragua's hydroelectric dam project was obtained through other nations, President Carter pressured those nations to cancel these financing arrangements.

- After the "Famous Twelve" had been enjoined, the U.S. Ambassador pressured the Nicaraguan government to permit their return. These were known subversives and, under the umbrella of the U.S. State Department, they conducted treasonous activities in Nicaragua.

- When dollars were badly needed, Mr. Carter successfully pressured all shipping companies to boycott Nicaragua so that the coffee crop could not be exported.

- Under orders from the White House, the U.S. Department of Agriculture arbitrarily gave instructions to beef inspectors to shut down Nicaragua beef exports to the United States.

- The U.S. Embassy in Nicaragua called and advised businessmen of the opposition political party to transfer their dollars from Nicaragua to the United States. This was done so as to liquidate the dollar supply in Nicaragua and, thus, dollars would not be available to purchase arms and ammunition.

- Due to U.S. pressure, an Israeli ship destined for Nicaragua, and loaded with lifesaving arms and ammunition, was forced to return to Israel.

- Mr. Carter, the U.S. State Department, and the OAS were repeatedly advised of international law violations by Panama and Costa Rica. No action was taken.

- Mr. Carter, the U.S. State Department, and the OAS were repeatedly advised as to Communist staging areas in Costa Rica. This area was never investigated.

- Mr. Carter successfully closed all markets where Nicaragua could purchase arms and ammunition.

- The United States was successful in negating all treaties and mutual defense pacts which would have saved Nicaragua from a Marxist take-over.

- The United States, through President Carter's representative, broke her promise to preserve the Guardia Nacional of Nicaragua.

- As a result of Mr. Carter's policy toward Nicaragua, eight thousand loyal members of the Guardia Nacional are now in prison and waiting to be tried. They committed no crime, and the vast majority of these men and women will be sentenced to thirty years at hard labor.

- Mr. Carter's representative gave assurances that members of the Liberal Party would be treated fairly. Many members of the party are in prison on political charges, and all of the affluent members had their property confiscated.

- Using human rights as a pretext, Mr. Carter successfully destroyed Nicaragua and is guilty of aiding and abetting the Marxists. Since "his group," the Sandinistas, won, over three thousand men, women, and children of Nicaragua have been slaughtered. Until this date, President Carter has made no protest about the violation of their right to live, not to mention their human rights.

- Mr. Carter could have had a Nicaragua without the Somozas, which he wanted, and without Communism, but he chose to let the Marxists take the nation.

- Mr. Carter has now provided the Soviet Union with Atlantic and Pacific seaports in the Western Hemisphere. Nicaragua has both.

- Nicaragua was invaded by international aggressor forces, with Communist brigades from many countries. Mr. Carter, the State Department, and the OAS had this information and did nothing.

- The Nicaraguan Army was still intact at the end, some sixteen thousand strong. It was never defeated by the

Communist invaders. Mr. Carter saw to it that these
gallant anti-Communist troops simply had no ammunition with which to fight.

• Mr. Warren Christopher, on direct orders from President
Carter, advised me that I would not be welcome in the
United States. This was also less than six hours after I
had arrived in Miami, Florida on July 17, 1979. It was also
less than twenty-four hours after I had, in accordance
with an agreement reached with Ambassador Lawrence
Pezzullo in Managua, resigned as President and Chief of
the Army of Nicaragua. Ambassador Pezzullo had told
me that I would be welcomed in the United States as a
Chief of State, and that he was speaking for President
Carter.

The betrayal of Nicaragua was not perpetrated out of ignorance, but rather by design. This I know for a fact. One could
go down a long list of U.S. allies and ask why Carter turned
against these anti-Communist nations. Pinochet of Chile could
give you an answer — by design. And how about Korea, Taiwan
(The Republic of China), Pakistan, Thailand, Saudi Arabia,
Rhodesia, South Africa, and Argentina? No, a plea of ignorance
will not suffice. Carter might have been able to plead ignorance
once, but not over and over again.

One might have asked the late Shah of Iran if he thought
Carter's betrayal of Iran was by design or through ignorance.
The Shah said it himself, "I should never have listened to
Jimmy Carter." Carter's ignorance didn't topple the Shah. In
Iran, Carter used the same pretext he used in Nicaragua, and
that pretext was "human rights." As I know so well, Mr. Carter
can exert tremendous pressure and that pressure was dumped
on the Shah of Iran.

Perhaps an Iranian diplomat in Washington said it best,
"President Carter betrayed the Shah and helped create a
vacuum that will soon be filled by Soviet-trained agents and
religious fanatics who hate America."

Upon assuming office in 1976, Mr. Carter set about to dis-
mantle the U.S. military machine. He did this while the Soviet
Union went on a war production basis. That course of military

action coupled with the betrayal of steadfast anti-Communist allies places Mr. Carter in the company of evil worldwide conspiratorial forces. I repeat, the treacherous course chartered by Mr. Carter was not through ignorance, but by *design*.

Why am I so concerned about the disastrous path being taken by the United States? I am a man without a country, set adrift by forces beyond my control. The Communists took Nicaragua and, at best, the future for me is uncertain. At this point in my life, there is one overriding conviction, and perhaps this conviction will chart my destiny.

While I'm privileged to tread this planet called earth, I shall do all within my power to see that other free nations do not suffer the agonizing death which struck Nicaragua. In my own way, I am sounding the alarm. To be effective, this alarm must be heard in the United States of America. It is my wish, it is my impassioned hope that the freedom-loving people of the United States will hear the alarm and that they will respond without delay. There is no time for dalliance.

Like so many Americans, I have stood on the parade field and saluted Old Glory as she passed. I, too, have thrilled to the sight of the Stars and Stripes as the flag was raised at sunrise, and I have felt the melancholy that can touch a man's heart at the sound of "Taps." You see, I know the true meaning of the United States, and I thank God for that privilege. The United States has been, and is, the hope and inspiration of free men everywhere. May that torch of liberty, symbolized by the Statue of Liberty, burn ever so brightly — now and always. For I know for certain, that should that torch be extinguished, the dreams of free men everywhere die at that same moment. Like the people of Nicaragua, for those freedom-loving people there would be no tomorrow; "for their tomorrow was yesterday."

My country, my people, and I were betrayed. That betrayal does not rest with the American people, but with the President of the United States. My love for the United States and her people is as great as it ever was. My prayer is that those who now lead the United States will not betray humanity. If that happens, God help us all, for then it would be the entire free world, and not just Nicaragua BETRAYED.

The End

In Appreciation

I will always be indebted to President Alfredo Stroessner and the outstanding people of Paraguay. I was welcomed in their marvelous country when acceptance was of the utmost personal importance.

President Stroessner understands the Communist threat in Latin America and he was the only Western Hemisphere leader who truly understood the Marxist takeover in Nicaragua. In my hour of need he was the only president who extended an invitation to me. I shall never forget his generosity.

President Stroessner and the people of Paraguay represent the democratic principles and Western ideology so essential to peace and progress. His leadership is rapidly bringing Paraguay to the forefront of the Western Hemisphere. The future for this exceptional nation is indeed bright, and I am privileged and honored to reside in the Republic of Paraguay.

A. Somoza

APPENDICES
and
INDEX

Appendix A

ANALYTICAL CHRONOLOGY

In order to verify contentions that have been made, the following represents a chronological listing of some of the significant events that were publicly reported between March 27, 1977 and August 13, 1979:

1977

March 24: The U.S. House Subcommittee on Foreign Operations holds hearings on the "Military Assistance Program." Lucy Wilson Benson, Under Secretary of State for Security Assistance, is asked: "What would be the reaction of the State Department if this Committee were to suspend all aid to Nicaragua? What would be lost to the United States and would there be a violation of our security interests?" Mrs. Benson replies: "I cannot think of a single thing."

April 5: At hearings of the U.S. House Foreign Operations Subcommittee (House Appropriations Committee) Charles Bray, State Department Deputy Assistant Secretary for Inter-American Affairs, says: ". . . we will hold off signing a FY 1977 agreement [*with Nicaragua*] until it becomes clearer that there has been improvement in the [*human rights*] situation."

(Note: At this time the highest number of reported "human rights" cases was 350, out of a total population of 2.6 million. These charges were made by the militant anti-Somoza Washington Office on Latin America [WOLA], a self-appointed group that engaged in coaching and bringing anti-Somoza opponents before appropriate committees. One example is Congressman Donald Fraser's [D-Minnesota] Subcommittee on International Organizations [House International Relations Committee], which held hearings on June 8–9, 1976. Of the 350 cases now claimed to be "human rights violations," over 50 percent were peasants who "reportedly" had disappeared from areas in which fighting had taken place between the National Guard and the Sandinista terrorists. At the same time, over one hundred "jueces de mesta," appointed village

leaders who had government authority, had been murdered by
the FSLN — and most openly accounted for by name, date,
and locality in the FSLN communiqués.)

May 19: The U.S. House Subcommittee on Foreign Opera-
tions votes 5 to 4 on Congressman Edward Koch's (D-New
York) amendment to cut $3.1 million in military assistance to
Nicaragua on the basis of human rights violations.

May 27: The U.S. State Department receives a cable from
the U.S. Embassy in Nicaragua contradicting testimony by
anti-Somoza witnesses who were brought before the Subcommittee on Foreign Operations by the Washington Office on
Latin America (WOLA) on April 5. This information from the
U.S. Embassy is *not* relayed to anyone in the Congress.

June 14: An amendment to restore military assistance to
Nicaragua fails by a 22 to 21 vote before the full House
Appropriations Committee.

June 21: The Assistant Secretary of State for Latin American Affairs reaffirms to the U.S. House Appropriations
Committee an earlier statement made by Deputy Assistant
Secretary Charles Bray: "I give you the formal assurance of
this Administration that we will not sign a FY 1978 Security
Agreement [*with Nicaragua*] unless there is an improvement [*in
human rights*]; nor would we sign an agreement in FY 1978
without further consultation with this Committee designed to
assure that you and we agree that there has been an improvement in the human rights situation."

June 22: An amendment to restore the $3.1 million in U.S.
military assistance to Nicaragua is passed on the floor of the
House of Representatives by a 225 to 180 vote (Foreign Assistance Appropriations Bill).

September 19: President Somoza lifts the State of Siege in
Nicaragua.

September 27: U.S. Deputy Secretary of State Warren

Christopher signs an authorization for $2.5 million in military assistance but stipulates that the implementation be held in abeyance. He also orders that $12 million in economic aid be held up awaiting a better human rights record in Nicaragua.

1978

February 9: The U.S. State Department issues its annual *Country Reports on Human Rights Practices*. On Nicaragua, it states, "The number of reported abuses and their severity have decreased markedly over the past year." The report also notes that some persons earlier listed as having "disappeared" have reappeared.

February 16: The U.S. Deputy Assistant Secretary of State for Inter-American Affairs testifies before the Subcommittee on International Organizations (House International Relations Committee) that "in the case of Nicaragua, as a manifestation of our concern at the status of human rights, no shipment of military goods for the use of the National Guard has been authorized since early 1977."

February 22: Nicaragua is the only country denied the right to buy arms from the United States in the 1979 FY military aid budget announced by the Carter Administration. Reason: human rights. This is despite the improvement recorded in the February 9 *Country Reports on Human Rights Practices*.

March 9: Assistant Secretary of State for Inter-American Affairs Terence Todman reaffirms before the House Subcommittee on International Development: "We will continue . . . to impress on the Government of Nicaragua our concern regarding human rights violations and the effect that such violations have on the totality of our relations, not just our bilateral assistance programs."

April 18: Nicaragua's request for 101 revolvers for use by bank guards for protection against Sandinista bank holdups is blocked by the U.S. State Department, despite approval for the request by the U.S. Embassy in Nicaragua.

May 2: The sum of $160,000 in unexpended military credits for the purchase of hospital equipment is quietly released after having been blocked for months by the U.S. State Department. (*Washington Post*, May 16, 1978)

July 23: The *Washington Post* quotes a Carter Administration source as saying: "We have told Somoza that if he reimposes the state of siege, closes opposition papers, or arrests opposition political leaders, the U.S. Ambassador will be recalled and we might break relations. We are not intriguing against any opposition faction. The fact is, we're against Somoza."

August 9: Patricia Derian, the U.S. Assistant Secretary of State for Human Rights and Humanitarian Affairs, testifies before the House Subcommittee on Inter-American Affairs, saying: "It is our policy not to intervene in the internal affairs of any country."

September 5: Hodding Carter, the U.S. State Department spokesman, states: "Our policy remains one of nonintervention in the domestic politics of other countries . . . . We are not in the position of suggesting the overthrow or downfall or anything else of any government."

October 3: The OAS Inter-American Human Rights Commission arrives in Nicaragua at the invitation of President Somoza. It remains in the country until October 12 and only investigates human rights charges against the government. The Commission subsequently issues a one-sided report, excluding any comments by the Nicaraguan government.

October 6: The OAS-sponsored Commission of Friendly Cooperation and Conciliation arrives in Nicaragua after being invited by President Somoza to help seek a solution to the political differences between the Somoza government and the opposition. The trinational Commission is made up of the Dominican Republic, Guatemala, and the United States. Ambassador William Bowdler, the U.S. delegate, calls on President Somoza in a private meeting to resign.

October 12: U.S. Deputy Secretary of State Warren Christopher, speaking of Nicaragua before the World Affairs Council in Los Angeles, says: ". . . we are firmly committed to the principle of nonintervention in the internal affairs of our Latin neighbors."

November 1: The United States sponsors a move in the International Monetary Fund to deny Nicaragua a $20 million standby credit loan. Action is seen as a blatant politicization of the IMF.

November 9: The U.S. Bureau of Alcohol, Tobacco and Firearms (BATF) seizes weapons purchased by Jose Pujol, cargo manager of Air Panama, which Pujol says were "for the Nicaraguan Sandinista guerrillas."

November 10: BATF agents interview Edgardo Lopez, Panamanian consul in Miami, who admits supervising seven arms shipments on instructions from a G-2 intelligence officer in Panama.

November 11: President Somoza proposes a plebiscite to resolve political differences between the Nicaraguan government and opposition groups.

November 5–11: The Panamanian airforce flies crates containing AK-47 rifles, 50-caliber machine guns, and hand-held mortars from Cuba to Panama. (U.S. Intelligence Report, May 2, 1979)

November 28: According to an AFP story, generally reliable intelligence sources show Panama as a conduit for Cuban-financed aid and weapons to Nicaragua.

Hodding Carter, State Department spokesman, says of supposed Cuban/Panamanian aid to the FSLN: "Third country participation or intervention in the affairs of Nicaragua is something which we are opposed to.
"We have seen the reports that various governments, including Cuba, have sent assistance to the Sandinistas, some of it

allegedly through Panama. They are obviously being studied, though I am not able to confirm them. We have raised these reports and our concerns about them with the pertinent governments — specifically, if you ask me, yes, Cuba; yes, others. I am not going to comment any further on our representations, but let me just say that they were raised directly."

Panamanian Foreign Minister Carlos Ozores says Panama is not helping the Sandinistas or Costa Rica. Asked whether the government of Panama had been notified by the State Department about U.S. concern over alleged military aid to the Sandinistas, the Foreign Minister replies: "Absolutely not." (Circuito PRC-TV Panama)

December 5: The LATIN News Agency reports that five thousand foreigners, mostly Panamanians and Venezuelans, have joined the FSLN movement.

December 20: The OAS Commission of Friendly Cooperation and Conciliation submits to the Nicaraguan government a group of guidelines for conducting the plebiscite proposed by President Somoza that no sovereign nation could accept. Among the Commission's proposals are that the OAS not only observe the plebiscite, but that it also administer and supervise it; that there be no prior registration of voters; that President Somoza and his immediate family leave Nicaragua during the plebiscite campaign; a change in voting districts; and allowing Nicaraguans living abroad to vote.

December 27: A *Washington Post* story quotes a senior Carter Administration official as saying that a "Somoza rejection of [the] U.S. mediation proposal could affect 'the whole gamut' of U.S. relationships."

Former Panamanian Vice Minister of Health Hugo Espadafora confirms that twenty experienced FSLN guerrillas were in Panama the day the U.S. Senate voted on the ratification of the Panama Canal Treaties, and that they were prepared to blow up the Canal with Panamanian troops under the command of General Omar Torrijos.

December 28: The head of the U.S. Army Southern Command in Panama, Lt. Gen. Dennis C. McAuliffe, meets with President Somoza and calls on him to resign the presidency.

December 29: An ACAN-EFE story has Sandinistas admitting to the deaths of two Panamanians, Oriel Sanchez Orribarria and Erasmo Moreno, in clashes with the Nicaraguan National Guard.

December 30: The United States recalls from Nicaragua the U.S. representative on the international Commission of Friendly Cooperation and Conciliation, the U.S. Ambassador to Nicaragua, and the head of the U.S. Army Southern Command in Panama. A *Washington Post* story states: "In its harshest and most pointed criticism of Somoza since the mediation began three months ago, the State Department described Somoza's refusal to accept 'the fair and workable' mediators' proposal as 'a serious snag.' "

1979

January 9: U.S. Congressman George Hansen (R-Idaho), following a visit to Nicaragua for a firsthand assessment of the situation, charges the U.S. policy towards Nicaragua with encouraging bloodshed in that country. Hansen also blames alarmist State Department reports with frightening away tourists, investors, and businessmen.

(Note: Unofficial sources have revealed instances of a campaign of economic strangulation being silently waged against the Somoza government, e.g., subtle pressures to stop U.S. Department of Agriculture meat-packing plant inspectors from visiting Nicaragua. Without certification by these inspectors, Nicaraguan meat exports to the United States would have to cease.)

January 18: According to ACAN-EFE reports, General Omar Torrijos publicly states that "there are more arms than men" available for the attack on Nicaragua. He admits that Panamanians are fighting the Somoza government in Nicaragua.

February: Cuba promotes a meeting in Costa Rica of the Communist Parties of Central America, Mexico, and Panama. Cuba urges assistance for the Sandinistas including arms, training, supplies, and havens. (U.S. Intelligence Report, May 2)

February 8: A U.S. State Department briefing issued by spokesman Hodding Carter reads: "The three nation mediating group . . . has suspended its mediation efforts. The negotiation group has concluded that it cannot break the impasse between the government and the opposition caused by President Somoza's unwillingness to accept the essential elements of the mediators' most recent proposal [*December 20, 1978*]."

In a further action to force the resignation of President Somoza, the Carter Administration suddenly announces:

(1) withdrawal of the four-man military mission.

(2) termination of all military assistance that has been held up by the Carter Administration since September 22, 1978.

(3) reduction of Embassy staff and AID personnel by eleven employees apiece, representing approximately 50 percent of the Embassy complement.

(4) cancellation of two projects amounting to $10.5 million for nutrition and rural education for the poor.

(5) withdrawal of all twenty-one Peace Corps volunteers.

February 13: The U.S. Subcommittee on Inter-American Affairs (House Foreign Relations Committee) holds hearings on "Security Assistance to Latin America." Viron Vaky, Assistant Secretary of State for Inter-American Affairs, testifies: "El Salvador, Nicaragua, Paraguay, and Uruguay have significant, unresolved human rights problems, and both our implementation of the President's human rights policy and our interpretation of the provisions Congress has written into law required the elimination of security assistance to those countries."

March: A member of the Central Committee of the Costa Rican Communist Party says Cuba has begun to channel limited financial assistance to the Sandinistas through his party. (U.S. Intelligence Report, May 2)

Leaders of the three factions of the FSLN Sandinista movement meet with Fidel Castro in Cuba. Castro is reported to have insisted on unity in return for increased Cuban support in terms of money, arms, and ammunition. Castro urges the Sandinistas to play down the Marxist nature of their programs. (U.S. Intelligence Report, May 2)

March 13–16: Two vans carrying arms are intercepted on the Costa Rica-Nicaragua border. Discovered are forty-nine FAL 7.62 caliber Belgian-made rifles sold to Cuba in 1959, and seventy M-1 carbines which had been exported from Miami, Florida to Caza y Pesca S.A. (a G-2 intelligence front) in Panama. (*Novedades*, Managua)

April 13: An official of the Tercerista faction of the FSLN says that half his faction's regular combatants have received training in Cuba. Members of the FSLN "general staff" say that Cuba has trained three hundred FSLN combatants now in the field and that their inventory includes an undisclosed number of anti-tank rockets of Soviet and French manufacture that Cuba has provided via Panama. (U.S. Intelligence Report, May 2)

May 1: The Senate Foreign Relations Committee eliminates the $150,000 U.S. aid program to Nicaragua.

The Bureau of Alcohol, Tobacco and Firearms investigation leads to the indictment of five people for illegally shipping arms to Panama. Those indicted include Jose Pujol, Miami air cargo manager for Air Panama, and Carlos Wittgreen, president of Caza y Pesca, which according to informed sources is a Panamanian company and an intelligence source for Panama. According to the indictment, the five men conspired with Edgardo Lopez, former Panamanian consul in Miami, to ship U.S. weapons to Panama without obtaining export permits.

May 4: Former Panamanian Vice Minister of Public Health Hugo Espadafora publicly calls for recruits for a Panamanian brigade to fight in Nicaragua with the FSLN. (*Critica*, Panama City)

May 11: Panamanian President Aristides Royo holds a press conference in Washington, D.C. "We have enough intelligence, first, not to assign a consul to buy arms, second, or to put arms on commercial flights of Air Panama. If I am going to smuggle arms, as head of government we have planes in the Panamanian Air Force." (Note: The U.S. Intelligence Report of May 2 confirms that Panamanian airforce lanes were used to fly arms from Cuba to Panama and then from Panama to the Sandinistas in Costa Rica.)

Royo says he has received no pressure from the United States to stop "any kind of aid" to the Sandinistas and claims that Edgardo Lopez was not the consul in Miami at the time he was interviewed by BATF agents on November 10, 1978. Royo says Lopez had been replaced on October 11.

(Note: Records show that Lopez was not replaced until January, 1979 and was indeed Panamanian consul at the time of his interview by BATF agents.)

June 4: Gale McGee, U.S. Ambassador to the OAS, says that "we condemn intervention in the Nicaraguan situation, if such be proven." (OAS meeting, Washington, D.C.)

June 5: Panamanian President Aristides Royo writes to President Jimmy Carter: "Panama is not intervening [*in Nicaragua*] and will not intervene in the internal affairs of any country."

June 7: The Panama Canal Subcommittee of the House Committee on Merchant Marine and Fisheries holds hearings and hears testimony from Colonel James C. Thomas (Ret): "The Administration has long had extensive information indicating Cuban, Panamanian and Costa Rican — and at times, Venezuelan — support for the Sandinistas."

Lt. Gen. Gordon Sumner (Ret.) also testifies: "My personal knowledge of Panama's involvement came from a two-hour conversation with General Omar Torrijos in November 1977."

Sumner says that during his meeting with Torrijos, he brought up the subject of Panamanian support for the FSLN, "fully expecting a full-blown denial. Much to my surprise and chagrin, General Torrijos defended the Sandinistas and his support for their efforts. Further, he stated that he would continue and increase this support . . . . In light of the indictment in Miami last month of five persons closely connected with Panamanian Intelligence for illegally smuggling arms from the U.S. to the Sandinistas via Air Panama we have seen that Omar Torrijos lives up to promise."

June 21: In an OAS speech, U.S. Secretary of State Cyrus Vance calls for President Somoza's replacement by a transitional government of national reconciliation: "Such a solution must begin with the replacement of the present government with a transitional government of national reconciliation which would be a clear break with the past."

June 26: Assistant Secretary of State for Inter-American Affairs Viron Vaky testifies before the House Foreign Affairs Subcommittee: "No end to or resolution of the crisis is possible that does not start with the departure of Somoza from power and the end of his regime.

"No negotiation, mediation or compromise can be achieved any longer with a Somoza government."

A U.S. State Department briefing is reported in *The New York Times* for June 27: " 'When you wish to deliver a message it sometimes helps to get the message across if you can do it face to face,' Mr. Carter said today, in explaining the decision to maintain relations with General Somoza. When asked what the message was that the United States wished to deliver, Mr. Carter replied, 'Resign.' "

June 27: New U.S. Ambassador Lawrence Pezzullo arrives in Nicaragua but refuses to present his credentials to President Somoza.

A U.S. State Department briefing on Nicaragua issued by spokesman Tom Reston reads: "We certainly are in favor of the removal of the present regime."

The U.S. press widely publicizes the contents of a U.S.

intelligence memorandum that shows the extent of Cuban and Panamanian involvement in Nicaragua in terms of providing arms, training of men, supplies, and other financial and logistical support.

June 29: A U.S. State Department briefing issued by spokesman Tom Reston reads: "We in fact have intelligence reports which indicate that various aircraft, some of them bearing Panamanian Air Force markings, made flights between Cuba, Panama, and Costa Rica. We raised the question with both Panama and Costa Rica. Both governments denied their involvement. The U.S. government is therefore not in a position to confirm at this time that the government of Panama. . . . When we raise this question obviously we state our policy which is that we are opposed to the flow of materiel and persons to fuel this conflict from outside Nicaragua . . . . You know what our policy is, that we seek the removal of Somoza . . . ."

July 14: A *Washington Post* story for July 21 reads, in part: "When special U.S. envoy William Bowdler arrived early Saturday morning at the middle-class home where he conducted his negotiations with the rebel-backed Nicaraguan junta, he brought gifts for hostess Violeta Chamorro — a bottle of wine and a jump rope for Chamorro's granddaughter.

"For Chamorro and the two other junta members who had been meeting with Bowdler every day that week, the gifts were important symbols of hope.

" 'He called me Mr. Foreign Minister for the first time,' said Nicaraguan Maryknoll priest Miguel d'Escoto. 'He said, you are the new government of Nicaragua.' . . ."

July 22: A United Press International wire story reads: "The U.S. aim in Nicaragua since last fall has been to oust Anastasio Somoza — 'and we did it,' says the U.S. Ambassador. Ambassador Lawrence Pezzullo said, 'our role was to get Somoza out, and we did it.' "

July 25: U.S. President Jimmy Carter tells a press conference: "It's a mistake for Americans to assume or to claim that every time an evolutionary change takes place or even an abrupt change takes place in this hemisphere that somehow it's a result of secret, massive Cuban intervention . . . . I think that our policy in Nicaragua is a proper one . . . . I do not attribute at all the change in Nicaragua to Cuba."

August 13: An AFP wire story reads: " 'The Jimmy Carter Administration actively participated in the overthrow of the Somoza government,' states former U.S. Secretary of State Henry Kissinger."

Appendix B

A LETTER TO SOMOZA

Hon. Anastasio Somoza
Asuncion, Paraguay

Dear Mr. Somoza:

We are aware that this book has never been written. But you certainly did a good job of speaking it spontaneously in those three-hour sessions, twice daily over a three-months period. So did your very able friend, Mr. Cox, in putting what you had said together as a book. And we are very glad to have been given the opportunity of publishing it. For several reasons.

Most important, of course, is the huge help we think your *Nicaragua Betrayed* can give us, in our perennial job of trying to wake up enough of the American people to a realization of our own clear and present danger. For what has happened to Nicaragua since Jimmy Carter was elected President of the United States, as you have so dramatically revealed, is of extreme general importance. But for us it is a great deal more.

To make that clear we simply must repeat the well known program for Communist progress towards absolute rulership of the world, as laid down by Lenin almost sixty years ago. "First," he decreed, for his associates and successors, in terms and actions that have since been paraphrased as follows, "we shall take all of eastern Europe. Next the masses of Asia. Then we shall encircle that last bastion of capitalism, the United States of America. We shall not have to attack, because it will fall like overripe fruit into our hands."

For there is no doubt that the Communist subjugation of Nicaragua, through the combined trickery, power, and tactics of Jimmy Carter and Fidel Castro, was a frightening achievement towards fulfillment of the third step in Lenin's program. All of which has now become a Communist bible for guidance in most of their activities. In fact we do not know of any longrange general precept by a recognized leader in political action which has been more faithfully followed by his successors than this diabolic instruction of Nikolai Lenin.

In January, 1946, Stalin's henchmen proclaimed their "People's

Nicaragua Betrayed

Republic" in Albania. During that year they established themselves as the government of Hungary, with brutal execution of Hungarian patriots who had resisted the German invaders and now resisted the Russians. In July of 1946 Stalin's hatchet man, Tito, completed his crushing grasp of Yugoslavia by the public shooting of Mihailovich. In November, 1946, Stalin's agents took over Romania and Bulgaria. In January, 1947, the mock elections in Poland completed the horribly cruel subjugation of that country to Stalin's "Lublin Gang." In February of 1948 Stalin's lieutenants in Czechoslovakia pulled their coup d'état and formally placed that country behind the Iron Curtain. And in October, 1950, Stalin's lackeys formalized their puppet state of East Germany.

This meant that the Communists had practically completed the whole first part of Lenin's three-part program by thirty years ago. They had also made quite a start on the second step by finishing their incredibly murderous subjugation of all of mainland China. That confident progress has continued ever since, right up to the recent betrayal of Iran into Communist hands. But we shall not cover such a general advance in any detail, because our greatest real interest — and yours, we are sure — lies in Lenin's third and final project.

That encirclement of the United States, aimed at the eventual enslavement of the American people under the brutal worldwide Communist tyranny, really got under way in 1959 with the establishment of Castro's rule over Cuba. Which has been followed since by a steady increase in his reach and power; by the establishment of a Soviet puppet named Torrijos as the Communist dictator over Panama; by the surrender of our Canal in Panama into Communist hands; and finally by the merciless betrayal of your country — the strongest anti-Communist bastion in the whole central section of the Western Hemisphere — into those same Communist claws.

You know all of this, our very good friend, just as well as we do. We are merely trying to emphasize why and how we think your splendid book can be of so much help to us in bringing that same knowledge to a great many more of the American people. Not only as to the strategic Communist design for surrounding the United States with sources of Communist power and of Communist infiltration from all sides, but as to the means and methods by which such betrayal of our allies has been so continuously accomplished.

If you would take just ten former very good friends of ours, ranging from the very large to the very small, such as China, Poland, Hungary, South Vietnam, Cuba, Panama, El Salvador, Rhodesia, Iran, and Nicaragua, and study the history of their betrayal, you would find that in every case there have been just about a dozen different forms of undermining utilized in order to push them under Communist rule. One most powerful such action has been our government's embargo against shipment to the victim country of arms, ammunition, or any military material; with this embargo made more fatal, near the desperate end of that country's struggle, through pressures exerted by the United States to keep any nation or anybody from sending military supplies of any kind to the thus disarmed victim in the struggle.

Your country, and hence your book, has supplied excellent illustrations of almost every one of the ten or eleven other mean and dirty tactics that have been used so often and so effectively to crush the freedom fighter. Which becomes even more helpful in view of how standardized and positive these Communist attacks on political entities of the free world have become. And of how disgracefully the United States has come to be the most powerful and effective single force on earth in support of the Communist advance everywhere from Iceland to Madagascar.

But we are not writing this letter to say that all is darkness by any means. Even the apathetic American people are learning that Jimmy Carter has no interest in human rights, except as an excuse for helping the Communists to make increasing trouble for an anti-Communist country. More and more of our fellow citizens are beginning to believe that his real aim is simply to help the Communists to win. The mood and outlook here are really changing. And the more people we can get to read your book, the more and faster they will change.

So once again we want to tell you how grateful we are for all of the work and determination you put into producing so revealing a document. Also to assure you that we shall put a lot of similar effort behind its distribution. And to send you our most earnest wishes for a happier future.

Sincerely,

The Publishers

Western Islands

Index